# COGNITIVE-BEHAVIOURAL APPROACHES TO PSYCHOTHERAPY

# COGNITIVE-BEHAVIOURAL APPROACHES
# TO PSYCHOTHERAPY

**Edited by**

Windy Dryden, Goldsmiths' College, University of London
and
William L Golden, Institute for Rational-Emotive Therapy, New York

**Harper & Row, Publishers**
London

Cambridge
Philadelphia
New York
San Francisco

Mexico City
São Paulo
Singapore
Sydney

First published 1986

Harper & Row
28 Tavistock Street
London WC2E 7PN

**British Library Cataloguing in Publication Data**

Cognitive-behavioural approaches to psychotherapy.
  1. Cognitive therapy  2. Behavior therapy
  I. Dryden, Windy  II. Golden, William L.
  616.89′142      RC489.C63

  ISBN 0–06–318346–3

Typeset by Inforum Ltd, Portsmouth
Printed and bound by Butler & Tanner Ltd, Frome and London

*To our parents*
*and Louise Dryden and Carolyn McCarthy*

# CONTENTS

# THE EDITORS

**Windy Dryden** is one of Britain's leading counselling psychologists and counsellor educators. He was lecturer in counselling psychology at the University of Aston in Birmingham from 1975 to 1984 and is at present Lecturer in Psychology at Goldsmiths' College, University of London. He is an Associate of the British Psychological Society, Fellow of the International Academy of Eclectic Psychotherapists, Diplomate in Professional Psychotherapy of the International Academy of Professional Counseling and Psychotherapy, Associate Fellow and Training Faculty Member of the Institute for Rational-Emotive Therapy in New York and Director of the Institute for Rational-Emotive Therapy (UK).

He has practised as a counselling psychologist in student counselling, general practice, marriage guidance and private practice settings. He has published over sixty articles, book chapters, and monographs primarily on rational-emotive therapy and cognitive behaviour therapy and is the author of *Rational-Emotive Therapy: Fundamentals and Innovations* (Croom Helm, 1984) and *Therapists' Dilemmas* (Harper and Row, 1985). He is the editor of *Individual Therapy in Britain* (Harper and Row, 1984) and *Marital Therapy in Britain, Volumes 1 and 2* (Harper and Row). He was founding editor of the *British Journal of Cognitive Psychotherapy* and is at present co-editor of the *Journal of Cognitive Psychotherapy: An International Quarterly*.

**William Golden** is the Director of Stress Management Training at the Institute for Rational-Emotive Therapy in New York City, the Associate Director of the Institute for Behaviour Therapy in Briarcliff Manor, New York, and is on the faculty of Cornell Medical College. He has a private practice in New York City and in Briarcliff Manor. He serves on the editorial boards of the *Journal of Rational-Emotive Therapy* and the *Journal of Cognitive Psychotherapy: An International Quarterly*. He has published articles and chapters on cognitive-behaviour therapy, hypnosis and biofeedback, and his main interest is in the integration of these modalities.

# LIST OF CONTRIBUTORS

**Aaron T Beck:** Department of Psychiatry, University of Pennsylvania, USA.

**Albert Ellis:** Institute for Rational-Emotive Therapy, New York, USA.

**Fred Friedberg:** Nassau Pain and Stress Center, Mineola, New York, USA.

**Tony A Gore:** Department of Neuropsychiatry and Behavioral Science, University of South Carolina, USA.

**Sheenah W R Hankin-Wessler:** Multimodal Therapy Institute, New York, USA.

**Matt E Jaremko:** Department of Psychology, Terrell State Hospital, Texas, USA.

**Maurits G T Kwee:** Inpatient Department of Behaviour Therapy, 'Het Sint Joris Gasthuis' Mental Hospital, Delft, The Netherlands.

**Arnold A Lazarus:** Department of Psychology, Rutgers University, USA.

**Giovanni Liotti:** Institute of Psychiatry, University 'La Sapienza', Italy.

**Maxie C Maultsby Jr:** University of Kentucky College of Medicine, USA.

**David S Metzger:** Department of Mental Health Sciences, Hahnemann University School of Medicine, USA.

**Robert A Neimeyer:** Department of Psychology, Memphis State University, USA.

**Jerome J Platt:** Department of Mental Health Sciences, Hahnemann University School of Medicine, USA.

**Maurice F Prout:** Department of Mental Health Sciences, Hahnemann University School of Medicine, USA.

**Marjorie E Weishaar:** Private Practice, Providence, Rhode Island, USA.

**Richard L Wessler:** Department of Psychology, Pace University, Pleasantville, New York, USA.

# PREFACE

Cognitive-behavioural approaches to psychotherapy made their initial mark in the 1950s and early 1960s through the work of Beck, Ellis, Kelly, Phillips and Rotter among others. It was in the early 1970s, however, that these approaches began to come to the forefront of the psychotherapeutic scene due mainly to the work of Bandura, Goldfried and Davison, Lazarus, Mahoney, Meichenbaum and the continuing contribution of Beck and Ellis. A recent survey has shown that cognitive-behavioural approaches are now one of the leading forces in current psychotherapeutic practice (Smith, 1982). Different approaches to cognitive-behaviour therapy now exist and it is a major purpose of this present text to detail the unique features of each.

In chapter 1, Richard Wessler sets the scene by considering how cognitions are conceptualized in the cognitive-behaviour therapies. In chapters 2–10 the major approaches to CBT are outlined. Contributors were asked to write to a common chapter structure emphasizing the distinctive features of their approach. First, they were asked to address themselves to the historical development and theoretical underpinnings of their approach. Under this rubric, major theoretical concepts are considered and issues of conceptualizing clients' problems are detailed. Second, the contributors were invited to focus on practical applications. Here the relationship between therapist and client is outlined and major treatment strategies and techniques are presented. In addition, contributors were asked to address themselves to the issue of obstacles to client progress, how they are conceptualized and what tactics are used to overcome them. Finally a case example is presented to show how each approach is applied to clinical problems.

In chapter 11, Kwee and Lazarus outline the latter's multimodal therapy. This approach has its roots in cognitive-behaviour therapy but to some degree has moved beyond the cognitive-behavioural tradition. Their work was chosen as a representative example to show how even now some practitioners are using CBT as a springboard to pioneer new developments in clinical practice.

Finally, in chapter 12, we attempt a brief overview of the commonalities and divergences that exist among the presented approaches and outline one framework which may help to organize the conduct of cognitive-behaviour therapy. Our chapter only highlights some of the issues that emerge when the different cognitive-behavioural approaches to psychotherapy are the focus of study, since a thoroughgoing critical appraisal of all their similarities and differences would merit an entire separate volume.

Readers and reviewers will note that contributors were not asked to present research data on their respective approaches. This may be viewed by some as a significant omission. We are aware of this. However, our major aim was to present the theoretical and practical aspects of a *large* number of cognitive-behavioural approaches to psychotherapy *within the constraints of a single volume*. To have had each of the contributors present an *adequate* review of relevant research would again have necessitated a separate volume.

We wish to thank our contributors for their participation and for responding so readily to our editorial comments and the staff at the London office of Harper & Row for their help in bringing this project to fruition.

## Reference

Smith, D. (1982). Trends in counseling and psychotherapy. *American Psychologist*, *37*, 802–809.

*Windy Dryden, London*
*William Golden, New York*
September, 1985.

# CHAPTER ONE Conceptualizing Cognitions in the Cognitive-Behavioural Therapies
## Richard L. Wessler

## History and basic premises of the approaches

### Historical overview

The Cognitive-Behavioural Therapies (CBT) consist of a collection of assumptions about disturbance and a set of treatment interventions in which human cognitions are assigned a central role. Because these approaches have been derived from various sources and are not the product of a single mind, there is diversity in the assumptions adopted and the interventions preferred. It should come as no surprise that the key term 'cognition' has been defined and employed in diverse ways by the various proponents of CBT; the purpose of this chapter is to review the ways in which this term 'cognition' has been used in CBT.

Except for approaches that employ cognitions solely for the control of behaviour, cognitions are presumed to be crucial mediators in the creation of emotions and behaviours. The key figures in the development of CBT have used the term 'cognition' to refer to several different mental activities, including conceptions and ideas, meanings, images, beliefs, expectations, attributions, and others, including variations of the preceding terms. While several different strategies have been proposed for changing and modifying cognitions, in no instance is the cognition taken as a target of change in and of itself. Most forms of CBT assume that cognitions, as crucial mediators of emotions and behaviours, need to change in order to effect lasting changes in the target emotions and behaviours.

Cognition is no latecomer to academic psychology. From the time of Wundt and James, the study of consciousness and of cognitive activities has been a legitimate subject matter for psychology. The early *Gestalt* psychologists studied perceptual phenomena and accounted for learning by using mentalistic concepts. Ericsson and Simon (1981) reviewed the history of cognition in early psychology, including its eclipse by Watson's behaviourism. But psychology never entirely lost its cognitive constructs. They were well represented in mental testing, and at least one form of behaviourism, that of Tolman, contained explicit cognitive assumptions as the intervening variables needed to explain behavioural events.

Psychotherapy, until relatively recently, has not drawn much from academic psychology. Psychotherapy has been dominated by psychoanalysis to the extent that most lay persons and many mental health professionals (e.g. Eysenck 1966) equate psychotherapy with psychoanalytically orientated treatment. More recently, the so-called humanistic approaches and behaviour therapy emerged as major competitors to psychoanalysis. At times they are referred to as 'psychotherapy' and at times they are not; when they are not, it is usually to discriminate them from psychoanalysis. Cognition was not important in any of these approaches nor in any of the forms of treatment inspired by these, the big three forces in psychology. Neuropsychiatry, based on a biological model of disturbance rather than a psychological one, regards cognitions as manifestations of neurochemical processes; thus, cognitions are signs of pathology rather than causes or mediators of pathology.

Psychoanalysis today is as diverse as CBT if not more so. The various schools of psychodynamic thought share a common assumption about unconscious processes and content as primary in disturbance. Cognition, defined as conscious mental activity, had no important role in Freud's theories. He once called the ego (the aspect of the mind where conscious mental activity takes place) the clown of the unconscious. However, if cognition is defined as *any* mental activity, then Freud was a cognitive theorists of sorts. There are, in the unconscious portion of the mind, mental representations of id impulses. What Freud called primary process thinking features ideation initiated by instinctual impulse (*das Trieb*); because the object of the impulse is absent or unavailable, gratification occurs by means of hallucination or dream. In secondary process thinking (an ego function), gratification is delayed, with thoughts given to anticipations and plans for reaching goal objectives.

Behaviourism is very different from psychoanalysis in its approach to science. In its most radical forms it eschews all constructs in favour of observables. This rather naive logical positivism yields no theory, and postulates no inferred variables or constructs to explain data obtained through observation of behaviour. The result is that behaviour remains unexplained. Functional statements that correlate environmental events with behaviour are sought rather than cause and effect statements. If psychoanalysis overemphasizes internal determinants of behaviour, radical behaviourism overemphasizes external determinants.

The first behaviour therapists (e.g. Salter and Wolpe) emphasized the reconditioning of the nervous system. They attempted to explain therapeutic change by writing in Pavlovian language and claiming that their procedures resulted in the forming of new associational bonds between stimuli and responses. Salter (1949), like Pavlov, had difficulty in extending conditioning principles to humans, and regarded words as conditioned stimuli and part of a second signalling system. These ideas provided the basis for the covert conditioning model which treats thoughts as covert stimuli. Indeed they may be conceived of as covert stimuli; theorists have few alternatives to postulating covert stimuli if they are to retain a stimulus–response paradigm. However, in constructing covert stimuli and responses, they conflict with the radical behaviourists, for they have reintroduced cognition to psychology.

Constructs that sound suspiciously mentalistic creep into behavioural approaches, despite efforts to discard cognitions as significant mediating constructs. Watson reduced thought to subvocal speech, a position not taken seriously today for lack of supporting evidence. Skinner has an account of speech and language (verbal behaviour) that is convincing to committed behaviourists. His notion of rule-generated behaviour is somewhat more generally appealing, but he thought (e.g. Skinner 1980, p. 87) that this was less robust than reinforcement in affecting behaviour. The search for reinforcers goes on.

In the brief history of psychotherapy, human thoughts, statements, and self-reports of thoughts have received little credence as causes of disturbance. What people say has not been trusted by therapists, but has been viewed as open to intentional and unintentional distortions. People's statements have been regarded as determined by unconscious processes, or environmental factors, or underlying biological events. Since efforts to reason with disturbed people and to talk them out of their disturbances proved unsuccessful, there was no need to include cognitions in the treatment process.

The so-called humanistic therapies, e.g. the approaches of Rogers and Perls, ignored cognition in favour of 'feelings' – a term with several meanings that are discussed elsewhere in this chapter. Therapies which posit redistribution of energy (including *Gestalt* therapy and bioenergetics) or expression of emotion or both, seem to say that cognitions might change as a result of catharsis, but cognitive change is merely incidental or perhaps coincidental. The 'self' that so often appears in Rogers's writings is 'experienced' rather than thought about. Cognition and cognitive change seem unnecessary for their account of disturbance and prescribed targets for change.

In the early history of psychotherapy, there was at least one notable exception: Paul DuBois (1909). Raimy (1975) cites DuBois as a precursor of CBT in the early part of the twentieth century. But DuBois had no lasting impact on psychotherapy, probably because the system against which he reacted – hypnosis – was soon replaced by a nonhypnotic psychoanalysis. His advocacy of persuasion over 'sly suggestions' had to wait for a waning of traditional psychoanalysis and behaviour therapy for his 'logical psychotherapy' to gain stature.

*Sum, ergo cogito* is a self-evident truth about *Homo sapiens*, the species that thinks. In biological taxonomy, thinking distinguishes human creatures from all other organisms. Human thinking emerged in the course of evolution, and can be assumed to be adaptive in the organism's and species' struggle for survival. If thinking contributes to survival and is the distinguishing characteristic of our species, why has thinking had to struggle for a place in the psychological therapy of disturbance? An excerpt from *Crime and Punishment* sheds some light on the question:

'She has certainly gone mad!' [Lebenziatnikov] said to Raskolnikov, as they went out into the street. . . 'They say that in consumption, the tubercules sometimes occur in the brain; it's a pity I know nothing of medicine. I did try to persuade her, but she wouldn't listen.'

'Did you talk to her about the tubercules?'

'Not precisely of the tubercules. Besides, she wouldn't have understood! But what I say is, that if you convince a person logically that he has nothing to cry about, he'll stop crying. That's clear. Is it your conviction that he won't?'

'Life would be too easy if it were so,' answered Raskolnikov.

'Excuse me, excuse me; of course it would be rather difficult for Katerine Ivanona to understand, but do you know that in Paris they have been conducting serious experiments as to the possibility of curing the insane, simply by logical argument? One professor there, a scientific man of standing, lately dead, believed in the possibility of such treatment. His idea was that there's nothing really wrong with the physical organism of the insane and that insanity is, so to say, a logical mistake, an error of judgement, an incorrect view of things. He gradually showed the madman his error and, would you believe it, they say he was successful? But as he made use of douches too, how far success was due to that treatment remains uncertain. . . So it seems at least.'

Raskolnikov had long ceased to listen. Reaching the house where he lived, he nodded to Lebenziatnikov and went in at the gate. Lebenziatnikov woke up with a start, looked about him and hurried on.

In this brief excerpt we find (a) psychoanalytic-like doubt that logic influences behaviour very much, (b) faith in physiological reductionism as an explanation of behaviour (in the form of brain tubercules), and (c) criticism of an uncontrolled experiment as a source of reliable knowledge. But the antilogical forms of treatment and their theories proved neither effective enough nor robust enough to become known as 'the' remedy for psychopathology or disordered behaviour. Dissatisfactions with these approaches to treatment made the time ripe for a resurgence of DuBois's focus on logic and persuasion.

The early contributors to CBT were Albert Ellis and Aaron T. Beck. Both were trained in and practised psychoanalysis, but came to reject it as both theory and technique. Ellis (1962) replaced psychoanalytic passive listening with active, direct dialogues with clients about the philosophies they lived by. Like Freud, he believed that people could use reason to guide their lives. However, while Freud thought that one could only rely on reason when the id was subjugated by insight, Ellis believed that people could consciously adopt reason to replace the irrational thoughts they rather naturally lived by. Ellis assumed that people could also choose self-acceptance rather than achieve it only through interactions with an empathetic and accepting therapist, as Carl Rogers held.

Beck (1963), through his research, came to realize that the Freudian view of depression was incorrect. His research into the dreams of depressed persons failed to reveal themes of anger turned inward, as Freudian theory predicted. Instead, depressed persons saw themselves as victims in their dreams. Beck developed an alternative theory of depression in which negative thoughts about oneself, the world, and the future (the cognitive triad of depression) are key elements in depression. Negative thinking can be identified and replaced by collecting evidence against its validity. Whereas DuBois wrote of the therapist as the persuasive source of accurate statements about reality, Beck turned the client into a colleague who researches verifiable reality.

Bandura's (1977) work on learning by vicarious experience as opposed to direct reinforcement led to a reformulation of behaviourism and of behaviour therapy. The key concept is that of expectancy of reinforcement. The notion of expectancy is clearly cognitive, and therefore antithetical to radical behavioural approaches. This important shift in emphasis led to a legitimation of cognition within a scientific behavioural theory of human action. Another concept also helped to move theory away from explaining behaviour strictly in terms of environmental control. It was the idea of reciprocal determinism – the mutual influence of organism and environment (Mahoney and Arnkoff 1978); in fact, this concept was known in social psychology as social exchange theory and had been widely used at least since the late 1950s when Homans (1961) adopted Skinner's ideas to sociology.

In the mainstream of CBT, several seminal works appeared in addition to those already cited. Mahoney's (1974) and Meichenbaum's (1977) early work emphasized cognitive control of behaviour, if not the production of emotions and behaviours due to cognitive processes. Their work represents a departure from the environmental control of behaviour to self-control. In its most noncognitive form, humans simply create environments that will control their behaviour in desirable ways, an idea that was proposed independently elsewhere in social psychology (Barker 1968). A. A. Lazarus (1981) initially worked within the narrow confines of Wolpe's behaviour therapy, but began to evolve an approach in which mental activities (cognition and imagery, between which Lazarus makes and maintains a distinction) are therapeutically important and, indeed, essential for lasting changes.

In academic psychology, meanwhile, the study of mental activities had once more become respectable. CBT is not based on modern cognitive psychology, but there are correspondences here and there. A very good example is Guidano and Liotti's (1983) integration of some well-known findings, especially Piaget's, into clinical theory and practice. A result of these developments was a revised version of human nature. Psychoanalysis and behaviourism assumed that humans were passively driven by internal or external forces. CBT, as a whole, assumes that humans are processors of information and decision-makers in their own lives.

## Man as manager

From George Kelly (1955) through Ellis, Beck, Mahoney, and Meichenbaum, down to Guidano and Liotti, an explicit assumption appears that human beings are scientists. Humans naturally want to understand themselves and their world, and cannot function properly in their world without prediction and control. This is an attractive proposition for cognitively orientated therapies. Humans are assumed to pose and test hypotheses, as do scientists, and to acquire their information by experimentation – or at least by taking an attitude of empiricism toward knowing and believing. Troubled persons are seen as poorly functioning scientists who could help themselves by testing their hypotheses more effectively and discarding ones that do not fit data in favour of ones that fit better. The overall strategy of CBT reflects this assumption: knowledge is challenged not just on logical grounds but on empirical grounds as well.

It is probably no coincidence that this view of humans gained support at the same time that information-processing models of cognitive processes emerged. Both are highly compatible with the post-World War II development of electronic computers and of cybernetics. What is not so apparent is the implicit view of the scientist contained in the metaphor: scientists are themselves processors of information – but so are many nonscientists.

Is there something wrong with the human-as-lay scientist model? Good science need not result in any decisions or actions in the real world. Scientists may seek and process information and revise their hypotheses in a self-correcting feedback loop. But like the computer, the output of scientists is information. Scientists need not act on their information; humans must act on their information, however that information might be obtained. Humans cannot solely live by an information-in/information-out orientation.

Man as scientist is a case of man created in the image of psychologists. Because psychologists are supposed to be scientists who practise hypothesis-testing, it is easy for them to project their own bias that all humans do or should function as scientists. However, hypothesis-testing is not the exclusive domain of empirical science, and empirical science is not the only or always the best way of knowing. It is unfortunate to exclude such other ways of knowing as those of artists and theologians. Further, every repairman who searches for the cause of a malfunctioning machine tests hypotheses, and these are heuristic not just algorithms. The repairman acts more like a detective than a scientist; unlike the scientist, the repairman's investigations are supposed to result in corrective actions – to make the object of his investigations perform better.

Managers are similar in that they too not only seek information, they act on it. The information they seek leads to two cognitive activities: planning and decision-making. But these are means to ends and not ends in themselves. Although the goals of science may include prediction and control, the latter is not at all necessary in order to have pure science or basic research, in which the pursuit of knowledge is for it own sake. For scientists, the goals of hypothesis-testing are knowledge and understanding; their counterparts in psychological therapy are insight and self-understanding. For managers, the goal is effective action that results in a profit (or a satisfying application of funds in the nonprofit sector); the therapy counterpart is behavioural change that results in more satisfying or acceptable consequences. For scientists, the crucial question is, do my data support my conclusions? For managers, the crucial question is, are the plans and decisions I have translated into action profitable? Managers, of course, may nervously hesitate to put plans into action, just as clients and other humans may avoid behavioural change due to cognitive fears. Therefore, the model of humans as managers is proposed as an alternative to that of humans as lay scientists.

Humans draw upon more information than that which they actively seek. They have internalized information from past sources, particularly parents, siblings, peers, teachers, and other socializing agents. The hypotheses they hold about themselves can make the difference between acting on plans and procrastination. Further, the hypotheses they hold about themselves may severely limit what plans and decisions they are able to make. For example, managers in the transportation business who are unable to think in terms flexible enough to allow them to survive in a changing social and economic environment will fail to switch to aeroplanes when train travel is no longer profitable. Similarly, clients and other humans may be hampered by their mental set. They might not think of themselves as 'the kind of person who can act differently' and fail to implement cognitive plans and decisions because they are, in psychological terms, phenomenologically ego-dystonic.

The next section of the chapter describes the role of cognitions in general in human emotions and behaviour. The concluding section describes the variety of cognitions that have been featured in CBT.

## Cognitions, emotions, and behaviours

### Cognitive theories of emotion

Cognitive-behavioural approaches to psychotherapy are not a single variant or technique within behaviour therapy. There is diversity as well as uniformity. While there is no single model of emotions and behaviours to which all forms of CBT subscribe in detail, there are certain common general features that can be identified. All forms of CBT agree that cognitive mediators process stimuli to produce emotional and behavioural responses. Mahoney (1977) pointed out that CBT differs from traditional behaviour therapy by assuming that environmental events do not *per se* determine behaviour; rather, information encoded as symbolic representations of environments determines behaviour. No one goes so far as to claim that (a) cognitions are the sole determining variable; (b) some responses may not be cognitively mediated; or (c) cognitions are not in turn affected by emotions and actions. Indeed, it seems best to think of cognitions, emotion, and behaviour as interdependent. Bandura (1977), for example, points out that perhaps the most effective way to change cognitions is to change one's performance; while verbal persuasion – DuBois's method – is a wholly cognitive procedure and may be the least effective.

Although there is no single universally agreed-upon model within CBT, most forms of CBT, as A. A. Lazarus (1981) has noted, assume many features of Plutchik's (1980) theory of emotion. The main points of this theory are summarized in the following sequence:

(a) A stimulus event is
(b) cognitively processed, resulting in
(c) physiological arousal and subjective feeling states, which lead to
(d) impulses to action, and
(e) overt behaviour that
(f) has the effect of satisfying a motive or of adapting to circumstances in ways that promote survival.

Plutchik hypothesizes that cognition developed in the course of evolution to enable the human organism to predict future events. Such forecasts serve both biological and emotional needs. Cognitive processes include sensory input, evaluation, symbolization, and comparison with information already stored in memory. The broad categories of behaviour that cognitive processes permit include avoidance of danger, elimination of barriers, satisfaction of needs, acceptance of beneficial stimuli that result in nurturance, rejection of harmful things, sexual contact, replacement of nurturing persons, attention to new stimuli, and becoming familiar with one's environment. Emotions are triggered when stimuli in the environment are cognitively evaluated by an organism affected by those stimuli. Emotions are more than physiological arousal and/or subjective affective states; they are a complex of cognition, arousal, feeling states, and behaviours.

In many respects, Plutchik's theory resembles theories of emotion proposed by Arnold (1960) and R. S. Lazarus (1984) that give primacy to cognition in the emotional–behavioural sequence. Zajonc (1980b) has proposed an alternative view of emotion in which affect is primary and independent of cognition (although they are related in noncausative ways). His controversy with R. S. Lazarus hinges on the question, is cognition or affect primary? (See Zajonc 1984; R. S. Lazarus 1984, for an exposition of their dispute.) Plutchik's theory, however, does not take a position on which covert process – cognition or affect – is primary, and thus avoids the controversy (Plutchik 1985).

Both Plutchik's and Zajonc's accounts of emotion invoke evolution to justify their position. Both models agree that life-saving action must be taken. Survival depends on appropriate action, and mechanisms have evolved to maximize the chances of survival. They disagree on the particular mechanisms and on whether cognitions are involved. However, much of the disagreement seems to stem from *definitions* of which mental activities are truly cognitive and which are not. Plutchik says that a decision to act depends on predictions made on the basis of limited information; Zajonc says that a decision to act must be made quickly and on the basis of 'minimal cognitive engagement'.

There are several undefined terms that muddle the controversy about the primacy of cognition, and these have to do with the proper meaning of cognition. Zajonc used the term 'cognitive' differently from its use in most cognitive psychology; he often used it to contrast with the word behavioural, as an adjective referring to hypothetical covert processes rather than to overt observable behaviour. Further, Zajonc did not mention CBT; his article was a polemic against experimental cognitive psychology which neglects such ideas as affect, attitude, emotion, feeling, and sentiment. He asked that experimental cognitive psychology see the futility of trying to create a science of learning and of cognitive processes without including affect (Zajonc 1980a).

Clearly, CBT does not ignore affect, but without clarifying the various meanings of cognition in CBT, controversies about cognition, emotion, and action can easily continue. The next section of this chapter offers an elementary taxonomy to clarify the role of cognitions in emotion and behaviour, and the uses of cognition in the various forms of CBT.

## Varieties of cognitions

The word cognition, like other words in the English language, has changed its meaning over time and continues to change its meaning. A specialized field such as psychology may use a common word like cognition and give it new and highly technical meanings. A dictionary gives a history of how a word was used in the past and at the time of the dictionary's compilation, but such a history can only furnish clues, not definitive answers to questions about current meanings.

'Cognition', according to the *Oxford English Dictionary*, is a noun signifying an action or faculty of knowing, perceiving or conceiving, as opposed to emotion and volition. The emphasis is on knowing and on knowledge. The modern English language word comes from Middle English *cognicioun*, from Latin *cognitio*, from *cognoscere* (past participle *cognitus*, to get to know, to learn: *co + gnoscere*, to know). This brief etymological discussion is presented to highlight the traditional meaning of the word, and the resulting confusion that arises from failing to specify whether the traditional meaning or some other is intended. Cognition, if one is to be faithful to its etymology, should be restricted to mean what one knows. Knowledge can come from the perception of what one senses, from reasoning, from intuition, or from combinations of these. By expanding and therefore diluting its meaning, cognition has come to mean all higher mental processes.

**Symbolic representations**  Symbolic representations of the environment are descriptive statements about external events. Mahoney (1977) argued that environments do not directly impinge on people and thereby create behavioural responses; rather, symbols – words and images – are more proximal causes. There is a strong echo of Hume and the British empiricists contained within this position: knowledge is acquired through the senses and the only reliable knowledge is sensory knowledge. This is the version of cognition that fits most comfortably with traditional behaviour therapy. It agrees with a basic assumption of empirical psychology, that the mind is a *tabula rasa* on which experience writes messages. The environmentalist position, that heredity counts for little and that all human behaviour is learned, is a cornerstone of behavioural-learning accounts of disturbance and change. This position also provides the rationale for conceiving of therapy and presenting it to patients and the public as relearning or re-education.

**Misconception hypothesis**  Another version of cognition as knowing about the world was Raimy's (1975) statement of his misconception hypothesis: 'If those ideas or conceptions of a client or patient which are relevant to his psychological problems can be changed in the direction of greater accuracy where his reality is concerned, his maladjustments are likely to be eliminated' (p. 7). Raimy uses cognition in the sense of what one is phenomenologically aware of, i.e. conscious ideas about a real nonsubjective world. Adjustment – or the elimination of maladjustments – results from revising one's subjective version of reality, thus causing its convergence with nonsubjective reality. The therapist's task, according to Raimy and in the best spirit of DuBois, is to present evidence so that the client/patient can correct misconceptions, particularly misconceptions about oneself. Raimy wrote that the central commonality of all therapeutic approaches is the correction of misconceptions, although the methods for doing this will be as diverse as psychoanalysis and client-centred therapy on the one hand, and explicit attempts at re-education on the other. Although gross distortions in one's ideas and conceptions about reality are inconsistent with most pictures of mental health, it seems questionable to assume that self-deceptions are always harmful.

**Errors in logic**   Human thinking does not end with self-statements that describe reality. Humans reach conclusions about the events they symbolically represent. The process of reaching conclusions may follow the rules of logic, or they may be paralogical. Conclusions may be tested for empirical verification, although evidence may be used spuriously with superstitious results.

Among CBT writers, Beck (1976) has most extensively discussed errors in logic. Overgeneralization, selective abstraction, magnification–minimization, arbitrary interpretation, and other distortions he described read like a textbook in logic courses. They are, quite plainly, errors in thinking. Premises may be omitted or distorted to reach inaccurate conclusions. Even when one starts with 'good data', i.e. accurate symbolic representations, bad conclusions can result due to errors in logic. These too are misconceptions in Raimy's sense, and presumably lead to maladjustment.

**Predictions**   Predictions are conclusions that serve as forecasts of future events. Predictions play an important part in cognitive and social learning theories of personality. Kelly (1955) used the term 'anticipation' in his first or fundamental postulate, and wrote of it as a primary guide and determinant of behaviour. Kelly's personal construct theory assumed that behaviour is directed by the way an individual anticipates events. It is assumed in this theory that people hold predictive efficiency as their highest value, and that all personal constructs must be validated or revised in relation to predictive efficiency. Friedman (1975), writing along similar lines, stated that some inefficient prediction is also desirable: too much predictability results in boredom.

Rotter (1954) wrote of expectancies in his account of social learning theory, a trend away from strict S-R and R-R behavioural paradigms. An individual generates expectancies about the reinforcement possibilities that could result from a certain course of action. Expectancies about reinforcement serves as guides for behaviour. Thus, expectancies, and not necessarily reinforcement itself, influence behaviour. Woods (1985) expanded his taxonomy of instrumental conditioning to include the acquiring of expectancies through experiences that are differentially reinforcing; his scheme is an interesting and potentially useful merging of a cognitive perspective with a traditionally noncognitive behavioural approach.

Bandura (1977) showed that differential reinforcement of a model with whom a person identifies produces vicarious learning. In this manner, a person learns to anticipate reinforcing outcomes of certain behaviours. Bandura distinguishes between behaviour-reinforcement contingencies one knows about, and those one believes one is actually capable of performing. What one knows is, by definition, cognitive. Changing what one knows can come about in several ways, according to Bandura, but the most powerful method is hypothesized to be self-demonstration. Actually performing new behaviours that lead to anticipated outcomes is the most effective method of changing what a person knows about his/her capabilities; verbal persuasion and other methods are not ineffective, but are said to be less effective than self-demonstrations.

Predictive conclusions – anticipations and expectancies – are centrally featured in social learning accounts of personality and of social psychology. They represent a shift from assuming that past events are determinants of current behaviour (an assumption found in both psychoanalysis and behaviourism) to assuming that anticipations of the future are determinants of behaviour. The latter is not a new idea; it can be traced back to Tolman's purposive behaviourism in its academic lineage, and to Adler for its psychotherapeutic roots.

**Postdictive conclusions** Predictions say what will or is likely to happen, postdictions say what has happened and why. In logic, a postdiction is an after-the-fact explanation. Any theory in psychology is able to suggest one or more reasons to explain the occurrence of a behaviour. Some theories, like psychoanalysis, do better at postdiction than prediction.

Attributions of causation are explanations that may be used postdictively as well as predictively. Attribution theory is a label given to a set of interrelated attempts to describe how people understand and explain behaviour (Harvey and Weary 1981). Attributions focus on perceived causality, without which attempts to predict and control would be impossible. Heider (1958) introduced the attributional approach in psychology, and said that persons function as lay scientists who strive for an understanding of events in cause-and-effect terms. They are especially interested in the causes of personal events.

Various attributional styles have been identified, some of which have relevance for CBT. One important style dimension is variability versus stability; another is internal versus external causes. If a person attributes his/her problems to stable, external conditions, it is unlikely that any psychotherapeutic change will occur unless the causal attribution changes to variable and internal (Wessler and Wessler 1980). Abramson, Seligman and Teasdale (1978) introduced global versus specific attributions of causality in reformulating Seligman's (1975) learned helplessness account of depression. Depressed persons are likely to attribute their successes to luck (external, variable) and failures to personal characteristics (internal, stable) rather than to situational ones. Försterling (in press) has reviewed twelve studies which found that reattributional training programmes produced changes in cognitions and behaviours but not necessarily in affect. Typically, these programmes increase subjects' attributions about failure as due to lack of effort (internal, variable, and thus under one's control), and improve performance as well as persistence.

Attributions should be taken as personally formulated theories of causation, and thus as phenomenological data. Nisbett and Wilson (1977) show that people easily err in forming attributions and in making predictions. Nisbett and Ross (1980) and Tversky and Kahnemann (1981) show that people often ignore evidence in favour of unreliable data, or adopt viewpoints for reasons that are totally unrelated to evidence.

In other words, they do not function as very good lay scientists. These findings may reflect people's tendency to believe sources of information rather than the methods by which information was obtained regardless of source. Controlled observation, however valued by scientific-thinking psychologists, is not the only basis for perceptual and cognitive knowledge. Causal attributions often rest on assumption rather than data, and may resist revision despite disconfirming data.

Janis (1983) points out that nonrational, nonevidential processes are at work in the counselling situation, and therefore a relationship in which the client trusts, likes and believes the counsellor is essential if the counsellor wants to influence the client's thinking and acting. The work of Janis and others in the field of persuasion and attitude change make it clear that the changing of beliefs is not always a straightforward process of education or re-education. It is useful to regard changes in cognitive knowledge in Piagetian terms: assimilation of new information is possible when people have the relevant categories; when they do not, the creation of new categories is needed (a process called accommodation). Guidano and Liotti (1983) have discussed the relevance of Piaget's work to an understanding of the development of disturbance and of therapeutic change. But these notions describe shifts in understanding. There is another type of covert mental process – appraisal – that is a key element in emotional processes.

## Appraisals

The term 'evaluative cognitions' may be something of a misnomer. The term cognition has historically referred to what one consciously knows, both immediate perceptual awareness and knowledge in the sense of understanding about a thing. Evaluation refers to a different type of mental activity – that of appraising things and events.

Appraise means to evaluate or to judge, according to dictionary sources. The English language word comes from Middle English, *appraisen*, partly from *preise*, value. *Praise* comes partly from Old French *aprisier*, from Late Latin *appretiare*, to set value on; *ad + pretiare*, to value, from Latin *pretium*, prize. The etymology of the word shows that appraisals have not to do with what one knows, but with how one assigns value or worth to a person, thing, or event.

Strictly speaking, appraisals and evaluations are not cognitions, although one can have cognitions about one's appraisals and evaluations. In practice, however, it is the custom in psychology to use the term cognition to refer indiscriminately to almost all covert mental processes. Thus, Abelson (1963) distinguished between 'cold' and 'hot' cognitions – what one knows and how one appraises – and preserved a tradition in social psychology that maintains a distinction between the cognitive component of an attitude and the evaluative (or affective) component (Allport 1968).

Appraisals are key processes in many theories of emotion (Arnold 1960), including those that differ with respect to the primacy of cognition (Lazarus 1984) or of affect (Zajonc 1984). Plutchik (1980) theorizes, for example, that each emotion is triggered by some stimulus in the environment that is cognitively evaluated by the organism. When speaking of emotions, it seems essential to focus on appraisals. For the human organism, appraisals stem from an individual's moral principles and social values.

**Irrational beliefs**  The central concept of Ellis's rational-emotive therapy (RET) is the 'irrational' belief, which is more an appraisal than a cognition.

In his extensive writings and particularly most recent writings, Ellis states that irrational beliefs either are absolute imperatives or are derived from absolute imperatives – must-statements. He has coined a word *musturbation*, which he equates with irrational thinking. Extreme, exaggerated evaluations or appraisals, he says, are derived from must-statements. A major intervention in RET is to urge clients 'to look for the musts' when they experience intense 'inappropriate' emotions. Prescriptions of morally desirable behaviours (or values) appear to be involved in the so-called moral emotions – hostility, guilt, shame, jealousy, social anxiety, and some forms of depression (Sommers 1981). Ellis clearly emphasizes 'hot' cognitions in his RET, but they receive less explicit attention in other forms of CBT.

**Automatic thoughts**   Beck uses the term 'automatic thoughts' to identify cognitions active in the depressive disorders, and these automatic thoughts contain implicit appraisals. They are thoughts that seem to come automatically and involuntarily when the person is thinking negatively about self, the world, and the future (Beck's cognitive triad of negative thoughts). Negative cognitions are usually embedded in the interpretive errors of logic discussed earlier in this chapter, and Beck discusses them as empirical or logical conclusions rather than as derivative from values or attitudes.

That negative appraisals can be separated from nonevaluative cognitions for theoretical and therapeutic purposes is evident from the following example. Upon hearing a siren outside a building he was in, a man reported feeling anxious and thinking, 'My house might be on fire.' As reported, his statement is a cold cognition in that it states a possible fact that can be verified or refuted by gathering empirical data, as Beck's therapeutic strategy calls for. However, although Beck does not explicitly say so, there is also an implied hot cognition in that the phrase has some personal meaning to the speaker that goes beyond a mere statement of potential fact. One can only speculate about the nature of the hot cognition without knowledge of the speaker's moral principles and social values. Did the speaker regard his (possibly) burning house as good or bad? Bad, if he valued the house and its contents; good, if he had committed arson to collect insurance.

A comparison of Beck's and Ellis's characteristic cognitive interventions further highlights the difference between statements of presumed fact and appraisals. Beck's typical procedure is to ask for evidence about automatic thoughts; thoughts are taken as hypotheses to be tested by collecting data, e.g. is it logical to assume that my house is burning, and if so how can I empirically test this hypothesis? Ellis's intervention asks clients to justify an appraisal by citing evidence, e.g. to prove that it is awful if your house were to burn down.

Unless one is accustomed to separating the factual component from the evaluative component, it is possible to be misled by clients' statements, or to treat perceptions and understandings when values should be the focus. (Cf. work on the connotative meaning of concepts [Osgood, Suci and Tannenbaum 1957], in which the evaluative factor accounts for half the variance in typical factor analyses of semantic differential scores. Some implications of Osgood's work are discussed in Wessler and Wessler (1980)).

**Feelings** The term 'feelings', commonly used in several forms of psychotherapy, especially those identified as 'humanistic', can be better understood when one keeps in mind the hot versus cold cognition distinction. 'Feeling' has at least four meanings in the English language. They are: (a) bodily sensation, (b) tentative knowledge or opinion (also referred to as what one 'thinks' rather than 'knows' for certain), (c) appraisal or evaluation, and (d) emotional response. The last meaning – emotional response – can be further subdivided into physiological arousal or bodily sensation (and thus is covered by the first meaning of 'feeling'), subjective state (more a 'mental emotion' than a physiological one), and overt expression of emotion (although this last meaning is probably rare since people speak of 'hiding' their feelings). So, legitimate answers to the question, 'How do you feel about global disarmament?' are: (a) tense, (b) I'm not sure – I think it won't work, (c) I'm strongly against it, or (d) it scares me when I think that the other side won't disarm. Of these various meanings of the word feeling, two are cold cognitions (perception of bodily sensation and opinion), one clearly a hot cognition (appraisal), and the remaining meaning indeterminate.

**Self and other cognitions** The distinction between hot and cold can be applied to a set of cognitions that are prominantly featured in several forms of CBT (and in phenomenological-humanistic therapies, e.g. that of Carl Rogers). Ideas people have about who they are, and what they are and are not capable of, help explain their failure to change and overcome inertia.

Possibly the most indispensable cognitions in therapy are those that pertain to the self. As cold cognition, the self-concept or self-image consists of inferences and hypotheses about oneself – a personal theory of the self (Epstein 1973; Guidano and Liotti 1983; Raimy 1975). The inferences and hypotheses are drawn from the data of personal experience, and from messages received from other people, particularly in the early years of life. The tenacity with which they are held may determine whether new ideas will be easily assimilated through new experiences, for instance demonstrations of self-efficacy. They may determine whether one even attempts new actions that are inconsistent with self-image; accommodative shifts may be needed before new actions can be taken or the resulting experiences can be assimilated.

Self-evaluations or self-appraisals are hot cognitions. They have several pyschological names: self-regard, self-esteem, good (or bad) self-concept, good (or bad) self-image, self-rating, self-judgement. At times they are role-specific: good husband, good father, good psychologist. Negative thoughts about oneself are part of Beck's cognitive triad of depressive cognitions. They often appear as conditions of worth: 'I must achieve in order to consider myself a worthwhile person' (Ellis 1962, p. 63); or, 'I'm a poor father because my children are not better disciplined' (Beck 1963, p. 329). Thoughts about oneself may complement thoughts about other people, e.g. 'People don't like me because I am inadequate,' or, 'People will see that I am inadequate and take advantage of me.'

The theoretically and philosophically pure RET intervention in this case is to challenge the client to prove that he/she is worthless because he/she has not achieved as much as he/she demands (the irrational belief would be something to the effect 'I must achieve, otherwise I am worthless.'). Note that this intervention makes no reference to the truth or falsity of the 'factual' part of the statement; indeed, Ellis considers it less therapeutic to show the client that he/she has in fact achieved, for then he/she would continue to base self-evaluation on arbitrary conditions of worth. A typical Beck intervention might take the 'my children are not better disciplined' part of the statement and seek evidence to support or refute it, that is, seek factual evidence about the validity of the cold cognition. However, another Beck intervention would be to focus on the paralogical evaluative conclusion that one is a poor father because children at times misbehave, thereby raising questions about the appropriateness of the self-appraisal. (Incidentally, Ellis would initially sidestep the questionable validity of the cold cognition by supposing that it might be true that the client is a poor father. 'But how', he would ask, 'does that make you a worthless person?' He might later investigate the extent to which the children were undisciplined.)

## Nonphenomenological cognitions

It should be apparent by now that it may be a contradiction to speak of unconscious cognitions. Cognitions, by definition, refer to what is known, and unconscious thoughts are, also by definition, unknown or not in one's awareness. And yet, one can recall or recognize memories of which one had hitherto been unaware, when appropriate retrieval cues are presented. Memory improves when recall is attempted under conditions that resemble those when learning took place (state-dependent learning). Bower (1981), for example, presents data in support of a theory in which mood and memory are shown as interrelated – mood affects recall, and memories affect mood. Further, one may not attend to stimuli which later capture attention when they are pointed out, or become predominant due to novelty or other cues. Finally insight into relationships between various aspects of a problem may suddenly emerge from a period of cognitive incubation, or if the problem is reframed.

The foregoing description of 'unconscious' cognitive processes represents a position in current cognitive psychology. It is intentionally nonFreudian. Freudian and othe psychodynamic approaches assume a structure of the mind called the 'unconscious', with hidden motives and ego-protective mechanisms. Freud was not the first person in the history of science to speak of unconscious processes, nor the first to give them scientific status. Helmholz employed the notion of unconscious inference (*unbewußter Schluß*) to explain perceptual constancies.

Despite the Freudian taint that puts off some behaviourists, there seems good reason to assume the existence of processes that lie outside awareness which can be inferred from behavioural data, that is, nonphenomenological cognitions. Mahoney, for example, forecast an important role for a network of unconscious thoughts in the future direction of CBT: 'the existence of such a network is not only possible but very probable, and . . . the practical implications are both challenging and inescapable' (Mahoney 1980, p. 160). Many of the schemata for perceiving and acting which are described in the next section of this chapter fall outside one's immediate awareness.

One possibility resulting from assuming unconscious cognitions is that they connect with conscious ones, with only one or two of the conscious cognitions evident. Moore (1980) hypothesizes that inferences very often appear linked, one to another, in roughly causal sequence. The terminal link in the chain most often contains the most definitive statement of the situation, and the definition of the situation may range from highly probable to highly improbable. The appraisal or evaluation of the terminal link in the chain triggers the emotional responses. One implication of this chain of association model is that therapists who rely on clients' introspections of their cognitions limit their treatment efforts to those cognitions that the individual is aware of and able to report, if only to him/herself. An important therapist task, then, is to help the client to discover unspoken and unthought-of ideas, understandings, and appraisals (cold and hot cognitions).

Another implication concerns self-help procedures. Books, tape recordings, lectures, and workshops can produce only limited benefits for their audiences for three reasons. First, they do not and cannot deal with nonphenomenological cognitions. Thus an important source of influence on behaviour and emotion is inaccessible. Second, they deal in generalities, not the idiosyncratic cognitions that disturb an individual. Finally, they may present correct principles that the individual nevertheless finds confusing to apply appropriately. Also, the person may not take the time or trouble to start or continue the self-help programme for reasons which the programmes have no way of dealing with.

To elaborate the last point, consider the difficulty therapists have in correctly applying psychological principles to their clients' problems. If it were easy, no supervisor of therapy would be needed (Wessler and Ellis 1980). Further, resistance to change (or inertia, to use a term with fewer psychoanalytic connotations) is mysterious to both client and therapist; Freud, one may recall, called it the neurotic paradox. The mystery can be solved by delving into nonphenomenological cognitions, especially ideas about oneself or what one's life would be like were one to carry out the changes contemplated and for which the self-help methods were originally sought.

Guidano and Liotti (1983) have written about implicit and explicit ideas – ideas that are out of and within awareness, respectively. Only explicit ideas can be expressed in words. However, implicit ideas can become explicit. The same assumptions can be made for personal and social values, as well as the moral principles one holds. Such evaluations may not be explicit, but nevertheless provide an unconscious set of rules the individual follows in everyday life. Just as habits are mindless but can become mindful, so implicit thinking can become mindful, and when it does it can be rendered into spoken and written language. Cognitive-behaviour therapists often refer to these implicit ideas as schemata, a concept to be discussed in the next section.

Spoken language contains paralinguistic clues to underlying meaning. These are clues to what one thinks and understands, but more especially to one's appraisals. Calling someone a 'fool' can be affectionate or hostile, depending on the manner of delivery of the message and the context in which it occurs. Therapists should listen for meanings, not words. Statements represent thoughts; thoughts may be incompletely expressed. By pursuing the deep structure or underlying meaning of a statement, therapists can achieve a fuller understanding of clients' cognitions and make implicit thoughts explicit.

## Generalized versus specific cognitions

Cognitive-behavioural approaches include at least two lines of psychological tradition. One is that of behaviour therapy, and the other comes from cognitive social psychology. As behaviour therapy adopted educational procedures, e.g. assertiveness training, social skills training, and other forms of directly teaching appropriate skills, it opened the way for the addition of cognitions. Social psychology was dominated for several decades by Lewin's field theory, particularly in the form of Festinger's theory of cognitive dissonance. Some of these cognitive social psychology notions found their way into counselling and psychotherapy (Strong and Claiborn 1982), where George Kelly had already staked a claim for cognition. The point of this historical reminder is that cognitive-behavioural approaches to psychotherapy consist of two emphases: one in which cognitions were added onto behavioural analyses, and another in which cognitions always served as pivotal constructs from the outset.

The behaviourist tradition was heavily influenced by the intellectual and philosophical positions of empiricism and associationism. Associationism holds that molecular units of behaviour (and cognition) are acquired and pieced together by their temporal association with one another. Both classical and operant conditioning are examples. The *Gestalt* tradition, on which much of cognitive social psychology is based, rejected empiricism in favour of nativism, and associationism in favour of an emphasis on the irreducible, organized whole. (We leave to the psychology of perception the question of nativism.) Of concern here is the question of a piecemeal approach to understanding cognitions versus one that stresses organization.

Psychological studies of language in general seem to support the position that concepts, as well as memories, are organized, and that the organization is hierarchical. Thus, a specific cognition – either cold or hot – such as an automatic thought, may be situation-specific but is at the same time part of a larger cluster of similar thoughts. It does not seem useful to suppose that the specific thought has been learned in similar situations and will only be elicited by specific stimuli. If language depended exclusively on operant and classical conditioning, we could not generate novel sentences. In the same vein, we cannot think certain thoughts unless we can generate them from an organized set.

In therapy, specific thoughts are of interest because they account for certain emotions and behaviours. However, they are of greater interest when seen as representing clusters of thoughts. As Raimy noted, misconceptions seem not to exist as single events, but rather cluster together and bear some relationship to each other. An approach that seeks only to extinguish or replace specific thoughts about specific situations, e.g. self-statement modification techniques, lack generalizability (although the skill of replacing thoughts may be generalizable).

Relatively enduring and generalized cognitions may be termed cognitive structures (Meichenbaum 1977) or schemata that 'represent one's general knowledge about a given concept or stimulus domain' (Fiske and Taylor 1983, p. 13). Examples of schemata might be 'People are inherently good' or 'People cannot be trusted.' The self-concept may be seen as a self-schema, e.g. 'I am not worthy of people's love and affection.' Popularly held cultural beliefs may purport to speak truth about human behaviour, e.g. 'The world is fair, and people get rewarded and punished according to some divine or natural plan of justice.' This particular generalization, sometimes called the belief in a just world, explains failure to aid persons in distress, because victims presumably deserve their fate. Aphorisms can also be a source of comfort, as when one explains misfortune by saying that it is God's will.

Such generalizations, which are not usually within an individual's awareness, can distort one's thinking, as for example when one believes that stereotypes of people are true without exception. One may have inaccurate stereotyped beliefs about oneself. The generalization need not be factual to have impact on the person; the person need only believe that it is correct. As the American sociologist W. I. Thomas expressed in his famous dictum: 'If people define things as real, they are real in their consequences.' Specific thoughts and statements may be seen as generated from schemata about oneself, the world, and other people, and should be distinguished in therapy from specific cognitions. The relationship is not unlike that between surface structure and deeper underlying meaning. In a sense, every specific cognition may reflect underlying assumptions, which may be nonphenomenological.

One important task of therapy, then, is to make clients more aware of their underlying nonphenomenological schemata. In other words (certain to be unacceptable to radical behaviourists), the task is to make the noncon-scious conscious. Located outside awareness are organizing assumptions about self, other people, and the ways the world works. These ideas account for consistency of behaviour in psychologically similar situations, as well as for individuals' distinct ways of interacting which we call personality. Another name for these assumptions is 'world view', a concept used by Piaget. The therapeutic implications of world view have been discussed by Watzlawick (1978) and by Guidano and Liotti (1983). World view may be inferred by therapist and by client from specific statements the client reports about specific situations, and from actions that, because of their recurrence, seem to follow certain assumptions and rules. Such inferences may be particularly made when these specific statements and behaviours are consis-tent with one another.

Generalized cold cognitions are supposed truths about self, others, and the ways in which the world works; generalized hot cognitions are personal and social values and moral principles, that is, statements about what should be rather than what actually exists. Values and moral principles are acquired by learning from other people's explicit teachings and the examples they set, and by the sense that one makes of one's own experiences. Values and principles become guides for personal conduct and for making specific appraisals of things and events, and also of oneself. The author calls them personal rules of living to emphasize their regulatory function in each person's life (see the chapter on Cognitive Appraisal Therapy). Relatively enduring hot cognitions may also be called evaluative premises and the specific appraisals derived from them can be called evaluative conclusions (Wessler and Wessler 1980).

## Behavioural change

**Plans and decisions**  Whether one prefers the image of humans as personal scientists or, as was argued earlier in this chapter, as managers, an active rather than passive view of humans is postulated. People do not passively react either to their environments or to their mental representations of those environments. In other words, when one adopts the human-as-manager viewpoint discussed earlier, one also adopts an open-system view of people in which actions are partly, or perhaps probabilistically, determined, but not fully determined as in a closed system. Humans are assumed to choose a course of action as a consequence of processing information about alterna-tives.

**Problem-solving**   It can be presumed that when persons' thinking leads them astray, they get into behavioural difficulties. Skills deficits are cognitive deficits before they are behavioural deficits. Maladaptive or troublesome behaviours may be corrected by new information and new strategies for utilizing information. Thinking realistically about the consequences of one's actions is a necessary step in effective problem-solving.

Spivack, Platt and Shure (1976) have described a number of features of cognitive skills needed for social problem-solving. These include recognizing that a problem exists, for instance that two or more people are in conflict, and taking time to stop and think about the problem rather than act impulsively. An important element in this process is the capacity to discriminate fact from opinion (description from inference). They go on to describe alternative-solution thinking, a skill that involves the generating of a number of possible solutions to the problem; their emphasis is upon generating alternatives rather than merely recognizing them or passively following formulae or strategies proposed by others. Consequential thinking is another important element, and involves anticipation or expectations about reinforcing outcomes (cf. Bandura's and Rotter's views on this point discussed earlier in this chapter). Once the alternatives and their consequences are weighed, the best method for implementing the solution is considered (means-end thinking). Finally, the solution is verified from the actual experience of trying it out (an idea akin to self-demonstration).

In summary, the steps are: problem identification and specification; seeking alternative solutions and screening them for payoffs; selecting means of implementation; and evaluating (and perhaps improving on) the solution by trial-and-success or trial-and-error. Information is neccessary, but so are the cognitive processes for using information. Unstated but clearly underlying problem-solving are the notions of planning and decision-making. (This perspective is discussed further in the chapter by Platt, Prout and Metzger.)

Decisions about action imply thinking about one's actions, selecting courses of action to take, and instructing oneself to do this and not that. Without cognitions about plans and decisions, action might seem to stem automatically from internal forces (psychodynamic unconscious model) or external forces (S-R behavioural model). Decisions represent a somewhat existential dimension – they are also what makes therapeutic change possible.

A seeming paradox stems from the hybridization of cognitive and behavioural approaches. Most approaches to cognitive-behavioural therapy agree with Raimy's claim that cognitions must change in order for enduring behavioural changes to occur. Some behaviourists argue that cognitions are epiphenomenal rationalizations to explain behaviours that are determined by reinforcement; behaviours must change in order for cognitions to change. Bandura pointed out that verbal methods of inducing cognitive change are among the weakest, and that self-demonstrations of efficacy are better at producing cognitive change. Eysenck (1985) agrees, although he insists on the primacy of behavioural change – the view that cognitions catch up with what has already happened due to conditioning.

Cognitive-behavioural approaches, then, can be seen as having a chicken-and-egg dilemma. Cognitions must change in order for behaviours to change, but behaviours must change in order for cognitions to change, and so on. Unless a client decides to act differently despite the anxiety generated by long-standing interpretations and evaluations, and decides to act in opposition to uncomfortable feelings rather than to reduce or avoid discomfort, behavioural change will not occur. Stated more clinically, how can we get a client to engage in behaviours that will promote thoughts of competence and feelings of confidence, when he/she is too afraid to try anything new?

The paradox is resolved by inserting the notion of decision: cognitive decisions to act differently result in the performing of new actions which result in experiences which in turn result in changes in specific and general cognitions. Janis (1983) has researched and written extensively about decisions. He points out that there are several procedural criteria and stages in vigilant decision-making, although people do not follow these most of the time. They encounter two problems: excessive delay in arriving at closure and premature closure – procrastination and impulsiveness. Both are defensive strategies for reducing stress. Without detailing the procedures involved in the process of reducing stress and promoting effective decisions, it is sufficient to note that they involve exploring clients' expectations and anticipations, images and conceptions, especially self-images and self-conceptions, to determine whether the new actions are alien to one's knowledge and value schemata.

Clients may anticipate that beneficial changes will result from a new course of action, and yet worry that the emotional 'costs' of fear and anxiety will outweigh the hoped-for benefits. Cognitive rehearsal, analyses of reinforcing consequences (including self-reinforcement), coping imagery, and behavioural rehearsal help prepare the person for change. Nonetheless, at some point, the individual must decide to endure the unfamiliar and risk the unexpected. Self-instructional coping statements can help in the situation, and self-demonstrations of efficacy may then follow.

Some behaviourists argue that reinforcement contingencies, not decisions, account for the action of delaying immediate reinforcement in favour of postponed reinforcement. Of course, they can explain action by employing their own theoretical language. The success of therapeutic procedures can be explained by any alternative theory. For example, a client who avoided social situations because, he stated, people criticized him for not appearing adequate, was induced to enter such situations; his anxiety gradually diminished. RET would explain that he surrendered his irrational belief that it is awful to be criticized. Beck's cognitive therapy explanation might be that he learned that people in fact did not often criticize him. A behaviourist might say that his frequent in vivo desensitization trials were effective due to repeated exposure and response prevention. A social learning explanation might state that he demonstrated self-efficacy and thereby lost his fear and gained confidence. Raimy might say that his cognitions became more realistic and his adjustment consequently improved. Others might say that he revised his world view as a result of his experiences. The criterion of utility is usually employed in judging theories, and all of the above may prove useful in a particular instance.

**Insight and action**   There are several types of insight. Ellis, Beck, and others use the term 'insight' to refer to one's understanding that thought affects mood. This might be called theoretical insight. Personal insight consists of awareness of particular thoughts leading to specific emotional and behavioural consequences. Self-awareness that is not accompanied by a change in feelings is often called intellectual insight.

The CBT explorations of clients' thinking will usually reveal other types of personal insights. These insights are here-and-now revelations of nonphenomenological cognitions and structures. The development of cognitive structures, that is, how they developed and what their sources were, is also a matter of insight. Such insights into one's personal history not only satisfy one's need for a relatively simple cause-and-result explanation of personality, but they may reveal the source of cognitive impediments to change.

One such impediment might be, for example, believing that one will defy one's mother's or father's ideals if a new behaviour is attempted. Or that a cognition is not inaccurate because 'everyone knows' it is accurate, particularly significant others in one's past. In some cases, insight may prove worse than ignorance. Knowing that one is the source of one's difficulties and that change is possible may lead to feelings of guilt when one does not change or changes slowly. Just as trusting one's feelings can lead to inertia when they promote avoidance, insight can lead to inertia unless one can adopt a new view of one's past. Except for the work of Guidano and Liotti, little attention in CBT has been paid to past influences on present and future actions and emotions.

Inducing oneself to attempt new actions in order to have corrective experiences may prove more difficult than either gaining insights or intellectually questioning one's thoughts. If corrective experiences and learning from one's efficacious performances are essential for therapeutic change, therapists can help clients make plans and decisions that promote their values and are consistent with therapeutic goals. Personal experience may prove to be the best teacher, decisions may be the most important cognitions in CBT, and encouragement to make decisions and carry them out may be the most challenging and significant task of psychological therapists.

## A new challenge

Cognitive-behavioural approaches to psychotherapy have generally held that behaviour and affect are the results of cognitive variables. Zajonc (1980b) has challenged this view while promoting his own, that affect is both primary and independent of cognition. The debate over primacy of affect or cognition is hampered by definitions of what is cognitive and what is not (Plutchik 1985). Greenberg and Safran (1984) have proposed Leventhal's (1979) perceptual-motor model to integrate affect and cognition. This model features the simultaneous generation of perception and emotion and the input of perception and emotion into planning and decisions for action. Emotional experience is said to result from a preattentive process whose components lie outside focal awareness; therefore, 'conscious changes at the conceptual level will not necessarily produce changes at the affective level, since emotional experience is as much a function of changes that take place at a perceptual-motor, preconceptual level as it is a function of conceptual cognition' (Greenberg and Safran 1984, p. 568). However, they warn against falling into polarized thinking about affect and cognition.

Similarly, Tosi and Baisden (1984) propose a therapeutic model of awareness that addresses cognitive operations occurring at different levels of brain functioning, including the operations of the primitive (sub-cortical) brain. Tosi's cognitive-experiential therapy relies on hypnosis to affect nonconscious processes, and to overcome distortions in cognitive awareness resulting from selective inattention. (Tosi's approach is also known as rational stage-directed hypnosis and was derived from RET. If DuBois's reaction against hypnosis marks the beginnings of cognitive-behavioural approaches to psychotherapy, then perhaps its history has come full circle.) Both Greenberg and Safran and Tosi believe that the evoking of emotional states is necessary in order to employ procedures that result in achieving changes in the cognitions that take place in these states.

The evoking of emotional experiences may be done through hypnosis, in vivo procedures, or imagery. The purpose of their evocation would not be to relive an emotional experience, abreaction, or catharsis. Rather, they would be evoked in order to elicit the cognitions that are associated with these affects and that would otherwise remain implicit. Whether affect must be evoked in order to identify relevant cognitions and for therapeutic changes to occur is an important research question with relevance for both the theoretical foundations and practice of psychotherapy using cognitive-behavioural approaches.

# References

Abelson, R.P. (1963) Computer simulation of 'hot cognitions'. In S. Tomkins and S. Messick (eds) *Computer simulations of personality*. New York: Wiley.

Abramson, L.V., Seligman, M.E.P. and Teasdale, J.D. (1978) Learned helplessness in humans: Critique and reformulation. *Journal of Abnormal Psychology, 87*, 49–74.

Allport, G.W. (1968) The historical background of modern social psychology. In G. Lindzey and E. Aronson (eds) *The handbook of social psychology*, vol. 1. Reading, MA: Addison-Wesley.

Arnold, M.B. (1960) *Emotion and personality*. New York: Columbia University Press.

Bandura, A. (1977) *Social learning theory*. Englewood Cliffs, NJ: Prentice-Hall.

Barker, R.G. (1968) *Ecological psychology*. Stanford, CA: Stanford University Press.

Beck, A.T. (1963) Thinking and depression. *Archives of General Psychiatry, 9*, 324–333.

Beck, A.T. (1976) *Cognitive therapy and the emotional disorders*. New York: International Universities Press.

Bower, G.H. (1981) Mood and memory. *American Psychologist, 36*, 129–148.

DuBois, P. (1909) The method of persuasion. In W.B. Parker (ed.) *Psychotherapy: A course of reading in sound psychology, sound medicine, and sound religion*, vol. 3. New York: Centre Publishing.

Ellis, A. (1962) *Reason and emotion in psychotherapy*. New York: Lyle Stuart.

Epstein, S. (1973) The self-concept revisited: Or a theory of a theory. *American Psychologist, 28*, 404–416.

Ericsson, K.A. and Simon, H.A. (1981) Sources of evidence on cognition: A historical overview. In T.V. Merluzzi, C.R. Glass and M. Genest (eds) *Cognitive assessment*. New York: Guilford Press.

Eysenck, H.J. (1966) *The effects of psychotherapy*. New York: International Sciences Press.

Eysenck, H.J. (1985) Psychotherapy effects: Real or imaginary? *American Psychologist, 40*, 239–240.

Fiske, S.T and Taylor, S.E. (1984) *Social cognition*. Reading, MA: Addison-Wesley.

Försterling, F. (in press) Attributional retraining: A review. *Psychological Bulletin*.

Friedman, M.I. (1975) *Rational behavior*. Columbia: University of South Carolina Press.

Greenberg, L.S. and Safran, J.D. (1984) Integrating affect and cognition: A perspective on the process of therapeutic change. *Cognitive therapy and research, 8*, 559–578.

Guidano, V.F. and Liotti, G. (1983) *Cognitive processes and emotional disorders*. New York: Guilford Press.

Harvey, J.H. and Weary, G. (1981) *Perspectives on attributional processes*. Dubuque, IA: W.C. Brown.

Heider, F. (1958) *The psychology of interpersonal relations*. New York: Wiley.

Homans, G.C. (1961) *Social behavior: Its elementary forms*. New York: Harcourt, Brace.

Janis, I.L. (1983) *Short-term counseling: Guidelines based on recent research*. New Haven, CT: Yale University Press.

Kelly, G.A. (1955) *The psychology of personal constructs*. New York: Norton.

Lazarus, A.A. (1981) *The practice of multimodal therapy*. New York: McGraw-Hill.

Lazarus, R.S. (1984) On the primacy of cognition. *American Psychologist, 39*, 124–129.

Leventhal, H. (1979). A perceptual-motor processing model of emotion. In P. Pliner, K.R. Blankstein and I.M. Spigel (eds) *Advances in the study of communication and affect*, vol. 5 *Perception of emotions in self and others*. New York: Plenum.

Mahoney, M.J. (1974) *Cognition and behavior modification*. Cambridge, MA: Ballinger.

Mahoney, M.J. (1977) Reflections on the cognitive-learning trend in psychotherapy. *American Psychologist, 32*, 5–13.

Mahoney, M.J. (1980) Psychotherapy and the structure of personal revolutions. In M.J. Mahoney (ed.) *Psychotherapy process*. New York: Plenum.

Mahoney, M.J. and Arnkoff, D. (1978) Cognitive and self-control therapies. In S.L. Garfield and A.E. Bergin (eds) *Handbook of psychotherapy and behaviour change: An empirical analysis*. New York: Wiley.

Meichenbaum, D. (1977) *Cognitive behavior modification*. New York: Plenum.

Moore, R.H. (1980) Inference chaining. In M.S. Morain (ed.) *Classroom exercises in general semantics*. San Francisco: International Society for General Semantics.

Nisbett, R.E. and Ross, L. (1980) *Human inference: Strategies and shortcomings of social judgment*. Englewood Cliffs, NJ: Prentice-Hall.

Nisbett, R.E. and Wilson, T.D. (1977) Telling more than we can know: Verbal reports on mental processes. *Psychological Review, 84*, 231–259.

Osgood, C.E., Suci, G.J. and Tannenbaum, P.H. (1957) *The measurement of meaning*. Urbana, IL: University of Illinois Press.

Plutchik, R. (1980) *Emotion: A psychoevolutionary synthesis*. New York: Harper and Row.

Plutchik, R. (1985) On emotion: The chicken-and-egg problem revisited. *Motivation and Emotion, 9*, 197–200.

Raimy, V. (1975) *Misunderstandings of the self*. San Francisco: Jossey-Bass.

Rotter, J.B. (1954) *Social learning and clinical psychology*. Englewood Cliffs, NJ: Prentice-Hall.

Salter, A. (1949) *Conditioned reflex therapy*. New York: Strauss and Young.

Seligman, M.E.P. (1975) *Helplessness: On depression, development, and death*. San Francisco: Freeman.

Skinner, B.F. (1980) *Notebooks*. Englewood Cliffs, NJ: Prentice-Hall.

Sommers, S. (1981) Emotionality reconsidered: The role of cognition in emotional responsiveness. *Journal of Personality and Social Psychology, 41*, 553–561.

Spivack, G., Platt, J. and Shure, M. (1976) *The problem-solving approach to adjustment*. San Francisco: Jossey-Bass.

Strong, S.R. and Claiborn, C.D. (1982) *Change through interaction*. New York: Wiley.

Tosi, D.J. and Baisden, B. (1984). Cognitive experiential therapy and hypnosis. In W. Wester and J. Smith (eds) *Clinical hypnosis: A multidisciplinary approach*. New York: Lippincott.

Tversky, A. and Kahnemann, D. (1981) The framing of decisions and the psychology of choice. *Science, 211*, 453–458.

Watzlawick, P. (1978) *The language of change*. New York: Basic Books.

Wessler, R.A. and Wessler, R.L. (1980) *The principles and practice of rational-emotive therapy*. San Francisco: Jossey-Bass.

Wessler, R.L. (1984) A bridge too far: Incompatibilities of rational-emotive therapy and pastoral counseling. *Personnel and Guidance Journal, 63*, 264–266.

Wessler, R.L. and Ellis, A. (1980) Supervision in rational-emotive therapy. In A.K. Hess (ed.) *Psychotherapy supervision*. New York: Wiley.

Woods, P.J. (1985) Learning paradigms, expectancies, and behavioural control: An expanded classification for learned behaviour. *British Journal of Cognitive Psychotherapy, 3*, 43–58.

Zajonc, R.B. (1980a) Cognition and social cognition. In L. Festinger (ed.) *Retrospections on social psychology*. New York: Oxford.

Zajonc, R.B. (1980b) Feeling and thinking: Preferences need no inferences. *American Psychologist, 35*, 151–175.

Zajonc, R.B. (1984) On the primacy of affect. *American Psychologist, 39*, 117–123.

## CHAPTER TWO

**Cognitive-Behaviour Modification: The Shaping of Rule-Governed Behaviour**
*Matt E. Jaremko*

## History and underpinnings of cognitive-behaviour modification

*Historical development of cognitive-behaviour modification*

During the years 1975 to 1978, Donald Meichenbaum published the *Cognitive-Behavior Modification Newsletter*, an informal description of ongoing research on the role of cognitive processes in human behaviour. As much as any other source in cognitive-behaviourism, the *Cognitive-Behavior Modification Newsletter* captured the imagination and enkindled the enthusiasm of many researchers and therapists. Numerous important and challenging questions related to the cognitive control of behaviour were raised by Professor Meichenbaum. A virtual explosion of research and reconceptualization was stimulated by those newsletters and to many that period marked the beginning of the so-called 'cognitive bandwagon' in behaviour therapy (Mahoney 1977a).

One of the points frequently made by Meichenbaum in those newsletters was emphasis on the 'hyphen' in cognitive-behaviour modification. The interaction of cognitive activity with other behaviour, their mutual influence on each other, was a feature of human experience to which cognitive-behaviour modification therapists were directing attention in both treatment and research. In addition, the rapprochement of behavioural and cognitive psychology was called for (Mahoney 1974). Now, it is clear from a number of sources (cf. Kendall 1983) that psychology has indeed 'gone cognitive'. But can it also be concluded that is has gone 'behavioural' as well? It could well be that there is more 'cognitive' in cognitive-behaviour modification than 'behavioural'. Such a premise is explored in this chapter.

A comprehensive integration of cognitive and behavioural approaches requires attention to the origin and function of behaviour as well as its structure. A perspective integrating functional and structural aspects of responding can be the basis on which cognitive-behaviour modification techniques are explained and expanded. It is crucial for the cognitive-behaviour modification therapist to analyze how the client came under cognitive/verbal control in the first place. Especially important is the origin of cognitive activity variously referred to as cognitive structures (Meichenbaum

1977), schemata (Leventhal and Nerenz 1983; Turk and Speers 1983); or scripts (Abelson 1981). What is the nature of these processes? How are these overlearned, conceptualized classes of behaviour modified by the cognitive-behaviour modification therapist? This is a primary task of the present chapter in which the tenets of cognitive-behaviour modification are discussed from the perspective of a functional theory of behaviour, that of radical behaviourism (Skinner 1953, 1957, 1969, 1974).

Radical behaviourism is a philosophy of the science of behaviour in which internal behavioural events are given consideration as elements in ongoing sequences of responding. Contrary to methodological behaviourism in which inner events are ignored as much as possible (Mahoney 1974), radical behaviourism has as its primary task the development of a complete account of all behaviour, including internal events. At the same time, a key feature of the radical-behavioural approach is that these internal events cannot be used as explanations for other behaviour. Such 'mentalism' appeals to inner causes for external responding (Jaremko 1979a). Radical behaviourism seeks to provide explanations for both internal and external responding by using events outside of the behaving individual, that is, genetic and environmental factors, as causal factors.

A refinement of the techniques of cognitive/verbal control may be possible when consideration is given to the origins and functions of the client's cognitive/verbal processes. Moreover, consideration of the radical-behavioural perspective alongside the cognitive one may do more to make cognitive-behaviour modification a truly integrative approach. In short a better understanding of the 'hyphen' in cognitive-behaviour modification may be achieved.

## Major theoretical concepts

Since first being articulated as a force in modern psychology, cognitive-behaviour modification has had a difficult time establishing a firm theoretical stance (Mahoney 1974). As an integrative approach, elements of many different theories have been useful in understanding and elaborating cognitive-behaviour modification (Meichenbaum 1977). The few attempts to identify an overriding theoretical approach for cognitive-behaviour modification have themselves turned out to be amalgamations of several conceptual models (Kendall 1983). It is in the spirit of a continued search for a unifying theoretical position for cognitive-behaviour modification that radical behaviourism is discussed here as a unifying theory.

**The origins of cognitive/verbal control**   If cognitive/verbal control is to be used by cognitive-behaviour modification therapists to help overcome emotional and behavioural problems, it is important first to understand where such control comes from. There are, of course, numerous instances of behaviour controlled by cognitive processes. Why people floss their teeth, buckle seat belts, pay income taxes, and go to church are some examples from daily life. The notion of rule-governed behaviour (Skinner 1969) is the key radical-behavioural concept helpful in understanding such cognitive/verbal control.

Rule-following is taught to humans at very young ages, becoming so habitual as to seem automatic. But the process by which rule-following originates gives important clues to cognitive-behaviour modification. Much behaviour, if not all of it, occurs in the presence of various stimuli. Through the process of discrimination training, these stimuli come to exert influence over behaviour. Behaviour reinforced when a stimulus is present and not reinforced or punished when the stimulus is absent will eventually occur only when the stimulus is present (Whaley and Malott 1971). Further, there is almost no end to the variety of stimuli that can set the occasion for the reinforcement of behaviour. Time, location, other people, proprioceptive events, and specific sights and sounds are only some of the general classes. In human beings, the verbal responses of one's self and others comprise a very important class of events which gain stimulus control over responding. Some verbal responses specify contingent relationships within an environment and can be termed rules. These rules come to exert control over behaviour only when certain experiences have been present in an individual's past.

Contingency-specifying stimuli, or rules, are frequently presented throughout a human being's life cycle. A parent repeats the maxim, 'Good girls (boys) don't fuss when they take naps,' and provides reinforcement for appropriate compliance. An older sibling warns the younger child, 'Don't play with my erector set or I'll bop you,' frequently punishing non-compliance with the rule. A teacher says, 'Stay in your seat all day and you'll get a gold star by your name,' setting the occasion for the reinforcement of an academic survival skill and the punishment of noncompliance with it.

It isn't long in the lives of most children before rules begin to exert stimulus control. Moreover, following rules becomes generalized after a critical mass of history of being reinforced for compliance and/or punished for non-compliance has accumulated. The typical child will follow rules which have never before set the occasion for reinforcement (Whaley and Malott 1971). The child's behaviour is rule-governed when he/she consistently performs actions without having had direct contact with the consequences of the actions. In this sense, cognitive/verbal control allows for the transcendance of immediate incentives in an environment.

The most common source of rules for children is other people, particularly adults. If the child has a repertoire of rule-governed behaviour, his or her actions can be controlled by the verbal activity of the adults with the occasional back-up reinforcement of social approval for compliance. In such a case, there is little or no contact with the natural consequences of performance or non-performance of the behaviour in question. Rather, the child performs the behaviour because (a) a rule has been stated ('It's time to go to church'), (b) following rules has been rewarded in the past, and (c) social reinforcement for compliance with the component behaviours implied in the rule is presented ('Good, I see you have dressed yourself for church'). Again, the crucial point is that behaviour occurs without the child ever having contact with the natural consequences of performing or not performing the activity.

In this conceptualization social reinforcement is a crucial developmental ingredient. Social approval provides an intermediate incentive for following a rule without yet having had direct contact with the consequences specified in the rule. A parent's encouragement for teeth-flossing maintains a rate of the action sufficient to produce the long-term result of healthier teeth and gums. Thereafter the natural consequences of flossing will exert more control. However, the immediate and intermediate social reinforcement must occur first in order for the child to come in contact with the natural results of the behaviour, which in many cases are delayed.

Moreover, social reinforcement from parents can occasion another important process in the cognitive/verbal control of behaviour, that of 'self-reinforcement' (Mahoney 1976). In most cases, children have learned to model the behaviour of their parents (Bandura and Walters 1963). In fact imitative behaviour is rewarded so much that it becomes generalized in most children (Whaley and Malott 1971). Children imitate much of what their parents do, even if a specific imitative behaviour has not been reinforced directly itself. Theoretically, imitation can extend to the parents' delivery of social reinforcement. The child begins to deliver social reinforcement to himself or herself ('What a fine chap am I, I brushed my teeth!'). If this self-reinforcement activity occurs at a reliable level, the development of rule-following behaviour can proceed more quickly because 'self-reinforcement' can mediate between the following of a rule and contact with the natural consequences of the action in question.

An obvious ingredient in rule-governed behaviour is the statement of the rule. Verbal communities, other persons who reward and/or punish verbal activity, arrange consequences that encourage children to describe the world (Skinner 1957). By rewarding many different types of verbal responses, including the labelling of contingent relationships in the world, verbal communities increase the extent to which children and adults state rules.

Eventually the child provides the rule statements himself or herself. The individual flosses teeth because a relevant rule is produced, 'I must floss before I go to bed,' and the person has had a history of being reinforced for following rules, even self-given ones. A person begins to buckle the automobile seat belt when the rule, 'I'll be safer in this car if I'm buckled into it,' is stated and rule-following has been advantageous to the person in the past. In fact, any behaviour whose natural immediate effects are too weak to ensure action will be performed only if (a) immediate prompts and consequences are arranged by others, as in the case of parents 'standing over' a child while he or she brushes teeth, or (b) a tendency to follow rules has been established, and (c) the relevant rule has been stated in the situation. In the latter case, rule-following can be viewed as the method of 'cognitive' control by which humans are able to perform actions that have only distal beneficial effects or alternatively not perform actions that have distal detrimental consequences.

**Emotional responding**   A key element in human experience is emotional responding, the hormonal and endocrine changes resulting from exposure to environmental events (Malott and Whaley 1976). These emotional changes can, of course, be conditioned (Izard 1977). Conditioned emotional experience elicited by cognitive/verbal events appears to be a central component in affective disorders (Beck 1976).

From the respondent perspective, neutral stimuli come to elicit responses after having had sufficient association with unconditioned stimuli. In some cases the neutral stimulus is a cognitive/verbal response and the unconditioned stimulus elicited is emotional responding. Thus an individual punished for failure to comply with a rule statement may come to respond to the rule statement in a manner similar to the punishing stimuli, that is, emotionally. In later episodes of rule-following, the rule-specifying stimuli may elicit the emotional experience. Conditioned emotional responses, no doubt more compex than the above brief treatment would suggest (Blankstein, Pliner and Polivy 1980), must be considered in a full account of cognitive-behaviour modification treatment.

Treating emotional disorders by focusing on the cognitive/verbal activity eliciting the negative emotion is the essence of cognitive-behaviour modification for affective disorders. A typical cognitive-behavioural treatment of depression, for example, is to show how self-defeating cognitive behaviour leads to negative emotions. Usually that cognitive activity takes the form of false or harmful rule statements. Consider the depressed person who chronically considers himself a burden to others and who becomes depressed about it. The cognitive behaviour involved is a false and/or harmful rule. Thus, 'Others think I am incompetent. Incompetent people are worthless. I'm worthless,' and other false rule-specifying self-talk generates emotional behaviour. If cognitive/verbal behaviour of that sort occurs chronically, an affective disorder is the result. Thus cognitive-behaviour modification views such faulty cognitive/verbal control as the most important target of treatment in affective disorders.

**The structuralization of cognitive activity**   Writers on cognitive-behaviour modification have proposed a construct to explain instances of responding in which obvious forms of control are lacking (Turk and Speers 1983). The term cognitive structure is one common label used for this construct (Meichenbaum and Gilmore 1984). Behaviour under the influence of this proposed process appears reflexive yet often is quite complex. In such a process a number of divergent situations elicit an automatic response sequence. Presumably these so-called cognitive structures are central to an individual's identity (Kovacs and Beck 1978). The term 'structure' is used to imply that the cognitive activity is so overlearned that its habitual, automatic, or reflexive nature operates in a manner similar to a physical structure in the body. This cognitive-behavioural process is proposed to be an integral part of the person's physical system, always 'present' and ready to be stimulated.

Meichenbaum, Butler and Gruson (1981) illustrate the potential role of cognitive structures by referring to the variety of ways different persons can approach the same event, a social gathering. A shy person interprets the party as a threat where other people are passing harsh judgements. A boastful individual may view the party as an opportunity to impress others. A third person views the party as a relaxing chance to meet new people and to enjoy conversation, while a fourth is interested in meeting members of the opposite sex causing him or her to talk only to certain persons about certain topics. In most of these cases the person is not aware of an underlying 'cognitive structure' leading him or her to view the social event in ways different from others. Why the same event elicits different reactions is explained by appeal to the cognitive structure construct. The construct has proved useful to cognitive-behaviour modification writers who have used it to provide accounts of emotional reactions to physical symptoms (Leventhal and Nerenz 1983), perceptual sets (Broadbent 1977), self-systems (Kelly 1955), and many other phenomena (Meichenbaum and Gilmore 1984).

While the construct of cognitive structure has appeared repeatedly in the cognitive-behaviour modification literature, few if any analyses of the exact nature of the behaviours involved in the process have been provided. However, in order to understand the cognitive/verbal control of behaviour more fully, it is necessary to attempt to specify exactly what is meant by this construct. One conceptualization consistent with the notions of rule-governed behaviour is presented here with the caveat that there are a variety of forms and functions which possess the common elements of structuralized cognitive activity.

Structuralized cognitive behaviour may occur as the result of an extended history of being reinforced for following a certain rule. A particular rule statement continually sets the occasion for behaviour in a variety of situations. Each time the rule statement elicits compliance, a sequence of consequences inevitably follows. Some of the consequences are the natural results of the behaviour involved, and some are added social consequences from others. After many episodes of contact with the consequences, the rule statement becomes less and less necessary for the behaviour to be elicited. Gradually the actual amount of verbal behaviour involved in stating the rule also becomes diminished. The combination of direct control by the consequences of the rule-following behaviour and gradual abbreviation of the rule statement results in 'structuralized' cognitive/verbal control.

An often-used example will clarify this process (Meichenbaum 1977). When first learning to drive an automobile with a manually operated transmission, rule statements are extensive. But as the specified activities come to produce the results of a smoothly moving car, less rule statements are necessary. Moreover, the rule statements themselves become less formal, shorter, and more idiosyncratic. Thus, after a while, the experienced driver does not emit rule statements to control the complex acts of driving. To say that a 'cognitive structure' controls driving activity merely means that the behaviour began as rule-governed but became shaped by consequences as actual experience with driving accumulated and rule statements about operating the vehicle became less necessary and 'telescoped'.

A clinical example reveals the importance of the 'cognitive structure' process for cognitive-behaviour modification. A depressed woman learned as a child to respond to rule statements specifying passive role behaviour.

Rule statements such as, 'Children are seen not heard,' 'Little girls don't talk back,' and 'Woman's role is to serve' set the occasions for the reinforcement of behaviours characterized by 'quiet servitude'. Noncompliance when the rule statements were present produced harsh punishment. Accumulating episodes of this rule-governed activity brought the child into contact with more and more rewards for appropriate role behaviour and punishment for inappropriate role behaviour. At the same time the rule statements became shorter and less articulate while expressing the same ideas'. For example, 'Little girls don't talk back' became 'Be quiet,' and later became a specific pattern of autonomic arousal. Eventually, the original rule-governed behaviour became automatic without explicit statement of the rules. However, in the changed environment of adulthood, the woman experienced conflicting consequences for the 'structuralized' cognitive behaviour. The emotional processes of depression were elicited by contact with the conflicting results of her behaviour. Understanding that the woman's passive behaviour originated as rule-governed may be very helpful in its modification since changing the rules controlling her behaviour is readily suggested as a target of intervention. Attention to structuralized cognitive activity is a hallmark of cognitive-behaviour modification (Meichenbaum 1977). Understanding 'cognitive structures' as instances of rule-governed behaviour which gradually change to automatic and reflexive behaviour helps to point out the need for abolishing unproductive forms of rule-following and establishing productive ones, a major treatment goal in cognitive-behaviour modification.

## How client problems are conceptualized

**An integrative model of cognitive-behavioural-emotional responding**   Having discussed many of the important elements of human experience from a radical-behavioural perspective, an attempt to integrate the components of cognitive/verbal control can now be made. Figure 2.1 depicts a model of the origin and function of the cognitive, emotional, and behavioural aspects of responding as exemplified in post-traumatic stress disorders seen among combat veterans of the Vietnam war (Jaremko and Brown 1982). This model can be used to conceptualize a variety of clinical conditions and provides the basis for many cognitive-behaviour modification techniques.

Approximately 30 per cent of combat veterans of the Vietnam war are estimated to show the symptoms of post-traumatic stress disorder (Wilson 1977). These symptoms include the re-experience of combat trauma,

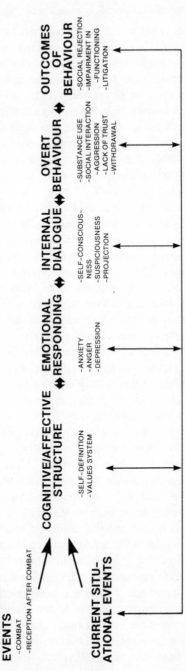

**Figure 2.1** An integrative model of cognitive-emotional-behavioural responding

numbing of emotional responses, and symptoms of stress and anxiety. Often the lives of such men are in chaos (Figley and Leventman 1980). As depicted in Figure 2.1, the powerful historical events of combat and the soldier's reception after combat have resulted in the development of cognitive/ affective structures continually stimulated by ongoing events. For the Vietnam veteran, a self-definition closely aligned with his status as a veteran causes him to be preoccupied with issues surrounding combat. Further, the combat experience has influenced the structure of the veteran's value system. Research shows that what the veteran considers important after combat has changed considerably from those things he valued prior to the trauma (Jaremko and Brown 1982).

Under certain conditions, such as employment conflict, these structural elements influence (and are influenced by) the ongoing stream of the veteran's behaviour. For example, not valuing accepted practices of main-stream society can trigger depression, and defining oneself as a cheated victim can elicit anger. These emotional responses stimulate internal dia-logues (Meichenbaum 1977) reflective of self-consciousness and suspicion ('My boss thinks I'm an anger-crazed person') or projection ('Why are these coworkers so afraid of me?'). What behaviour the veteran exhibits is then influenced by this emotional and cognitive activity. Social interaction can be affected as in strained interaction or social withdrawal. The potential for substance abuse is enhanced as the veteran is reinforced by the reduction of negative affect through mood-altering substances. Such activities have outcomes that can result in further contact with punishing and traumatizing circumstances. For some, these interactive streams of cognitive, emotional and behavioural responding continue for long periods of time, until in-tervention occurs (Williams 1980). In addition each element depicted in Figure 2.1 can influence each of the others. Only the original history is impervious to change. However, a central thesis of cognitive-behaviour modification, emphasizing both 'cognitive' and 'behavioural', is to create a new history with the client, adding to the existing elements of his or her cognitive and behaviour repertoire (Goldfried and Robins 1983). But it is important first to recognize the existing cognitive-behavioural chains pre-sented by the client before attempting to modify them. In the interest of illustration, the cognitive-behavioural chains often found in depressed clients will now be considered from the perspective of Figure 2.1 before discussing the practical applications of cognitive-behaviour modification.

While the developmental histories of persons with affective disorders continue to be a matter of scrutiny (Hammen and Peters 1977), there is some support for the notion that such individuals have had numerous failure experiences in their pasts (Abramson, Seligman and Teasdale 1978). These experiences are typical of the historical events referred to in Figure 2.1 and help to formulate cognitive structures reflective of negative self-evaluation and perceived social rejection. A person with major episodes of depression is often influenced by the processes of these structuralized negative self-images. When in certain situations, such as being evaluated harshly by a punitive boss, the cognitive structures of negativity about the self are stimulated. These structual elements may take the form (when analyzed by therapist and client) of a perceived inability to do anything right and continual inability to please significant others (a punitive parent, for example). Depressed affect, of course, is the result of this interaction of evaluative situations with the cognitive structures of depression.

The sadness then influences what the depressed person says to himself or herself. Failure expectations are expressed explicitly in internal dialogue processes: 'It's no use applying for a promotion, I can't do the work anyway. What's the use of continuing?' etc. Self-talk such as this influences the actions performed by the person. He or she may remain inactive for long periods of time, for example. Further detrimental outcomes are experienced as a result of the behaviours of depression. The entire process outlined in Figure 2.1 can recycle in a chronic manner should the cognitive, emotional and behavioural elements proposed here go unchallenged. The role of the cognitive-behaviour modification therapist is to show the client, through collaborative effort, how his or her depression stems from a process similar to the one shown in Figure 2.1. Having achieved such insight, the client can begin to refute the elements in the depressive cycle by learning to follow more adaptive rules. It is to the practical methods used by the therapist to achieve such goals that the chapter now turns.

## Practical applications

### *The undercontrol and the overcontrol of behaviour*

A basic tenet of cognitive-behaviour modification is to discover the nature of a disorder prior to attempting to remedy it. Meichenbaum (1977) called this a cognitive-functional approach in which the structure as well as the function of disordered behaviour is task analyzed. Two dimensions of psychopathology are especially helpful in analyzing the role of cognitive/verbal processes in emotional and behavioural disorder: behavioural undercontrol and behavioural overcontrol (Achenbach and Edelbrock 1978).

In the case of undercontrol, the client is more likely to respond to the immediate effects of his/her actions and less likely to wait for delayed yet favourable consequences or to perform behaviours leading to these delayed effects. Often disordered states result from this hypersensitivity to the immediate effects of one's behaviour (Davison and Neale 1982). Impulsive children fail to delay gratification when they act inattentively in situations requiring concentration (Meichenbaum 1977). Individuals with substance abuse problems intake harmful substances in part because of the quick and powerful biochemical and cognitive effects of the substance (Cappell 1975). Persons said to have personality disorders exhibit behaviour having mildly favourable immediate results but strong self-defeating distal effects (Chesno and Kilmann 1975). Moreover, hypersensitivity to immediate behavioural consequences is a component of many ordinary problems, including obesity, anxiety states, marital disruption, and parenting difficulties (cf. Malott 1980).

The crucial dimension common to these problems is that behaviour which has both immediate and distal effects is influenced more by its immediate effects. However, the distal effects are often more important to the person's overall wellbeing than are the immediate effects. The failure to delay immediate gratification produces more ultimate misery and pain than the effort of behavioural control, but because this misery is passively endured by the individual while behavioural control involves an active and repeated acceptance of avoidable discomfort or even pain, the effort of such control is often beyond the individual concerned. The impulsive child's failure to learn to read well produces more long-term cost (though the child does not comprehend this) than the minor inconvenience of attentiveness. The smoker's diseased respiratory system is more significant, at least to an outsider, than the absence of the pleasant short-term benefits of cigarette smoking. And the histrionically behaving mother loses more love, attention and respect from family and friends than the small victories gained by pandering for social approval. In short, failure to control hypersensitivity to immediate behavioural effects is a key dimension of many everyday difficulties as well as much abnormal behaviour.

Behavioural overcontrol is implicated in disorders which involve maladaptive cognitive processes. Depressed persons have learned to attribute failure experiences to stable, internal causes (Abramson, Seligman and Teasdale 1978). Socially anxious persons believe themselves to be less capable than others of smooth social discourse (Jaremko 1983). Thought-disordered individuals falsely believe that others blame them for undesirable circumstances (Cohen, Nachmani and Rosenberg 1974). Unassertive people expect acceptable social responses to yield punishing results (Fiedler and Beach 1978). In each of these disorders, thinking and believing in a certain way results in unproductive behaviour. That is, behaviour is over-controlled by irrational and/or erroneous cognitive activity.

The cognitive activity involved in the behavioural and emotional problems of overcontrol has a variety of forms, each of which has been the target of considerable research. The appraisal of coping resources and task demands has occupied the attention of stress researchers (Lazarus 1966; Meichenbaum and Jaremko 1983). The investigation of expectations about personal effectiveness has characterized much research on depression (Bandura 1977). Internal dialogue and self-talk have been investigated by researchers of test anxiety (Wine 1982). And structuralized cognitive activity has recently been the focus of cognitive-behaviour modification researchers and clinicians (Goldfried and Robins 1983; Turk and Speers 1983). Each variety of cognitive activity is researched by first attempting to assess it, followed by analysis of its relationship to other behaviour and, finally, examination of its role in treating disorders. But the common feature of such cognitive-behavioural analysis has been the belief that cognitive responses play a critical role in the development and maintenance of problem and abnormal behaviour.

In summary, then, two commonly considered dimensions of psychopathology are very important in cognitive-behaviour modification. In the first case, individuals are hypersensitive to the immediate consequences of their behaviour, resulting in life difficulties or disordered states. In the second case, behaviour is overcontrolled by cognitive activity in maladaptive ways. Understanding these two dimensions of psychopathology is a crucial first step in cognitive-behaviour modification. In point of fact, the undercontrol and overcontrol of behaviour are simply parts of the same process. In the case of undercontrol, a lack of cognitive activity results in hypersensitivity to behaviour's immediate effects while in overcontrol, ill-advised cognitive control leads to unproductive behavioural tendencies. The task of cognitive-behaviour modification, therefore, is to understand the exact nature of cognitive/verbal control so that problems of undercontrol can be remediated by the learning of cognitive skills and problems of overcontrol can be ameliorated by the replacement of maladaptive cognitive/verbal responses with adaptive ones (Meichenbaum 1977).

Treating emotional and behavioural problems through cognitive-behaviour modification involves collaboration between therapist and client to (a) achieve an understanding of the client's own instances of behavioural overcontrol and/or undercontrol and (b) establish stimulus control over emotional and behavioural responses with new, more coping-orientated cognitive activity (or adaptive rules). In short, the client learns to control maladaptive responses by replacing unproductive rule control with control by adaptive rules. A variety of specific coping techniques are used by the cognitive-behaviour modification therapist but the overriding goal is to enhance adaptive rule-following with stimulus control by adaptive rules. The rules the client learns may be stress-coping skills (Jaremko 1984; Meichenbaum and Jaremko 1983), problem-solving skills (D'Zurilla and Nezu 1982), or communication and social skills (Guerney 1977); but in each case the cognitive-behaviour modification therapist tries to establish a generic attitude of 'personal science' (Mahoney 1977b) so that the client deals better with the many challenges to which he or she will be exposed. Cognitive-behaviour modification, therefore, is a preventive approach which attempts to achieve maximum generality in treatment effects by training generic cognitive skills. Table 2.1 offers a checklist for cognitive-behaviour modification intervention.

**Table 2.1**   Checklist for cognitive-behaviour modification intervention

**(A)   Establish therapeutic relationship**
- Make client feel special by rapport establishment methods (reflection, self-disclosure, social reinforcement)
- Avoid argumentative encounters with client
- Encourage some degree of 'immediacy' interaction to overcome resistance
- Couch treatment in terms of collaboration rather than teaching

**(B)   Conceptualize client problem(s)**
- Socratic dialogue to establish determinants of problem(s)
- Behaviour analysis of simpler problems
- Distinguish between overcontrol and undercontrol
- Self-monitoring assignments to procure facts about problems
- Develop action-orientated conceptual model integrating elements of disordered responding

**(C)   Enhance following of appropriate metarules**
- Research areas of client's life to discover rules for proper living in each area
- Prioritize rules as they relate in importance to target problem(s)
- Evaluate statement of and compliance with rules through self-monitoring
- Arrange environmental incentives for relevant rule-following activity
- Use self-management techniques for compliance failure
- Develop social support system for maintenance of rule-following behaviour
- Adjust strategies according to progress and changing needs

## The therapeutic relationship

As with most approaches to psychological treatment (Strupp 1973), the therapist is a key ingredient in cognitive-behaviour modification. The major task of the therapist is to reinforce the client when new verbal behaviour is performed (Krasner 1962). The therapist role is important because new rules can gain stimulus control over the client's behaviour only when rule compliance is reinforced in the presence of rule statements. In the early stages of treatment, the cognitive-behaviour modification therapist is frequently the only source of this reinforcement. Encouraging the client to investigate new ways of thinking and behaving as well as providing reinforcement for increasingly sophisticated attempts at cognitive coping may be the cognitive-behaviour modification therapist's most important activity (Goldfried and Robins 1983).

Therefore, it is important that the therapist become a source of reinforcement. Most commonly this is accomplished by performing behaviours which establish rapport with the client (Egan 1975): reflection, social reinforcement, ingratiation, and self-disclosure, to name only a few. A common condition of many clients with emotional problems is that they fail to think that anyone else considers them to be worthwhile and special; that is, these clients make assumptions that others don't value them (Hammen and Peters 1977). By explicitly making a client feel special through the above-cited techniques, the cognitive-behaviour modification therapist may more quickly establish himself or herself as a source of reinforcement (Egan 1975). Even therapists who purportedly use confrontive and challenging methods demonstrate this necessary warmth, albeit 'New York' warmth (Ellis 1973).

A helpful dictim to consider when establishing the therapist as a reinforcer is to avoid arguments with the client. Often argumentative interchanges fail to be productive because (a) they tend to associate the therapist with negative emotional experience, eroding his or her reinforcement value, and (b) the unproductive verbal behaviour to which the therapist is responding may have a disguised function, one the therapist is serving by arguing with the client. For instance, the often-heard client statement, 'I'm a worthless person,' may be what Skinner (1957) termed an 'impure tact', a response that appears to be a label but functions as a request. Should the therapist argue with the statement by refuting it, 'No, of course, you're not worthless,' he or she unwittingly reinforces a less direct and possibly troublesome form of social interaction. Even though the form of the client's response is, 'I'm a worthless person,' the function is, 'I'm insecure, tell me I'm all right.' Thus arguments with clients may prevent realization by the client of an undesirable way of responding, making modification of such behaviour impossible.

The therapeutic relationship in cognitive-behaviour modification remains crucial throughout intervention, including follow-up. The rule statements which are being established as sources of stimulus control may change, becoming increasingly generic as treatment progresses; but the therapist is typically the person who reinforces such cognitive mediation. Until the client begins to reap the benefits of cognitive/verbal control in terms of a life with less emotional pain and more productivity, the therapist's social support is frequently the only reason the client attempts personal experimentation with alternative methods of coping. It may be that the therapist who explicitly nurtures this process will be more influential with clients (Mahoney 1980).

## Strategies of treatment

With rapport established, the client and therapist are ready to collaborate on achieving a working understanding of the problem(s) presented by the client. A variety of assessment and teaching techniques are used (Meichenbaum and Cameron 1983), the goal of which is an analysis similar to the one presented in Figure 2.1 which can be used as a guide to teach how response elements interact to result in disordered states. Some of the methods by which the client is taught to conceptualize his/her problem(s) are listed in Table 2.1 Worth special mention is Socratic dialogue, used by the therapist to teach cognitive-behaviour analysis. The overriding goal of cognitive-behaviour modification is, of course, to establish stimulus control by appropriate self-generated rule statements. Didactic presentation of such rules to a client in a expository fashion may promote a passive attitude by the client. However, by asking questions which the therapist believes will lead the client to a particular conclusion, an active, problem-solving approach is encouraged, one that can be selectively reinforced by the therapist (Frank 1974). In short, indirect questioning of the client by the therapist produces more behaviour by the client. This behaviour can then be shaped into more sophisticated forms of behaviour analysis and rule-governed activity.

In like manner, conceptualization of a client's problem may be enhanced if analysis of simpler behaviour is first conducted by the client. For example, teaching the client to understand why he or she engages in a mildly unpleasant, but nevertheless necessary, health maintenance task can readily be shaped and faded to an understanding of the central problem(s) brought to treatment. The eventual result could be a working conceptualization of the target behaviour(s). In this way, conceptualizing the problem is not only a diagnostic activity but a therapeutic goal. Should the client learn to analyze his or her own behaviour, an important skill in its own right will have been learned in the early part of intervention.

Another aid in conceptualizing client problems may be to view problem behaviour from its key dimensions. Characterization of a target problem, for example, as overcontrol or undercontrol might suggest action strategies for remediation. Thus, the excessive smoker may see more clearly the need to learn cognitive mediation skills when he or she comes to view the substance abuse as an undercontrolled activity. Or the obsessive worrier might accept more readily the necessity of replacing unwanted internal dialogue if he or she can conceptualize the worry as overcontrol by false or harmful rules. Similar effects might be obtained by having clients view problems as either behavioural excesses or behavioural deficits (Goldiamond 1965). Likewise, the dichotomy of anxiety-generated performance failure versus skill deficit could also be helpful in order to set up action-orientated assessment and treatment activities (Meichenbaum and Cameron 1983).

Ultimately, conceptualization of the client's problem must be accomplished through the collection of facts about its rate, topography, and situational control. The achievement of this goal is made possible by teaching the client to monitor aspects of his or her own behaviour. Self-monitoring is not considered just an assessment tool. In the generic preventive approach of cognitive-behaviour modification, the validity of accurate self-monitoring is a major goal of treatment (Rehm 1982). When a client can and does monitor his or her own behaviour with reliability and validity, a major step toward personal science has been taken. In many cases, then, the cognitive-behaviour modification therapist will spend a great amount of time on the teaching of self-monitoring (Meichenbaum 1977), telling the client that it is a generic skill necessary for future management of his or her affairs. In other words, collecting data about relevant behaviours is one of the rule-governed behaviours the client is taught to perform. The data collected during the self-monitoring activities can then be used to formulate an integrative model of the client's problem.

## Major treatment techniques

The next step in treatment, usually overlapping somewhat with the previously discussed phases, is to implement procedures that will increase the following of appropriate rules. Emphasis here will be given to the enhancement of following generic self-control rules, or metarules (Malott 1980), but the approach can be applied to any behaviour-consequence relationship (rule) determined by the client or therapist to be of importance.

## Generic cognitive control

A hallmark of cognitive control is stimulus control by 'executive' cognitive processes. Put another way, rules about rule-following may be the most effective type of cognitive control (Carver and Scheier 1983). When one is controlled by such 'metarules' the tendency to follow the rules stated in the metarules may also be greatly increased. In addition to, and sometimes instead of, focusing on rule-following specific to a target problem (e.g., when depressed increase pleasurable activities), cognitive-behaviour modification often attempts to increase the control exerted by metarules, assuming that successful control by these rules also ensures successful control by the rules specified in the metarule. The rules presented below can be considered as some of the targets of generic cognitive control.

**Research life for proper rules**   The client considers the rules in those aspects of his/her life that would most likely enhance living. For example, what rules would enhance living in the areas of health care, diet, hygiene, exercise, home management, safety, travel, time management, interpersonal interaction, parenting, work and career, recreation, community involvement, and family life? These rules are prioritized as they relate to the client's target problem(s). Once enumerated, they become the targets of the client's improvement and/or rehabilitation. It also is helpful to check periodically the adequacy of the list of rules so derived. Additionally, the task of writing a list of life-enhancement rules is easily accomplished. A sense of self-effectiveness often results from such an easily obtainable goal early in treatment.

**State rules in relevant situations**   The client and therapist then choose from among the rules listed and begin to establish proper control by the chosen rule. At times it may be best to begin with an easy rule for the client to follow, while in other circumstances a central, though more difficult, rule would be the best first target. In any case the client is instructed and motivated to state the rule prior to and during the relevant situations. Such self-instruction appears to remind the client of the major variables involved in a behavioural episode, thus increasing the chances of compliance with the rule. Much has been written about how to achieve such self-instruction (Meichenbaum 1977). The techniques of behavioural rehearsal and fading are often the most used procedures in this segment of treatment.

**Evaluation of rule-statement and compliance**    Through self-monitoring, the client is assigned the task of determining how often he or she states the rule and complies with it. Procedures for the shaping of this important activity have been alluded to and are contained in several sources (e.g. Karoly and Kanfer 1982). For instance, a useful approach is to use electronic devices, such as pagers, to assist clients in recognizing their own behaviour. A randomly controlled beeper can greatly increase the amount of attention paid to rule-statement behaviour.

**Arrange incentives for rule-following**    Perhaps the most crucial 'behavioural' component of cognitive-behaviour modification is the use of contingency management. Clients, with the aid of the therapist, must arrange tangible rewards for rule-compliance and concrete punishers for non-compliance. These incentives will, of course, mediate between the rule-following and its long-range effects. There are many sources describing behaviour contracting or contingency management (e.g Kanfer and Phillips 1970), but this metarule about arranging incentives is the essence of the 'behavioural' aspect of cognitive-behaviour modification. Formal and informal behaviour contracts are an excellent way to motivate otherwise unperformed acts.

## Targeted cognitive control: stress inoculation training

The cognitive-behaviour modification movement has produced a variety of specific treatment packages that can be helpful in overcoming targeted behavioural and emotional disorders (Kendall 1983). One of the most commonly used cognitive-behaviour modification treatment packages is stress-inoculation training (Meichenbaum and Jaremko 1983). Stress-inoculation training has been evaluated in a variety of clinical situations and with a variety of clinical problems (Meichenbaum 1977) and has been shown to be an effective treatment approach. The stress-inoculation training approach will be briefly presented here as it relates to establishing rule-following in persons with specific stress and anxiety disorders.

Meichenbaum and Cameron (1983) have provided a detailed description of stress-inoculation training, a general treatment package designed to reduce and/or prevent stress and anxiety problems. The transactional model of stress and coping (Lazarus 1966) provides the basis for stress-inoculation training. In this model anxiety and stress reactions are the result of discrepancies between the demands placed on a person and the person's perception of his/her resources to cope with the demands. When a person feels that there are more demands than resources to cope with them, stressful responding results.

Stressful responding is characterized by an ongoing and continuous cycle of unpleasant physiological arousal, global cognitive appraisal and specific negative self-talk (Jaremko 1979b, 1984). The stress cycle sets up a strong potential for avoidance because it is experienced as unpleasant to the stressed individual. When avoidance responding does occur, future encounters with the stress-inducing situation may be more difficult to handle. The goal of stress-inoculation training is to train, practice and apply specific coping skills to slow down the stress cycle and to preclude untoward avoidance behaviour. Consider the following example of social anxiety presented by Jaremko (1983):

A young man has occasion to be around a woman he would like to ask out for a date. In this situation, he experiences a racing heartbeat, sweaty palms and 'butterflies.' He interprets these physiological phenomena as 'anxiety.' This global appraisal makes it likely that the young man will emit idiosyncratic negative self-evaluations and self-references. He may say to himself, 'She will not find me attractive,' or 'She looks too old for me.' These negative references lead to further physiological arousal, which keeps the cycle of stress going. The young man may face the stressor by talking to the woman and, if he possesses social skills, his social stress will probably decrease when and if he judges the interaction successful. If he faces the stressor but is awkward and unskilled, he may have a failure experience and experience an increase in social anxiety in the future. Finally, the man can avoid the interaction (by procrastinating, devaluing the person's attractiveness, etc.). In this case it will probably be more difficult for him the next time he has occasion to talk to a woman. His social anxiety will only continue and may even get worse. (p. 420)

Stress-inoculation training attempts to teach rules about coping with stress to persons with stress-related problems. There are three phases to the stress-inoculation training approach: conceptualization, skills training, and

**Table 2.2** A flow chart of stress inoculation training

**Phase One: Conceptualization**

(a) Data collection–integration
- Identify determinants of problem via interview, image-based monitoring, and behavioural observation
- Distinguish between performance failure and skill deficit
- Formulate treatment plan; task analysis
- Introduce integrative conceptual model

(b) Assessment skills training
- Train clients to analyze problems independently (e.g. to conduct situational analyses and to seek disconfirmatory data)

**Phase Two: Skills acquisition and rehearsal**

(a) Skills training
- Train instrumental coping skills (e.g. communication, assertion, problem-solving, parenting, study skills)
- Train palliative coping skills as indicated (e.g. perspective-taking, attention diversion, use of social supports, adaptive affect expression, relaxation)
- Aim to develop an extensive repertoire of coping responses to facilitate flexible responding

(b) Skills rehearsal
- Promote smooth integration and execution of coping responses via imagery and role-play
- Self-instructional training to develop mediators to regulate coping responses

**Phase Three: Application and follow-through**

(a) Induce application of skills
- Prepare for application using coping imagery, using early stress cues as signals to cope
- Role-play (a) anticipated stressful situations and (b) client coaching someone with a similar problem
- 'Role-play' attitude may be adopted in real world
- Exposure to in-session graded stressors
- Use of graded exposure and other response induction aids to foster in vivo responding and build self-efficacy

(b) Maintenance and generalization
- Build sense of coping self-efficacy in relation to situations client sees as high risk
- Develop strategies for recovering from failure and relapse
- Arrange follow-up reviews

*Source*: Adapted from Meichenbaum and Cameron (1983).

application. Table 2.2 presents a flow chart of stress-inoculation procedures. The client and the therapist collaborate to develop a conceptualization of the stressful transaction. An integrative model similar to that presented by Jaremko (1984) is a useful guide in outlining this conceptualization. Once again, quoting from Jaremko (1983), social anxiety provides a clear picture of a typical conceptualization guiding stress-inoculation training. The model of stress and coping was the following:

> Talking to an opposite-sex person may lead to a readily predictable cycle of external and internal behaviour. . . . The goal of treatment is to make the person aware of this cycle, especially at the incipient stages where prodromal cues are evident, and then interrupt and break the cycle with the consequence of encouraging social interaction. In short the cycle involved a repeating process in which the stressor may set off uncomfortable physiological activity that contributes to the appraisal process of the situation as potentially harmful. This negative appraisal engenders a series of negative self-statements and images that in turn cause the physiological processes to increase, triggering the cycle once again. . . . Three sets of coping skills can be used to combat and control the negative cycle and make it more likely that the client would be able to cope. (p. 436)

Once the stressful responding has been conceptualized, the client begins to learn stress-coping skills designed to break or slow the stress cycle down enough to allow task completion in the stressful situation. A variety of specific skills can be practised using the behavioural approaches alluded to earlier in the section under arranging incentives for rule-following. In each case the learning of a new skill can be viewed as a rule to be followed, the eventual result of which may be reduced stress. For example, the rule that daily exercise will result in less anxiety can be taught, followed and evaluated. Similarly, other skills taught in stress-inoculation training are rules to be followed and evaluated for their impact on control of the targeted disorder. These skills include instrumental coping skills such as communication, assertion, and so on; and palliative skills such as attention diversion, physical relaxation and the like.

Stress-inoculation training also involves the rehearsal of skills in increasingly more stressful situations. Much practice is devoted to rehearsing coping skills in both role-playing and in vivo conditions. In fact, it is the extensive graduated practice of stress-coping skills that provides the rationale for the 'inoculation' aspect of stress-inoculation training. This preventive approach allows the organization of many specific cognitive and behavioural techniques in a manner that allows the client to test out the effectiveness of adaptive rule-following in coping with stress. A number of sources provide more detail about stress-inoculation training (cf. Meichenbaum and Jaremko 1983).

As a practical example of stress-inoculation training the case of helping severely burned adults cope with pain can be considered (Wernick, Jaremko and Taylor 1979). After learning a three-phase cycle of stressful pain responding incorporating physiological arousal, cognitive appraisal, and negative self-talk, patients practised deep breathing and muscle relaxation as physical methods to endure the intense discomfort of burned tissue. A variety of cognitive strategies were also practised so as to allow the patient something on which to focus when pain was especially bad or when intrusive medical treatments for burns were being conducted. Finally, patients learned and practised how to use cognitive restructuring (or self-instruction) to combat specific negative self-talk. This technique involved identifying specific negative statements the patient made when in pain, devising positive or coping-orientated statements that refuted the negative statements, and imaginal and in vivo practice replacing the negative statements with the positive ones. Finally, the patients practised combining the skills with the help of the therapist as a coach during the actual conduct of the medical procedure known as 'tanking' in which dead tissue is scraped from the burned area.

The entire stress-inoculation training package was conducted by specially trained nurses in five in vivo sessions of training on a burn and trauma ward. Wernick, Jaremko and Taylor (1979) showed that patients were much better able to cope with the burn pain than nontreated patients on a number of relevant measures (pain medication requests, global assessments and treatment compliance). In effect the project showed that severely burned persons could be taught to follow better pain management rules by the use of stress-inoculation training.

## Overcoming obstacles to client progress

**Self-management techniques for rule-following failures** When the client fails to follow an agreed-upon rule, a frequent occurrence with clients having emotional and behavioural disorders, self-management techniques can be implemented to accomplish the tasks of cognitive/verbal control. Procedures such as eliminating competing contingencies and incentives, breaking the task into smaller segments, establishing clear-cut criteria for success, and getting frequent feedback are some of the procedures that have been successful in building behavioural repertories (Goldfried and Merbaum 1973). The client is continually reinforced by the therapist for such attempts as effective personal science. It may also be important to proceed slowly in difficult cases, not expecting quick gains. By carefully building a history of being rewarded for rule-following, even the most resistant client can come to appreciate his or her own potential for self-control.

**Develop social support systems**     The goal of cognitive-behaviour modification is, of course, a permanent increase in the following of the targeted rule(s). Once achieved, the client and therapist collaborate to establish a social support system that would continue to provide social reinforcers for rule compliance. The client's family, friends, coworkers, theme-orientated clubs, and other groups are some of the social support systems that can provide the needed back-up reinforcers for a client's behaviour.

**Adjust strategies and expand to other rules**     Once rule-following is accomplished and maintained in one area, a new rule can become the target. However, if enhanced rule-following does not occur, client and therapist must adjust strategies using more elementary targets, different reinforcers, or even a different conceptualization of the disorder. The therapist provides liberal social reinforcement for coping attempts both in times of progress as well as when progress is lacking. It is through persistence and continued effort that new histories of being reinforced for adaptive rule-following are achieved. Client resistance could well be caused by an unacceptable analysis of the client's problem. Changing that conceptualization might overcome the resistance.

## Case example

To illustrate how the cognitive-behaviour modification therapist conceptualizes and treats a client's problem, a Vietnam combat veteran's anger control problem will be considered. A thirty-two-year-old man was referred to a veteran's outreach centre by the courts where he was awaiting trial for attempted murder. While in a restaurant, late one night, the client was challenged by an inebriated customer. The client became so angry he left the restaurant, procured a hand gun from his vehicle, returned to the restaurant and continued the argument. In a scuffle, both the veteran and the other man were shot, neither seriously. Unfortunately, such a scenario was not uncommon for the client. A number of times each week, the client entered into arguments with coworkers, bosses, or even complete strangers. He had had over fifty jobs in ten years. He was frequently alone and took alcohol excessively.

The development of trust with this client took many weeks, involving all of the techniques cited in Table 2.1 with emphasis on 'immediate' here and now interaction with the therapist. A trusting relationship between therapist and client allowed the beginning of teaching the client to recognize elements similar to those depicted in Figure 2.1. Socratic probing helped the client to realize that he felt cheated by his culture for the way he was treated after serving his country in Vietnam, a common cognitive structure in Vietnam combat veterans (Figley and Leventman 1980). In addition the conceptual behaviour of placing no importance on many of society's values was identified and called a 'values vacuum' by client and therapist. Such conceptual responding was stimulated in many of the client's interactions and led to frequent emotional outbursts. The client was taught to view his anger as an instance of overcontrol by a structuralized rule. That is, he was shown how reflexive self-statements pertinent to being cheated by an uncaring government made him likely to behave aggressively. He agreed that it was very important to determine how and why he engaged in this structuralized rule-stating.

He was given two important assignments designed to increase a personal science perspective. First the client was required to write an analysis of three or four 'habitual' behavioural excesses and deficits. A very factitious individual, he described why he spent so much time grooming. He also discussed how he had come to control his smoking behaviour as well as a daily habit of exercise running. These analyses were discussed in treatment sessions and the client was shaped to give more and more accurate accounts of the origin and nature of his behaviour in these areas.

Secondly, the client was given an electronic pager which was activated by the therapist five or so times a day. The client was to count these pages and to record any anger incidents and/or structualized responses ongoing when paged. Structuralized responses included criticism of cultural values, expressions or thoughts of inequity, and references to the hopelessness of his life. In a triple column format (Hollon and Kendall 1980), the client rated the emotional changes that resulted from these structuralized behaviours as well as his behavioural responses and the consequences, immediate and distal, of those acts. The triple-column data allowed the client to see at a glance the specifics of several episodes of anger outbursts. In the first column he described the situation by coding several dimensions (others present, time, place, location, etc.). In the second column he recorded his responses, both overt and covert. And in the third column, he described what resulted from these previous events. During a crucial session approximately three months into treatment, the client was led to sketch a model of his anger outbursts, indicating how the anger was controlled by the cognitive structures mentioned. The model was similar to Figure 2.1 and set the stage for the implementation of the next phase of cognitive-behaviour modification, that of enhancing rule control.

A couple of sessions were then devoted to devising and prioritizing a three-page list of rules the client could follow to enhance his life. Two crucial targets from that list were to restrict alcohol use and to enhance communication with a girlfriend by daily talks at lunch. While there were many other rules this client learned to follow, these two can illustrate the components of cognitive-behaviour modification for achieving generic cognitive/verbal control. The client entered into a behaviour contract to consume alcohol only during two hours of the day and while at home. During these times, he could also only drink a limited amount. The contract was checked daily by both the client's girlfriend and an assistant to the therapist. After initially slow progress, the client's drinking came under control with adherence to the drinking rule nine out of ten days. Parenthetically, it might be mentioned that the client discontinued attending a particular night club where he had previously had many of his altercations. The terms of the drinking contract involved monetary loss upon violation. The few violations were strictly enforced, perhaps aiding in the establishment of rule control. Further, accuracy of the self-report data was validated by random breathalizer tests. In short, the client had entered a contract agreement that demanded compliance and that could detect noncompliance.

Daily talks with the girlfriend were accomplished by arranging the lunch time talks at a place where they could be observed by a third party, usually the therapist's assistant. Agendas for the talks were prepared a week in advance and the client was required to submit daily summaries of the talks. Ground rules for the types of communication allowed were also established, such as a minimum number of open-ended questions by each person, active listening, and descriptive language. Verification of adherence to the ground rules was obtained in conference with the girlfriend. Almost immediate compliance with the daily talks was achieved with very few exceptions. As a result of the talks, the client's relationship with his girlfriend matured into a reliable source of social support.

In weekly sessions, the client and the therapist reviewed the effects of enhanced rule control and planned strategies for the extension of rule control. The client continued to work on rule control for two years, while awaiting trial and serving parole. During this time he held a job in construction work, married his girlfriend, and developed an active hobby in amateur theatre. His anger problems diminished after establishment of rule control by the initial rules mentioned above. Eventually the client discontinued alcohol consumption altogether and maintained control over anger and other strong emotions.

Admittedly, the case illustrated here has been simplified and told in an overly favourable light. There were setbacks as there always are. But they were viewed as problems to be solved and chances to enhance the generality of the treatment effects. There were also more complex influences involved in the treatment, but the generic approach to cognitive-behaviour modification can be identified as the guiding strategy used to deal with the details of clinical intervention. Shaping rule-governed behaviour is indeed a complex process. The approach presented in this chapter is offered as an aid in achieving the modification of cognitive/verbal control.

# References

Abelson, R.P. (1981) Psychological status of the script concept. *American Psychologist*, *36*, 715–729.

Abramson, L., Seligman, M. and Teasdale, J. (1978) Learned helplessness in humans: Critique and reformulation. *Journal of Abnormal Psychology*, *87*, 49–74.

Achenbach, T. and Edelbrock, C. (1978) The classification of child psychopathology: A review of empirical efforts. *Psychological Bulletin*, *85*, 1275–1301.

Bandura, A. (1977) Self-efficacy: Toward a unifying theory of behavioral change. *Psychological Review*, *84*, 191–215.

Bandura, A. and Walters, R. (1963) *Social learning and personality*. New York: Holt, Rinehart, and Winston.

Beck, A.T. (1976) *Cognitive therapy and the emotional disorders*. New York: International Universities Press.

Blankstein, K., Pliner, P. and Polivy, J. (eds) (1980) *Assessment and modification of emotional behavior*. New York: Plenum.

Broadbent, D. (1977) The hidden preattentive processes. *American Psychologist*, *32*, 109–119.

Cappell, H. (1975) An evaluation of tension models of alcohol consumption. In R. Gibbons, Y. Israel, H. Kalant, R. Popham, W. Schmidt, and R. Smart (eds) *Research advances in alcohol drug problems*, vol. 2. New York: Wiley.

Carver, C. and Scheier, M. (1983) A control-theory approach to human behavior, and implications for problems in self-management. In P. Kendall (ed.) *Advances in cognitive-behavioral research and therapy*, vol. 2. New York: Academic Press.

Chesno, F. and Kilmann, P. (1975) Effects of stimulation intensity on sociopathic avoidance learning. *Journal of Abnormal Psychology*, *84*, 144–151.

Cohen, B., Nachmani, G. and Rosenberg, S. (1974) Referent communication disturbances in acute schizophrenia. *Journal of Abnormal Psychology, 83*, 1–14.

Davison, G. and Neale, J. (1982) *Abnormal Psychology* (3rd edn). New York: Wiley.

D'Zurilla, T. and Nezu, A. (1982) Social problem-solving in adults. In P. Kendall (ed.) *Advances in cognitive-behavioral research and therapy*, vol. 1. New York: Academic Press.

Egan, G. (1975) *The skilled helper*. Monterey, CA: Brooks/Cole.

Ellis, A. (1973) *Humanistic psychotherapy*. New York: McGraw-Hill.

Fiedler, D. and Beach, L. (1978) On the decision to be assertive. *Journal of Consulting and Clinical Psychology*, *46*, 537–546.

Figley, C. and Leventman, S. (eds) (1980) *Strangers at home*. New York: Praeger.

Frank, J. (1974) *Persuasions and healing* (2nd edn). New York: Schocken Books.

Goldfried, M. and Merbaum, M. (eds) (1973) *Behavior change through self-control*. New York: Holt, Rinehart and Winston.

Goldfried, M. and Robins, C. (1983) Self-schema, cognitive bias, and the processing of therapeutic experiences. In P. Kendall (ed.) *Advances in cognitive-behavioral research and therapy*, vol. 2. New York: Academic Press.

Goldiamond, I. (1965) Self-control procedures in personal behavior problems. *Psychological Record*, *17*, 851–868.

Guerney, B. (1977) *Relationship enhancement*. San Francisco: Jossey-Bass.

Hammen, C. and Peters, S. (1977) Interpersonal consequences of depression: Responses to men and women enacting a depressed role. *Journal of Abnormal Psychology, 37*, 322–332.

Hollon, S. and Kendall, P. (1980) In-vivo assessment techniques for cognitive-behavioral processes. In P. Kendall and S. Hollon (eds) *Assessment strategies for cognitive-behavioral interventions*. New York: Academic Press.

Izard, C. (1977) *Human emotions*. New York: Plenum.

Jaremko, M.E. (1979a) Cognitive-behavior modification: Real science or more mentalism? *The Psychological Record*, *3*, 175–184.

Jaremko, M.E. (1979b) A component analysis of stress-inoculation training: Review and perspectus. *Cognitive Therapy and Research, 3*, 35–48.

Jaremko, M.E. (1983) Stress inoculation training for social anxiety with specific emphasis on dating anxiety. In D. Meichenbaum and M. Jaremko (eds) *Stress reduction and prevention*. New York: Plenum.

Jaremko, M.E. (1984) Stress-inoculated training: A generic approach for the prevention of stress-related disorders. *Personnel and Guidance Journal, 28,* 544–550.

Jaremko, M.E. and Brown, R. (1982) The role of values structure in the etiology and maintenance of post-traumatic stress disorders, Unpublished manuscript, available from M. Jaremko, Terrell State Hospital, Terrell, Texas 75160, USA.

Kanfer, F. and Phillips, J. (1970) *Learning foundations of behavior therapy.* New York: Wiley.

Karoly, P. and Kanfer, F. (eds) (1982) *Self-management and behavior change.* Elmsford, NJ: Pergamon.

Kelly, G. (1955) *The psychology of personal constructs.* New York: Norton.

Kendall, P. (ed.) (1983) *Advances in cognitive-behavioral research and therapy,* vol. 2. New York: Academic Press.

Kovacs, M. and Beck, A. (1978) Maladaptive cognitive structures and depression. *American Journal of Psychiatry, 135,* 525–533.

Krasner, L. (1962) The therapist as a social reinforcement machine. In H. Strupp and L. Luborsky (eds) *Research in psychotherapy,* vol. 2. Washington, DC: American Psychological Association.

Lazarus, R.S. (1966) *Psychological stress and the coping process.* New York: McGraw-Hill.

Leventhal, H. and Nerenz, D. (1983) A model for stress research with some implications for the control of stress disorders. In D. Meichenbaum and M. Jaremko (eds) *Stress reduction and prevention.* New York: Plenum.

Mahony, M.J. (1974) *Cognition and behavior modification.* Cambridge MA: Ballinger.

Mahony, M.J. (1976) Terminal terminology: A self-regulated reply to Goldiamond. *Journal of Applied Behavior Analysis, 9,* 515–517.

Mahony, M.J. (1977a) Cognitive therapy and research: A question of questions. *Cognitive Therapy and Research, 1,* 5–16.

Mahony, M. (1977b) Personal science: A cognitive learning therapy. In A. Ellis and R. Grieger (eds) *Handbook of rational emotive therapy.* New York: Springer.

Mahoney, M. (ed.) (1980) *Psychotherapy process: Current issues and future directions.* New York: Plenum.

Malott, R. (1980) Rule-governed behavior in the achievement of evasive goals. Unpublished manuscript available from R. Malott, Department of Psychology, Western Michigan University, Kalamazoo, MI, USA.

Malott, R. and Whaley, D. (1976) *Psychology.* New York: Harper.

Meichenbaum, D. (ed.) (1975, 1976, 1977, 1978) *Cognitive-behavior modification newsletter.* Waterloo: University of Waterloo.

Meichenbaum, D. (1977) *Cognitive-behavior modification: An integrative approach.* New York: Plenum.

Meichenbaum, D. and Cameron, R. (1983) Stress inoculation training: Toward a general paradigm for training coping skills. In D. Meichenbaum and M. Jaremko (eds) *Stress reduction and prevention.* New York: Plenum.

Meichenbaum, D. and Gilmore, J. (1984) The nature of unconscious processes: A cognitive-behavioral perspective. In K. Bowers and D. Meichenbaum (eds) *The unconscious reconsidered*. New York: Wiley.

Meichenbaum, D. and Jaremko, M.E. (eds) (1983) *Stress reduction and prevention*. New York: Plenum.

Meichenbaum, D., Butler, L. and Grunson, L. (1981) Towards a conceptual model of social competence. In J. Wine and M. Smye (eds) *Social competence*. New York: Guilford Press.

Rehm, L. (1982) Self-management in depression. In P. Karoly and F. Kanfer (eds) *Self-management and behavior change*. Elmsford, N.J.: Pergamon.

Skinner, B.F. (1953) *Science and human behavior*. New York: Macmillan.

Skinner, B.F. (1957) *Verbal behavior*. New York: Appleton-Century-Crofts.

Skinner, B.F. (1969) *Contingencies of reinforcement*. New York: Appleton-Century-Crofts.

Skinner, B.F. (1979) *About behaviorism*. New York: Knopf.

Strupp, H. (1973). On the ingredients of psychotherapy. *Journal of Consulting and Clinical Psychology*, *41*, 1–8.

Turk, D. and Speers, M. (1983) Cognitive schemata and cognitive processes: Going beyond the information given. In P. Kendall (ed.) *Advances in cognitive-behavioral research and therapy*, vol. 2. New York: Academic Press.

Wernick, R., Jaremko, M. and Taylor, P. (1979) Stress-inoculation with severely burned adults. *Journal of Behavioral Medicine*, *4*, 5–9.

Whaley, D. and Malott, R. (1971) *Elementary principles of behavior*. New York: Prentice-Hall.

Williams, D. (1980) *The treatment of post-traumatic stress disorders in Vietnam veterans*. Cincinnati: Disabled Veterans of America.

Wilson, J. (1977) Identity, ideology, and crisis: The Vietnam veteran in transition, part 1. Unpublished manuscript, Cleveland State University.

Wine, J. (1982) Evaluation anxiety: A cognitive attentional construct. In H. Krohne and L. Laux (eds) *Achievement, stress, and anxiety*. Washington, DC: Hemisphere.

# CHAPTER THREE   Cognitive Therapy

*Marjorie E. Weishaar and Aaron T. Beck*

## History and underpinnings of cognitive therapy

Cognitive therapy is a system of psychotherapy based on a theory of psychopathology which maintains that how an individual perceives and structures his experiences determines how he feels and behaves (Beck 1967, 1976). Cognitive therapy is related on a theoretical level to cognitive psychology, information processing theory, and social psychology. It is founded in empirical investigation and is, by nature, a collaborative process of investigation, reality testing, and problem-solving between therapist and patient. The patient's maladaptive interpretations and conclusions about events are treated as hypotheses to be tested. Behavioural experiments and verbal examination of alternative interpretations are used to generate contradictory evidence and to bolster more adaptive beliefs, thus leading to therapeutic change. Thus, cognitive therapy is active, structured, time-limited and present-centred, although the sources of the patient's under-lying assumptions (schemata) are explored in order to clarify the function they may have served and the contribution they have made throughout the patient's development.

Cognitive therapy has been used successfully in the treatment of a variety of problems and disorders, most notably depression (Beck *et al.* 1979), anxiety, phobias and agoraphobia (Beck and Emery 1979, 1985; Coleman 1981), psychosomatic disorders, pain problems (Beck and Emery 1979), marital conflict (Epstein 1983), and loneliness (Young 1981).

Cognitive therapy is derived from findings that psychological disturbances frequently stem from specific, habitual errors in thinking (Beck 1967). These cognitive distortions arise from maladaptive assumptions which are triggered by environmental stimuli. When stressed, patients may reason on the basis of self-defeating assumptions, incorrectly interpret life situations, judge themselves too harshly, or fail to generate adequate strategies to deal with external problems. Thus, an event may trigger anxiety because the individual perceives it as dangerous either by attributing idiosyncratic meaning to the event or by exaggerating the likelihood of disaster. At the time of arousal, these assumptions are plausible, consistent, and highly salient to the patient although they may not reflect the objective risk of the situation. For example, patients may be able to judge the likelihood of a person getting stuck in an elevator or being in a plane crash in terms consistent with known statistics when they are not in that situation. However, as they approach the elevator or the airport, their predictions of danger increase, often to the point of absolute certainty that they themselves will be harmed.

The cognitive model does not assume that cognitions operate exclusive of biochemistry or behaviour in the etiology of psychopathology. They represent one level of analysis and are viewed as the problem, not its cause. Cognitive techniques combine verbal procedures with behaviour modification techniques in order to find evidence for or against a patient's assumptions, to modify beliefs, and to build necessary skills. Behavioural techniques may play an instrumental role in cognitive change by providing the experience necessary to elicit new cognitions and change maladaptive assumptions. Cognitive techniques are explicitly designed to help the patient identify, test, and correct distorted conceptualizations and the dysfunctional beliefs underlying these cognitions. By thinking and acting more realistically and adaptively, according to tested hypotheses rather than assumed principles, the patient is expected to experience improvement in symptoms and functioning.

## Historical development of cognitive therapy

Cognitive therapy, as formulated by Beck, has been shaped by a variety of approaches to psychopathology and the process of therapy. The phenomenological approach in which the individual's view of self and one's personal world is central to the determination of behaviour is traced to Greek Stoic philosophers. Later, Kant's (1798) emphasis on conscious subjective experience was influential in the phenomenological approach to psychology. More contemporary expressions of this approach are found in the writings of Alfred Adler (1936), Alexander (1950), Horney (1950), and Sullivan (1953).

Structural theory, as elucidated by Freud's concept of hierarchical structuring of cognitions into primary and secondary processes, has also shaped cognitive theory. However, while Freud was concerned with thoughts – unconscious and conscious – they were deemed to be less important than instinctual drives in determining behaviour and emotion.

More modern developments in cognitive psychology have emphasized the notions of cognitive structures and nonconscious cognitive processing as demonstrated in the work of George Kelly (1955). Kelly is credited with being the first to describe the cognitive model through his use of 'personal constructs' and the role of beliefs about the self in behaviour change. Cognitive theories of emotions posited by Magda Arnold (1960) and Richard Lazarus (1966) have also influenced cognitive therapy.

Albert Ellis's (1962) work on the association between dysfunctional beliefs and emotion provided impetus to the further development of cognitive therapy by emphasizing the primacy of 'irrational beliefs' in dysphoria. Concurrent with Ellis's and Beck's work was the rise of behaviour therapy in the USA which, despite its initial exclusive focus on overt behaviour change, provided techniques and an empirical approach to therapy that is similarly the hallmark of cognitive therapy.

Beck's formulation and development of cognitive therapy began in the early 1960s with clinical observations of depressed patients and investigations of their treatment with traditional psychoanalysis. Rather than finding retroflected anger underlying depression, Beck observed cognitive distortions as the core process in depression. He reformulated the view of depression to incorporate the negative bias in cognitive processing apparent in depressed individuals.

While influenced on philosophical and theoretical levels by the phenomenological, structural, and cognitive psychology schools, Beck's cognitive therapy was also shaped in terms of style and process by recent and contemporary psychologists. The focus on here-and-now problem-solving is also found in the work of Albert Ellis (1962). The style of questioning and probing for personalized meanings is similar to that in Rogers's (1951) client-centred therapy. The attention paid to the individual's development, particularly in regards to assumptions or schemata, reflects the influence of Piaget (1960). And the identification of common themes in a patient's emotional reactions, narratives, and memories as well as the concept of pre-conscious cognitions are derived in part from psychoanalytic approaches.

Since the 1960s, the developments of behaviour therapy, from its roots in behaviour modification, and of cognitive therapy have interacted with each other so that the term 'cognitive-behaviour therapy' presently reflects the approach of roughly 40 per cent of new psychologists in USA colleges and universities (Klesges, Sanchez and Stanton 1982). As mentioned above, the empirical nature of cognitive therapy is shared by behaviour therapy and was strongly influenced by the work of Bandura (1977), Frank (1961), Goldfried and Davison (1976), Mahoney (1974), Meichenbaum (1977), and Kazdin and Wilson (1978). The influence of behaviour therapy is apparent in the structure and process of cognitive therapy, for it includes setting the agenda for the session, eliciting feedback, setting goals for therapy, operationalizing problems, testing hypotheses, problem-solving techniques, and assigning homework. Currently, the role of cognitions in behaviour change is being investigated systematically in a number of disorders, from depression to agoraphobia.

While recognizing the historical contributions of other schools of psychotherapy, cognitive therapy differs from its antecedents and contemporaries in a number of ways. Active collaboration between patient and therapist in all phases of therapy, focus on present problems rather than childhood recollections, and the lack of interpretation of unconscious factors distinguish cognitive therapy from psychoanalysis. Cognitive therapy also contrasts with behaviour therapy in terms of its focus on internal experiences, such as thoughts, attitudes, and images. The empirical investigation shared with behaviour therapy is used on the patient's cognitions rather than on overt behaviours. While focusing on beliefs, like rational-emotive therapy, cognitive therapy investigates the unique and idiosyncratic cognitions of the patient as opposed to applying the fixed number of 'irrational beliefs' proposed by Ellis (1962). In further contrast to rational-emotive therapy, the method of questioning patients is Socratic rather than directive or exhortive. In cognitive therapy, a patients's beliefs are not directly challenged or argued but tested through a process called guided discovery.

## Major theoretical concepts

The cognitive model maintains that the way an individual structures situations or events largely determines affect and behaviour (Beck 1967, 1979). Cognitions (thoughts or images) about an event are based on attitudes or assumptions (schemata) derived from previous experience which are used to classify, interpret, evaluate, and assign meaning to that event. The interpretation of a potentially stressful situation is an active, continuous process that includes successive appraisals of the external situation, the individual's coping abilities or resources, and the risks, costs, and gains of various strategies. If the person's impression indicates that vital interests are at stake, the primitive, egocentric cognitive system is activated and the person is primed to make extreme, one-sided, absolutistic, and global judgements. Typical conceptualizations of this nature are danger, loss and self-enhancement which correspond, respectively, to anxiety, sadness and affection. Thus, cognitive structuring of a situation triggers affect and behavioural mobilization or demobilization based on hyperactive schemata specific for the syndrome manifested. The cognitive content of syndromes (e.g. anxiety disorders, depression) have the same theme (danger or loss, respectively) as found in 'normal' experience, but cognitive distortions are more extreme and, consequently, so are affect and behaviour. Moreover, each individual has unique vulnerabilities and sensitivities which predispose him or her to psychological distress. Thus, what may trigger distress in one individual is benign for another. Individual learning experience, developmental history, and personality differences account for variations in sensitivities to stressors. For example, an individual whose personality is organized largely around autonomy and independence is susceptible to experiences representing a thwarting of his or her freedom of choice or goal attainment. More socially dependent people are likely to react to situations of interpersonal loss.

Deviations in the thinking process play a role in affective and behavioural responses in several respects. As mentioned above, when vital interests are at stake, cognitive processing tends to be overinclusive and rigid. In addition, there is a loss of volitional control over thinking and a reduced ability to 'turn off' the intense schemata. Finally, there is a reduction in the ability to concentrate, recall and reason. Because of these features and the fact that the individual's construction of the situation contains only a subset of information to begin with, maladaptive schemata may be maintained and reinforced. In situations of interpersonal difficulties, both individuals bring to bear maladaptive cognitive reactions which tend to be mutually reinforcing.

## How client problems are conceptualized

**Model of psychopathology** Cognitive therapy views psychopathological disorders on a continuum with 'normal' cognitive-affective-behavioural responses to life situations. Thus, they are exaggerated forms of normal emotional reactions. Similarly, an individual shows the same physiological responses to psychosocial or symbolic threats as to actual physical threats. Therefore, each cognitive, affective, behavioural, or physiological response serves some 'function', but becomes hyperactive and maladaptive in cases of pathology. Each of the four basic emotions has cognitive (perceptual) and behavioural correlates. Sadness is evoked when there is a perception of defeat, loss or deprivation. The behavioural consequence is to withdraw.

Elation follows from perceived gain and reinforces activity toward the goal. Anxiety is triggered by perceived vulnerability and threat, and the behavioural consequence is to withdraw, 'freeze', or prepare for defence. Anger, in contrast, is directed to the offensive qualities of the threat, and the behavioural inclination is to attack.

Normal and psychopathological syndromes are conceptualized as being mediated by primal cognitive processes (analogous to Freud's 'primary process') which tend to interpret a situation in global and relatively crude terms. In normal reactions, initial perceptions are refined and tested against reality, correcting global and primal conceptualizations (analogous to Freud's 'secondary process'). In psychopathology, these corrective functions are impaired and emotions become exaggerated. Cognitive processing is the mechanism involved in the development of psychological disorders.

The cognitive models of depression and anxiety will be discussed below to exemplify the role of cognitions in psychopathology.

**Cognitive model of depression**   Depression is characterized by the 'cognitive triad' (Beck 1967), reflecting the patient's negative view of the self, the world, and the future. The depressed person sees himself or herself as deficient, inadequate, deserted and lacking in qualities that are essential for self-worth and happiness. The patient's negative view of the world is reflected in beliefs that exorbitant demands have been put upon him or her, that there are insurmountable obstacles to achieving life goals, or that the world is devoid of pleasure or gratification. The individual perceives defeat or deprivation, an environment which is overwhelming, and himself or herself as bereft of resources. The patient's negative view of the future is apparent in beliefs that current troubles will persist indefinitely and may, indeed, get worse, and in the hopelessness which can lead to suicidal ideation.

The motivational, behavioural and physical symptoms of depression are derived from these negative cognitive patterns. The observed 'paralysis of will' is due to an expectation of failure and the belief in one's lack of ability to cope or to control the outcome of an event. Thus, there is a reluctance to commit oneself to a goal and, often, a desire to avoid all challenges. Suicidal wishes also stem from pessimism and hopelessness and often reflect a desire to escape uncontrollable, unbearable problems. The increased dependency often observed among depressed patients reflects the negative view of the self as inept, an overestimation of the difficulty of normal life tasks, the expectation that things will turn out badly, and the desire that someone more competent take over. Indecisiveness is similarly derived from the belief that one is incapable of making the right decision. The physical symptoms of depression – loss of energy, fatigue and inertia – are also related to negative expectancies. Work with depressed patients indicates that initiating activity actually reduces retardation and fatigue, and the refutation of negative expectations and demonstration of motor ability play important roles in recovery.

Negatively biased thinking is a core process in depression. The predisposition to focus on the negative is likely to come early in life through personal experience, identification with significant others, and the perception of others' attitudes towards one. Thus, attitudes and beliefs learned by children may persist and influence future cognitive processing. These constructs used to subsequently classify, interpret, evaluate, and assign meanings to events are called schemata. Personal schemata may be adaptive or maladaptive, positive or negative, idiosyncratic or universal (Wright and Beck 1984). In the case of depression, they are maladaptive, negative, and idiosyncratic. Depressogenic schemata are of the order 'I am a failure,' 'Nothing ever works out for me,' and the like.

A particular schema may be latent at any given time and is activated by certain kinds of circumstances, such as those analogous to the original experience leading to the negative attitude, or in reaction to a series of nonspecific traumatic experiences which surpass the individual's coping threshold or shift the balance away from his or her adaptive schemas. Thus, events in themselves are not conceived of as producing depression unless the person is predisposed by cognitive schemas to be sensitive to that type of event. This explains why some people are able to withstand a number of life stress events while others become depressed over seemingly minor occurrences.

As depression deepens, thinking is dominated by negative themes and the patient loses the ability to view these negative thoughts and any other information objectively. The hypervalent, dominant schemata underlie systematic errors in reasoning called *cognitive distortions*. These include (see Beck 1967):

(a) Arbitrary inference – drawing a specific conclusion in the absence of substantiating evidence or even in the face of contradictory evidence.
(b) Selective abstraction – conceptualizing an experience on the basis of a detail taken out of context, ignoring other more salient information.
(c) Overgeneralization – drawing a general rule from one or a few isolated incidents and applying the concept broadly to related or unrelated situations.

(d) Magnification and minimization – assigning a distorted value to an event, seeing it as far more significant or less significant than it actually is.
(e) Personalization – attributing external events to oneself in the absence of any such connection.
(f) Absolutistic, dichotomous thinking – categorizing experiences in one of two extremes; for example, completely good or totally bad.

Recent categorization of cognitive distortions breaks these six down further (Burns 1980): (a) arbitrary inference includes emotional reasoning ('I feel it therefore it must be true') and jumping to conclusions; (b) selective abstraction contains mental filtering (dwelling on a negative detail) and disqualifying the positive; (c) overgeneralization includes labelling (labelling someone in highly emotional terms when it is the behaviour you object to), and 'should' statements (absolute rules used to motivate self or judge others); (d) magnification (catastrophizing) or minimization; (e) personalization; and (f) dichotomous or 'all-or-nothing' thinking.

**Cognitive model of anxiety disorders**   Anxiety disorders are conceptualized as the expression of excessive functioning or malfunctioning of normal survival mechanisms. As in the case of depression, symptoms reflect the operation of specific systems: cognitive, affective, behavioural, motivational and physiological. The basic mechanisms for coping with threat are the same for a normal person as an anxious person: decisions are made quickly and physiological responses prepare the body for escape or defence. These physiological responses are the same for a psychosocial threat as for a physical danger. The difference between the 'normal' individual and the anxious one is that the anxious individual's perception of danger is incorrectly based on false premises or is excessive while the normal response is based on a more accurate assessment of risk and magnitude of danger. Further, among normal individuals the misperception of danger can be corrected by reality testing. In the anxious patient, reality testing is impaired and cues of safety and self-efficacy are screened out. In extreme cases, as in panic, the patient seems unable to recall even previous successful coping as if a 'cognitive bypass' were preventing rational thought from operating. Thus, in cases of anxiety, cognitive content revolves around danger and the individual is likely to maximize the risk of harm and minimize his or her ability to deal with physical or social threats. The magnitude of harm is also likely to be exaggerated, thereby increasing both the value and the probability of an undesirable event occurring.

The cognitive appraisal of danger triggers the operation of other systems. Affectively, the person feels nervous and the motor system responds by increasing or decreasing muscle tension as the body prepares to fight, flee, freeze, or faint. This motor component is facilitated by the autonomic nervous system which may innervate (sympathetic nervous system) or conserve (parasympathetic nervous system) resources. The wish to flee is the motivational response, but paradoxically, the behavioural system may respond with inhibition of speech and movement. The cognitive system further responds with multiple fears, catastrophic interpretations, and inhibition of memory of past coping.

The function of autonomic activity is to mobilize the individual to deal with actual danger by regulating blood supply, metabolism and temperature. However, in the absence of objective danger, such responding is excessive and counterproductive. The situation is further confounded by the fact that the individual cannot develop and apply active coping skills since no actual danger exists. Nevertheless, autonomic arousal is derived from specific cognitive sets based on the perception of danger and the assessment of vulnerability. For example, a 'hypervigilant set' prepares for flight or defence and is manifested in rigid posture, increased blood pressure and increased heart rate due to the activation of the sympathetic nervous system. In contrast, the parasympathetic nervous system is activated by a 'helpless cognitive set' and corresponds to a slump, fall or faint response with decreased blood pressure and heart rate.

**Cognitive model of phobias**   The main difference between phobias and other anxiety disorders is that phobias are fears of specific situations or objects and the anxiety they generate may be prevented by avoiding the situations. Other anxiety patients cannot as easily avoid the stimuli which trigger anxiety, for the cues tend to be more multiple, diffuse and internal (Beck and Emery 1979). Cognitively, phobias differ from other anxiety disorders in specificity of content. In phobias, cognitive content is more directly related to the stimulus situation than in other anxiety disorders. Phobias are similar to other anxiety disorders, however, to the extent that cognitive distortions, physical symptoms and behavioural inclinations are activated.

The cognitive model of phobias differs from both the behavioural and psychoanalytic perspectives. Behaviour therapists argue that the phobic individual is not afraid of the phobic object because of any intrinsic danger, but because of conditioning. Wolpe (1969) describes the development of a phobia thus: first, a frightening incident occurs and produces anxiety. Concurrently, a neutral stimulus is present during the frightening event. Second, the neutral stimulus becomes linked to the anxiety by this temporal association. Thereafter, the person becomes anxious in the presence of the 'neutral' stimulus.

Psychoanalysts similarly postulate an indirect association between the source of fear and the specific content of fear experienced by the patient. According to psychoanalytic theory, the phobic individual displaces his or her real fear onto a more socially acceptable one. Thus, a woman with anxiety-provoking fantasies about behaving sexually in public might develop street phobia (Snaith 1968).

In contrast to these perspectives, the cognitive approach to phobias is to investigate directly what the patient expects to have happen in the phobic situation. In other words, reports from patients indicate that it is not the object, event or situation in itself that they fear, but the anticipated consequences of being in the situation. For example, a patient who reported a 'fear of crowds' was actually afraid of how he might behave in a crowd, afraid that he would lose control in some way, faint, vomit, or become hysterical (Beck and Emery 1979). Another patient, with a fear of doctors and hospitals, had actually had a traumatic incident occur in surgery. Her surgeon had begun an incision on her throat before she was fully anaesthetized and her fear of hospitals was directly related to the belief that, under a doctor's care, she might stop breathing. Based on patient reports then, it is important to discover the specific cognitions associated with anticipated consequences. The same phobic situation may not evoke the same thoughts and images in different individuals. In addition, by exploring cognitions, the therapist is likely to find a central theme or common denominator in the case of multiple phobias.

Phobias may develop from normal or innate fears or may be exaggerated versions of socially instigated fears experienced by the general population. Snaith's study of phobic patients (1968) found that their fears closely matched those of a control group of normal individuals. More recent work (Kirkpatrick 1984) reflects how specific fears are related to age, sex, and cultural factors. Some fears (e.g. of strangers) may be innate and serve a protective function until the child matures enough to operate according to a less absolute system. However, in other cases, fear may actually be perpetuated and reinforced by parents who have the same fears (Beck and Emery 1979). What differentiates a phobia from a fear is the magnification of the amount of risk and the degree of harm expected in a situation. Thus, the nature of phobias may relate quite directly to real but unlikely dangers, to traumatic events, to childhood fears, or to vicarious learning from significant others.

The cognitive model views phobias in terms of the organism's response to threat and thus the rules for promoting survival in cases of actual danger apply in the phobic situation: decisions to act must be made quickly and are served by unambiguous, inclusive, and absolute rules rather than by probabilistic or relative ones.

**Cognitive model of agoraphobia**   Recent interest in agoraphobia has provided impetus to investigating its nature, etiology and treatment. Investigations have focused on phobic avoidance of being outside the home alone, on panic attack as the core disturbance and on the anticipatory fear of panic attacks (Wolfe 1984), fear of fear (Chambless and Goldstein 1980), or 'a heterogeneous collection of phobias and a varied assortment of other psychological problems' (Williams 1985, p. 110).

The cognitive set of the agoraphobia is one of vulnerability, from the perceptions of external and internal danger to the loss of interpersonal effectiveness. The individual's concept is that, when alone, he or she is vulnerable at any time to serious medical, mental or emotional disorder. He or she believes the disorder can be remedied if there is a quick, unobstructed access to safety. Interpreting autonomic arousal as a sign of impending disaster accentuates fear and may enhance somatic symptoms further leading to a full-blown panic attack.

The situations precipitating anxiety (e.g. stores, tunnels, bridges, subways) have usually been explained as blocking access to help. However, it is possible that they pose dangers besides threatening the lifeline to safety. An agoraphobic patient who had panic attacks in department stores was fearful of being accused of shoplifting, of stumbling on the escalator, and of getting stuck in the elevator and suffocating. Similarly, tunnels and subways can cave in and the patient could get crushed or suffocate. Bridges collapse and the patient can get killed. Automobiles get into collisions. Escape from aversive situations may be as important as getting help.

The onset of agoraphobia may begin with such perceptions of opportunities to be immobilized, humiliated, crushed, suffocated or attacked. Many of these fears are childlike, yet the patient believes he or she has no defence against external danger. Further, the patient's autonomic reactions are interpreted as internal disaster, reinforcing the notion of being a victim of

uncontrollable events. Agoraphobics are unlikely to recognize the association between life events and their affective, behavioural, and physiological
responses (Chambless and Goldstein 1980; Guidano and Liotti 1983), and
tend to attribute their reactions to a decrement in their competencies. The
lost of self-confidence resulting from their multiple inhibitions, submissive
tendencies, and negative appraisals of themselves leads to disequilibrium in
relationships and a sense of being trapped and dominated by other people.

Cognitive conflicts centring on the fear of constraint and the fear of
loneliness, on protection and freedom (Guidano and Liotti 1983) and on
dependency, control, and autonomy (Beck and Emery 1985) are apparent in
agoraphobic patients. Research at the Center for Cognitive Therapy finds
that the agoraphobic patient has a greater investment in mobility for its own
sake and sensitivity to being restrained or controlled than other psychiatric
patients. Yet most use a strategy of depending on a caretaker for reassurance and medical assistance.

The symptoms of panic attack frequently occurring in agoraphobic patients are interpreted as specific signs of immediate disaster. Thus, deperso-
nalization may be viewed as evidence of 'going crazy', increased heart rate as
a sign of heart attack, and hyperventilation as evidence that one will stop
breathing altogether. Anticipated consequences include death by heart
attack, stroke, or cessation of breathing, being a public disgrace by fainting
or screaming, or losing control of one's impulses and killing someone.

Some patients can train themselves to head off a full-blown panic attack
through distraction or cognitive restructuring (that is, viewing the symptoms
as an emotional reaction and not a sign of catastrophe). For many others, or
as panic escalates, cognitive techniques are not readily accessible. There is
an inhibition of high-level evaluation processes, a 'cognitive bypass', so that
patients have problems in applying reason or objectivity or even in drawing
on memory of previous 'false alarms'. In these cases, distraction, activity,
and techniques such as respiratory control (Clark, Salkovikis and Chalkley
1985) may be more immediately efficacious and may ultimately undermine
assumptions of lack of control over internal disorder.

## Practical applications

Cognitive therapy is a learning experience in which the therapist plays an
active role in helping the patient to uncover and modify cognitive distortions
and dysfunctional assumptions. The proximal goal is to promote cognitive
restructuring through the modification of systematic bias in thinking. It is

designed to be a short-term therapy and an effort is made to induce the patient to carry out homework designed to identify and respond to negative cognitions, master cognitive and behavioural skills learned in sessions, and test hypotheses. Thus, much work is done by patients outside the session, allowing for more rapid change and for the patient to learn to become his or her own cognitive therapist.

## The therapeutic relationship

The cognitive therapist serves a dual function as a guide to understanding how beliefs and attitudes influence affect and behaviour and as a catalyst to promote corrective experiences that will promote adaptive cognitions and skills. Therapy is a collaborative effort between patient and therapist, thus underscoring the importance of relationship factors: warmth, accurate empathy, and genuineness (see Rogers 1951). Without these qualities, it is unlikely that the therapist will be able fully to appreciate the patient's personal world view. While showing warmth, the therapist plays an active role in pinpointing problems, focusing on important areas and proposing and rehearsing specific cognitive-behavioural techniques.

The empirical orientation of therapy converts the patient's closed belief system into an open system. Questioning is the major therapeutic device and behavioural experimentation is a primary way to investigate the validity of specific assumptions. Such experimentation and the purpose and goals of these assignments are done with the full understanding and endorsement of the patient. Moreover, feedback from the patient – about the session, the therapist, the direction of therapy, and the like – is elicited to maintain rapport, trust and collaboration. Issues of 'transference' and 'resistance' are dealt with directly in terms of underlying dysfunctional beliefs, therapist factors (e.g. lack of rapport or understanding, failure to provide a rationale for the assignment or line of questioning), or lack of consensus on the aims, purposes, and goals of therapy (Beck *et al*. 1979; see also Golden 1983 for a review of sources of resistance).

## Strategies of treatment

Initially, the therapist focuses on symptom relief and problem definition and describes the nature of cognitive therapy and the rationale behind the treatment. Collaboration begins at the outset, as patient and therapist investigate how and what the patient thinks, the basis for such thinking, and the practical benefits and costs which result from such thinking. The patient contributes the 'raw data' and the therapist guides the patient about what data to collect and how to use it therapeutically. Early on, patients may need to learn to recognize that they have ideation which intervenes between a stimulus and their emotional reaction to it. As patients are socialized to therapy, they are trained to identify these thoughts which occur continuously, which seem to come from nowhere, and which usually remain unchallenged. These are called 'automatic thoughts'. Patients learn that these thoughts are modifiable when treated as hypotheses to be investigated logically either verbally or behaviourally.

After a review of presenting concerns and symptoms, it is possible to reduce an often extensive problem list by looking for common denominators and deciding with the patient which problems to work on first. A treatment plan is formulated by the therapist, ideally containing the following information: the patient's habitual patterns of reaction, specific vulnerabilities, stresses impinging on these vulnerabilities that activate the pattern of symptoms, early developmental factors, and how the patient is handling current problems in view of this background.

Along with an overall treatment plan, each session is planned in the first few minutes by setting an agenda, deciding which problems will be addressed, eliciting feedback from the previous session, and reviewing homework. Setting an agenda reflects the active nature of cognitive therapy, helps the therapist and patient use their time efficiently, and further encourages teamwork.

In eliciting data about thoughts and images, the therapist teaches the patient that cognitions may or may not reflect actual circumstances. This is done verbally by direct questioning about the evidence for such conclusions, alternative explanations, and the process by which the patient reached such conclusions. The therapist may also use metaphor and analogy when appropriate. In this process of investigation, the patient and therapist not only formulate concrete hypotheses to test, but design experiments to test them, and further explicate the assumptions which underlie them. Testing hypotheses is largely done outside the therapy session as homework. For example, a woman who assumed her friend had not called her because she was angry called her friend to check out her conclusion. Similarly, a man who assumed that all eyes would be on him in a restaurant, dined out only to observe that others were more intent on their meals and dining companions than on him. Finally, a law student whose perfectionistic style caused anxiety and depression acted against her belief that 'If I can do something I must do it,' and chose not to compete for a prestigious award she did not really want. This gave her a greater sense of internal control and decreased her dysphoria.

Collaborative empiricism and guided discovery are hallmarks of cognitive therapy. The alliance between patient and therapist, the focus on concrete goals and a problem list, and the investigation of the thoughts and images underlying present problems are all part of the empirical approach. Guided discovery is a way, through Socratic dialogue, of teaching the patient how to identify maladaptive cognitive processing and how to uncover assumptions and reality test them by opening them up to alternatives. (See section entitled 'Disputing Irrational Beliefs' in Golden and Friedberg's chapter for an example of such dialogue.) By evaluating dysfunctional cognitions, the therapist and patient may produce shifts in thinking to a more realistic level. Behavioural experiments, designed to test dysfunctional cognitions and try more adaptive interpretations, assist in cognitive change. Structural change is achieved through the analysis of assumptions that have restricted the patient's response repertoire, the adoption of more adaptive assumptions which fit more closely with the reality of the situation, and the practice of behaviours congruent with these new assumptions.

## Major treatment techniques

Cognitive therapy applies a number of specific treatment techniques, both verbal and behavioural, depending on the nature of the presenting problem and the needs of the individual patient. Cognitive techniques are directed at identifying and testing specific misconceptions.

This approach consists of highly specific learning experiences designed to teach the patient the following operations: (1) to monitor his negative, automatic thoughts (cognitions); (2) to recognize the connections between cognition, affect, and behaviour; (3) to examine the evidence for and against his distorted automatic thought; (4) to substitute more reality-oriented interpretations for these biased cognitions; and (5) to learn to identify and alter the dysfunctional beliefs which predispose him to distort his experiences. (Beck *et al.* 1979, p. 4)

Verbal techniques are used to explore the logic behind and basis for specific conclusions. Behavioural techniques are used not only to change behaviour, but to elicit thoughts. For example, exposure therapy has value not only as a counterconditioning, desensitization, or response-prevention technique, but because it elicits thoughts and images that may be at the base of the agoraphobic's avoidance.

Major cognitive and behavioural techniques used in cognitive therapy are reviewed below.

**Cognitive techniques**   Automatic thoughts are among the most accessible cognitive data available to the patient. Yet, patients are often unaware of their stream of thoughts, their interpretations, and their judgements. Eliciting and recognizing automatic thoughts is thus the first technique used by the therapist and taught to the patient. Patients are trained to observe the sequence of external events and their reactions to them. Automatic thoughts precede affect and are consistent with it. They reflect thematic content specific for various symptoms (e.g. threat is specific for anxiety; loss, deprivation, or defeat for depression). Automatic thoughts may be demonstrated in the session by drawing attention to mood shifts, using imagery or role-playing, and even by discussing the patient's expectations about therapy. Patients are trained to identify the thoughts juxtaposed between an event and their emotional response. Automatic thoughts may be further demonstrated by assigning the patient homework to observe the sequence of external events during the week and their reactions to them.

Automatic thoughts are often taken for granted by patients as 'the truth' rather than as one perspective on reality, so they often have not considered their ability to modify their thoughts. Moreover, automatic thoughts seem plausible and valid to the individual and recur despite trying to block them out (Beck 1967). Because of their power, then, automatic thoughts and particularly the beliefs underlying them need to be repeatedly framed as hypotheses rather than firm conclusions.

By increasing objectivity and perspective on events, patients may begin to see the distortions in their thinking. It is very often helpful to label these cognitive errors (e.g. arbitrary inference, dichotomous thinking), along with identifying how they shape further judgments, emotion and behaviour.

Testing automatic thoughts proceeds in a scientific manner by gathering data, evaluating evidence and drawing conclusions. As Beck and Young (1984) point out, patients learn, by designing experiments that subject their automatic thoughts to objective analysis, that one's view of reality can be quite different from what actually takes place. They also learn the process of rational thinking through collaborative empiricism and this maintains gains after formal therapy ends.

cant manage to walk *unobviously* but she does all the time

Automatic thoughts can be tested in a variety of ways (Beck and Young 1984). One is to have the patient recall previous experience and list evidence for and against the hypothesis. For example, a female patient stated, 'No man will find me sexually attractive unless I lose a lot of weight.' This was clearly contradicted by the number and quality of love affairs she had had at her present weight. Another way is to design an experiment to test a given hypothesis. In this case, the patient predicts an outcome and proceeds to gather data. Data may either contradict or confirm a patient's hypothesis, so it is important for the therapist not to dismiss automatically the patient's hypothesis as irrational. Finally, in cases in which automatic thoughts are not easily tested through experimentation, therapists may produce evidence from their own or others' experience. For example, a patient who concluded that lack of satisfaction in one job predicted total failure in all careers was presented evidence about the career changes of Albert Schweitzer (a former musician), Michael Crichton (physician turned novelist), and others who made rewarding transitions to new careers. The therapist can also ask questions designed to uncover a logical error inherent in the patient's beliefs. A patient who had had surgery the previous year had persistent pain which had decreased markedly over the months, so that at times it was merely annoying discomfort. His automatic thought, 'I can't take this pain,' was contradicted by the fact that not only could he take the pain (e.g. function in work, family, and social roles) but he had been able to take worse pain in the previous year. (Indeed, he identified only 'going to smokey parties and playing volleyball' as the things pain prevented him from doing.) His adaptive response to this recurring automatic thought became, 'I don't like this pain, but I've certainly taken worse.'

In framing hypothesis for testing, it is necessary to make them specific and concrete. Thus, global labels, generalities, or vague terms need to be operationally defined. A man who believed, 'I'm not an adult,' was asked to list as many adult attributes as he could and to rate himself on each of them. Similarly, a depressed patient who concluded, 'I'll never be the person I was before' identified the qualities she liked about herself in the past (e.g. friendliness, initiative, optimism), further operationalized them into specific behaviours (e.g. asking others about themselves, asking a friend to lunch, identifying positive thoughts) and monitored those behaviours over the next few weeks. Using global labels to define oneself often combines the distortions of labelling (Burns 1980), overgeneralization, and dichotomous thinking. Refining terms, developing criteria, and building a continuum for evaluation (e.g. 'I am 0 per cent success as a parent' to 'I am 100 per cent success as a parent') help to undermine these maladaptive thinking patterns.

Reattribution techniques are used to test assumptions by considering alternative causes of an event. Depressed and anxious patients often blame themselves for external events and even for their disorders (e.g. 'I think wrong and that's why I'm sick'). Through a review of the many factors impinging on the situation and by applying logic to the available evidence, the patient may make a more realistic assessment of his or her responsibility. This makes working on the problem far less overwhelming for the patient and may, in cases of misattribution, relieve guilt. It also enhances problem-solving as in the example of an anxious woman who tearfully explained that she was making herself nauseated, lightheaded, feverish and weak by 'being an anxious person'. After considering alternative explanations, she visited her physician and learned she had an intestinal virus.

Decentring is a technique used with patients who feel that they are the centre of attention. They view themselves as being continuously vulnerable to other people's judgements of them. They may easily feel ridiculed, rejected, or suspicious. One young man who believed that people would find him stupid if he didn't appear completely confident and sure of himself had postponed his dream of going to college. As his registration day grew near, he designed an experiment to expose his uncertainty. On registration day, he asked several fellow students for directions, for information regarding schedules, and for a translation of a confusing computerized list. He reported that '100 per cent' of the students were friendly and often as confused as he. By gathering information with his questions, he was also able to be of help to other lost students.

Self-monitoring of behaviours is a traditional behavioural technique which can be applied to cognitive endeavours. The simplest application is in the counting and recording of automatic thoughts. It is also used in specific instances to monitor affective levels among depressed and anxious patients. Depressed patients or those with chronic pain may think their depression or pain is constantly at a high level. By monitoring it they may see fluctuation, often in association with times of day or activity level. Observing shifts in mood or comfort helps to modify the belief that pain or depression is constant, intense and unremitting. Monitoring anxiety level allows the patient to recognize that, even during a panic attack, anxiety has a beginning, a peak, and a decline. This knowledge may be used to encourage remaining in a situation rather than fleeing it. Remaining in the situation disconfirms the patient's belief that the worst will happen and provides information that the person can survive anxiety, that it is time-limited, and that he or she merely has to wait for the wave of anxiety to pass.

Decatastrophizing, also referred to as the 'what if' technique (Beck and

Emery 1979), is used with anxious patients to explore their worst case scenarios. By posing questions about the extent and duration of the patient's predicted consequences, the therapist attempts to widen the range of information on which the individual bases his predictions, and broaden the individual's time perspective. A typical use of decatastrophizing and time projection is presented by Beck (1976) with a medical student whose fear of public speaking included the belief that he could never live down appearing foolish to his classmates. In this case, the therapist questioned the patient about what exactly would happen if he were to appear ridiculous to his peers. Would his career be ruined? Would his family disown him? Would he feel badly? For how long? Then what would happen? The use of questions allowed the patient to conclude for himself that he had exaggerated the significance of the public-speaking assignment. Moreover, the use of time projection (e.g. 'For how long?' 'And then what?') conveys the notion that anxiety, and even possible embarrassment, would be time-limited. Decastrophizing and exploring the patient's worst fears also exposes misinformation that patients have (e.g. about mental disorders, physical disorders, 'normal' behaviour) and allows for the reduction of distress through education.

The use of imagery procedures is endorsed by the finding that 90 per cent of anxious patients report visual images prior to and concurrent with anxiety (Beck, Laude and Bohnert 1974). Indeed, some patients describe themselves as 'imagers' rather than 'thinkers' and find it much easier to report visual fantasies than automatic thoughts. Spontaneous or autonomous pictorial images provide rich data about the patient's conceptual system; induced fantasies, long used by behaviour therapists in relaxation and skills training, are finding new use in dream restructuring (Freeman 1981); and specific imaginal procedures can be used to modify cognitions.

By asking for details of fantasies, the therapist and the patient begin to identify the patient's conceptualization of and reaction to the pictured situation. If the given fantasy is of a future event and cognitive distortions are encouraging avoidance or negative affect, then the distortions can be corrected. Other techniques for modifying images follow (Beck and Emery 1979):

1. Turn-off technique: Like thought-stopping, images of traumatic events and memories can be interrupted by a loud noise or shouting, 'Stop it!' A pleasant fantasy can be substituted for the upsetting one.
2. Repetition (Raimy 1975): In some cases, successive repetitions of a fantasy become more reasonable and realistic in content, and the fantasy

changes from a less probable to a more probable outcome. In other cases, anxiety is substantially reduced or even eliminated with successive imaging although the content of the fantasy does not change.

3. Time projection: When a person is upset about a particular event, imaging the situation six months, a year, or several years from the present allows detachment about the significance of the upsetting event.

4. Metaphors: Vivid metaphorical images can present alternative views of a situation in a creative way.

5. Decatastrophizing image: Often anxious patients imagine a situation without considering any positive features or 'rescue factors' in it. Discussing the image and pointing out the missing data allow the patient to distinguish between fantasy and reality.

6. Induced imagery: By gradually changing an image from negative to neutral or positive, the patient can experience an increase in his or her sense of control, and fantasize behaviour that is more adaptive than current behaviour.

7. Goal rehearsal: Rehearsing a desired behaviour in one's mind, problem-solving in advance, and practising positive self-instructions are likely to increase one's sense of self-efficacy.

8. Positive imagery: Positive images can be relaxing, provide distraction and can be used as substitutes for negative images in the 'turn-off' techniques.

9. Coping imagery: Several types of coping imagery have been advocated, ranging from Lazarus's (1976) 'step up' or hierarchical technique whereby the patient imagines dealing with a range of possible outcomes from best to worst, to imagining how someone else would handle the situation (covert modelling), to changing features of the image to make it less threatening.

Because both the therapist and the patient maintain an open attitude towards the patient's cognitions, the therapist does not rule out realistic life problems or skills deficits as sources of distress. Cognitive therapy is reality-orientated and takes a problem-solving approach. It does not assume that patient's problems are 'in their imagination'. Patients often accurately report life problems which require action or show skill deficits which contribute to their problems. Generating alternatives within a problem-solving framework is an active intervention and, in the case of severely depressed patients or those incapacitated by anxiety, the therapist may take a dominant role in identifying alternative courses of action. Teaching skills is similarly done as a problem-solving technique.

Maladaptive assumptions are less accessible to patients than are thoughts and images and are identified by discerning themes within automatic thoughts covering a variety of situations and over time. These assumptions are rules used by individuals to interpret events and guide behaviour. They are maladaptive in the sense that they are rigidly held, absolute, unrealistic, and used too frequently and inappropriately. They are also associated with strong emotions, and emotion evoked during the investigation of an assumption is a clue to its importance.

When the therapist believes that an assumption has been identified, concurrence is sought from the patient either by asking the patient to abstract a general rule from his or her automatic thoughts collected over time or by directly asking the patient if the hypothesized assumption seems plausible. Together, the patient and therapist reach accord on the most accurate statement of the patient's underlying assumption. When presented with a list of possible assumptions, an anxious and depressed patient (who had lost both parents tragically and who had recently given birth to a daughter) emotionally endorsed the assumption, 'I expect to lose what I value most.' A salesman in job jeopardy had the assumption, 'In order to be happy I must be wealthy.' These assumptions reflect specific vulnerabilities, possibly based on deeply held values, which may be exposed by life events.

As with automatic thoughts, changing maladaptive underlying assumptions is best served by questions, not counterarguments. Beck and Young (1984) identify several ways of analyzing the validity of assumptions. One is to ask the patient if the assumption seems reasonable, productive or helpful. If the patient sees no problem with the universal application of the assumption, the therapist may pose questions to explore the problems. For example, a physician who believed that in order to have a successful practice he had to put 100 per cent effort into everything had not considered the possibility of burn-out. Questioning the logic and consequences of maladaptive assumptions can also be approached by asking the patient to list the evidence against an assumption or by listing the advantages or disadvantages of modifying the assumption. Finally, in cases in which patients are acting on imperatives, on how they 'should' ideally behave, an experiment is designed to challenge that assumption. In this experiment, analogous to response prevention, the patient acts contrary to a 'should' and observes whether the actual consequences are the same as the ones predicted.

**Behavioural techniques** Behavioural techniques are used throughout the course of cognitive therapy both in the pursuit of behavioural goals and as the means to a cognitive end. Behavioural techniques are particularly useful in engaging and increasing the activity level of severely depressed patients. They are also primary in skills training through modelling, role-playing, and rehearsal. Moreover, since a significant proportion of therapeutic change results from the application of cognitive principles outside the therapy session, behavioural assignments serve a major function in *homework*. Such assignments typically focus on self-observation, structuring time effectively, and implementing specific procedures for dealing with concrete situations.

Behavioural techniques also provide the opportunity and experience to modify automatic thoughts and assumptions. A depressed patient who believed, 'I can't be with people,' began to change her belief by going to an office party with the goal of staying twenty minutes and greeting three people. Her attitude became more positive through a series of *graded tasks* of increasing difficulty including going to a picnic for one hour (she chose to stay for two hours) and joining coworkers at a holiday luncheon. *Scheduling activities* similarly provides structure to the depressed person's day and undermines his or her belief that they are inactive because of some inherent defect.

Scheduling activities not only counteracts inertia, loss of motivation, hopelessness, and excessive rumination but helps patients increase their enjoyment and sense of accomplishment on a daily basis through *mastery and pleasure ratings*. By rating each activity of the day (using a 0–10 scale) for both mastery and pleasure, patients are able, at least on a superficial level, to contradict the beliefs that they cannot accomplish or enjoy anything any more.

*Behavioural rehearsal and role-playing* are used to practise the techniques to be applied during the week and also to elicit automatic thoughts which can be dealt with in the session. *Cognitive rehearsal* allows the patient to imagine taking the steps necessary to complete a task and can be used to anticipate obstacles that make the assignment difficult.

*Self-reliance training* (Beck and Young 1984; Emery 1980) is often effective with depressed patients who have come to rely on others to take care of their daily needs. One patient whose self-esteem suffered as a result of her dependence on others began keeping track of her 'not helpless behaviour' which included cooking again and resuming other routine activities as well as restricting her crying to a specific time and situation (alone in the laundry room). Thus, she claimed more responsibility for her daily functioning and more control over her emotional reactions.

*Diversion techniques* can reduce strong affect and decrease negative thinking. Such techniques include physical activity, social contact, work, play, and visual imagery. One agoraphobic patient carried coins in her pocket and tried to identify them through touch alone as distraction when anxious. Another anxious patient used jogging to disperse physiological arousal. Still another depressed patient found that volunteer work with the elderly diverted her focus of attention from herself and improved her mood.

*Hypothesis testing* has both cognitive and behavioural components. Each 'mini-experiment' is specifically designed to test a hypothesis in a concrete fashion. Before entering the experimental situation, the patient predicts an outcome consistent with his or her automatic thoughts. The patient then carries out the agreed-upon behaviour and evaluates the evidence in light of the new experience.

*Exposure therapy* allows for a particular type of hypothesis testing among anxious patients. Patients with driving phobias, for example, can report level of anxiety, physiological symptoms, thoughts, and images while driving. In this way, they gather data on the number of 'false alarms' they have physiologically and how their negative predictions (e.g. of driving off the road, of a bridge collapsing) are not borne out. After numerous excursions with a paraprofessional recording cognitions, a patient compiled a list of negative, false forecasts which she laughingly called, 'Ellen's Famous Predictions'. She was able to view her recorded prophecies as evidence that anxiety is not correlated with real danger and that she is not good at predicting the future. From this evidence she was able to devise more realistic coping thoughts.

## Overcoming obstacles to client progress

Beck and Young (1984) identify two types of problems in therapy: difficulties in the therapist–patient relationship, and problems in which therapy seems not to be working. Therapists with a less than full understanding of cognitive therapy may view it as a technique-orientated approach and fail to appreciate the centrality of the relationship between patient and therapist. Although cognitive therapy is directive and structured, therapists must remain flexible and be prepared to depart from the standard therapy format when appropriate.

When the therapist perceives a patient to be dissatisfied, angry, hostile, or withdrawn, it is vital to address that observation directly. The therapist can check with the patient about the accuracy of that perception, the patient's feelings, and the thoughts the patient may have about the therapist. Having feedback as part of every therapy session is designed, in part, to maintain a good relationship between patient and therapist and to prevent automatic thoughts from persisting uncorrected. However, automatic thoughts about the therapist or therapy may occur outside the session and the patient may bring those thoughts and feelings into the session, sometimes catching the therapist by surprise.

It is important that therapists remember that many interventions can be misinterpreted in a negative way and much confusion and faulty attributions may result when the therapist fails to provide a comprehensive rationale for interventions, paces the session or the process of therapy too fast or too slowly for the patient, or does not adapt his or her style to the needs of the patient. For example, therapists may choose to use more self-disclosure when perceived as impersonal and may do more frequent checking on patients' reactions when patients believe the therapist does not understand them. In this case, too, the therapist may ask more frequently for feedback on his or her formulations of the patients' thoughts.

When misinterpretations occur, they are treated like other thoughts. Patients are given as much time as they need to present their interpretations of events and consequent feelings. The therapist plays an active role, through questioning, in making these thoughts explicit. Together they gather data and search for alternative explanations. The therapist, too, has automatic thoughts about the patient and him/herself which may hinder therapeutic progress. In this case, too, it is imperative to explore one's own distortions and assumptions and to re-evaluate the evidence for one's conclusions. It is also important not to be judgmental or to label the patient as passive-aggressive, resistant, or irrational. Such labelling actually inhibits learning more about the patient's responses and misinterpretations in relationships.

Problems with the rate of progress in therapy may come from several sources. Patients may have difficulty completing assignments because they do not understand them, do not expect them to be helpful, or do not think they will do them correctly. Explaining assignments completely and rehearsing them, cognitively or behaviourally, assists patients in completing assignments. Expectations about the helpfulness of homework can be dealt with as automatic thoughts. It also helps to remind patients that the assignment is a natural experiment that can be redesigned following data collection. Reviewing the disadvantages and advantages of maintaining the belief that problems cannot be solved by doing homework may be discussed or the therapist can ask the patient to experiment before reaching that conclusion. Setting aside time for homework or 'scheduling an appointment with yourself' to do homework also helps patients who are not used to doing an activity regularly. A system of self-reward can also reinforce a patient for doing homework. Finally, if patients are inhibited by performance anxiety and the thought, 'I can't do this right,' it is important to explain that self-help assignments cannot be failed, that partial completion is more helpful than not trying, and that most learning occurs by successive attempts and self-correction.

Unrealistic expectations about the rate of progress may be held by either the patient or the therapist or both. Research on the efficacy of cognitive therapy for depression has demonstrated its effectiveness in twenty sessions over a twelve-week period (Rush *et al.* 1977). Many patients familiar with these findings enter therapy with the expectation that they will be 'cured' in that amount of time. Some patients, depending on their diagnosis, personality, skills repertoire, and effort with homework, may need more than the recommended fifteen to eighteen sessions.

In contrast, some patients may make rapid progress through the initial stages of therapy and wish to terminate treatment upon symptom removal or before basic assumptions have been altered. In such cases, it is best to reassess the patient's goals for therapy, review the fundamental role of basic assumptions or schemata in daily problems, and assess with the patient the evidence for cognitive change. Patients satisfied with symptom relief may, of course, choose to end therapy at that point, but booster sessions every few weeks may be used to maintain contact should problems recur.

Therapists may find it helpful to remind the patients and themselves that 'ups and downs' are to be expected and, in fact, 'downs' provide opportunities for the patient to apply newly learned skills or to observe himself or herself in a challenging situation. One therapist even congratulated a patient on having a panic attack in a department store, saying, 'Great! The goal is to have a panic attack in as many different places as possible without leaving. That way, you'll see you can survive them all.' When working with severely depressed patients, the therapist must often work hard not to share the patient's negative expectations and hopelessness. In this instance, the therapist must often work at correcting misconceptions about the process of change and the nature of depression before further progress can occur, for the negative bias in depression can lead to minimizing any gains.

Another problem in therapy is that cognitive techniques may be misapplied. They may be applied incorrectly, incompletely, too rigidly, or at an inappropriate time. While it is necessary to stay with a particular technique long enough to give it an adequate trial, trying an alternative technique when the patient does not improve may be more efficacious. Further, a patient may not respond to a technique because it is applied prematurely or is too threatening. At this time it is important to get feedback from the patient about the intervention, to assess alternatives, to address the anxiety or to slow down.

Finally, there may be little progress in therapy because the patient and therapist are working on a secondary or tangential problem. They may have made substantial progress on the problem without a change in overall depression or anxiety because the real problem is being withheld by the patient. Beck and Young (1984) describe a patient who presented difficulty at work as the major problem while marital problems, which were too threatening to discuss, contributed to the work difficulties. Another example is provided by a woman who professed wanting to lose weight, but whose self-image difficulties were really based on her confusion over sexual preference. In contrast are patients who show 'progress' in terms of decreased anxiety who are not experiencing anxiety because they are avoiding the stimulus situations. Thus, notions of progress in therapy must be in terms of mutually agreed-upon goals, multiple avenues of change (e.g. behavioural change, cognitive change, emotional change), and with realistic expectations of rates of progress.

## Case example

In this case example, we describe the course of treatment for an anxious patient in order to illustrate both behavioural and cognitive techniques used in cognitive therapy.

### Presenting problem

The patient is a twenty-nine-year-old, single male who had been in treatment with three previous therapists for his anxiety. In the past year, he had been medicated on Xanax, Dalmane, and Elavil with no relief for his anxiety and depression. His history of anxiety was lifelong and he had been hospitalized five times since childhood for 'nervous stomach'. During one hospitalization, he reported, chunks of food were removed from his intestine. His anxiety prevented him from eating, working, dating, and travelling far from home.

The patient lived in a rural New England town with his parents and older sister. Unemployed for nearly a year, he spent his days at home, watching television, smoking cigarettes, and trying to avoid confrontations with his sister, who dominated the household with her tantrums, unpredictable behaviour, and unreasonable demands. The patient's pre-eminent fear was of vomiting after eating, making a mess, and infuriating his sister. Consequently, he had restricted his eating, had lost weight, and had not eaten a meal with the other family members in five months. He also regarded clearing his throat in the morning and expectorating as 'vomiting', proof that he had stomach trouble. His fear of vomiting in front of others led him seriously to limit his social life, seeing only neighbours and not dating. His fear of getting lost caused him to restrict more and more the distance travelled from home.

The patient's parents were described as 'overprotective', not letting him spend the night with friends or relatives as a child and discouraging him as a young adult from moving to his own apartment because of his lack of furniture, saying 'If you can't do things completely right, don't do them at all.'

## The first sessions

The first sessions focused on generating a problem list, educating the patient about anxiety, and doing functional and cognitive analyses of anxiety-evoking situations. Functional and cognitive analyses are used to identify the eliciting stimuli, the behaviours, the thoughts and the feelings in situations. Symptom removal was begun in the first session by teaching the patient basic relaxation skills to use prior to eating and on the train ride to therapy sessions.

The problem list generated in the first session included: (a) being unable to eat because of anxiety, (b) procrastination, (c) avoiding bars, restaurants, parties, and shopping malls, (d) being unable to work because of anxiety. There were specific automatic thoughts associated with these problems. The thought associated with being unable to eat was, 'I'll get nauseated, vomit, and make a mess.' In terms of procrastination it was, 'I give up when I feel lousy.' Avoidance of bars, restaurants, and the like centred on thoughts of vomiting in front of others, making them angry and consequently being an outcast, being approached sexually by a woman, and being looked at by other people. His thoughts about being unable to work were, 'I can't do a good (perfect) job unless I am anxiety-free,' relating to messages from his mother about not doing something unless you can do it right.

The first problem addressed was eating. The patient was instructed to record his thoughts prior to eating. These were generally negative predictions ('My sister will come home and be angry'). He was also instructed to eat when he was hungry, to chew each mouthful fifteen times, and to put his fork down between bites to slow his speedy ingestion of food. In this way, he worked behaviourally on reducing the probability of discomfort and cognitively on testing negative predictions. Education about anxiety also helped him to distinguish between physical symptoms and emotions, to relabel emotions as such and not as a sign of organic illness.

The volitional nature of the patient's vomiting became apparent in exploring the meaning of the act with him. He said, 'I've been sick all my life. Everyone's said, "Something's wrong with that boy." To prove it was physical, to show I was sick, I'd vomit.' The patient was instructed in alternative ways of seeking relief from anxiety including saying to himself, 'It only has to go this far,' breathing slowly, and distracting himself from the physical sensations. He substituted relaxation exercises for gagging. In reviewing his history, he recognized that gagging had been a way to avoid school and, later, work. As he demonstrated competence through graded task assignment in later sessions, he avoided fewer situations and relied less on this behaviour. It also became clear that the patient avoided activities his parents chose for him. Assertion training in later sessions also aided him in making his own decisions and acting on them without resorting to sick role behaviour.

Acting contrary to his schema, 'I'm a sick person,' was a powerful tool for Ted. To help him do this, he was asked to use self-instruction ('I'm just gagging, I don't have to throw up'), list the ways in which he was not a 'sick person' (e.g. able to do odd jobs, take care of himself), record levels of anxiety and observe fluctuations, and relabel nausea as a sign of anxiety and not physical illness. He was also assigned graded tasks designed to increase his activity outside the home (e.g. accepting carpentry work in his neighbourhood, eating in a neighbourhood café), decrease his agoraphobic avoidance (e.g. travel increasing distances by himself), and decrease his procrastination by breaking tasks down into manageable steps (e.g. enrolling in a community college began with calling for an appointment).

His procrastination was also addressed in sessions, working on his automatic thought, 'I can't do anything unless I feel good.' This thought prevented him from calling the college's guidance counsellor to set up an appointment. In the therapy session, he phoned another therapist who role-played a guidance counsellor with much credibility. Prior to the role-play, Ted was asked to rate his anxiety from 0–100 (he stated it was 70 per cent), state his thoughts ('I'll be too nervous to speak'), and predict his success from 0 to 100 per cent. Following the role-play, he rated both the credibility of the therapist as guidance counsellor (100 per cent) and his anxiety during the role-play (20 per cent). He was also asked about his prediction of silence (he actually asked more questions than planned) and his belief that he cannot function if he feels any symptoms of anxiety (proven false by role-play). This combination of cognitive and behavioural techniques helped decrease his anxiety in this practice situation and he actually visited the college during the following week.

## Later sessions

Later sessions focused on issues of autonomy and independence from his family. He was able to rehearse cognitively an imagined scene with his sister with his response to any tirade being, 'You might be right.' Work on assertion began with his thoughts about acting on his own behalf ('It's not nice to upset a family member') and continued with questioning the assumption that being assertive is hurtful, listing the advantages and disadvantages of acting in his best interest in the family, and behavioural rehearsal. He found, while learning assertiveness skills, that it was helpful to carry two flashcards with him. On one was the automatic thought, 'Mother says I'll fail,' with the adaptive response, 'Opinions are not facts,' on the reverse side. On the other card was simply the message, 'My parents exaggerate how dangerous the world is.'

The patient ceased taking Elavil and Dalmane after the fourth session of cognitive therapy and rarely took Xanax. Currently, he is doing very well at a local college, eats comfortably in the school cafeteria, drives to school, and socializes with classmates. He continues to test his negative predictions and has a new attitude about risk-taking: that it is the only way to make progress.

## References

Adler, A. (1936) The neurotic's picture of the world. *International Journal of Individual Psychology, 2,* 3–10.

Alexander, F. (1950) *Psychosomatic medicine: Its principles and applications.* New York: Norton.

Arnold, M. (1960) *Emotion and personality,* vol.1. New York: Columbia University Press.

Bandura, A. (1977) *Social learning theory.* Englewood Cliffs, NJ: Prentice Hall.

Beck, A.T. (1967) *Depression: Clinical, experimental, and theoretical aspects*. New York: Hoeber. (Republished as *Depression: Causes and treatment*. Philadelphia: University of Pennsylvania Press, 1972).

Beck, A.T. (1976) *Cognitive therapy and the emotional disorders*. New York: International Universities Press.

Beck, A.T. and Emery, G. (1979) *Cognitive therapy of anxiety and phobic disorders*. Philadelphia: Center for Cognitive Therapy.

Beck, A.T. and Emery, G. (1985) *Anxiety and phobias: A cognitive approach*. New York: Basic Books.

Beck, A.T., Laude, R. and Bohnert, M. (1974) Ideational components of anxiety neurosis. *Archives of General Psychiatry, 31*, 319–325.

Beck, A.T., Rush, A.J., Shaw, B.F. and Emery, G. (1979) *Cognitive therapy of depression*. New York: Guilford Press.

Beck A.T. and Young, J.E. (1984) Cognitive therapy of depression. In D. Barlow (ed.) *Clinical handbook of psychological disorders: A step-by-step treatment manual*. New York: Guilford Press.

Burns, D.D. (1980) *Feeling good: The new mood therapy*. New York: New American Library.

Chambless, D.L. and Goldstein, A.J. (1980) Anxieties: Agoraphobia and hysteria. In A.M. Brodsky and R. Hare-Mustin (eds) *Women and psychotherapy*. New York: Guilford Press.

Clark, D.M., Salkovskis, P.M. and Chalkley, A.J. (1985) Respiratory control as a treatment for panic attacks. *Journal of Behavior Therapy and Experimental Psychiatry, 16(1)*, 23–30.

Coleman, R.E. (1981) Cognitive-behavioral treatment of agoraphobia. In G. Emery, S. Hollon and R.C. Bedrosian (eds) *New directions in cognitive therapy*. New York: Guilford Press.

Ellis, A. (1962) *Reason and emotion in psychotherapy*. New York: Lyle Stuart.

Emery, G. (1980) Self-reliance training in depression. In D.P. Rathjen and J.P. Foreyt (eds) *Social competence: Interventions for children and adults*. Elmsford, NY: Pergamon Press.

Epstein, N. (1983) Cognitive therapy with couples. In A. Freeman (ed.) *Cognitive therapy with couples and groups*. New York: Plenum Press.

Frank, J.D. (1961) *Persuasion and healing*. Baltimore: Johns Hopkins Press.

Freeman, A. (1981) Dreams and images in cognitive therapy. In G. Emery, S. Hollon and R.C. Bedrosian (eds) *New directions in cognitive therapy*. New York: Guilford Press.

Golden, W.L. (1983) Resistance in cognitive-behaviour therapy. *British Journal of Cognitive Psychotherapy, 1(2)*, 33–42.

Goldfried, M.R. and Davison, G.C. (1976) *Clinical behavior therapy*. New York: Holt, Rinehart and Winston.

Guidano, V.P. and Liotti, G. (1983) *Cognitive processes and emotional disorders*. New York: Guilford Press.

Horney, K. (1950) *Neurosis and human growth: The struggle toward self-realization*. New York: Norton.

Kant, I. (1798) *The classification of mental disorders*. Konigsberg, Germany: Nicolovius.

Kazdin, A.E. and Wilson, G.T. (1978) *Evaluation of behavior therapy: Issues, evidence, and research strategies*. Cambridge, MA: Ballinger.

Kelly, G. (1955) *The psychology of personal constructs*. New York: Norton.

Kirkpatrick, D.P. (1984) Age, gender and patterns of common intense fears among adults. *Behaviour Research and Therapy, 22(2)*, 141–50.

Klesges, R.C., Sanchez, V.C. and Stanton, A.L. (1982) Obtaining employment in academia: The hiring process and characteristics of successful applicants. *Professional Psychology, 13*, 577–586.

Lazarus, A. (1976) *Multi-modal behavior therapy*. New York: Springer.

Lazarus, R. (1966) *Psychological stress and the coping process*. New York: McGraw-Hill.

Mahoney, M.J. (1974) *Cognition and behavior modification*. Cambridge, MA: Ballinger.

Meichenbaum, D. (1977) *Cognitive-behavior modification: An integrative approach*. New York: Plenum.

Piaget, J. (1960) *The moral judgment of the child* (trans. M. Gabain). Glencoe, IL: Free Press. (Original work published 1932.)

Raimy, V. (1975) *Misunderstandings of the self*. San Francisco: Jossey-Bass.

Rogers, C. (1951) *Client-centered therapy*. Boston: Houghton Mifflin Co.

Rush, A.J., Beck, A.T., Kovacs, M. and Hollon, S. (1977) Comparative efficacy of cognitive therapy and imipramine in the treatment of depressed outpatients. *Cognitive Therapy and Research, 1*, 17–37.

Snaith, R.P. (1968) A clinical investigation of phobias. *British Journal of Psychiatry, 144*, 673–697.

Sullivan, H.S. (1953) *The interpersonal theory of psychiatry*. New York: Norton.

Williams, S.L. (1985) On the nature and measurement of agoraphobia. *Progress in Behavior Modification, 19*, 109–144.

Wolfe, B.E. (1984) Gender imperatives, separation anxiety, and agoraphobia in women. *Integrative Psychiatry*, March–April, 57–61.

Wolpe, J. (1969) *The practice of behavior therapy*. New York: Pergamon Press.

Wright, J.H. and Beck, A.T. (1984) Cognitive therapy, In E. Reinhardt (ed.) *Depression*. Munich: GMBH.

Young, J.E. (1981) Cognitive therapy and loneliness. In G. Emery, S. Hollon and R.C. Bedrosian (eds) *New directions in cognitive therapy*. New York: Guilford Press.

# CHAPTER FOUR  Structural Cognitive Therapy
*Giovanni Liotti*

## History and underpinnings of structural cognitive therapy

*Historical development of structural cognitive therapy*

Structural approaches to cognitive therapy are primarily concerned with the *relationship* between the various aspects and levels of cognition, that is, with the *organization* of personal knowledge of self and the world.

During the historical development of cognitive-behavioural therapies, many theorists have concerned themselves with structural issues. Kelly (1955) and the exponents of personal construct therapy (see the chapter by Neimeyer) are to be credited with particularly fruitful expositions of some structural features of human cognition. The basic theory of rational-emotive therapy highlights an important structural theme in its 'ABC' model of the perceptual/cognitive/emotional/behavioural episode (see the chapter by Dryden and Ellis). Beck and his collaborators have hinted at the relations between central value systems (superordinate schemata), lower order schemata and ongoing cognitions like automatic thoughts (Beck, Epstein and Harrison 1983).

Other writers who have emphasized the importance of structural issues in cognitive therapy include Arnkoff (1980), Landau and Goldfried (1981), Mahoney (1980, 1982) and Sollod and Wachtel (1980).

In the early eighties, Guidano and I tried to develop a comprehensive model of the overall structure of self-knowledge. This model would have to be complex enough (so that it could take into account the major issues raised by cognitive-developmental psychology, evolutionary epistemology and contemporary research on the self) and at the same time be simple enough to be usable in the daily clinical practice of cognitive psychotherapy (Guidano and Liotti 1983).

*Major theoretical concepts*

The basic assumptions of a fully developed structural approach to human cognition are as follows:

**Order** In an individual's stream of consciousness, various events take place. Perceptions, dream-images, memory-images, verbalized thoughts and feelings occur in varying succession and intertwine with each other. Below the surface chaos of the changing content of the stream of consciousness, structural theory assumes the existence of an underlying order, or structure.

A man awakens from a sad dream. On leaving his bed, he feels tired and gloomy. The images of the dream come back to him, while he looks out of the window. His gaze stops for a brief moment on the colourful geranium upon the window-sill, and then dwells on the bare trees of the garden. 'My life – like this winter – is as barren as these trees,' he thinks, 'but my winter will not change into a spring.' Memories of his lonely childhood are automatically summoned to his attention, as if to prove the hopelessness of his entire life – past as well as future. The prospects of the day seem to him an unbearable burden of meaningless activities.

There is a structure, an order, underlying the interlaced elements in the stream of consciousness of the protagonist in this vignette. The dream-images, the sadness, the selective attention on the bare trees rather than on the colourful flowers, the inner dialogue of hopelessness, the unhappy memories, the negative evaluation of the daily activities, form a piece of depressive experience. What Beck (1976) has called 'the cognitive triad of depression' (see chapter by Weishaar and Beck) is an aspect of the structure connecting the fragments of the protagonist's perceptual, imaginal, emotional and intellectual experience.

**Hierarchical structure** The structure of human cognition is conceived of as hierarchical in nature, and strictly interconnected with emotion and behaviour. The higher levels of the hierarchy specify the fundamental goals of action, while decisions on details are left to subordinate levels (see the review of control theories of motor behaviour by Stelmach and Diggles (1982)).

In a depressive's cognitive organization, a hierarchically high level defines most actions as meaningless, and states that it is therefore 'wiser' to spare the effort of engaging in them (Beck 1976; Cohen *et al.* 1982; Guidano and Liotti 1983). The subordinate levels of the cognitive structure apply this general rule (to spare the effort of 'meaningless' action) according to environmental contingencies: when free to choose whether to stay at home or to go out and meet friends, the patient will select the former; when forced to take part in a conversation, the patient will utter as few sentences as possible and avoid direct gaze; when invited to join friends in any future social activity, the patient will stubbornly refuse; and so on.

**Constructive activity**    Human beings have an active role in constructing both models (representations) of the self and models of the 'reality' to which they respond. We are 'active problem solvers' (Popper and Eccles 1977, p. 46). From childhood, we tend to treat the puzzling, difficult or adverse aspects of the physical and social environments we are actively exploring as problems to be solved. We incorporate the procedures of problem-solving and the solutions we are able to find into our representational models of the self and the world (see Weimer's (1977) discussion of the 'motor theories of the mind'). Tacit, unconscious processes, it should be remembered, play an important role in human problem-solving strategies (Nisbett and Wilson 1977). It is also worth remembering that the gamut of human problem-solving strategies is limited by biological constraints.

**Biological constraints**    The active construction of models of self and reality proceeds from, and is limited by, inborn predispositions or rules of behaviour. Experience and learning progressively shape such inborn rules, but cannot completely abolish them.

A depressive may construe himself as being lonely, and believe that others reject him. He can develop rules of behaviour that compulsively aim at self-sufficiency. These representational models and these rules of behaviour, however, cannot abolish the inborn predisposition to make affectional bonds with others (Bowlby 1977, 1980, 1982).

**Tacit processes**    There is a level of mental activity which is unconscious, or 'tacit'. The structural theory here explained, far from equating the tacit processes of the human mind with Freud's idea of the 'unconscious', approaches them from the vantage point of contemporary neuropsychology.

Tacit processes seem to be constantly at work in the human mind, and to operate through: (a) the appraisal of contrasts between current sensory excitation and the stored models of prior experience; (b) the elimination of discrepancies between current sensory inflow and the representations (schemata) of previous information (see, e.g. Neisser 1976; Pribram 1971).

In Piaget's terminology, the tacit processes of the human mind operate through the dynamics of accommodation and assimilation (Flavell 1963). New experiences – which are partly different from similar ones that have previously been encoded into memory schemata – are first accommodated (appraisal of contrasts) and then assimilated (elimination of discrepancies) within the pre-existing cognitive structures. According to this theory, one cannot even perceive (let alone conceive) a sudden, absolutely novel piece of information.

The tacit matching processes which constantly abstract the key features of the ongoing interaction with reality are therefore of central importance in the organization, maintenance and change of our knowledge of ourselves and of the world.

An example of the processes of accommodation is provided, in clinical practice, by the patient who states that he 'intellectually' understands and accepts an explanation (or interpretation) offered by the therapist, but still 'feels' and is prone to act according to his former representation of self and reality. The new belief, derived from the 'acceptance' of the therapist's intervention, is accommodated into the patient's cognition, but not yet assimilated into his cognitive structures.

**Historical dimension** Cognitive structures are made up of elements gathered in different periods of one's life. Episodic memories of childhood, early emotional schemata[1] and verbalizable beliefs acquired later in life may all contribute to the appraisal and evaluation of ongoing events, to present problem-solving strategies, and to daily plans of action.

**Organization** The various aspects and levels of an individual's cognition can be represented in a formal model, that is, as elements of an integrated organization. To envisage such an organization, it is useful to compare the structure of scientific research programmes (Lakatos 1970) with the overall structure of personal knowledge of self and reality.[2]

Every scientific research programme, according to Lakatos, is centred around a 'metaphysical' hard-core. This hard-core is a set of basic assumptions that must not be questioned or disproved during the development of the research programme, since they are the very source of the general hypothesis upon which the entire programme is based. Stemming from these core assumptions, scientists *heuristically* develop a number of auxiliary hypotheses. The auxiliary hypotheses make up the *protective belt*, that can be schematically visualized as placing itself around the hard-core (see Figure 4.1a).

The protective belt preserves the core assumptions from refutations: unexpected outcomes of research are attributed to the failure of the auxiliary hypotheses, rather than to the weakness of the basic assumptions. When the matching between the outcomes of research plans and the auxiliary hypotheses leads to a proper restructuring, correction or corroboration of the protective belt, the research programme is said to undergo a progressive shift. When unexpected results of the research plans are confronted by the construction of new, defensive, ad hoc hypotheses, one can speak of a 'thickening' of the protective belt, and say that the research programme is undergoing a regressive shift.

One may identify three levels in an individual's cognitive organization that correspond, respectively, to the 'metaphysical' hard-core, the protective belt, and the level of actual research plans (i.e. the level defined by the procedures and the outcomes of research): see Figure 4.1b.

The *core level* of an individual's cognitive organization comprises schemata that have been formed, usually, during childhood and adolescence, and that are tacitly held by the individual as unquestionable assumptions about some important aspect of self and reality. The following factors contribute to the impossibility, for the individual, of doubting the validity and of limiting the generalization of these early schemata, once they are formed:

(a) The child has a limited ability of distancing and decentring during the long stages of early cognitive development characterized by pre-operative thinking and concrete operations (Flavell 1963); the child, therefore, cannot easily reflect on his/her own thinking, nor compare it critically with that of other persons.

(b) The situations that elicit regularly recurring emotions, for every child, are mainly those created by family interactions. The style of family interaction, for each family, is remarkably constant over time. Therefore, the child's emotional schemata that have been formed during any emotionally intense family interaction are likely to be repeatedly reinforced and confirmed by subsequent interactions – thus leading to strongly held beliefs about the character of oneself and of other people.

(c) The child's modelling upon the attachment figures (Bandura 1977; Bandura and Huston 1961; Guidano and Liotti 1983) is also a repeatedly

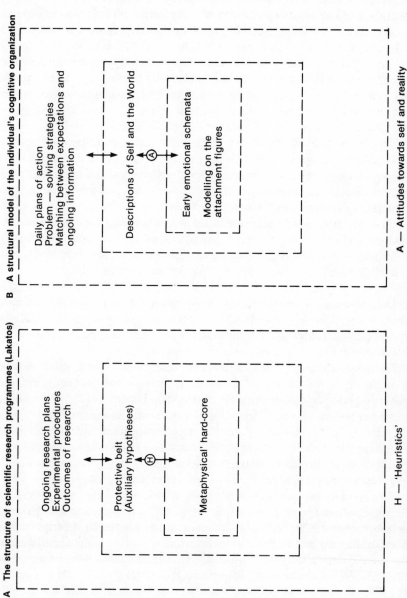

**A** The structure of scientific research programmes (Lakatos)

Ongoing research plans
Experimental procedures
Outcomes of research

Protective belt
(Auxiliary hypotheses)

'Metaphysical' hard-core

H — 'Heuristics'

**B** A structural model of the individual's cognitive organization

Daily plans of action
Problem — solving strategies
Matching between expectations and
ongoing information

Descriptions of Self and the World

Early emotional schemata

Modelling on the
attachment figures

A — Attitudes towards self and reality

**Figure 4.1** A comparison between the structure of scientific theories and the organization of personal knowledge

reinforced and confirmed learning process, leaving little room for possible alternative views of one's personal identity.

(d) Dogmatic descriptions of the child's character, or of significant aspects of reality, can be so forced upon the child by parents, caregivers and educators, that he or she cannot help but accept them as unquestionably true. When these dogmatic descriptions are strongly in contrast with the child's own first-hand experiences, the basis for future serious psychopathology may be laid in the child's developing cognitive organization (Bowlby 1979, 1985; Guidano and Liotti 1983).

One not infrequently finds, during the psychotherapy of depressives, that one of the patient's parents (having perhaps had a very unhappy childhood) is afraid of being reminded of past misfortunes, and believes that to dwell on sad memories will inevitably cause the onset of a depression. The patient may then recall having been required by this parent always to appear happy, and to *believe* that the world is *always* nice and pleasant. One of Bowlby's patients is reported (Bowlby 1985) as having finally commented upon his childhood experience thus: 'I see now that I was terribly lonely as a child, but I was never allowed to *know* it.'

The *intermediate level* of the cognitive organization comprises verbalizable, explicit descriptions of the self, other people and the world. Kelly (1955) and his followers (see the chapter by Neimeyer) have stressed the polarized, dichotomous character of these constructs.

The relationship between the explicit descriptions of the intermediate level and the core emotional schemata is akin to that between semantic memory and episodic memory (Bowlby 1980; Tulving 1972). The explicit self-descriptions of the intermediate level seem able to function as a 'protective belt' with regard to the core assumptions, as some recent experimental studies, performed by Swann and Hill (1982), suggest.

It is surprisingly easy to change a self-description: it is sufficient to offer an alternative, *verbal* description while the individual is engaged in a neutral cognitive task and prevented (through distraction) from engaging in a dialogue with the person who is offering the alternative description. However, after a few minutes or hours, the individuals whose self-description has been so changed engage themselves in an inner or outer dialogue concerning the theme of the changed description, at the end of which their former view of themselves is reaffirmed (Swann and Hill 1982).

These experimental studies suggest that explicit, verbalizable self-descriptions are matched (in an automatic, tacit way) with core assumptions, and that this matching process has a strongly confirmatory bias. The verbalizable, communicable aspects of personal identity (in themselves rather easily changeable) protect the tacit assumptions of 'self-knowledge' from refutations. It seems, therefore, that this confirmatory matching process between self-descriptions and core assumptions affords stability to the explicit aspects of personal identity.

A useful concept for exploring the dynamic relationship between core assumptions and verbal self-descriptions is that of 'attitude toward oneself' (Guidano and Liotti 1983). Examples of what I mean by 'dispositions' or 'attitudes' about oneself can be found in contemporary cognitive-behavioural literature under such rubrics as 'selective attention to the self' (Mischel, Ebbesen and Zeiss 1973, 1976), 'self-reinforcement or self-regulatory style' (see Kirschenbaum and Tomarken 1982, for a review of recent literature on this topic), 'deindividuation' (Diener 1979), 'self-deception' (Gur and Sackeim 1979), 'blindness to oneself' and 'standing back to oneself' (Hamlyn 1977).

In the metaphorical comparison between Lakatos's model of scientific research programmes and cognitive organization, the attitudes toward oneself may be likened to scientists' heuristic procedures of deriving auxiliary hypotheses from core assumptions.

The *peripheral level* of the cognitive organization reflects the plans of action and the problem-solving strategies that each individual is able to develop in the day-to-day confrontation with the environment. The appraisals and evaluations of internal (e.g. emotional) and external (e.g. interpersonal) events can also be conceived of as processes taking place at this level. Through processes of causal attribution, new experiences are accommodated at the peripheral level, before being assimilated within the pre-existing structures of the intermediate level.

## How client problems are conceptualized

One could envisage an ideal model of the 'healthy' cognitive organization, starting from such concepts as 'basic trust' (Erikson 1965) and 'secure attachment'[3] (Ainsworth 1982; Bowlby 1982). The basis assumptions making up the hard-core of such an organization would, then, imply:

(a) The appraisal of other people as basically helpful and available should one need their presence;
(b) A positive view of oneself with regard to one's ability to cope with the

normal difficulties and nuisances of everyday life – and also with regard to one's trustworthiness and lovableness in the relationship with significant others.

It has been proved that secure attachment is positively correlated with a confident and constructive attitude toward the exploration of novel environments and meetings with strangers (Ainsworth 1982; Bowlby 1973b, 1982). Such a confident exploratory attitude toward the environment would probably develop (when cognitive growth, after adolescence, allows for it) into a confident exploratory attitude toward oneself, that is, toward the 'inner world' of one's feelings and thoughts. The self-descriptions of the intermediate level of the cognitive organization, then, would never acquire a dogmatic, absolutistic or defensive character. The belief system of the individual would remain open to changes, readjustments and learning. The set of explicit descriptions of self and the world would not function as a *rigid* protective belt around the core assumptions; the individual, therefore, would probably become able consciously to know his/her own presuppositions about the nature of self and reality, from which the explicit self-descriptions have originated. Contradictions and inconsistencies in these basic premises would then be acknowledged, and eventually amended. Correspondingly, the day-to-day plans of action, the strategies of problem-solving, and the rules for assimilating new experiences (i.e. the regulation of the processes of appraisal, evaluation and causal attribution of ongoing stimulation) would remain flexible and lead to adaptation.

Various kinds of deviation from this 'ideal' pattern are conceivable. In what follows, four examples of such deviations, corresponding to the major 'neurotic' patterns of emotion and behaviour, will be illustrated.[4]

**Agoraphobia and related multiple phobias**     The core level of this cognitive organization conveys a basic dilemma: freedom, which is desirable, implies loneliness, which is fearful – and conversely company or protection implies being subject to other people's coercive influences.

Companionship and protection are to be paid for with a strong reduction of one's personal freedom for autonomous exploration and enjoyment of the environment. Protective people are also expected, according to the individual's basic assumptions, to be coercive and overcontrolling. Strangers are viewed as potentially hostile, dangerous, or at least indifferent to one's difficulties and insensitive to one's sufferings. The 'self' is frequently perceived as 'weak' and prone to physical illnesses. The pattern of anxious attachment (Bowlby 1973a) is likely to be the origin of this 'hard-core' of the cognitive organization.

In the personal history of agoraphobic patients, one may frequently identify an attachment figure who:

(a) was overprotective (thereby reducing the child's freedom for exploration, and inducing a view of the child's self as 'weak' and 'ill');
(b) was overcontrolling;
(c) was scarcely available to the child's requests for companionship and help;
(d) frequently threatened to leave the child alone, sometimes as a way of disciplining him/her;
(e) suffered from anxiety disorders, thereby providing a model for the construction of fearful assumptions about the nature of self and reality (Guidano and Liotti 1983, 1985; Tearnan, Telch and Keefe 1984).

In order to solve the problems created by the conflict between freedom–loneliness and protection–constriction, the future agoraphobic develops, usually during childhood, an overcontrolling attitude both toward self and toward other people. By controlling one's 'weaknesses' (e.g. a feeling of malaise) one may, for instance, avoid the alarm and overprotection of an anxious mother, and therefore be allowed by her to go out and play with peers. Should such a weakness be revealed to her, one would never be allowed, perhaps for many days, to go out and enjoy onself, or would even be forced to remain in bed. By controlling other people's behaviour – through aggression, shows of personal 'power', or through subtle 'seduction' – one may obtain their company when wished, but also get rid of them should they become oppressive.[5] Thanks to this overcontrolling disposition, children may become able to cope with various environmental contingencies and with their own emotional arousal.

As cognitive growth proceeds, it is through the filter of this overcontrolling disposition that children develop articulate and verbalizable descriptions of themselves and of interpersonal reality. These descriptions, after adolescence and before the onset of the clinical syndrome, will be expressed by statements centring on themes of personal freedom, an unwillingness to tolerate even minimal dependency on others, self-sufficiency, and personal (physical, social or moral) 'strength'. With this kind of protective belt placed around the hard-core of anxiety-ridden assumptions about the nature of self and reality, these adolescents are frequently able to grow up in an apparently healthy and lively way, and often become enterprising young men and women who are popular with their peers and quite successful in their chosen vocations. There is, however, a weak point in this cognitive organization. To become able quickly to control personal ('weak') emotions and to manipulate interpersonal relationships is not the best way to develop an articulate knowledge of them. The urge to exert control *as soon as possible* over a given phenomenon in order to suppress it or modify its course is largely incompatible with the possibility of carefully exploring that phenomenon. Self-control, if it comes before proper self-observation, tends both to become ineffective and to hamper the development of self-knowledge. This is particularly true of one's own unpleasant emotions, which need to be endured for a while in order to understand their relationship with one's overall psychological and interpersonal life. To strive *immediately* to control a distressing emotion is like sending a messenger to sleep before he has spelled out the message (see Mahoney 1982, pp. 100–106).

Careful descriptions of an important set of personal emotions and interpersonal realities, therefore, will be lacking in the 'protective belt' of the persons predisposed to develop agoraphobia. When these persons meet with life events that imply an increased risk of loneliness or of reduced personal freedom,[6] and that are beyond their power to control, they find themselves unable to assimilate the corresponding emotional experiences. The patients try to control, rather than to endure and understand, their own emotions and the interpersonal situations eliciting them. Upon finding themselves unable to do so, they tend to develop inaccurate (ad hoc) hypotheses about the nature of their unpleasant emotional experiences. When they are unable to control their emotions, they find it difficult to regard them as being of a personal, internal nature (what is personal, in their self-description, is also controllable) and tend to attribute these emotional reactions to something outside the self: typically, to an illness threatening their ability to maintain control over themselves (cf. the typical fears of 'losing control', of 'madness', of fainting, etc.). Of course, this mistaken causal attribution is able to evoke further fear reactions, and to close a typical neurotic vicious circle of unpleasant emotions and distorted thoughts.[7]

The only way to control the misunderstood fear reactions, at this point in the onset of the syndrome, is to avoid the situations in which they are most likely to appear (which, by the way, are obviously situations of 'loneliness', in which no one is likely to help the 'ill' patient should he/she have one of his/her 'attacks'). This leads to the development of phobic avoidance behaviour.

**Depression** The core level of the cognitive organization corresponding to clinical 'neurotic' depression is characterized by the view of the self as 'destined' to loneliness. Frequently, this basic assumption originates from the experience of actual losses during childhood (Adam 1982; Bowlby 1980; Brown 1982). Symbolic losses (loss of the parents' presence or love, rather than actual death of the attachment figure) are also possible antecedents of early emotional schemata centring around the theme of one's unavoidable loneliness.

Two causal attributions may be associated with the helplessness (Seligman 1975) of the individual who has grieved over an irretrievable loss. One is an internal attribution: the self is held responsible for the helplessness or even for the loss that has caused it. The other is an external attribution: the outside reality is evil, and responsible for the loss and for the individual's subjective experience of helplessness. The self-descriptions that may develop from such an internal causal attribution can be easily imagined: the self will be construed as basically unlovable, and deserving the sadness and loneliness that is being experienced. Equally easy to imagine are the descriptions of outside reality at large that may follow the external causal attribution for a loss: the world, and the people in it, will be perceived as cold, rejecting, cruel, unloving. It is no wonder, in such situations, that the degree of intimacy with the surviving parent, and the family's support for and understanding of the child who has experienced an early loss, have been recognized as strong protective factors against the development of future clinical depression in adult life (Brown and Harris 1978). When such understanding, support and intimacy is lacking, the child who has experienced a real or symbolic loss is left with only one solution to the problem of loneliness: to *exert every possible effort* in order both to overcome the alleged, imagined defects and faults of the self (internal attribution) and to cope with the hostile, rejecting world (external attribution) by developing what has been called 'compulsive self-reliance' (Bowlby 1973b, 1977, 1980).

Like the controlling attitude of the agoraphobic, the disposition to exert every possible effort in the face of life's difficulties allows for a partially satisfactory adaptation. If one tries hard, if one has enough willpower, if one is able to stand suffering and strive nevertheless for success or for making oneself acceptable to people, then perhaps one will succeed in avoiding the expected loneliness and misery. Self-descriptions are then built on this basic attitude. In these descriptions, a strong propensity toward global value judgements, 'shoulds' and 'musts', is, of course, to be expected. Correspondingly, to forgive one's faults or other people's misdeeds will be almost impossible (Rowe 1984). In day-to-day plans of action and problem-solving strategies, the central theme will be the idea of the solitary, strenuous striving allegedly needed to overcome the difficulties and obstacles which are the focus of the individual's selective attention. To enjoy oneself and relax will be possible only after ever 'due' effort has been exerted.

When, notwithstanding one's best efforts, life provides new occasions for experiencing losses or symbolic losses (Beck 1976), the depressive cognitive organization loses its fragile compensatory power. The same may happen after having reached the goal of one's striving – a rather typical example is a professional success – and noticing thereupon that one is as 'alone' as ever. Then, all of a sudden, *every* effort seems useless to the depressive.

The idea that every effort is useless, of course, dominates, on the cognitive side, the clinical picture of depressives' apathy, withdrawal, decreasing rate of behaviour, and loss of interest or motivation. Not protected any more by the self-descriptions based on the formerly positive attitude toward effort, the depressive's basic assumptions about self and reality spring out of the cognitive hard-core. The typical cognitive triad of depression flows into the patient's stream of consciousness.

**Obsessive-compulsive patterns**   The core level of this kind of cognitive organization is characterized by a symmetric view of self and others in which each pole of the dyad, self–other, is either 'good' or 'bad', so that if one is 'good' ('white', positive) then the other is 'bad' ('black', negative). Moreover, each pole of the dyad, self–other, oscillates between the 'good' and the 'bad' position. Both the self and the attachment figure, in other words, are represented as positive *and* negative with clear equipollence.

The pattern of ambivalent attachment (Ainsworth 1982; Bowlby 1973b, 1982) is likely to correspond to this cognitive hard-core. An ambivalently attached child shows frequent alternations of approaching to and avoidance of the attachment figure. There are various patterns of caregiving that may be related to ambivalent attachment of the child (Guidano and Liotti 1983). An example is provided by a rigid, emotionally cold and righteous parent, who is strongly committed to the moral education and physical care of the children but is also consistently unavailable to their requests for playful and tender expressions of love and care. The children would have equal reasons for assuming that such a parent is 'good' (i.e. concerned with their physical and moral wellbeing, and therefore loving) and for considering he or she is 'bad' (i.e. rejecting, not really loving them). They may consider themselves 'bad' when they remember their avoidance of the 'good' parent, or, reciprocally, 'good' when they ponder on how right it had been to detach themselves from such a 'bad' parent.

Such a double, dichotomized view of self and others creates a condition of unbearable uncertainty. Either solution of the dilemma, 'Am I good, and the other bad, or is the reverse the case?' is unpleasant, but to have such a doubt without any definite answer is even worse. Therefore, the child is likely to search for *absolutely certain* solutions to his/her dilemma. A perfectionistic attitude toward self and others is developed. Mistakes and faults are regarded as proof of the absolute, 100 per cent certain 'badness' of self or others, and therefore avoided as much as possible. The descriptions of 'ideal' self and others that are built in this way are likely to be abstract, extreme and rigid, as well as idealized. When concrete human beings (with their more or less positive, negative, and neutral deeds) have to be rated according to such an abstract code of values, the rating becomes either impossible or dogmatically extreme. Proper knowledge (adaptive descriptions) of self and others is obviously hampered, and the ground is prepared for the development of a variety of problematic patterns of emotional reactions and behavioural responses in the face of many life events.

**Eating disorders** People suffering from anorexia nervosa, from various patterns of overeating leading to obesity, and from the so-called dietary chaos syndrome (Palmer 1979) share a similar cognitive hard-core. Affectional bonds, or love relationships, are represented as situations of mutual, complete understanding and unconditional acceptance, and at the same time as situations leading to painful disappointments and disillusionments.

The partner in an affectional bond, when not showing *flawless* understanding and acceptance, is immediately rated as disappointing, and a defensive emotional detachment is thereupon developed. It is as if the schemata representing love relationships do not allow for intermediate conditions between an absolutely perfect relationship and a painful, totally disappointing relationship to which the person cannot commit him/herself, even to a minimal degree. People that are not suited to the role of the perfect partner (according to the patient's standards) tend to be considered as unable or unwilling to understand the patient, and prone to criticize his/her behaviour or physical makeup and to intrude upon him/her.

A family environment in which the expression of one's thoughts and emotions is steadily discouraged, so that any discordance in feeling and belief among family members may be (hypocritically) concealed, is likely to facilitate the construction of this cognitive hard-core. A hypocritical view of affectional bonds characterized, from the beginning, by total mutual under-standing (almost without need of words) is thus transmitted to the children. When these children discover that this view of love does not correspond to what is really going on between father and mother, or between their parents and themselves, the resultant experience of disillusionment is unavoidable and extremely painful.

In order to protect oneself from disappointments, it seems logical to avoid self-exposure and self-commitment to anybody who has not proved him/herself to be 'perfect' and perfectly loving, so as to make disillusionment impossible. Of course, this attitude makes the expression of one's more personal and vulnerable feelings and thoughts a very rare event indeed. Verbal descriptions of personal feelings and thoughts are rarely produced, and therefore the verbalizable aspects of one's personal identity related to the 'inner world' of thinking and emotions come to be only vaguely represented in the patient's cognitive organization. Personal identity thus remains represented, in many important meaning domains, as body-identity.

Whenever a self-perception marked by unpleasantness is evoked (e.g. by a critical comment about the client's behaviour or physical makeup made by peers or by some significant person), this perception shapes itself, in the internal representation, into a negative body image; typically, a body image disfigured by fat. Obese patients seem sadly to accept this body image, while anorexic patients strenously fight against it, up to the point of starving themselves.

**Concluding remarks on abnormal cognitive organizations**	The sketches of 'abnormal' cognitive organizations outlined in the previous paragraphs are, of course, overschematized. In clinical practice, many combinations of the elements of these four organizations may be found in some individual patients. For instance, a patient may show a cognitive organization in which the elements of the agoraphobic and of the depressive cognitive structures are blended and combined. Another may present a mixed cognitive orga-nization comprising depressive and obsessive-compulsive elements, and so on.

Some patients change their cognitive organization during their life, although this is a rare occurrence according to my clinical experience. An example is a female patient who was mildly anorexic during her adolescence, developed a severe anorexic reaction during her first marriage, divorced, recovered from anorexia, married again, and reacted with an agoraphobic syndrome to the jealousy and control of her second husband.

# Practical applications

## The therapeutic relationship

A co-operative relationship between patient and therapist has been advocated as one of the hallmarks of successful treatments by Beck and his collaborators (Bedrosian and Beck 1980; Young and Beck 1982). Structural cognitive therapy fully subscribes to this view. Both therapist and patient will enjoy a rewarding sense of a common purpose by sharing commonly set goals and participating in joint plans to achieve them.

In a co-operative therapeutic relationship, many forms of resistance to the therapist's behavioural prescriptions and to other therapeutic manoeuvres will not emerge, or will appear in a more manageable and usable way than in other types of relationships (Bedrosian and Beck 1980; Guidano and Liotti 1983; Wachtel 1982).

If one succeeds in creating a co-operative, relaxed therapeutic relationship, one can expect that the patient will experience it as a 'secure base' (Bowlby 1977) for the exploration of the more painful aspects of his/her emotional life and personal identity.

Knowledge of the more common 'abnormal' cognitive organizations, and of the corresponding patterns of untoward parenting and 'deviant' attachment, is a valuable aid to therapists in their efforts to establish co-operative relationships with patients. To co-operate with a patient in pursuing his/her goal of increasing wellbeing entails first of all recognizing and respecting the patient's personal identity. The personal identity of agoraphobic patients is largely built on the need to be in control of the relationships in which they engage themselves, at least until they learn to trust the other person. The therapist, therefore, would be advised to leave the agoraphobic patient a wide margin of control in the early therapeutic relationship.

Depressive patients have usually built their personal identity on the idea of 'effort'. The therapist, therefore, would show them that he/she acknowledges and respects this aspect of their identity by asking such questions as, for instance, 'Do you believe that you have anything to lose if you prepare yourself to exert the effort required by joining me in an exploration on the nature of your sufferings?'

A patient suffering from an eating disorder is likely to be reluctant to respond to any direct request for self-exposure and for explicit commitment to a therapeutic contract. The therapist would probably be wise to acknowledge explicitly that the patient would have had good reasons, in her life, for not exposing her thoughts and feelings to a stranger – as the therapist surely is in the beginning phase of a therapeutic relationship. The therapist would be advised to accept the evasiveness of anorexic or obese patients during the first sessions, and avoid seeking detailed information until considerable therapeutic progress has been achieved.

Many obsessional patients show an evident ambivalence toward treatment during the first interview. On the one hand, they protest that they are prepared to undergo any sacrifice in order to get well. On the other hand, they express fear that they may suffer too much in order to get well (and they seem to imagine an unbearable kind of *total* 'perfect' suffering). The therapist may safely ask the patient, then, to be prepared to maintain a little 'nucleus' of his/her current attitude at the end of the treatment – just that little nucleus that will be needed in order to avoid unnecessary emotional suffering while being able to conduct an otherwise normal and satisfactory life. In this way, the therapist will also partly satisfy the obsessional's need for certainty by showing him that accurate predictions of the end goal of the treatment are possible. At the same time, the therapist will indirectly undermine the patient's assumption that only 'perfect' (100 per cent) solutions of any problem are conceivable; partial but nevertheless satisfactory solutions can be imagined and pursued.

In structural cognitive therapy, some phenomena strictly pertaining to the therapeutic relationship may become the objects of the conjoint exploratory activity of patient and therapist. Noteworthy among these are the ways in which the patient tends to construe the therapist's behaviour in the relationship. Expedient cues for the assessment and change of the interrelations between the different levels of the patient's cognitive organization can be found in this way. An agoraphobic woman, for instance, may plan to discuss a recent episode of anxiety and avoidance behaviour with her therapist, and know that this is in keeping with a mutually agreed upon therapeutic contract. While she is explaining the episode during the session, she tacitly matches the ongoing interaction with her ideal self-description (i.e. a self-sufficient person who would not allow herself to be dependent on anybody). This ideal self-description is related to a core schema representing unhappy interactions with an oppressive father who used to force her into doing things she strongly disliked, threatening to leave her alone in the street if she refused to comply. During the session, the therapist becomes aware of a change in the patient's attitude. Now she seems to construe his questions concerning the episode of avoidance behaviour as if they were pressures aimed at forcing her into an abrupt and painful exposure to the avoided situations. In response to the therapist's questions about her change of attitude, she first explains her fears of dependency ('I am afraid that I'll come to depend too much on you, doctor'), and then her dim apprehension of the therapist as an 'omnipotent' man trying to compel her to engage in distressing activities like being alone in the street.

Noticing the discrepancy between this way of construing the present situation and her own plans for dealing with her anxiety in a co-operative atmosphere, this patient was able to recollect the painful episodes of her interaction with her severe father. It should be incidentally noticed that these were not at all 'unconscious' memories. Simply, the patient did not put these memories in relation to her fear of dependency and to her current way of appraising many interpersonal situations.

It is likely that the causal theory she had developed about her anxiety (i.e. the idea of being physically or mentally ill), and her preoccupation of maintaining control over herself and other people, prevented her from exploring the relationships between her past experiences, her belief system, and her present pattern of thoughts, emotions, appraisals and actions.

## Strategies of treatment

When a new therapeutic relationship is begun, the therapist's[8] hope is that the patient will, in the course of it:

(a) Develop his/her competence in tasks of self-observation;
(b) Grasp at least some aspects of the structural properties of his/her own cognitive organization;
(c) Proceed autonomously to modify and regulate, on the basis of the above described achievements, those aspects of his/her psychological life that afford unnecessary, 'neurotic' suffering.

The strategic process required to attain or approximate these goals is a dynamic, sequential interplay of observational and change procedures that is set into motion by the definition of the therapeutic contract.

**The therapeutic contract**   As a rule, during the first meetings, the therapist gently questions the patient about their treatment goals. Thereupon, the therapist makes it explicit that he is available and willing, within the limits of his engagement with the patient being of a professional nature, to join the patient in *their* efforts to achieve *the patient's* goals. Except in extreme cases (e.g. a patient expressing the intention to harm him/herself or others) the therapist carefully avoids denying the validity or plausibility of the patient's aims. Even when the expressed goals evidently stem from the patient's basic problem, the therapist tries to reformulate them rather than to dismiss them as morbid aims or irrelevant wishes. An example is provided by Clara's case.

Clara, sixteen years old, suffered from a mild form of anorexia nervosa. She stated that she wished to go on losing weight, and asked me to help her in her plans of self-starvation. I replied that I was not a dietician, and in any case I was doubtful that *limiting herself* to a search for hypocaloric diets could be a reasonable approach to *all* her problems. If she would find it useful, however, I could accept joining her in an exploration of her wishes to lose weight, and of her problems with eating and body shape.

In this way, the therapist tries to put into practice the definition of the therapeutic relationship as a co-operative one, and moreover to make it clear that he is supposed to co-operate with the patient, rather than vice versa.

From this vantage point, the therapist can enquire into the solutions that patients have already attempted to apply to their problems, and the outcomes of these attempts. This procedure provides valuable information about the functioning of the peripheral level of their cognitive organization.

Clara, accepting my idea of co-operating in an exploration of her eating problems, stated that her reasons for wishing to lose weight were twofold. First, she had been criticized by a peer, some months before, for being overweight, and she was now strongly determined to avoid the repetition of such an experience. In order to be sure of not being criticized in the future, she felt the need to prove to herself that she was able to resist hunger, go on with the diet, and stay *very* thin. Second, she wanted to assert herself against her parents' pressures and intrusions (her parents were trying to force her into a normal eating pattern).

One learns from such an account a good deal about Clara's cognitive activity (at the peripheral level of the cognitive organization). Clara selectively heeds other people's criticism and intrusions upon her private domain of autonomous decisions and choices. Her problem-solving strategies do not include dialogue with parents, selection of uncritical or more accepting friends, and so on; rather, they are limited to striving to attain what she believes to be an acceptable physical shape and an unshakeable personal willpower. Attributions and causal theories relating her ongoing emotions to other aspects of her psychological and interpersonal life are limited to the idea that everything negative she may have experienced is due to her having been 'too fat' and unable to resist her parents' intrusiveness.

**Self-observation and change at the peripheral level**  The first techniques that the therapist proposes to a patient are usually aimed at inducing a change at the peripheral level. In order to achieve this goal, the therapist may choose one among a number of cognitive-behavioural techniques: in vivo exposure, coping imagery, assertiveness training, thought stopping, and problem-solving procedures (see Guidano and Liotti 1983, pp. 145–151, for a discussion of the value of these techniques in a strategic process of cognitive change).

I explained to Clara that she could benefit from assertiveness training and social skills training. She agreed to use these techniques, and after a while her interpersonal life become easier and more pleasant, while her urge to lose weight, although diminished, did not disappear.

As an adjunct or alternative to therapeutic techniques, and as a home-work assignment, the therapist always asks his patients to keep a diary of their distressing experiences. The records in the diary should report on the occurrences of those unpleasant emotions, moods or untoward behaviours that have been proposed by the patient as the target of treatment. Each such entry in the diary should show in outline form:

(a)  the environmental events preceding and accompanying the emotional/behavioural episode;
(b)  the evaluative thoughts concurrent with those events;
(c)  the subsequent plans of action envisaged by the patient.

In essence, up to this point the strategy and the procedures are quite similar to those advocated by Beck (Beck *et al.* 1979; Bedrosian and Beck 1980).

**Observation and change at the intermediate level**  This, as has been repeatedly stated in this chapter, is the level of explicit descriptions of personal identity. Personal identity regulates much of peripheral cognitive activity, and needs constancy of such activity in order to maintain its invariance through time. The therapist who is trying to induce a change at the peripheral level should therefore expect to meet with at least some minor resistance emerging from this 'deeper' level.

When Clara developed an attraction toward a male peer in her school, she actively refused to use the social skills she was learning in her relationship with him. She strongly believed that any expression of her feelings would have been unproductive and even harmful to the relationship she hoped to develop with the boy.

The first task of the therapist facing these forms of resistance is to help the patient (through careful and considerate questioning) to verbalize them clearly. A number of self-statements is likely to be then produced by the patient. In the case of severely disturbed patients, many of these statements and the related beliefs will be unrealistic, dogmatic, absolutistic, irrational, self-damning, 'awfulizing', 'masturbating' (Ellis 1962, 1983; Ellis and Whiteley 1979) and so on.

Clara's statements concerning her reasons for avoiding any form of self-exposure to the boy she liked, centred around the theme that affectional bonds may be the beginning of an extremely painful experience of disappointment. The boy could misunderstand her feelings, intrude upon her private life, prove untrustworthy, and so on. Or else, she could prove herself not acceptable in his eyes, once he had come to know her well enough. When asked how she believed she could disappoint him, Clara answered, assuredly: 'Because I am too fat.'

Here, the therapist comes to a crossroads. One can confront the patient with the irrationalities of his/her cognition; or alternatively one can try to discover, inside the patient's cognitive organization, the source of the mistaken self-conception. The structural-cognitive point of view favours the second alternative, although most structural-cognitive therapists can readily acknowledge that the challenging of the patient's self-descriptions through various therapeutic techniques (e.g. semantic, disputing or 'fixed role' methods) may help foster the exploration of core schemata. The main reason for favouring a rather more exploratory than disputing or attacking strategy is the acknowledgement of the active role humans play in the construction of their experiences. Here as in other aspects of the therapeutic strategy there is agreement between two structural approaches, the present one and Kelly's personal construct theory (cf. the concept of 'creativity cycle' in Kelly 1955).

**The exploration of the core level**  Once the maladaptive aspects of the self-description have been defined and verbalized, the ground is set for a progressive disengagement from them. An implicit yet powerful way to achieve decentring and disengagement with regard to one's own self-description is to examine its origin in one's personal history. In order effectively to help a patient to trace how he or she has come to use a given representational model of self, the clinician should have an extensive knowledge of 'deviant' patterns of attachment. A line of enquiry to be recommended is to ask the patient whether a given view of him/herself has been autonomously developed on the basis of his or her own first-hand experience, or whether it corresponds to something that parents have constantly told him/her. If patients state that their self-descriptions reflect their own experience of themselves one may enquire into the interpersonal contexts in which these experiences initially occurred. The possibility that such experiences stem from attempted solutions at early interpersonal problems should be borne in mind.

Clara had had, since childhood, a very limited communication with her mother. When Clara tried to speak of her dreams and wishes, her mother usually replied with criticisms, and sometimes even with sarcasm. Clara's father was more available to listen to the child, but much more frequently absent from home than Clara's mother. Clara, when eleven years old, discovered that her father had been engaged in an extramarital affair, and was very disappointed by the discovery. It was rather easy to understand how Clara had developed the expectation that nothing very promising could follow the expression of her wishes, feelings and thoughts to a beloved person. At the same time, it was the discovery that she had *learned* to construe interpersonal relationships as disappointing that helped Clara to become wary of generalizations from her family experiences to other, new relationships.

Relevant to enquiries at the core level of the cognitive organization are experimental findings that prove the existence of selective exclusion of information within human cognitive processes (for a discussion of the clinical implications of these laboratory findings, see Bowlby 1980, 1985). Such experimental results tend to confirm the hypothesis that some episodes may be recorded in memory and thus influence a person's thoughts, feelings and behaviour, while at the same time being actively excluded from the ongoing stream of consciousness and therefore not easily retrievable on request. Should a therapist suspect that this process is operative within a particular patient, he/she is advised to be wary of conjuring up 'interpretations' of experiences that perhaps are not within the patient's awareness, and rather admit that some unknown facts are still beyond the scope of the therapeutic exploration. Conditions for overcoming the process of selective exclusion of information are:

(a) a co-operative, relaxed therapeutic relationship, fostering continued exploration;
(b) the repeated noting of discrepancies between a patient's appraisal of a given situation at the peripheral level and ongoing cognitive activity at other levels;
(c) the questioning of beliefs related to 'shame' and fear of discomfort (Ellis 1983).

The relationship between episodic memories (Tulving 1972) of early experiences, explicit self-descriptions and ongoing evaluation of emotional and interpersonal occurrences should be repeatedly stressed. The old structure of memory, self-concept and peripheral cognition should then be contrasted with alternative and more adaptive representational models, to be envisaged both by the patient and the therapist. Only after this process has been gone through many times are the revised models likely to be stable.

Clara clearly understood that her self-description as 'disappointing' and her evaluation of interpersonal realities as always implying criticism, sarcasm, intrusion and disillusionment were related to her memory of episodes in her family life. This understanding helped her to express more freely her likes and dislikes to new acquaintances, and to the boy toward whom she felt attracted. She progressively constructed, in this way, new representational models of self and others, in which the expectation of disillusionment was less strong and generalized than in the old ones. During this process of progressive construction of new cognitive models, Clara needed to discuss the daily occurrences of her interpersonal life with her therapist. She and her therapist repeatedly enquired into how likely it was that a new interpersonal situation had been misconstrued according to the old representational models.

Experiences of assertiveness and self-exposure were thus the occasion, for Clara, to recognize that her old models were sometimes still at work in her internal dialogue. At the age of eighteen, when she was engaged in a love relationship with a boyfriend, Clara commented: 'It is as if an inner voice still warns me against disillusionment, while I know that such a danger is minimal or unlikely with Bob. I must remember that Bob is not just like my father or my mother – only then can I find the courage to tell him how I feel or what I am thinking.'

## Notes on the use of treatment techniques

The therapist approaching treatment from a cognitive-structural point of view may use almost any technique described in the literature on cognitive-behavioural therapies (see the other chapters in this book). Even metaphors and 'teaching tales' such as those devised by Milton Erikson (see, e.g., Rosen 1982) can be fruitfully employed in the process of cognitive restructuring or reframing.[9] There are no major treatment techniques specific to the approach described here. Any technique that may be used is conceived of as a behavioural experiment or a logical challenge aimed at uncovering deeper structures *while* modifying more superficial ones. Many therapeutic interactions that do not have the features of a technique are conceived of in the same way.

Any technique that could foster the *practice* of new skills by the patient will be, on equal grounds, favoured over others. Thus, self-observation (perhaps the main 'technique' in this approach) is favoured over the therapist's explicit hinting at irrational beliefs immediately followed by forceful disputing of those beliefs. This is because 'a procedure cannot be really understood unless one is actually able to proceed on it . . . the understanding is embedded in, inseparable from, the undertaking: and thus, if the undertaking, the power of action, is arrested, so too is the understanding, the power of thought' (Sacks 1982, p. 291). If Berkeley's motto 'Esse est percipi' is true, even more so is Leibniz's maxim 'Qui non agit non existit' – whoever (or whatever) does not act, does not exist.

## Overcoming obstacles to client progress

Resistance to change that is related to the structure of the patient's identity should be expected and regarded more as 'grist for the cognitive therapeutic mill' (Glass and Arnkoff 1982, p. 65) than as true obstacles to therapeutic progress. Emotionally charged pieces of episodic memory that are being actively shut off, that is, selectively excluded from the ongoing processing of information about the self (resistance at the *core level*), may be considered as impediments to therapeutic change in the more proper sense of the expression. In the preceding paragraph I have pointed to some ways of overcoming these obstacles. Here I shall add that the therapist facing this kind of resistance may also choose to go on disputing the maladaptive contents of the peripheral and intermediate levels, on the basis of the following structuralistic assumption: if a change is achieved at one level of the cognitive organization, it is likely that this change will also affect the other, interrelated levels. Even temporary modifications of a self-description may therefore afford changes in the frame of reference within which past memories are appraised and evaluated. If a painful and shameful episode is seen within a different meaning structure, the patient will find it easier to remember it and report on it.

There are also types of cognitive organization that are scarcely amenable to classical cognitive interventions. Noteworthly among these are the multiple personalities, in which various distinct control structures ('consciousnesses') compete for the regulation of the overall course of thought, feeling and action (Hilgard 1977). Multiple personality and related disorders, which seem much more common than was once thought (Bliss 1980; Bliss, Larson and Nakashima 1983; Rosenbaum 1980), have been treated with therapeutic formats that are compatible with a cognitive-behavioural approach (see, e.g., Schatzman 1980). It is clear, however, that clinical procedures should be very creatively adapted to the special requirements of these cases, and supported by extensive clinical experience and notable therapeutic skills.[10]

Therapeutic progress can also be hindered by environmental, and notably, by interpersonal influences continuously active in the patient's daily life. The parents or the partner in an affective relationship can keep confirming the patient's representational models of self and reality, in a way that can hardly be manageable within the setting of individual psychotherapy. In such cases, family therapy may be indicated. Interviews with family members can also afford valuable information for the reconstruction of the processes through which core schemata and self-descriptions were formed – information concerning episodes of family life of which the patient has become unaware or has never been aware (Bowlby 1979, 1985; Guidano and Liotti 1983, pp. 77–78).

## Case example

### *The first meeting*

Vito showed up at my office in the company of his wife, his son of five and his father. He had been referred to me by a well-known psychiatrist, who recommended behaviour therapy for Vito's agoraphobia. Vito had developed agoraphobia six years before his referral to me, and his ailments had proven drug-resistant (both standard doses of diazepam and of amytriptiline had been tried for years). In 1975, there was no therapist with a wide experience of behavioural treatment of agoraphobia in Sicily, where Vito (then thirty-four years old) lived and worked as a very successful architect. Therefore, Vito decided to take leave from work and stay in Rome for two months, where I agreed to meet him every working day. Forty sessions were thus planned.

During the first session a very typical picture of the agoraphobic syndrome emerged. The first panic attack had been experienced in 1968, while Vito and his wife were travelling by train on the first day of their wedding trip. Before 1968 Vito had even travelled abroad, without any problem whatsoever. The honeymoon was interrupted, and since then Vito experienced recurrent anxiety attacks and developed avoidance behaviour both toward situations in which he would be alone, far away from places of safety or trustworthy persons, and toward situations from which he could not escape quickly (e.g. the barber's chair, crowded public places, buses, trains, joining a line in a store, etc.). He travelled to Rome in his own car on provincial and national roads, but avoided motorways on which he could not reverse and have access to an 'easy' escape. In order to feel secure enough to stand the trip from Sicily to Rome, Vito had to take with him not only his wife, but also his seventy-year-old father. In Sicily, he told me, the company of each of them – but not of his anxious mother – would be reassuring enough to enable him to leave home and even move outside town (provided they were in his car) without experiencing anxiety.

When, toward the end of the first session, I questioned Vito about what he wanted to achieve from therapy, he answered that he wished to regain self-control, now threatened (he felt) by his illness. I concluded the session by explaining a gamut of therapeutic methods potentially able to help him *start* to move towards his goal: systematic desensitization and graded in vivo exposure, self-observation during exposure, biofeedback training, and exploration of interpersonal and marital problems. Vito and I eventually agreed on beginning with graded self-exposure to the avoided situations (to be guided and assisted by me) and careful self-observation during such exposure (to be commented upon during each subsequent session).

## Peripheral aspects of the cognitive organization

Vito was quite successful in gradually exposing himself to the less fearful among the situations he usually avoided. For instance, by the fifth session he was able to stay unaccompanied in a bus and travel the distance of three bus-stops. Immediately before, during and immediately after these exposures he was also able to observe – in a clearer way than he did before – such phenomena as:

(a) The fearful expectation of experiencing anxiety (cf. the *fear of fear* concept – Mathews, Gelder and Johnston 1981; and *discomfort anxiety* – Ellis 1979);
(b) The evaluation of anxiety as something that may lead to fainting, having a heart attack, or to screaming and acting 'like a madman', with the concurrent fantasies of making himself ridiculous in the face of unknown bystanders;
(c) The planning of avoidance behaviour by asking a trustworthy person to be ready to help him in any circumstance and by trying always to have a quick way of escape towards a place of safety;
(d) The *effort of keeping control* over anxiety, with the concomitant *fear of losing control* and the related fantasies of fainting, having a heart attack or becoming mad.

The self-perpetuating properties of this kind of circular cognitive-behavioural organization are immediately evident. One should also notice that in this type of cognition anxiety is appraised more as the sign of an illness than as a component of the range of personal emotions.

Because of such a causal attribution of anxiety, Vito was unable to make any sense out of the fact that his first panic attack had occurred during the first day of his wedding trip. This was to him a most unfortunate coincidence, and nothing more than an odd coincidence since, he stated, he was very much in love with his wife and quite willing to marry her because she was faithful, affectionate and very pretty. Their sexual life was full of harmony and a reciprocal source of joy.

From a structural cognitive point of view, Vito's difficulty in including anxiety within the class of personal emotions – and therefore to relate it meaningfully to the main events in his life – can be regarded as a major resistance to therapeutic change. Independently of how much 'control' he might be able to regain over his avoidance behaviour as an outcome of behavioural therapeutic techniques, he would never properly understand either what happened in his 'inner life' when he married or the overall structure of his own emotional and cognitive activity, unless this resistance was overcome. I started dealing with this resistance by asking Vito whether or not he had noticed a discrepancy in his appraisal and evaluation of anxiety. On the one hand, he was saying to himself that this was the sign of an illness, in a sense quite similar, for instance, to diabetes; on the other hand, he believed that a witness of one of his 'crises' would judge him negatively and ridicule him. One usually does not find ridiculous a fellow man suffering from diabetes. Moreover, he felt that he should exert control over anxiety. Now, one knows that it is possible to exert some control over the expression of one's personal emotions and may perhaps come to believe that one *should* exert such control; but how can one control the metabolic abnormalities of diabetes or their expression in the form of a diabetic coma *through a similar kind of willpower*?

## The intermediate level of the cognitive organization

My questioning of Vito along these lines elicited a set of self-statements, expressed beliefs and reasonings that can be summarized as follows.

A 'true' man, according to Vito and also to the Sicilian culture to which he belonged, was not supposed to betray his weaknesses and to show 'woman-ish' emotions such as fear or sadness. Vito had learned to control these emotions quite early in his life, and since he found himself unable to suppress even the outward manifestations of his first panic attack, he concluded that, although his panic attack was similar to the experience of fear, it could not be understood as an emotion. If it had been fear that he had experienced during his honeymoon, he would have controlled it.

Besides, there was nothing during his wedding day or his honeymoon which he should have feared. However, anxiety did look like fear, and casual onlookers would rate him as a 'weak' or 'crazy' man should they witness one of his 'crises'. Only familiar people who knew that he was really ill would prove helpful on such occasions, and would not judge him.

Vito's description of himself as a man able to control 'womanish' emo-tions, and of other people as prone to ridicule him because of his 'crises', could be traced back to some aspects of Vito's personal history.

## *The core level of the cognitive organization*

I began, then, to question Vito about the following themes: Did he witness, in his childhood, somebody else's 'womanish' emotional displays? How did he, and how did his parents, judge this (or these) person(s)? How would he rate the self-control skills of his parents during his childhood? Did his parents discourage his tantrums when he was a child and, if so, how?

Gradually, the following story was reconstructed.

Vito's mother was very prone to unduly worry over dangers she felt to be looming up for her beloved husband and her son. Sudden illnesses and hooligan assaults befalling her husband were frightening scenes she frequently depicted to herself and to her son when Vito's father was not at home. She became uncontrollably anxious when her husband was late coming home at night, and on such occasions she screamed and cried, imagining him lying in a dark alley, wounded or perhaps killed by the Mafia, by hoodlums or by robbers – or maybe the victim of a sudden heart attack. Vito was forced to picture these frightening scenes to himself, too, and also to imagine himself as a lonely child facing the perils of an inimical world. Initially, he joined his mother in screaming and crying, but his father, on finally coming back and finding wife and son in such an emotional state, scolded him. Ever since he was three years old, Vito was told by his father that he was a 'man', and was not supposed to let himself go and cultivate such 'silly' fears.

Vito strove bravely, during his childhood years, not to express the emotion elicited by his mother's behaviour when his father was late, and finally succeeded in his efforts. His mother's 'hysterical' tantrums then became so unbearable to him that he decided never to get married in order to avoid suffering 'womanish' emotions.

Another reason for Vito's childhood decision not to get married was that his mother, while never proving overtly affectionate or loving, maintained that men always need the care of mothers and wives since they are poorly endowed with physical health in comparison with women. In this respect, she believed, nature had gifted women more generously because they have to endure the bodily stresses of childbearing and delivery. According to this belief, she conceived of Vito as a boy of weak constitution who needed his mother's constant attention and protection, and never allowed him to move freely outside the home. Despite having to absorb this description of himself as prone to a myriad of physical dangers and illnesses, this oppressive aspect of the relationship between a man and a woman reinforced Vito's decision to become self-sufficient and never to get married. He decided to cultivate his physical strength as much as possible, and began (with the help and approval of his father, and notwithstanding his mother's opposition) to practice various sports. He made a point of never revealing to his overcontrolling mother any pain from minor wounds, any sickliness from colds, or any fears of such things as having to fight a stronger peer. In this way, he strove to become free from her overprotective influence through the development of an overcontrolling attitude toward himself.

As a teenager, Vito was an outgoing, handsome, clever, brave and seemingly self-confident boy. Girls soon proved very attracted to him. He gradually forgot his decision to remain independent and never to get married. Then, one day, he fell in love with the woman who became his wife.

After having decided to marry her, and as the wedding day approached, Vito had some forewarning of an impending mishap, some dim feelings of something wrong in his life. However, he had also developed an almost life-long disposition to control such 'silly' feelings and 'womanish' worries over imaginary impending dangers, so he easily managed quickly to discard these forewarnings. The wedding took place.

## The onset of agoraphobia as transformation of the cognitive organization

We can envisage the deep, core level of Vito's cognitive organization as signalling a danger or reduced personal freedom, and the intermediate level as denying validity to these signals.

During the honeymoon, the 'silly', denied feelings of impending danger became, one can now rather safely infer, more and more difficult to control while remaining impossible to understand. An unexplained autonomic arousal was appraised in a negatively biased way (Marshall and Zimbardo 1979; Maslach 1979). Vito found himself prey to an incomprehensible and uncontrollable 'something' that, precisely because of the function 'control' played in his view of himself, became a direct threat in his self-esteem and to his very sense of personal identity. Vito panicked. The cognitive structure accommodated the information conveyed by this panic attack as 'the sign of an illness'. Vito strove to control this 'illness' through the use of tranquillizers and through the avoidance of those situations in which the 'illness' seemed prone to manifest itself. Why such situations should be able to elicit the symptoms of an illness remained difficult for Vito to explain. Vito's self-description acquired a new element: 'I *am* ill,' and the illness was conceived of as mysterious in its nature and able to undermine his self-control.

The information conveyed by his emotional suffering was then assimilated into Vito's pre-existing cognitive structures. Doctors provided the label for the assimilated information: Vito became agoraphobic.[11]

## The outcome of treatment

Vito's treatment developed along two dimensions. On the one side there was the programme of graded in vivo exposure; on the other side there was the reconstruction of Vito's story, summarized in the above narration.

While Vito reflected upon the ways in which he learnt to control 'womanish' emotions, and discovered how these ways were connected to fearful images of loneliness, to oppressive experiences of reduced personal freedom, and to paternal injunctions of 'machismo', he also understood how self-control prevented him from trying to understand his own emotions.

The idea that he was suffering from a mysterious illness that physicians were unable to cure with their psychotropic drugs gradually faded away in Vito's mind. His motivation to proceed with the programme of graded in vivo exposure was sustained and apparently increased by this understanding and growing self-knowledge. The limits of cultural bias, such as the labelling of a group of emotions as 'womanish', were also spontaneously acknowledged by Vito without any rational criticism of these beliefs on the part of the therapist. Briefly, one could say that Vito disengaged himself from his old self-description. He did not drastically change his self-description, but became decidedly less prone to overvalue the power of self-control. He also understood that what he once kept saying to himself (e.g. 'I am a "true" man; I should not let myself feel silly emotions') was something he had learned to believe. Besides that, by understanding that he deeply feared the general idea of marriage (equated to loss of freedom), and was not unconsciously rejecting his wife as a person, Vito was able to improve the quality of his marriage. An exercise that I suggested to him, and that he appreciated, was to define exactly, on every possible occasion offered to him by his daily marital life, the different attitudes of his mother and his wife. Before the treatment Vito was automatically prone to emphasize the similarities between mother and wife.

Vito has remained either free of anxiety or able to cope with it (now regarded as a personal emotion) since 1975. He is able to travel *alone* within his town and all over Sicily. He comes to see me in Rome every year, sometimes for a single session and sometimes for a few sessions distributed over the course of a week. During these sessions we have repeatedly contrasted his old *structure* of memory, self-concept and peripheral cognition (a structure that obviously still emerges in periods of stress) with various other representational models of self and reality. In these new models, the idea of 'being in control' of imaginary, more or less likely dangers, has been replaced by the idea of 'learning from one's emotions' when facing possible dangers.

Only in 1983 Vito dared to travel outside Sicily for destinations other than Rome. On finding himself free from anxiety during his 1983 trip, Vito experienced a mild feeling of unreality. 'It seemed to me', he reported later, 'that it was not really *me* doing such a thing. The uncanny aspect of the whole trip was that I was not controlling anything in my emotional world, and yet I was anxiety-free.' And, with a smile of complicity, 'You know, as soon as I realized this, I started feeling a little bit anxious,' he concluded.

## Notes

1  According to Leventhal (1979), emotional schemata are made up by key perceptual features of emotion-eliciting situations, by autonomic reactions that accompany these situations, and by representations of one's own expressive motor patterns. They make up 'feeling memories', and can best be retrieved through imaginative procedures.

2  There is a tradition of using the metaphor of 'person-as-scientist' in cognitive psychology and therapy. This tradition was introduced by Kelly (1955), and has been used by many other theorists. Theorists of cognitive therapy who use this metaphor in a more consistent way also tend to agree on many other aspects of their clinical theories and their related therapeutic applications. Instances of such an agreement are the favouring of an invitational-exploratory style of therapeutic strategy over a directive-disputational one, and the relatively reduced role attributed to pure logic in psychological health (cf. Guidano and Liotti 1983; Mahoney 1980, 1982; Neimeyer 1985 and chapter by Neimeyer in this volume).

3  Attachment theory (Bowlby 1973a, 1977, 1980, 1982) is the conceptual framework for the idea of 'secure attachment'. The emotional bonding and the attachment behaviour of the child to the caregivers are regarded as the foundations for the development of the representational models of self and others. Research findings (Ainsworth 1982; Bowlby 1982; Main and Weston 1982) show that children rated as securely attached to their mothers are active in exploring new situations, and show little or no fear when they meet adult strangers who make friendly overtures. These children use mother as a secure base for their explorations; they exchange glances with mother while in novel environments, and from time to time return to mother and enjoy contact with her. The mothers

of securely attached children are rated highly on scales of acceptance–rejection, co-operation–interference, and accessibility–ignoring. They are 'smiling' mothers, available and responsive to the child's requests and needs.

4   For a more extensive description of these 'abnormal' cognitive organizations, and for an outline of the clinical method through which they were identified in a wide sample of 'neurotic' patients, see Guidano and Liotti (1983), and Liotti (1984).

5   In this context, the observation that many school-phobic children show an overcontrolling attitude toward their parents and peers (Millar 1983) may be of some interest.

6   Examples of these life events are easy to find in the literature on the precipitating factors of agoraphobia (see Guidano and Liotti 1983; Tearnan, Telch and Keefe 1984). Increased physical or affective loneliness is to be expected when one wishes to break an unsatisfactory marriage; after a significant loss; when one is near to one's wedding day and therefore to leaving the parents' home; when one needs to move to a new city; and so on. Reduced personal freedom is frequently implied by marriage and by the birth of one's children; by the beginning of a relationship with a jealous lover; by increasing difficulties in one's job that cannot be left because of financial considerations; by the prospect of a physical illness that may perhaps require hospitalization; and so on.

7   In this context, one should also remember the experimental studies suggesting that emotions deprived of proper cognitive labels and causal attributions are recognized as very alarming ones, and develop themselves into an increasingly unpleasant autonomic arousal (Marshall and Zimbardo 1979; Maslach 1979). The panic attacks that frequently mark the onset of agoraphobia could possibly develop in this way.

8   My style of establishing therapeutic relationships is in keeping with the structural cognitive theory that I have endorsed. It is, however, *my* style and other styles (more or less directive, empathic, interpretative, or pedagogic than mine) may well be equally in keeping with the theory.

9   The analogical mode of thought (i.e. the non-lexical, imaginal one) has many interesting properties that have not been covered in this chapter due to constraints of space. Metaphors and tales appeal to these properties, and also require an active engagement of the listener for their understanding (see the essays on 'metaphor and thought' edited by Ortony 1979). This active engagement of the listener, according to the activity postulate of structural cognitive theory, accounts for the power of metaphors in cognitive restructuring. It is also worth noting that the imaginal stream of thought probably comprises direct ways through which deep structures of self-knowledge can feed new material to the other levels of cognitive processing (see Guidano and Liotti 1983).

10   One should be ready, for instance, to ask a patient, either in an hypnotic state or during a therapeutic session in which no hypnotic induction has previously been performed, actively to reproduce his or her 'hysterical' hallucinations. When the patient succeeds in doing so, the theory is disproved that the frightening 'voices'

or visual scenes come from outside the self, that is, the self-description changes from 'I am seeing or hearing so and so' to 'I am somehow actively imaging or daydreaming so and so'. The next step would be the reconstruction of the childhood experiences that have led the patient to discover daydreaming (in these cases reaching the level of self-hypnosis) as a 'solution' to interpersonal problems (see Bliss 1980; Bowlby 1985; Schatzman 1980).

11   Exploiting the analogies between the cognitive organization and Lakatos's model of research programmes (see Figure 4.1), one could envisage in Vito a 'hard-core' made of images conveying a feeling of restricted freedom, frightening loneliness, hostile environments outside the home, personal 'weakness' and proneness to illnesses. Problem-solving strategies based on self-control are expedient in making him construe himself as a self-sufficient person ('protective belt'), but also prevent him from the critical appraisal of the assumptions encapsulated in his hard-core.

Starting with the first panic attack, many of the core assumptions seemed confirmed: Vito 'is' weak, prone to illnesses, in need of protection, surrounded by potentially hostile people who would despise him. To all these expected dangers, Vito has nothing to oppose but 'control'. His protective belt is thickened by the new, ad hoc hypothesis that he is now an ill man, the illness being envisaged as a threat to self-control. The 'research programme' undergoes a regressive shift. In order to avoid this, both the protective belt and the hard-core need to be revised.

# References

Adam, K.S. (1982) Loss, suicide and attachment. In C.M. Parkes and J. Stevenson-Hinde (eds) *The place of attachment in human behavior*. London: Tavistock.

Ainsworth, M.D.S. (1982) Attachment: Retrospect and prospect. In C.M. Parkes and J. Stevenson-Hinde (eds) *The place of attachment in human behavior*. London: Tavistock.

Arnkoff, D.B. (1980) Psychotherapy from the perspective of cognitive theory. In M.J. Mahoney (ed.) *Psychotherapy Process*. New York: Plenum Press.

Bandura, A. (1977) *Social learning theory*. Englewood Cliffs, NJ: Prentice Hall.

Bandura, A. and Huston, A.C. (1961) Identification as a process of incidental learning. *Journal of Abnormal and Social Psychology*, *63*, 311–318.

Beck, A.T. (1976) *Cognitive therapy and the emotional disorders*. New York: International Universities Press.

Beck, A.T., Epstein, N. and Harrison, R. (1983) Cognitions, attitudes and personality dimensions in depression. *British Journal of Cognitive Psychotherapy*, *1*, 1–16.

Beck, A.T., Rush, J.A., Shaw, B.F. and Emery, G. (1979) *Cognitive therapy of depression*. New York: Guilford.

Bedrosian, R.C. and Beck, A.T. (1980) Principles of cognitive therapy. In M.J. Mahoney (ed.) *Psychotherapy process*. New York: Plenum.

Bliss, E.L. (1980) Multiple personalities: A report of 14 cases with implications for schizophrenia and hysteria. *Archives of General Psychiatry, 37*, 1388–1397.

Bliss, E.L., Larson, E.M. and Nakashima, S.R. (1983) Auditory hallucinations and schizophrenia. *Journal of Nervous and Mental Disease, 171*, 30–33.

Bowlby, J. (1973a) *Attachment and loss*, vol. 2: *Separation: Anxiety and anger*. London: Hogarth Press.

Bowlby, J. (1973b) Self-reliance and some conditions that promote it. In R.G. Gosling (ed.) *Support, innovation and autonomy*. London: Tavistock.

Bowlby, J. (1977) The making and breaking of affectional bonds. *British Journal of Psychiatry, 130*, 201–210, 421–431.

Bowlby, J. (1979) On knowing what you are not supposed to know and feeling what you are not supposed to feel. *Canadian Journal of Psychiatry, 24*, 403–408.

Bowlby, J. (1980) *Attachment and loss*, vol. 3: *Loss*. London: Hogarth Press.

Bowlby, J. (1982) *Attachment and loss*, vol. 1: *Attachment* (2nd edn). London: Hogarth Press.

Bowlby, J. (1985) The role of childhood experience in cognitive disturbance. In M.J. Mahoney and A. Freeman (eds) *Cognition and psychotherapy*. New York: Plenum.

Brown, G.W. (1982) Early loss and depression. In C. Parkes and J. Stevenson-Hinde (eds) *The role of attachment in human behaviour*. London: Tavistock.

Brown, G.W. and Harris, T.O. (1978) *Social origins of depression*. London: Tavistock.

Cohen, R.M., Weingartner, H., Smallberg, S.A., Pickar, D. and Murphy, D.L. (1982) Effort and cognition in depression. *Archives of General Psychiatry, 39*, 593–597.

Diener, E. (1979) Deindividuation, self-awareness, and disinhibition. *Journal of Personality and Social Psychology, 37*, 1160–1171.

Ellis, A. (1962) *Reason and emotion in psychotherapy*. New York: Lyle Stuart.

Ellis, A. (1979) Discomfort anxiety: A new cognitive-behavioural construct, 1. *Rational Living, 14*, 3–8.

Ellis, A. (1983) Rational-emotive therapy (RET) approaches to overcoming resistance. 1: Common forms of resistance. *British Journal of Cognitive Psychotherapy, 1*, 28–38.

Ellis, A. and Whiteley, J.M. (eds) (1979) *Theoretical and empirical foundations of rational-emotive therapy*. Monterey, CA: Brooks/Cole.

Erikson, E. (1965) *Childhood and society*. London: Hogarth Press.

Flavell, J.H. (1963) *The developmental psychology of Jean Piaget*. New York: Van Nostrand.

Glass, C.R. and Arnkoff, D.B. (1982) Think cognitively: Selected issues in cognitive assessment and therapy. In P.C. Kendall (ed.) *Advances in cognitive-behavioral research and therapy*, vol. 1. New York: Academic Press.

Guidano, V.F. and Liotti, G. (1983) *Cognitive processes and emotional disorders*. New York: Guilford.

Guidano, V.F. and Liotti, G. (1985) A constructivistic foundation for cognitive therapy. In M.J. Mahoney and A. Freeman (eds) *Cognition and psychotherapy*.

New York: Plenum Press.

Gur, R.C. and Sackeim, H.A. (1979) Self-deception: A concept in search of a phenomenon. *Journal of Personality and Social Psychology, 37*, 147–169.

Hamlyn, D.W. (1977) Self-knowledge. In T. Mischel (ed.) *The Self: Psychological issues*. Oxford: Basil Blackwell.

Hilgard, E.R. (1977) *Divided consciousness: Multiple controls in human thought and action*. New York: Wiley.

Kelly, G.A. (1955) *The psychology of personal constructs*. New York: Norton.

Kirschenbaum, D.S. and Tomarken, A.J. (1982) On facing the generalization problem: The study of self-regulatory failure. In P.C. Kendall (ed.) *Advances in cognitive-behavioral research and therapy*, vol. 1. New York: Academic Press.

Lakatos, I. (1970) Falsification and the methodology of scientific research programmes. In I. Lakatos and A. Musgrave (eds) *Criticism and the growth of knowledge*. Cambridge: Cambridge University Press.

Landau, R. and Goldfried, M.R. (1981) The assessment of schemata: A unifying framework for cognitive, behavioral, and traditional assessment. In P.C. Kendall and S.D. Hollon (eds) *Assessment strategies for cognitive-behavioral interventions*. New York: Academic Press.

Leventhal, H. (1979) A perceptual-motor processing model of emotion. In R. Pliner, K. Blankstein, and I. Spigel (eds) *Perception of emotions in self and others*. New York: Plenum Press.

Liotti, G. (1984) Cognitive therapy, attachment theory and psychiatric nosology: A clinical and theoretical inquiry into their interdependence. In M.A. Reda and M.J. Mahoney (eds) *Cognitive Psychotherapies*. Cambridge, MA: Ballinger.

Mahoney, M.J. (1980) Psychotherapy and the structure of personal revolutions. In Mahoney, M.J. (ed.) *Psychotherapy Process*. New York: Plenum Press.

Mahoney, M.J. (1982) Psychotherapy and human change processes. In J.H. Harvey and M.M. Parks (eds) *Psychotherapy research and behavior change*. Washington, DC: American Psychological Association.

Main, M. and Weston, D.R. (1982) Avoidance of the attachment figure in infancy: Descriptions and interpretations. In C.M. Parkes and J. Stevenson-Hinde (eds) *The place of attachment in human behavior*. London: Tavistock.

Marshall, G.D. and Zimbardo, P.G. (1979) Affective consequences of inadequately explained physiological arousal. *Journal of Personality and Social Psychology, 36*, 970–988.

Maslach, C. (1979) Negative emotional biasing of unexplained arousal. *Journal of Personality and Social Psychology, 36*, 953–969.

Mathews, A.M., Gelder, M.G. and Johnston, D. (1981) *Agoraphobia: Nature and treatment*. New York: Guilford Press.

Millar, T.P. (1983) School phobia: An alternative hypothesis. *Annals RCPSC, 16*, 549–554.

Mischel, W., Ebbesen, E. B. and Zeiss, A.R. (1973) Selective attention to the self: Situational and dispositional determinants. *Journal of Personality and Social Psychology, 27*, 129–142.

Mischel, W., Ebbesen, E.B. and Zeiss, A.R. (1976) Determinants of selective memory about the self. *Journal of Consulting and Clinical Psychology, 44*, 92–103.

Neimeyer, R.A. (1985) Personal constructs in clinical practice. In P.C. Kendall (ed.) *Advances of cognitive-behavioral research and therapy*, vol. 4. New York: Academic Press.

Neisser, U. (1976) *Cognition and reality: Principles and implications of cognitive psychology*. San Francisco: Freeman.

Nisbett, R.E. and Wilson, T.D. (1977) Telling more than we can know: Verbal reports on mental processes. *Psychological Review, 84*, 231–259.

Ortony, A. (ed.) (1979) *Metaphor and thought*. Cambridge: Cambridge University Press.

Palmer, R.L. (1979) Dietary chaos syndrome: A useful new term? *British Journal of Medical Psychology, 52*, 187–190.

Popper, K.R. and Eccles, J.C. (1977) *The self and its brain*. Berlin: Springer Int.

Pribram, K. (1971) *Languages of the brain*. Englewood Cliffs, N.J.: Prentice-Hall.

Rosen, S. (1982) *My voice will go with you: The teaching tales of Milton H. Erickson*, New York: Norton.

Rosenbaum, M. (1980) The role of the term schizophrenia in the decline of diagnoses of multiple personalities. *Archives of General Psychiatry, 37*, 1383–1385.

Rosenberg, M. (1979) *Conceiving the self*. New York: Basic Books.

Rowe, D. (1984) The advantages of being depressed. Paper read at the 14th E.A.B.T. Conference, Brassels, 17–19 September 1984.

Sacks, O. (1982) *Awakenings* (rev. edn) London: Picador-Pan.

Schatzman, M. (1980) *The story of Ruth*. New York: Putnam's Sons.

Seligman, M.E.P. (1975) *Helplessness: On depression, development and death*. San Francisco: W.H. Freeman.

Sollod, R.N. and Wachtel, P.L. (1980) A structural and transactional approach to cognition in clinical problems. In M.J. Mahoney (ed.) *Psychotherapy process: Current issues and future directions*. New York: Plenum.

Stelmach, G.E. and Diggles, V.A. (1982) Control theories in motor behavior. *Acta Psychologica, 50*, 83–105.

Swann, W.B. and Hill, C.A. (1982) When our identities are mistaken: Reaffirming self-conceptions through social interaction. *Journal of Personality and Social Psychology, 43*, 59–66.

Tearnan, B.H., Telch, M.J. and Keefe, P. (1984) Etiology and onset of agoraphobia: A critical review. *Comprehensive Psychiatry, 25*, 51–62.

Tulving, E. (1972) Episodic and semantic memory. In E. Tulving and W. Donaldson (eds) *Organization of memory*. New York: Academic Press.

Wachtel, P.L. (ed.) (1982) *Resistance*. New York: Plenum.

Weimer, W.B. (1977) A conceptual framework for cognitive psychology: Motor theories of the mind. In R. Shaw and J. Bransford (eds) *Acting, perceiving and knowing: Toward an ecological psychology*. New Jersey: Erlbaum.

Young, J.E. and Beck, A.T. (1982) Cognitive therapy: Clinical applications. In A.J. Rush (ed.) *Short-term psychotherapies for depression*. New York: Wiley.

# CHAPTER FIVE  Rational-Emotive Therapy (RET)
*Windy Dryden and Albert Ellis*

## History and underpinnings of rational-emotive therapy

### Historical development of RET

Rational-emotive therapy (RET) was founded in 1955 by Albert Ellis, a New York clinical psychologist who began his career in the helping professions in the early 1940s. As a result of research he was doing at that time for a massive work to be entitled *The Case for Sexual Liberty*, Ellis gained a local reputation for being an authority on sexual and marital relationships. He was consulted by his friends on their sexual and relationship problems and discovered that he could be successful in helping them with these problems in a short period of time. He decided to pursue formal training in clinical psychology after discovering that there were no formal training possibilities then offered in sexual and marital counselling. After getting a PhD degree in clinical psychology, he chose to be trained in psychoanalysis, believing then that it was the deepest and most effective form of psychotherapy available. He decided on this course of action because his experiences as an informal sex-marital counsellor had taught him that disturbed relationships were really a product of disturbed persons, 'and that if people were truly to be helped to live happily with each other they first had better be shown how they could live peacefully with themselves' (Ellis 1962, p. 3).

Ellis initially enjoyed working as a psychoanalyst partly because it allowed him to express both his helping and problem-solving interests. However, he became increasingly dissatisfied with psychoanalysis as an *effective* and *efficient* form of treatment. In the early 1950s, Ellis began to experiment with different forms of therapy, including psychoanalytic-orientated psychotherapy and eclectic-analytic therapy. But although he became more effective with his clients, he remained dissatisfied about the efficiency of these methods. During this period of experimentation, Ellis returned to his lifelong hobby of reading philosophy to help him with his search for an effective and efficient form of therapy. One of the major influences on his thought at that time was the work of the Greek and Roman Stoic philosophers (e.g. Epictetus and Marcus Aurelius). They emphasized the primacy of philosophic causation of psychological disturbances – a viewpoint which was not popular in America in the 1950s – and de-emphasized the part played by psychoanalytic psychodynamic factors. In essence, the Stoic viewpoint which stated that people are disturbed not by things but by their view of things, became the foundation of RET, in particular, and this perspective (following Ellis's pioneering formulations) remains at the heart of present-day cognitive-behavioural approaches to psychotherapy.

Kelleyan Influences

**Major philosophical influences**   Apart from Stoicism, present-day RET owes a philosophical debt to a number of other sources that have influenced its development: (a) Immanuel Kant's writings on the power (and limitations) of cognition and ideation strongly impressed Ellis (1981a) and the work of Spinoza and Schopenhauer was also important in this respect. (b) Philosophers of science, such as Popper (1959, 1963), Reichenbach (1953), and Russell (1965), were influential in helping Ellis see that all humans develop hypotheses about the nature of the world. Moreover, these philosophers stressed the importance of testing out the validity of such hypotheses rather than assuming that they are necessarily correct. Ellis has frequently argued that the practice of RET is synonymous, in many respects, with the logico-empirical methods of science (Ellis 1962, 1979a). Ellis (1983a, 1985a) also stresses the flexibility and antidogmatism of the scientific method and holds that RET opposes all dogmas, just as science does, and that rigid absolutism is the very core of human disturbance (Ellis 1985b). (c) Although the philosophy of RET, as found in Ellis's writings, is at variance with devout religiosity, in one respect Christian philosophy has been most influential. RET's theory of human value (which will be discussed later) is similar to the Christian viewpoint of condemning the sin, but forgiving the sinner (Ellis 1983a; Hauck 1972; Powell 1976). (d) Due to its stand on self-acceptance and its bias against all forms of human rating, RET allies itself with the philosophy of ethical humanism (Russell 1950, 1965) which opposes the deification and devil-ification of humans. Since RET considers that humans are at the centre of their universe (but not of *the* universe) and have the power of choice (but not of unlimited choice) with regard to their emotional realm, it has its roots in the existential philosophies of Heidegger (1949) and Tillich (1977). Indeed, Ellis (1973) often portrays RET as having a pronounced humanistic-existential outlook. (e) Ellis was influenced, particularly in the 1960s, by the work of the general semanticists (e.g. Korzybski 1933). These theorists outlined the powerful effect that language has on thought and the fact that our emotional processes are heavily dependent on the way we, as humans, structure our thought by the language we employ.

**Major psychological influences**     Ellis, in developing RET, has similarly been influenced by the work of a number of psychologists. (a) Ellis, himself, received a training analysis from an analyst of the Karen Horney school and Horney's (1950) concept of the 'tyranny of the shoulds' was certainly an early influence on his emphasis on the primacy of absolute, dogmatic evaluative thought in the development and maintenance of much psychological disturbance. (b) The work of Adler was important to the development of RET in several respects.

Adler (1927) was the first great therapist to really emphasize inferiority feelings – while RET similarly stresses self-rating and the ego anxiety to which it leads. Like Adler and his Individual Psychology, RET also emphasizes people's goals, purposes, values and meanings. RET also follows Adler in regard to the use of active-directive teaching, the stress placed on social interest, the use of a holistic and humanistic outlook, and the employment of a highly cognitive-persuasive form of psychological treatment. (Ellis 1981b)

(c) Although RET was originally termed 'Rational Psychotherapy', it has always advocated the use of behavioural methods as well as cognitive and emotive techniques in the practice of therapy. Indeed, Ellis utilized some of the methods advocated by some of the earliest pioneers in behaviour therapy (Dunlap 1932; Jones 1924; Watson and Rayner 1920), first in overcoming his own early fears of speaking in public and of approaching women, and second in the active-directive form of sex therapy which he practised in the early 1950s. This behavioural active-directive emphasis remains prominent in present-day RET.

In its thirty years' existence, RET has been practised in various therapeutic modalities (individual, group, marital and family), by many kinds of helping professionals (e.g. psychologists, psychiatrists, social workers) with a variety of client populations (e.g. adults, children, the elderly) suffering from a wide range of psychological problems and disorders. Apart from its use in counselling and psychotherapy, rational-emotive principles have been applied in educational, industrial, and commercial settings. A very recent development has been the application of RET to public education in the form of nine-hour intensive workshops. In this respect, it is playing a significant role in the field of preventative psychology. RET is practised throughout the world and there are RET 'Institutes' in the United States, Italy, West Germany, Holland, Australia, England and Mexico. It is thus a well-established form of cognitive-behavioural therapy.

*Major theoretical concepts*

RET is based on a set of assumptions which stress the complexity and fluidity of human beings. Given this fundamental view of human nature RET rests on the follow theoretical concepts.

**Goals, purposes and rationality**    According to RET theory, humans are happiest when they establish important life goals and purposes and actively strive to attain these. Ellis argues that human beings, in establishing and pursuing these goals and purposes, should consider the fact that they live in a social world and that a philosophy of self-interest, where a person places him or herself first, also implies putting others a close second. This is in contrast to a philosophy of selfishness where the desires of others are neither respected nor regarded. Given that humans will tend to be goal-directed, *rational* in RET theory means 'that which helps people to achieve their basic goals and purposes, whereas "irrational" means that which prevents them from achieving these goals and purposes' (Dryden 1984a, p. 238). Thus, rationality is not defined in any absolute sense, but is relative in nature.

**The interaction of psychological processes and the place of cognition**    RET theory has, from its inception, stressed an interactive view of human psychological processes. Cognitions, emotions and behaviours are not experienced in isolation and often, particularly in the realm of psychological disturbance, overlap to a significant degree. Recently, Ellis (1984a) has stressed the inferential nature of Activating events and has shown how events (or more correctly how we perceive events) again interact with our cognitive evaluations, emotions and behaviours. This point will be amplified in the section entitled 'An expanded ABC framework'.

   Given this interactional view, it is true, however, that RET is most noted for the special place it has accorded cognition in human psychological processes, particularly the role that evaluative thought plays in psychological health and disturbance. One of RET's unique contributions to the field of cognitive-behaviour therapy lies in its distinction between 'rational' and 'irrational' Beliefs. 'Rational' Beliefs are evaluative cognitions of personal significance which are preferential (i.e. non-absolute) in nature. They are expressed in the form of 'desires', 'preferences', 'wishes', 'likes' and 'dislikes'. Positive feelings of pleasure and satisfaction are experienced when humans get what they desire, whereas negative feelings of displeasure and dissatisfaction (e.g. sadness, concern, regret, annoyance) are experienced when they don't get what they desire. These negative feelings (the strength of which is closely related to the importance of the desire) are regarded as appropriate responses to negative events and do not significantly interfere with the pursuit of established or new goals and purposes. These Beliefs, then, are 'rational' in two respects. First, they are relative, and second, they do not impede the attainment of basic goals and purposes.

'Irrational' Beliefs, on the other hand, differ in two respects from 'rational' Beliefs. (a) They are absolute (or dogmatic) in nature and are expressed in the form of 'musts', 'shoulds', 'oughts', 'have-tos', etc. As such they (b) lead to negative emotions which largely interfere with goal pursuit and attainment (e.g. depression, anxiety, guilt, anger). Ellis (1982a) notes that 'rational' Beliefs strongly tend to underly functional behaviours, whereas 'irrational' Beliefs underpin dysfunctional behaviours such as withdrawal, procrastination, alcoholism, substance abuse, etc.

*Psychoanalysis*

**Two basic biological tendencies** Unlike most other theories of therapy which stress the impact of significant life events on the development of psychological disturbance, RET theory, mainly through the writings of Ellis (1976a), hypothesizes that the biological tendency of humans to think irrationally has a notable impact on such disturbance. Ellis's hypothesis that irrational thinking is heavily determined by biological factors (always interacting with influential environmental conditions) rests on the seeming ease with which humans think crookedly and the prevalence of such thinking even among people who have been rationally raised (Ellis 1976a). Ellis (1984a) notes that 'even if we had the most rational upbringing, virtually all humans would often take their individual and social preferences and irrationally escalate them into absolutistic demands on (a) themselves, (b) other people, and (c) the universe around them.'

However, Ellis further argues that humans have a second basic biological tendency, namely, to exercise the power of human choice and to work towards changing their irrational thinking. Thus, they have (a) the ability to see that they make themselves disturbed by the irrational views they bring to situations, (b) the ability to see that they can change their thinking and, most importantly, (c) the ability to work actively and continually towards changing this thinking by the application of cognitive, emotive, and behavioural methods. While RET theory asserts that humans have a strong biological tendency to think irrationally (as well as rationally), it holds that they are by no means slaves to this tendency and can transcend (although not fully) its effects. In the final analysis, then, the RET image of the person is quite an optimistic one.     *Image of Person.*

**Two fundamental human disturbances**   Ellis (1977a, 1984a) has argued that humans can make absolute demands on self, other people and the world. However, if these demands are more closely investigated they can be seen to fall into two major categories of psychological disturbance: ego disturbance and discomfort disturbance (Ellis 1979f, 1980b).

In ego disturbance, a person makes demands on self, others and the world and if these demands are not met in the past, present, or future, the person becomes disturbed by damning 'self'. As Dryden (1984a) has shown, self-damnation involves (a) the process of giving my 'self' a global negative rating and (b) 'devil-ifying' my 'self' as being bad or less worthy. The rational and healthy alternative to self-damnation is self-acceptance which involves (a) refusing to give one's 'self' a single rating (because it is an impossible task, due to one's complexity and fluidity; and because it normally interferes with attaining one's basic goals and purposes) and (b) acknowledging one's fallibility.

In discomfort disturbance, the person again makes demands on self, others and the world which are related to dogmatic commands that comfort and comfortable life conditions exist. When these demands are not met in the past, present, or future then the person becomes disturbed. Tolerating discomfort in order to aid goal attainment and long-range happiness is the healthy and rational alternative to demands for immediate gratification.

It can thus be seen that self-acceptance and a high level of frustration tolerance are the two main cornerstones of the rational-emotive image of the psychologically healthy human being (Ellis 1979a).

*How Client problems are conceptualized – an expanded ABC framework*     *Cognitive Framework.*

When RET was originally established, Ellis (1962) employed a simple ABC assessment framework to conceptualize clients' psychological problems. In this schema, 'A' stood for the Activating event, 'B' represented a person's Belief about that event, and 'C' denoted the person's emotional and behavioural responses, or Consequences, to holding the particular Beliefs at 'B'. The major advantage of the ABC framework lay in its simplicity. However, its simplicity was also a disadvantage in that important distinctions between different types of cognitive activity were glossed over (Wessler and Wessler 1980). It is important to note that different RET therapists use different expanded versions of the original ABC framework (Ellis 1984a; Raitt 1984; Wessler and Wessler 1980). There is thus no absolutely correct way of conceptualizing clients' problems according to such an expanded schema. What is presented below is one version of the expanded ABC framework.

*expanded version of ABC framework which take into account the subtlety of cognitive activity*

**Activating events or Activators (A) of cognitive, emotional, and behavioural Consequences (C)**    The RET theory of personality and personality disturbances begins with people trying to fulfil their Goals (Gs) in some kind of environment and encountering a set of Activating events or Activators (As) that tend to help them achieve, or tend to block, these Goals. The As they encounter usually are present or current events or their own thoughts, feelings, or behaviours as a result of these events; but they may be embedded in memories or thoughts (conscious or unconscious) about past experiences. People are prone to seek out and respond to these As because of (a) their biological or genetic predispositions; (b) their constitutional history; (c) their prior interpersonal and social learning, and (d) their innately predisposed and acquired habit patterns (Ellis 1976a, 1979b, 1983a).

In fact, As (Activating events) virtually never exist in a pure or monolithic state; they almost always interact with and partly include Bs and Cs. People bring themselves (their goals, thoughts, desires and physiological propensities) to As.    *A*

*B*

**Beliefs (Bs) about Activating events (As)**    According to RET theory, people have almost innumerable Beliefs (Bs) – cognitions, thoughts, or ideas – about their Activating events (As); and these Bs importantly and directly tend to exert strong influences on their cognitive, emotional and behavioural Consequences (Cs). Although As often seem directly to 'cause' or contribute to Cs, this is rarely true, because Bs normally serve as important mediators between As and Cs and therefore more directly 'cause' or 'create' Cs (Bard 1980; Ellis 1962; Goldfried and Davison 1976; Grieger and Boyd

1980; Wessler and Wessler 1980). People largely bring their Beliefs to As; and they prejudicially view or experience As in the light of these biased Beliefs (expectations, evaluations) and also in the light of their emotional Consequences (Cs). Therefore, humans virtually never experience A without B and C; but they also rarely experience B and C without A.

Bs take many different forms because people have many kinds of cognitions. In RET, however, we are mainly interested in their rational Beliefs (rBs), which we hypothesize lead to their self-helping behaviours, and in their irrational Beliefs (iBs), which we theorize lead to their self-defeating (and anti-social) behaviours. We can list some of the main (but not the only) kinds of Bs as follows:

1. *Nonevaluative observations*. Example: '(I see) the man is walking' – such observations do not go beyond the available data. They are nonevaluative because they are not relevant to our goals. When such observations are relevant to our goals they become evaluative; for example, when the man walking is my father who has just recovered from a car accident. The evaluative aspects of such *evaluative observations* are often implicit – e.g. '(I am pleased that) the man is walking.'

2. *Nonevaluative inferences*. Example: 'The man who is walking is going to the post office' – cognitions are called inferences because they go beyond the available data. All we are able to observe in this example is a man walking in a certain direction. Although he is proceeding in the direction of the post office he may or may not be 'going to the post office'. As such, inferences may be viewed as hypotheses about our observations which may or may not be correct. These inferences are nonevaluative when they are not relevant to our goals. When such inferences are relevant to our goals they become evaluative; for example, when the man will bring us back our birthday parcels if indeed he does go to the post office. The evaluative aspects of such *evaluative inferences* are again often implicit – e.g. '(it is good that) the man who is walking is going to the post office.'

   It is helpful to realize, for assessment purposes, that inferences are frequently chained together (Moore 1983) and that it is often important to find the most relevant inference in the chain, that is, the one that overlaps with the person's musturbatory evaluations. Thus, if a client reports experiencing anger at his wife for forgetting the shopping, shopping may not actually be the 'event' that triggers his anger-producing evaluation. The inference chain may be revealed thus: wife forgets shopping ⟶ I will mention this to her ⟶ she will nag me ⟶ I won't be able to watch the football game on TV in peace. Any of these inferences may trigger anger-creating evaluations and it is often important to involve clients as fully as possible in the assessment process by asking questions to help them provide reliable information concerning their most relevant inferences in particular chains.

3. *Positive preferential evaluations.* Example: 'I prefer people to approve of me' or 'I like people to approve of me (but they do not have to).' These cognitions are termed 'positive preferential evaluations' because they are relative and non-absolute (statements like 'but they do not have to' are rarely stated but are implicit in such cognitions); and they refer to what the person evaluates as positive – 'people approving of me.' They are often termed 'rational' in RET theory since they tend to aid and abet a person's basic goals and purposes.

Let us assume that a man who holds the Belief 'I prefer people to approve of me' observes a group of people laughing and infers that they are laughing *with* him. Ellis (1984d) has noted that this person may conclude the following based on the positive preferential evaluation that he likes approval and the inference that they are laughing with him:

(a) '(I presume) they think I am funny.'
(b) '(I presume) they like me.'
(c) '(I presume) their liking me has real advantages.'

These cognitions are all positive nonabsolute inferences since they go beyond the available data; they are relevant to the person's goal (he is getting what he values); and they are not held with absolute conviction.

(d) 'My ability to make them laugh is good.'
(e) 'It's pleasant to hear them enjoy themselves.'

These cognitions are both positive nonabsolute evaluations since this man is appraising his ability to make them laugh and their pleasure at laughing in a positive but relative manner.

4. *Positive musturbatory evaluations.* Example: 'I must have people approve of me.' Such cognitions are termed 'positive musturbatory evaluations' because they are absolute and dogmatic; and they refer to what the person evaluates as positive in a devout manner. They are often termed 'irrational' in RET theory in that they tend to impede and inhibit a person from achieving his or her other basic goals and purposes.

Let us again assume that a group of people are laughing with a man and presumably like him. Ellis (1984d) has noted that he may conclude the following based on his above positive musturbatory evaluations – thinking errors are categorized in brackets:

(a) 'I am a great, noble person!' (overgeneralization)
(b) 'My life will be completely wonderful!' (overgeneralization)
(c) 'I deserve to have only fine and wonderful things happen to me!' (demandingness and deification)

Cognitions (a), (b) and (c) are all positive absolute evaluations. The evaluations of 'I' and the 'world' are positive and grossly exaggerated.

(d) 'I am sure they will always like me.' (delusions of certainty)
(e) 'I am convinced that I will always please them.' (delusions of certainty)

Cognitions (d) and (e) are both positive absolute inferences since they go beyond the data at hand; they are positively relevant to the person's goal; and they are held with absolute conviction.

5. *Negative preferential evaluations.* Example: 'I prefer people not to disapprove of me' or 'I dislike people disapproving of me (but there's no reason why they must not disapprove of me).' These cognitions are termed 'negative preferential evaluations' because, once again, they are relative and nonabsolute (statements like 'but there's no reason why they must not . . .' are also rarely stated but are again implicit in such Beliefs); and they refer to what the person evaluates as negative – 'people disapproving of me'. They are also termed 'rational' in RET theory since they again tend to aid and abet a person's basic goals and purposes.

This time let us assume that a man who holds the Belief 'I prefer people not to disapprove of me' observes a group of people laughing but infers that they are laughing *at* him. Ellis (1984d) has noted that this man may conclude the following based on the above negative preferential evaluation:

(a) '(I presume) they think I am stupid.'
(b) '(I presume) they don't like me.'
(c) '(I presume) that their not liking me has real disadvantages.'

Cognitions (a), (b) and (c) are all negative nonabsolute inferences since they go beyond the data at hand; they are relevant to the person's goal (he is getting what he dislikes); and they are not held with absolute conviction.

This man may further conclude:

(d) 'It's unfortunate that they are laughing at me.'
(e) 'It would be bad if I have some unfortunate trait.'

Cognitions (d) and (e) are both negative nonabsolute evaluations. The evaluations of his 'situation' and of his 'unfortunate trait' are negative and nondevout.

6. *Negative musturbatory evaluations*. Example: 'I must not have people disapprove of me.' Such cognitions are termed 'negative musturbatory evaluations' because they are absolute and dogmatic; and they refer to what the person evaluates as negative in a devout manner. They are further examples of 'irrational' Beliefs in that they tend to impede the achievement of a person's basic goals and purposes.

If we assume again that a group of people are laughing at a man and presumably disapprove of him, he may conclude the following (Ellis 1984d) based on the above negative musturbatory evaluations – again the categories of thinking errors are listed in brackets.

(a) 'I am an incompetent, rotten person!' (overgeneralization, self-downing)
(b) 'My life will be completely miserable!' (overgeneralization, awfulizing)
(c) 'The world is a totally crummy place!' (overgeneralization, awfulizing)
(d) 'I deserve to have only bad (or good) things happen to me!' (demandingness and damnation)
(e) 'This is awful, horrible and terrible!' (awfulizing, catastrophizing)
(f) 'I can't bear it!' (I-can't-stand-it-itis)

Cognitions (a) to (f) are all examples of negative absolute evaluations. The people and things appraised are all evaluated in a negative and grossly exaggerated manner.

(g) 'I will always act incompetently and have significant people disapprove of me.' (overgeneralization)

(h) 'They know that I am no good and will always be incompetent.' (non sequitur; jumping to conclusions; mind-reading)

(i) 'They will keep laughing at me and will always despise me.' (non sequitur; jumping to conclusions; fortune-telling)

(j) 'They only despise me and see nothing good in me.' (focusing on the negative; overgeneralization)

(k) 'When they laugh with me and see me favourably, that is only because they are in a good mood and do not see that I am fooling them.' (disqualifying the positive; non sequitur; phoneyism)

(l) 'Their laughing at me and disliking me will definitely make me lose my job and lose all my friends.' (catastrophizing; magnification)

(m) 'They could only be laughing because of some foolish thing I have done and could not possibly be laughing for any other reason.' (personalizing; non sequitur; overgeneralization)

Cognitions (g) to (m) are all examples of negative absolute inferences since they go beyond the data at hand; they tend to sabotage the person's goals; and they are held with absolute conviction.

## Consequences (Cs) of Activating events (As) and Beliefs (Bs) about As    Cs (cognitive, affective, and behavioural Consequences) follow from the interaction of As and Bs. We can say, mathematically, that $A \times B = C$; but this formula may actually be too simple and we may require a more complex one to express the relationship adequately. C is almost always significantly affected or influenced, but not exactly 'caused', by A – because humans naturally to some degree react to stimuli in their environments. Moreover, when A is powerful (e.g. a set of starvation conditions or an earthquake) it tends to affect C profoundly.

When C consists of emotional 'disturbance' (e.g. severe feelings of anxiety, depression, hostility, self-deprecation, and self-pity), B usually (but not always) mainly or more directly creates or 'causes' C. Emotional 'disturbance', however, may at times stem from powerful As – for example, from environmental disasters such as floods or wars, or from personal tragedy. Emotional disturbance may also follow from factors in the organism – for example, hormonal or disease factors – that are somewhat independent of yet may actually 'cause' Consequences (Cs).

When strong or unusual As significantly contribute to or 'cause' Cs, or when physiological factors 'create' Cs they are usually accompanied by contributory Bs, too. Thus, if people are caught in an earthquake or if they experience powerful hormonal changes and 'therefore' become depressed, their As or their physiological processes probably are strongly influencing them to create irrational Beliefs (iBs), such as, 'This earthquake shouldn't have occurred! Isn't it awful! I can't stand it!' These iBs, in turn, add to or help create their feelings of depression at C.

Cs usually consist of feelings and behaviours but may also consist of thoughts (e.g. obsessions). Cs (Consequences) that follow from As and Bs are virtually never pure or monolithic but also partially include and inevitably interact with A and B. Thus if A is an obnoxious event (e.g. a job refusal) and B is, first, a rational Belief (e.g. 'I hope I don't get rejected for this job!') as well as, second, an irrational Belief (e.g. 'I must have this job! I'm no good if I don't get it!'), C tends to be, first, healthy feelings of frustration and disappointment and, second, unhealthy feelings of severe anxiety, inadequacy, and depression.

So A × B = C. But people also *bring* feelings (as well as hopes, goals and purposes) to A. They wouldn't keep a job unless they desired or favourably evaluated it or unless they enjoyed some aspect of it. Their A therefore partially includes their B and C. The two, from the beginning, are related rather than completely disparate.

At the same time, people's Beliefs (Bs) also partly or intrinsically relate to and include their As and their Cs. Thus, if they tell themselves, at B, 'I want to get a good job,' they partly create the Activating events at A (going for a job interview), and they also partly create their emotional and behavioural Consequences at C (feeling disappointed or depressed when they encounter a job rejection). Without their evaluating a job as good they would not try for it nor have any particular feeling about being rejected.

A, B, and C, then, are all closely related and none of them tends to exist without the other.

In RET, A and C are normally assessed before B and are usually assessed in the order that clients report them. C refers to both emotional and behavioural Consequences of the preferential or masturbatory evaluations made at B. Careful assessment of emotional Cs is advocated in RET, since they serve as a major indicator of what type of evaluations are to be found at B. In this regard, Ellis (1980a) has argued that it is important to differentiate between 'appropriate' and 'inappropriate' negative emotions. Emotions such as sadness, regret, annoyance, concern are termed 'appropriate' in RET in that they are deemed to stem from rational, preferential evaluations at B and encourage people to attempt to change, for the better, obnoxious situations at A. The 'inappropriate' versions of the above emotional states are: depression, guilt, anger, and anxiety. These are deemed to stem from 'irrational', musturbatory evaluations at B and tend to interfere with people's constructive attempts to change undesirable situations.

When emotional Cs are being assessed, it is important to realize three important points. First, clients do not necessarily use affective terminology in the same way as RET therapists do. It is often helpful to inform them about the nature of the unique discriminations made between emotional states so that therapist and client can come to use a shared emotional 'language'. Second, emotional Cs are often 'chained' together in a manner similar to the way inferences are chained. For example, anger is frequently chained to anxiety in that one can experience anger to 'cover up' feelings of inadequacy, and one can feel depressed after a threat to one's self-esteem emerges (Wessler 1981). Finally, rational-emotive therapists had better realize that clients do not always want or need to change every technically 'inappropriate' negative emotion as defined by RET theory; that is, a particular 'inappropriate' emotion (e.g. anger) may not be truly 'inappropriate' or self-defeating, depending on the circumstances. Thus, a good deal of flexibility and clinical acumen is called for in the assessment of emotional Cs to be targeted for change.

While we have chosen to highlight the assessment of emotional Cs, similar points can be made about the assessment of behavioural Cs. As noted earlier, withdrawal, procrastination, alcoholism, and substance abuse are generally regarded as dysfunctional behaviours and related to 'irrational', absolute evaluations at B (Ellis 1982a).

**Other issues in problem conceptualization**    There are a number of other important issues in the assessment stage of RET. First, therapists had better be alert to problems in *both* the areas of ego disturbance and discomfort disturbance. In particular, ego and discomfort disturbance often interact and careful assessment is often required to disentangle one from the other. Second, clients often have secondary problems about their primary problems and these require careful assessment for effective therapy. RET therapists often had better help clients with their secondary problems before the primary problems can be productively tackled. Common secondary problems found in dealing with clients' psychological problems include: anxiety about anxiety (e.g. in panic disorders) and guilt about anger; although numerous permutations are found in clinical practice. Third, RET practitioners pay particular attention to other ways that humans perpetuate their psychological problems and attempt to assess these carefully in therapy. Thus, humans often seek to defend themselves from threats to their 'ego' and sense of comfort. Therapists are often aware that much dysfunctional behaviour is defensive and help their clients to identify the irrational Beliefs that underlie such defensive dysfunctional behaviour. In addition, psychological problems are sometimes perpetuated because the person defines their consequences as payoffs. These payoffs also require careful assessment if productive therapeutic strategies are to be implemented.

Assessment occurs throughout therapy and becomes particularly relevant when therapeutic obstacles are encountered. While rational-emotive therapists may not use formal modes of assessment (e.g. DSM-III), since they rarely add significant material to that derived from the practice of therapy, there is nothing to prevent the utilization of such conceptualization systems in RET.

## Practical applications

### The therapeutic relationship

RET is an active-directive form of psychotherapy in that therapists are active in directing their clients to identify the philosophical source of their psychological problems, and in showing them that they can challenge and change their irrational, absolute evaluations. As such, RET is an educational form of therapy. Ellis (1979d, 1984c) has sometimes conceptualized the role of the effective RET therapist as that of an authoritative (but not authoritarian!) and encouraging teacher who strives to teach his or her clients how to be their own therapist once formal therapy sessions have ended.

**Therapeutic conditions**  Given the above role, RET therapists strive to *accept unconditionally* their clients as fallible human beings who often act self-defeatingly, but who are never essentially bad (or good). No matter how badly clients behave in therapy, the RET therapist attempts to accept them as people but will frequently, if appropriate, let them know his or her reactions to the client's negative behaviour (Ellis 1973).

Ellis (1977b), writing about his approach to the therapeutic relationship, says that he strives to be as open as therapeutically feasible and will not hesitate to give highly personal information about himself should his clients ask for it, except when he judges that clients would use such information against themselves. RET therapists often disclose examples from their own

lives concerning how they experienced similar problems and more importantly how they have gone about solving these problems. Thus, they strive to
be *therapeutically genuine* in conducting sessions.

RET therapists tend to be *appropriately humorous* with most of their
clients since they think that much emotional disturbance stems from the fact
that clients take themselves and their problems, other people, and the world
*too* seriously and thus strive to model for their clients the therapeutic
advantages of taking a serious but humorously ironic attitude to life. They
endeavour, however, not to poke fun at clients themselves but rather at the
clients' self-defeating thoughts, feelings and actions (Ellis 1977c, 1977e,
1981c). In the same vein and for similar purposes, RET therapists tend to be
informal and easygoing with most of their clients. However, RET opposes
therapists' unethically indulging themselves in order to enjoy therapy
sessions at their clients' expense (Ellis 1983b).

RET therapists show their clients a special kind of empathy. They not only
offer them 'affective' empathy (i.e. communicating that they understand
how their clients feel), but also offer them *'philosophic' empathy* (i.e.
showing them that they understand the philosophies that underlie these
feelings).      *Personal philosophys.*

Thus, with certain modifications, they agree with Rogers's (1961) views
concerning therapist empathy, genuineness and unconditional positive regard. However, rational-emotive therapists are very *wary* of showing the
vast majority of their clients *undue warmth*. Ellis (1977b, 1982b) has argued
that if RET therapists get really close to their clients and give them
considerable warmth, attention, caring and support, as well as unconditional acceptance, then these therapists run two major risks.

The first major risk is that therapists may unwittingly reinforce their
clients' dire needs for love and approval – two irrational demands which are
at the core of much human disturbance. When this happens, clients appear
to improve because their therapists are indeed giving them what they believe they must have. They begin to 'feel better' but do not necessarily 'get
better' (Ellis 1972b). Their 'improvement' is illusory because their irrational
philosophies are being reinforced. Since they seem to improve, their
therapists have restricted opportunities to identify these ideas, show them
how they relate to their problems, and help them challenge and change
them. Consequently, while such clients are helped by their therapists, they
are not shown how they can help themselves and are thus vulnerable to
future upset.

The second major risk concerns therapists unwittingly reinforcing their
clients' philosophies of low frustration tolerance (LFT) – a major form of

discomfort disturbance. Clients with LFT problems

almost always try to seek interminable help from others instead of coping with life's difficulties themselves. Any kind of therapy that does not specifically persuade them to stop their puerile whining and to accept responsibility for their own happiness tends to confirm their Belief that others *must* help them. Close relationship therapy is frequently the worst offender in this respect and thereby does considerable harm. (Ellis 1977b, p. 15).

However, since RET is relative in nature and is against the formulation of absolute, dogmatic therapeutic rules, it does recognize that under certain conditions (e.g. where a client is extremely depressed, accompanied by powerful suicidal ideation), distinct therapist warmth may be positively indicated for a restricted period of time.

**Therapeutic style**   While Ellis (1979b) recommends that RET therapists adopt an active-directive style with most clients and a particularly forceful version of that style with some very disturbed and resistant clients, not all RET therapists concur with this view. Some recommend a more passive, gentle approach under specific, or even most, conditions with clients (e.g. Garcia 1977; Young 1977). Eschenroeder (1979) notes that it is important to ask in RET 'which therapeutic style is most effective with which kind of client?' (p. 5). In the same vein, recent proponents of eclectic forms of therapy argue that the style of therapeutic interaction needs to be varied to meet the special situation of individual clients (Beutler 1983; Lazarus 1981). While this is a scantily researched area in RET, it may be best for RET therapists to avoid (a) an overly friendly, emotionally charged style of interaction with 'hysterical' clients, (b) an overly intellectual style with 'obsessive-compulsive' clients, (c) an overly directive style with clients whose sense of autonomy is easily threatened (Beutler 1983), and (d) an overly active style with clients who easily retreat into passivity. This line of reasoning fits well with the notion of flexibility which rational-emotive therapists advocate as a desirable therapeutic quality. Varying one's therapeutic style in RET does not mean departing from the theoretical principles on which the content of therapy is based. As Eschenroeder (1979) points out, in RET 'there is no one-to-one relationship between theory and practice' (p. 3).

## Strategies of treatment

Ellis (1979c, 1980a) has pointed out that there are two forms of RET – preferential and general. He says that general RET is synonymous with cognitive-behaviour therapy (CBT) while preferential RET is unique in a number of important respects. Since a major aim of the chapters in this book is to present the distinctive features of different forms of CBT, the emphasis here will be on preferential RET (although it should be noted that RET therapists routinely use strategies derived from both forms of RET). The major goal of preferential RET is an ambitious one: to encourage clients to make a profound philosophic change in the two main areas of ego disturbance and discomfort disturbance. This involves helping clients, as far as humanly possible, to give up their irrational musturbatory thinking processes and to replace them with rational nonabsolute thinking, as discussed in the expanded ABC framework section above.

In preferential RET, the major goals are to help clients pursue their long-range basic goals and purposes and to help them do so as effectively as possible by fully accepting themselves and tolerating unchangeable uncomfortable life conditions. Practitioners of preferential RET further strive to help clients obtain the skills which they can use to prevent the development of future disturbance. In encouraging clients to achieve and maintain this profound philosophic change, rational-emotive therapists implement the following strategies. They help their clients see that:

(a) Emotional and behavioural disturbances have cognitive antecedents and these cognitions normally take the form of absolutistic devout evaluations. RET practitioners train their clients to observe their own psychological disturbances and to trace these back to their ideological roots.

(b) People have a distinct measure of self-determination and can thus *choose* to work at undisturbing themselves. Thus, clients are shown that they are not slaves to their biologically based irrational thinking processes.

(c) People can implement their choices and maximize their freedom by actively working at changing their irrational musturbatory Beliefs. This is best achieved by employing cognitive, emotive, and behavioural methods – often in quite a forceful and vigorous manner (Ellis 1979b).

With the majority of clients, from the first session onward, RET therapists are likely to use strategies designed to effect profound philosophic change.

The therapist begins therapy with the hypothesis that this particular client may be able to achieve such change and thus begins preferential RET, which he or she will abandon when and if he/she collects sufficient data to reject the initial hypothesis. Ellis regularly implements this viewpoint, which is based on the notion that the client's response to therapy is the best indicator of his or her prognosis. It is not known what proportion of RET therapists share and regularly implement this position.

When it is clear that the client is not able, or does not wish, to achieve philosophic change, whether on a particular issue or in general, the therapist often switches to general RET and uses methods to effect inferential and behavioural-based change. A good example of this change in strategy is one often reported by a therapist of our acquaintance. He was working with a middle-aged married woman who reported feeling furious every time her ageing father would telephone her and enquire, 'Noo, what's doing?' She inferred that this was a gross invasion of her privacy and absolutistically insisted that he had no right to do so. The therapist initially intervened with a 'preferential RET' strategy by attempting to Dispute this client's dogmatic Belief and tried to help her see that there was no law in the universe which stated that he *must* not do such a thing. Meeting initial resistance, the therapist persisted with different variations of this theme – all to no avail. Changing tack, he began to implement a 'general RET' strategy designed to help the client question her inference that her father was actually invading her privacy. Given her father's age, the therapist enquired, was it not more likely that his question represented his usual manner of beginning telephone conversations rather than an intense desire to pry into her affairs? This enquiry proved successful in that the client's rage subsided because she began to reinterpret her father's motives. Interestingly enough, although he returned to the 'preferential' strategy later, the therapist never succeeded in helping this client to give up her irrational musturbatory Belief! However, some clients are more amenable to re-evaluating their irrational musturba-tory beliefs *after* they have been helped to correct distorted inferences. We had better do research on this topic if we are to answer the question: 'Which strategy is most appropriate for which clients at which stage in therapy?' Meanwhile, it is important to note that RET therapists, if they follow Ellis's lead, are unique in that they are more likely to challenge musturbatory cognitions and to dispute self-defeating Beliefs in their clients much earlier in the therapeutic process than do other cognitive-behavioural therapists.

**Therapeutic strategies in a 'typical' RET session** What therapeutic strategies do Rational-Emotive therapists employ in a 'typical' session of preferential RET? The following is meant to be a flexible guide rather than a rigid framework:

*Homework*

1. *Check on any homework assignments that the client agreed to do since the previous session (if relevant).*
   (a) If these assignments have been executed successfully, enquire what the client gained from doing them.
   (b) Troubleshoot any problems that emerged as a result, particularly if the assignment was not attempted. Assess the possible existence of irrational beliefs that prevented the client from doing the homework assignment. Dispute these Beliefs and reassign the task (if appropriate).

2. *Ask for the client's most pressing primary problem.*
   (a) Assess this problem using the expanded ABC framework.
   (b) Identify the most relevant inference that provided the context for the emotional and/or behavioural problem.
   (c) Assume that the inference is correct for the moment and urge the client to do the same.
   (d) Check whether the client has a secondary problem (e.g. depression about feeling depressed). If so, do an ABC analysis of this problem and proceed as below, having explained to the client the advisability of working on the secondary problem first and getting the client's agreement to do so. This step can also occur before 2(a) above.

3. *Help the client see the relationship between (a) musturbatory irrational Beliefs and their absolute evaluative conclusions and (b) the emotional and/or behavioural problem, and how the former tend to 'create' or 'cause' the latter.*
   Show the client the desirability of disputing irrational Beliefs in order to promote constructive and desired emotional and behavioural changes.

4. *Dispute the client's irrational musturbatory Beliefs and/or their absolute evaluative conclusions by asking for any evidence that truly supports them.*
   (a) Show the client that any evidence provided is usually in support of 'rational' Beliefs but not of 'irrational' Beliefs – e.g. there is evidence that it is preferable for clients to perform well and be approved but not that they therefore *must* succeed.
   (b) Repeat 4(a) until the client acknowledges that the evidence justifies the existence of the 'rational' Beliefs but not that of the 'irrational' Beliefs.

(c) Help the client see the relationship between the rational Beliefs and the constructive and desired emotional and behavioural changes.

5. *Help the client see the advisability of continuing to Dispute the irrational Beliefs in this and other relevant situations.*

6. *Negotiate a homework assignment which will give the client an opportunity to Dispute the irrational Beliefs and act on the new rational Beliefs.*

   (a) Troubleshoot possible obstacles to the successful completion of the assignment in advance.

   (b) Conduct in-session practice in which the client can rehearse the assignment using imagery or simulated exercises (if relevant).

7. *Identify and correct any distorted inferences which were assumed to be true in 2(c) (if time allows).*

The above framework indicates clearly that the 'typical' RET session is sequentially structured. It is highly desirable if the client can make sense of and agree to his or her active participation in this structure.

## Major treatment techniques

RET represents a major form of eclecticism known as 'theoretically consistent eclecticism' (Dryden 1984b) in that techniques are liberally borrowed from other therapeutic systems, but employed for purposes usually consistent with RET's underlying theory. In particular, RET therapists are mindful of the short-term and long-term effects of particular therapeutic techniques and will rarely employ a technique that has beneficial immediate, but harmful long-range, Consequences. While rational-emotive therapists employ a large number of cognitive, emotive, and behavioural techniques, only the major ones will be discussed here. It should be noted at the outset that probably all the following techniques have cognitive, emotive, and behavioural elements to them and that 'pure' techniques (e.g. purely cognitive) probably do not exist. Techniques are grouped below to show which psychological process predominates.

**Cognitive techniques** Probably the most common technique employed by RET therapists with the majority of their clients is the *disputing of irrational beliefs*. There are four sub-categories of Disputing (Ellis 1977a). DETECTING consists of looking for irrational Beliefs – particularly musts, shoulds, oughts, and have tos – that lead to self-defeating emotions and behaviours.

DEBATING consists of the therapist asking a number of questions which are designed to help the client give up irrational Beliefs. Questions such as 'Where is the evidence . . .?' 'In what way does this Belief have truth or falseness?' and 'What makes it so?' are frequently employed. The therapist proceeds with such questioning until the client acknowledges the falseness of his or her irrational Belief and, in addition, acknowledges the truth of its rational alternative. DISCRIMINATING involves the therapist helping the client to distinguish clearly between his or her nonabsolute values (his wants, preferences, likes and desires) and his or her absolutistic values (his needs, demands and imperatives). DEFINING involves the therapist helping the client to make increasingly accurate definitions in the language that he or she employs when referring to his or her Beliefs (Dryden 1984c). Rational-emotive therapists are often very creative in their use of Disputing sequences (e.g. Young 1984a, 1984b, 1984c) and sometimes employ such methods in a highly dramatic fashion (Dryden 1984c). A formal version of Disputing that includes some of its main components is known as *DIBS* (Disputing irrational Beliefs). Ellis (1979d) outlines its form thus: (4)

(5) Disputing Irrational Beliefs                    Defining

| Question 1: | What irrational Belief do I want to dispute and surrender? |
| Answer: | I must be as effective and sexually fulfilled as most other women. |

| Question 2: | Can I rationally support this Belief? |
| Answer: | ................................................................ |

| Question 3: | What evidence exists of the truth of this Belief? |
| Answer: | ................................................................ |

| Question 4: | What evidence exists of the falseness of my Belief that I must be as orgasmic as other women are? |
| Answer: | ................................................................ |

| Question 5: | What are the worst possible things that could actually happen to me if I never achieved the orgasm that I think I must achieve? |
| Answers: | ................................................................ |

| Question 6: | What good things could happen or could I make happen if I never achieved the heights of orgasm that I think I must achieve? |
| Answers: | ................................................................ |

(Ellis 1979, pp. 79–80)

DIBS is one example of *cognitive homework* that is frequently given to clients to do between sessions after the client has been trained to use them. Other examples appear in Figures 5.1 and 5.2. The purpose of these forms is to provide a clear framework for clients to learn to do Disputing for themselves.

Clients who do not have the intellectual skills necessary to perform cognitive Disputing are usually helped to develop *rational self-statements* which they can memorize or write out on 3 × 5 cards and repeat at various times between sessions. An example developed by one of us (WD) with a client was 'Just because my being overweight is bad, doesn't mean that I am bad. My overeating makes me too heavy and is therefore wrong, but I can correct it and get better results.' Two cognitive methods which are often employed by RET therapists to help clients reinforce their new rational philosophy are *bibliotherapy* where clients are assigned self-help books to read (e.g. Ellis and Becker 1982; Ellis and Harper 1975; Young 1974) and *the use of RET with others* – a technique which gives clients an opportunity to practise thinking through rational arguments with their friends and relatives.

**Emotive techniques**   RET, as a therapeutic system, has often been falsely accused of being too intellectual and insufficiently emotive. However, this is far from being true, and rational-emotive therapy sessions are frequently charged with emotion. The practice of effective RET is based upon the therapist offering the client the emotional attitude of *unconditional acceptance* (as discussed in the section on the therapeutic relationship). From this foundation, RET therapists frequently and judiciously employ *humorous techniques* to reduce the client's irrational Beliefs to absurd, amusing conclusions; the use of rational humorous songs (Ellis 1977c, 1977e, 1981c); and amusing anecdotes, all of which are designed to encourage the client to think rationally by not taking him or herself, others and the world *too* seriously.

Moreover, RET therapists strive to serve as good *rational role models* both in their interactions with their clients and in their disclosures concerning how they handle their own psychological problems. In doing so, they employ a good measure of *therapist self-disclosure*. They encourage the use of role-playing and, in particular, *rational role reversal* where the therapist may adopt the irrational side of the client and encourage the client to Dispute irrational Beliefs from his or her rational side – a technique which is particularly employed with clients who have gained some mastery of the

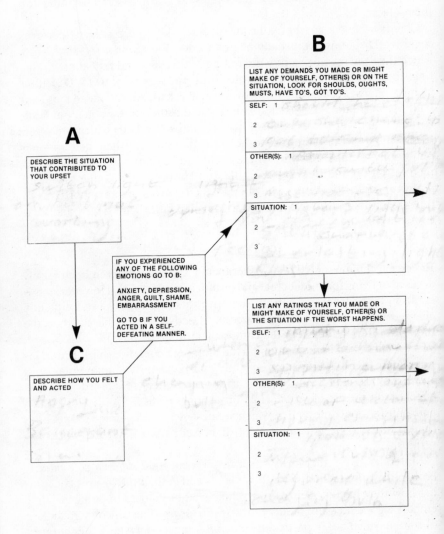

**Figure 5.1** A guide for solving your emotional and behavioural problems by re-examining your self-defeating thoughts and attitudes (Dryden 1982)

# D

| QUESTION YOUR DEMANDS |
|---|
| SELF: 1 |
| 2 |
| 3 |
| OTHER(S): 1 |
| 2 |
| 3 |
| SITUATION: 1 |
| 2 |
| 3 |

| RATIONAL ANSWER |
|---|
| SELF: 1 |
| 2 |
| 3 |
| OTHER(S): 1 |
| 2 |
| 3 |
| SITUATION: 1 |
| 2 |
| 3 |

| NEW FEELING AND ACTION |
|---|
|  |

| QUESTION YOUR RATINGS |
|---|
| SELF: 1 |
| 2 |
| 3 |
| OTHER(S): 1 |
| 2 |
| 3 |
| SITUATION: 1 |
| 2 |
| 3 |

| RATIONAL ANSWER |
|---|
| SELF: 1 |
| 2 |
| 3 |
| OTHER(S): 1 |
| 2 |
| 3 |
| SITUATION: 1 |
| 2 |
| 3 |

## RET SELF-HELP FORM

Institute for Rational-Emotive Therapy
45 East 65th Street, New York, N.Y. 10021
(212) 535-0822

**(A) ACTIVATING EVENTS,** thoughts, or feelings that happened just before I felt emotionally disturbed or acted self-defeatingly: _____

_____

**(C) CONSEQUENCE or CONDITION**—disturbed feeling or self-defeating behaviour—that I produced and would like to change: _____

_____

| (B) BELIEFS—Irrational BELIEFS (IBs) leading to my CONSEQUENCE (emotional disturbance or self-defeating behaviour). Circle all that apply to these ACTIVATING EVENTS (A). | (D) DISPUTES for each circled IRRATIONAL BELIEF. Examples: "Why MUST I do very well?" "Where is it written that I am a BAD PERSON?" "Where is the evidence that I MUST be approved or accepted?" | (E) EFFECTIVE RATIONAL BELIEFS (RBs) to replace my IRRATIONAL BELIEFS (IBs). *Examples: "I'd PREFER to do very well but I don't HAVE TO." "I am a PERSON WHO acted badly, not a BAD PERSON." "There is no evidence that I HAVE TO be approved, though I would LIKE to be."* |
|---|---|---|
| 1. I MUST do well or very well! | | |
| 2. I am a BAD OR WORTHLESS PERSON when I act weakly or stupidly. | | |
| 3. I MUST be approved or accepted by people I find important! | | |
| 4. I am a BAD, UNLOVABLE PERSON if I get rejected. | | |
| 5. People MUST treat me fairly and give me what I NEED! | | |
| 6. People who act immorally are undeserving, ROTTEN PEOPLE! | | |
| 7. People MUST live up to my expectations or it is TERRIBLE! | | |
| 8. My life MUST have few major hassles or troubles. | | |
| 9. I CAN'T STAND really bad things or very difficult people! | | |
| 10. It's AWFUL or HORRIBLE when major things don't go my way! | | |

**Figure 5.2** RET self-help form (Sichel and Ellis 1984)

| | | |
|---|---|---|
| 11. I CAN'T STAND IT when life is really unfair! | | |
| 12. I NEED to be loved by someone who matters to me a lot! | | |
| 13. I NEED a good deal of immediate gratification and HAVE TO feel miserable when I don't get it! | | |
| *Additional Irrational Beliefs:* | | |
| 14. | | |
| 15. | | |
| 16. | | |
| 17. | | |
| 18. | | |

**(F) FEELINGS and BEHAVIOURS** I experienced after arriving at my EFFECTIVE RATIONAL BELIEFS: _____

**I WILL WORK HARD TO REPEAT MY EFFECTIVE RATIONAL BELIEFS FORCEFULLY TO MYSELF ON MANY OCCASIONS SO THAT I CAN MAKE MYSELF LESS DISTURBED NOW AND ACT LESS SELF-DEFEATINGLY IN THE FUTURE.**

Joyce Sichel, Ph.D. and Albert Ellis, Ph.D.

ABC framework and Disputing methods. Another frequently used emotive technique is that of *rational-emotive imagery* (Ellis 1979d; Maultsby and Ellis 1974). Here clients gain practice at changing their 'inappropriate' emotions to 'appropriate' ones while keenly imagining the negative event. What they are in fact doing is learning to change their self-defeating emotions by changing their underlying philosophy.

Finally, clients are encouraged to act and think in forceful but rational ways (Ellis 1979b). They are urged to do regular *shame-attacking exercises* where they practise their newly acquired philosophies of discomfort toler-ance and self-acceptance while doing something that they consider 'shame-ful', but not harmful to themselves or others. Examples might include: requesting to buy a pair of trousers in a bookstore or wearing different coloured gloves for a whole day. Repeating rational self-statements in a *passionate and forceful* manner is often used in conjunction with such exercises and also at other times.

*In vivo rather/self Statements than Imaginal*

**Behavioural techniques**   The use of a wide variety of behavioural techni-ques is advocated wherever possible since it is realized that cognitive change is very often facilitated by behavioural change (Ellis 1979e; Emmelkamp, Kuipers and Eggeraat 1978). However, some behavioural techniques are favoured over others. Thus in vivo rather than imaginal techniques are preferred because 'live' exposure presents clients with more opportunities for philosophic change than 'imagined' exposure (Ellis 1983c). For the same reason, RET therapists often encourage their clients *fully to expose* them-selves to, say, feared events, although in practice compromises often have to be reached concerning how fully clients are prepared to expose themselves (Dryden 1985).

Other behavioural methods often used in RET include: (a) *'stay-in-there' activities* (Grieger and Boyd 1980) which give clients an opportunity to raise their level of frustration tolerance by encouraging them to remain in uncomfortable (but not harmful or traumatic) situations for a period of time while tolerating their feelings of chronic discomfort; (b) *anti-procrastination exercises* where clients are encouraged to push themselves to start tasks earlier rather than later, thus Disputing their dire need for comfort-of-the-moment (Ellis and Knaus 1977); (c) various *skill training methods* which equip clients with key skills in which they are deficient (e.g. assertion and social skills training), and which are usually employed after cognitive Disputing methods have been used and some philosophic change has been encouraged (Ellis 1977d); and (d) the use of *rewards and penalties* which are

*Learning Assertion — Social Skill Theory*

Rewards - Penalties

used to encourage clients to implement self-change programmes.[1]

## Overcoming obstacles to client progress

When RET is practised efficiently and effectively and when clients understand and are prepared continually to implement its basic concepts, then it can achieve remarkable results. However, frequently (and perhaps more frequently than most therapists are prepared to admit!), various obstacles to client progress are encountered in the practice of RET (and indeed all other forms of therapy). Three major forms of obstacles are deemed to occur in RET: (a) relationship obstacles; (b) therapist obstacles; and (c) client obstacles (Ellis 1985a).

3 obstacles to change.

**'Relationship' obstacles to client progress** These can be first attributed to poor therapist–client matching. Such mismatching may occur for many reasons. Thus, clients 'may have a therapist who, according to their idiosyncratic tastes or preferences, is too young or too old, too liberal or too conservative, too active or too passive' (Ellis 1983d, p. 29). If these 'relationship match' obstacles persist, then it is preferable for that client to be transferred to a therapist with more suitable traits. Other relationship obstacles may occur because the therapist and client may get on 'too well' and get distracted from the more mundane tasks of therapy. In such cases, the paradox is that if the client improves, the 'life' of the satisfactory relationship is threatened. As a result, collusion may occur between therapist and client to avoid making therapy as effective an endeavour as it might otherwise be. This problem can be largely overcome if the therapist helps first himself or herself and then the client to overcome the philosophy of low frustration tolerance implicit in this collusive short-range hedonism.

**Therapist obstacles to client progress** There are two major types of therapist obstacles: skill-orientated obstacles and disturbance-orientated obstacles. When obstacles to client progress can be mainly attributed to therapist skill deficits, these may appear in a variety of forms but most commonly therapists may impede client progress by:

(a) Improperly inducting clients into therapy and failing to correct unrealistic expectations such as 'my therapist will solve my problems for me.'

(b) Incorrectly assessing clients' problems and thus working on 'problems' that clients do not have.

(c) Failing to show clients that their problems have ideological roots and that C is largely (but not exclusively) determined by B and not by A – inexpert therapists often fail to persist with this strategy or persist with an ineffective strategy.

(d) Failing to show clients that the ideological roots of their problems are most frequently expressed in the form of devout, absolutistic 'musts' or one of the three main derivatives of 'musturbation'. Instead, inexpert RET therapists frequently dwell too long on their clients' anti-empirical or inferentially distorted thinking.

(e) Assuming that clients will automatically change their absolute thinking once they have identified it. Inexpert RET therapists either fail to Dispute such thinking at all or use disputing methods sparingly and/or with insufficient vigour. In addition, inexpert therapists routinely fail to: give their clients homework assignments which provide them with opportunities to practise disputing their irrational Beliefs; check on their clients' progress on these assignments; and help their clients to identify and change their philosophic obstacles to working continually at self-change.

(f) Failing to realize that clients often have problems about their problems and thus working only on a primary problem when the client is preoccupied with a secondary problem.

(g) Frequently switching from ego to discomfort disturbance issues within a given session so that clients get confused and thus distracted from working on either issue.

(h) Working at a pace and a level inappropriate to the learning abilities of clients so that these clients are insufficiently involved in the therapeutic process due to confusion or boredom.

For these reasons it is highly desirable for RET therapists to strive continually to improve their skills by involving themselves in ongoing supervision and training activities (Dryden 1983; Wessler and Ellis 1980, 1983).

Client progress can also be hindered because therapists may bring their own disturbance to the therapeutic process. Ellis (1983b) has outlined five major irrational Beliefs that lead to therapeutic inefficiency.

(a) 'I *have* to be successful with all my clients practically all of the time.'

(b) 'I *must* be an outstanding therapist, clearly better than other therapists I know or hear about.'

(c) 'I *have to* be greatly respected and loved by all my clients.'

(d) 'Since I am doing my best and working so hard as a therapist, my clients *should* be equally hard working and responsible, *should* listen to me carefully and *should* always push themselves to change.'

(e) 'Because I am a person in my own right, I *must* be able to enjoy myself during therapy sessions and to use these sessions to solve my personal problems as much as to help clients with their difficulties.'

In such cases, it is recommended that RET therapists apply RET principles and methods to search for and dispute their own self- and client-defeating Beliefs which may (a) impede them from confronting their clients; (b) distract them and their clients from getting the therapeutic job done; (c) foster undue therapist anxiety and anger; and (d) encourage inappropriate behaviour antithetical to the practice of effective and ethical therapy.

**Client obstacles to client progress**   In order really to benefit from RET, clients had better achieve three forms of insight, namely: (a) Psychological disturbance is mainly determined by the absolutistic Beliefs that they hold about themselves, others, and the world. (b) Even when people acquired and created their irrational Beliefs in their early lives, they perpetuate their disturbance by re-indoctrinating themselves in the present with these Beliefs. (c) Only if they constantly work and practise in the present and future to think, feel and act against these irrational Beliefs are clients likely to surrender their irrationalities and make themselves significantly less disturbed.

In a study by Ellis (1983e) on the characteristics of clients who 'failed' in RET, the following categories of 'failure' client emerged: (a) Clients who did poorly in RET failed to do consistent *cognitive* self-disputation. They were characterized amongst other factors by extreme disturbance, by grandiosity, by lack of organization, and by plain refusal to do these cognitive assignments. (b) Clients who refused to accept responsibility for their 'inappropriate' emotions and refused to change forcefully and *emotively* their Beliefs and actions, were more clingy, more severely depressed and inactive, more often grandiose and more frequently stubbornly rebellious than clients who benefited from RET. (c) Clients who did poorly in the *behavioural* aspects of RET showed 'abysmally low frustration tolerance, had serious behavioural addictions, led disorganized lives, refrained from doing their activity homework assignments, were more frequently psychotic and generally refused to work at therapy' (Ellis 1983e, p. 165).

Thus, clients' own extreme level of disturbance is a significant obstacle to their own progress. While a full discussion of what 'special' therapeutic methods and techniques the therapist should employ with such clients is outside the scope of this chapter (see Ellis 1983d, 1983f, 1984b, 1985a, 1985c), therapists can adopt a number of strategies to enhance therapeutic effectiveness with these DCs ('difficult customers'). Amongst other tactics, therapists had better, first, be consistently and forcefully encouraging in their therapeutic interactions with these clients, showing them that they can do better if they try. Second, therapists would be wise to keep vigorously showing these resistant clients that they (the therapists) do, in fact, unconditionally accept them with all their psychological difficulties and that they can indeed accept themselves in the same way. Third, therapists can often be successful with such clients by consistently showing them that their refusal to work on their problems will generally lead to bad consequences and needless suffering. Fourth, therapists had better be flexible in experimenting with a wide range of therapeutic techniques (including some unusual ones!) in their persistent efforts to help their 'difficult' clients. Above all, rational-emotive therapists had better be good representatives of their therapeutic system and accept themselves and tolerate the discomfort of working with difficult clients while sticking to the therapeutic task!

## Case example

Ted J., a forty-year-old garment salesman, came to therapy because he was severely depressed, constantly angry, and sexually inadequate with his wife. He had been married for four years to a personable and very attractive twenty-five-year-old woman whom he described as 'exceptionally sweet and kind' but for whom he no longer had any sexual desire and with whom he either lost his erection soon after starting intercourse or remained erect but was unable to achieve orgasm. Within a few months after marrying, he had returned to his old habits of having regular sex contacts with prostitutes and with occasional homosexual pickups. He was guilty over lying to his wife about his extramarital escapades and over his lack of feeling for her, and he was extremely ashamed of his homosexual acts. He was also depressed about his depression and ashamed of his sexual 'inadequacy'. He thought of either killing himself or running away to another part of the country where he would 'get away from all my troubles by just disappearing'.

I (AE) saw this client for sixteen sessions over a period of seven months. After teaching him the ABCs of RET, I first worked with him on his secondary symptoms – especially on his depression about his depression and on his shame about his sexual 'inadequacy'. His main irrational Beliefs (iBs) behind these secondary disturbances were:

(a) 'Being depressed is weak and shameful. I *must* not feel this way!'
(b) 'All my life I have been sexually potent and now I can't even keep it up and come with my beautiful, young wife. Almost any man with balls would be dying to screw her, and I can't. I *should* be able to do so and I am a wimp if I can't!'

Teaching this client to do RET Disputing, I showed him how to keep asking himself, 'Granting that depression is a weakness, why is it *shameful* for me to be weak? Where is it written that I *must* not be depressed?' And he was able to answer himself, after a few sessions: 'It's highly *inconvenient* but never *shameful* to be weak and depressed. There is *no* reason why I *must* not be depressed, though I can think of many reasons why I don't *want* to be this way.'

He also, under the guidance of RET, kept Disputing: 'Why do I *have* to be potent with my beautiful wife? Why am I not *allowed* to find her sexually unarousing?' And he was soon able to answer – and to *convince* himself – 'I don't *have* to be sexually potent with her – or, for that matter, with anyone! Losing my erection or not coming to orgasm is damned frustrating – but it hardly makes me a worthless shit!'

Once he began to accept himself *with* his primary symptoms of depression and of sex failure with his wife, Ted was directed to working on his primary symptoms of depression and anger. These largely originated in his irrational Beliefs (iBs): 'I must love and want to stay married to my exceptionally sweet and kind wife, even though I'm quite bored to be with her.' And: 'She *shouldn't* expect me to be great in bed with her all the time when I've been used to screwing around with a large number of sexy women for the last twenty years and when I really *need* that kind of variety to keep myself sexually alive!'

When Ted actively Disputed these iBs, he was able to come up with these rational Beliefs (rBs) in their stead: 'Even though my wife is a fine, kind, lovely person, and in many ways is an ideal mate, I don't *have* to find her sexually exciting and I am *allowed* to feel that she is somewhat boring.' And: 'My wife has a perfect right to expect regular sex from me even though I've been used to more exciting partners for many years. If I really want exciting sex rather than a good, solid, companionable marriage, maybe I'd better not be married at all. She didn't *force* me to marry her; and if she wants more than I care to give, that's too bad but it certainly doesn't make her a rotten person!'

As he worked at debating and surrendering his irrational Beliefs, Ted lost his guilt and depression over being bored and over being sexually unexcited with his wife; and he became much less angry with her. He then was able to have fairly good sex with her about twice a week and had no trouble coming to orgasm.

In addition to Disputing his irrational Beliefs and replacing them with rational self-statements, Ted was shown how to use rational problem-solving methods and how to employ a long-term hedonic calculus in deciding whether it might be worth his while to stay with his wife or to leave her (Ellis and Abrahms 1978; Ellis and Whiteley 1979; Goldfried and Davison 1976).

One of the main RET methods that Ted found useful in overcoming his depression and anger was his reading of some of the rational-emotive self-help literature, particularly *A New Guide to Rational Living* (Ellis and Harper 1975), *A Guide to Personal Happiness* (Ellis and Becker 1982), and *How to Live With – and Without – Anger* (Ellis 1977f). Audio cassettes that he found especially helpful included *Conquering Low Frustration Tolerance* (Ellis 1976b) and *Solving Emotional Problems* (Ellis 1972a). I also encouraged him to use another cognitive RET technique – that is, to use his knowledge of RET to understand his wife and his business associates and to try to talk them out of some of their irrational ideas (Bard 1980; Ellis 1973). He reported that doing so helped him appreciably to practise using RET on himself and to hone his Disputing skills so that he could use them more effectively on himself.

The main emotive techniques that I employed with Ted were, first, unconditionally accepting him, in spite of his unethical behaviour (especially his lying to his wife) and showing him that he could finally accept himself even *with* this undesirable activity (Ellis 1973; Ellis and Harper 1975). Second, I encouraged Ted to do several shame-attacking exercises (Ellis 1971; Ellis and Abrahms 1978), in the course of which he forced himself to do acts in public (e.g. singing loudly while walking on the street) that he considered 'shameful' and, simultaneously, worked on his feelings so that he did *not* feel embarrassed or humiliated while doing them. Third, I had him regularly practise rational-emotive imagery (Maultsby and Ellis 1974), during which he imagined 'terrible' things happening (such as his wife discovering his homosexual encounters) while he made himself feel *only* appropriately sorry and disappointed but *not* inappropriately horrified and depressed.

Finally, I monitored Ted so that he practised several RET behavioural methods. In particular, I gave him the homework assignments – which, because of his guilt, he at first was too terrified to carry out – of forcing himself to be increasingly honest with his wife about his lack of sex and love feelings for her and about his desires to return to bachelorhood. He avoided doing this assignment for several weeks; but when he contracted (with himself and me) to have outside affairs only *after* he had had an honest talk with his wife about his feelings for her, he immediately began to have such talks – and to feel much less guilty and depressed after each talk. Behaviourally, Ted was also induced to stop avoiding having sex with his wife and to make sure that he satisfied her noncoitally if he didn't function in intercourse (Ellis 1960, 1976c). Ironically, as soon as he began to follow this suggestion, he was able almost always to get and keep his erections and come to orgasm within ten minutes of intromission.

After two months of therapy, Ted completely overcame his sex problems with his wife and was able to discuss his feelings with her in a friendly, unguilty manner. Their relationship improved considerably and he no longer dreaded coming home after work or being with her on weekends. He still felt bored with his marriage, however, and he was able, without guilt, depression, and anger, to show his wife that she was not responsible for his boredom and that he just was not, at that time, suited to marriage with her or probably with any other woman. She sadly but courageously accepted this reality and decided to leave him and arrange for an amicable divorce. Once they separated, he kept working in RET sessions to overcome his guilt and depression about the separation; and by the time he left therapy he was doing quite well in this regard.

Although Ted rarely discussed his job problems during therapy, he reported that he started applying RET principles to his relationships with his sales manager and with the two partners who ran his company. Doing so, he lost virtually all his long-standing rage at the 'unfair' ways in which he thought they were treating him and he was consequently able to perform much better at his job.

I still see Ted every month or two when he chooses to observe my regular Friday night workshop, 'Problems of Everyday Living', in the course of which I publicly interview volunteers who bring up their emotional problems. Two and a half years subsequent to his RET sessions, he reports that he is functioning well sexually, has a regular mistress with whom he leads an interesting sex and companionable life, is doing better than ever at work – and rarely feels seriously depressed or angry. He still reads RET writings, actively uses rational-emotive Disputing to help his friends with their emotional problems, and refers a number of them to RET practitioners when they continue to be disturbed. As he recently said to me, 'RET is still a way of life for me – and I expect to keep using it forever!'

## Note

1  For a full discussion of techniques and methods avoided or used minimally in RET, the reader is advised to consult Ellis (1979d, 1983c).

## References

Adler, A. (1927) *Understanding human nature.* New York: Garden City.
Bard, J. (1980) *Rational-emotive therapy in practice.* Champaign, L.: Research Press.
Beutler, L.E. (1983) *Eclectic psychotherapy: A systematic approach.* New York: Pergamon.
Dryden, W. (1983) Audiotape supervision by mail: A rational-emotive approach. *British Journal of Cognitive Psychotherapy, 1(1),* 57–64.
Dryden, W. (1984a) Rational-emotive therapy. In W. Dryden (ed.) *Individual therapy in Britain.* London: Harper and Row.
Dryden, W. (1984b) Issues in the eclectic practice of individual therapy. In W. Dryden (ed.) *Individual therapy in Britain.* London: Harper and Row.
Dryden, W. (1984c) *Rational-emotive therapy: Fundamentals and innovations.* Beckenham, Kent: Croom Helm.
Dryden, W. (1985) Challenging but not overwhelming: A compromise in negotiating homework assignments. *British Journal of Cognitive Psychotherapy, 3(1),* 77–80.
Dunlap, K. (1932) *Habits: Their making and unmaking.* New York: Liveright.
Ellis, A. (1960) *The art and science of love.* Secaucus, NJ: Lyle Stuart.
Ellis, A. (1962) *Reason and emotion in psychotherapy.* Secaucus, NJ: Lyle Stuart.
Ellis, A. (speaker) (1971) *How to stubbornly refuse to be ashamed of anything* (cassette recording). New York: Institute for Rational-Emotive Therapy.
Ellis, A. (speaker) (1972a) *Solving emotional problems* (cassette recording). New York: Institute for Rational-Emotive Therapy.
Ellis, A. (1972b) Helping people get better: Rather than merely feel better. *Rational Living, 7(2),* 2–9.
Ellis, A. (1973) *Humanistic psychotherapy: The rational-emotive approach.* New York: McGraw-Hill.
Ellis, A. (1976a) The biological basis of human irrationality. *Journal of Individual Psychology, 32,* 145–168.
Ellis, A. (speaker) (1976b) *Conquering low frustration tolerance* (cassette recording). New York: Institute for Rational-Emotive Therapy.

Ellis, A. (1976c) *Sex and the liberated man*. Secaucus, NJ: Lyle Stuart.

Ellis, A. (1977a) The basic clinical theory of rational-emotive therapy. In A. Ellis and R. Grieger (eds) *Handbook of Rational-Emotive Therapy*. New York: Springer.

Ellis, A. (1977b) Intimacy in psychotherapy. *Rational Living, 12(2)*, 13–19.

Ellis, A. (1977c) Fun as psychotherapy. *Rational Living, 12(1)*, 2–6.

Ellis, A. (1977d) Skill training in counselling and psychotherapy. *Canadian Counsellor, 12(1)*, 30–35.

Ellis, A. (speaker) (1977e) *A garland of rational humorous songs* (cassette recording). New York: Institute for Rational-Emotive Therapy.

Ellis, A. (1977f) *Anger – how to live with and without it*. Secaucus, NJ: Citadel Press.

Ellis, A. (1979a) The theory of rational-emotive therapy. In A. Ellis and J.M. Whiteley (eds) *Theoretical and empirical foundations of rational-emotive therapy*. Monterey, Calif.: Brooks/Cole.

Ellis, A. (1979b) The issue of force and energy in behavioral change. *Journal of Contemporary Psychotherapy, 10(2)*, 83–97.

Ellis, A. (1979c) Rejoinder: Elegant and inelegant RET. In A. Ellis and J.M. Whiteley (eds) *Theoretical and empirical foundations of rational-emotive therapy*. Monterey, Calif.: Brooks/Cole.

Ellis, A. (1979d) The practice of rational-emotive therapy. In A. Ellis and J.M. Whiteley (eds) *Theoretical and empirical foundations of rational-emotive therapy*. Monterey, CA: Brooks/Cole.

Ellis, A. (1979e) A note on the treatment of agoraphobics with cognitive modification versus prolonged exposure in vivo. *Behaviour Research and Therapy, 17*, 162–164.

Ellis, A. (1979f) Discomfort anxiety: A new cognitive behavioral construct. Part 1. *Rational Living, 14(2)*, 3–8.

Ellis, A. (1980a) Rational-emotive therapy and cognitive behaviour therapy: Similarities and differences. *Cognitive Therapy and Research, 4(4)*, 325–340.

Ellis, A. (1980b) Discomfort anxiety: A new cognitive behavioral construct. Part 2. *Rational Living, 15(1)*, 25–30.

Ellis, A. (1981a) The place of Immanuel Kant in cognitive psychotherapy. *Rational Living, 16(2)*, 13–16.

Ellis, A. (1981b) *New developments in rational-emotive therapy*. Address given at the First European Conference on Cognitive Behavioural Therapies, Lisbon, Portugal.

Ellis, A. (1981c) The use of rational humorous songs in psychotherapy. *Voices, 16(4)*, 29–36.

Ellis, A. (1982a) The treatment of alcohol and drug abuse: A rational-emotive approach. *Rational Living, 17(2)*, 15–24.

Ellis, A. (1982b) Intimacy in rational-emotive therapy. In M. Fisher and G. Striker (eds) *Intimacy*. New York: Plenum.

Ellis, A. (1983a) *The case against religiosity*. New York: Institute for Rational-Emotive Therapy.

Ellis, A. (1983b) How to deal with your most difficult client: You. *Journal of Rational-Emotive Therapy, 1(1)*, 3–8.

Ellis, A. (1983c) The philosophic implications and dangers of some popular behavior therapy techniques. In M. Rosenbaum, C.M. Franks and Y. Jaffe (eds) *Perspectives in behavior therapy in the eighties*. New York: Springer.

Ellis, A. (1983d) Rational-emotive therapy (RET) approaches to overcoming resistance 1: Common forms of resistance. *British Journal of Cognitive Psychotherapy, 1(1)*, 28–38.

Ellis, A. (1983e) Failures in rational-emotive therapy. In E.B. Foa and P.M.G. Emmelkamp (eds), *Failures in behavior therapy*. New York: Wiley.

Ellis, A. (1983f) Rational-emotive therapy (RET) approaches to overcoming resistance 2: How RET disputes clients' irrational resistance-creating beliefs. *British Journal of Cognitive Psychotherapy, 1(2)*, 1–16.

Ellis, A. (1984a) Foreword. In W. Dryden, *Rational-emotive therapy: Fundamentals and innovations*. Beckenham, Kent: Croom Helm.

Ellis, A. (1984b) Rational-emotive therapy (RET) approaches to overcoming resistance 3: Using emotive and behavioral techniques of overcoming resistance. *British Journal of Cognitive Psychotherapy, 2(1)*, 11–26.

Ellis, A. (1984c) Rational-emotive therapy. In R.J. Corsini (ed.) *Current psychotherapies*. Itasca, IL: Peacock.

Ellis, A. (1984d) Expanding the ABCs of RET. *Journal of Rational-Emotive Therapy, 2(2)*, 20–24.

Ellis, A. (1985a) *Overcoming resistance*. New York: Springer.

Ellis, A. (1985b) How counselling and psychotherapy can help prevent a nuclear holocaust. Invited address to the American Association for Counseling and Development, 2 April 1985.

Ellis, A. (1985c) Rational-emotive therapy (RET) approaches to overcoming resistance 4: Handling special kinds of clients. *British Journal of Cognitive Psychotherapy, 3(1)*, 26–42.

Ellis, A. and Abrahms, E. (1978) *Brief psychotherapy in medical and health practice*. New York: Springer.

Ellis, A. and Becker, I. (1982) *A guide to personal happiness*. North Hollywood, CA: Wilshire.

Ellis, A. and Harper, R.A. (1975) *A new guide to rational living*. North Hollywood, CA: Wilshire.

Ellis, A. and Knaus, W. (1977) *Overcoming procrastination*. New York: New American Library.

Ellis, A. and Whiteley, J.M. (eds) (1979) *Theoretical and empirical foundations of rational-emotive therapy*. Monterey, CA: Brooks/Cole.

Emmelkamp, P.M.G., Kuipers, A.C.M. and Eggeraat, J.B. (1978). Cognitive modification versus prolonged exposure in vivo: A comparison with agoraphobics as subjects. *Behaviour Research and Therapy, 16*, 33–41.

Eschenroeder, C. (1979). Different therapeutic styles in rational-emotive therapy. *Rational Living, 14(1)*, 3–7.

Garcia, E.J. (1977) Working on the E in RET. In J.L. Wolfe and E. Brand (eds) *Twenty years of rational therapy: Proceedings of the first national conference on rational psychotherapy*. New York: Institute for Rational Emotive Therapy.

Goldfried, M. and Davison, G. (1976) *Clinical behavior therapy*. New York: Holt, Rinehart and Winston.

Grieger, R. and Boyd, J. (1980) *Rational-emotive therapy: A skills-based approach*. New York: Van Nostrand Reinhold.

Hauck, P.A. (1972) *Reason in pastoral counseling*. Philadelphia: Westminster.

Heidegger, M. (1949) *Existence and being*. Chicago: Henry Regnery.

Horney, K. (1950) *Neurosis and human growth*. New York: Norton.

Jones, M.C. (1924) A laboratory study of fear: The case of Peter. *Journal of Genetic Psychology*, *31*, 308–315.

Korzybski, A. (1933) *Science and sanity*. San Francisco: International Society of General Semantics.

Lazarus, A.A. (1981) *The practice of multimodal therapy*. New York: McGraw-Hill.

Maultsby, M.C., Jr and Ellis, A. (1974) *Technique for using rational-emotive imagery*. New York: Institute for Rational-Emotive Therapy.

Moore, R.H. (1983) Inference as 'A' in RET. *British Journal of Cognitive Psychotherapy*, *1(1)*, 17–23.

Popper, K.R. (1959) *The logic of scientific discovery*. New York: Harper and Bros.

Popper, K.R. (1963) *Conjectures and refutations*. New York: Harper and Bros.

Powell, J. (1976) *Fully human, fully alive*. Niles, IL: Argus.

Raitt, A. (1984) Weight control: A rational-emotive approach. *British Journal of Cognitive Psychotherapy*, *2(1)*, 51–60.

Reichenbach, J. (1953) *The rise of scientific philosophy*. Berkeley, CA: University of California Press.

Rogers, C.R. (1961) *On Becoming A Person*. Boston, Houton Mufflin.

Russell, B. (1950) *The conquest of happiness*. New York: New American Library.

Russell, B. (1965) *The basic writings of Bertrand Russell*. New York: Simon and Schuster.

Tillich, P. (1977) *The courage to be*. New York: Fountain.

Watson, J.B, and Rayner, R. (1920). Conditioned emotional reactions. *Journal of Experimental Psychology*, *3*, 1–14.

Wessler, R.A. (1981) So you are angry: Now what's your problem. *Rational Living*, *16(1)*, 29–31.

Wessler, R.A. and Wessler R.L. (1980) *The principles and practice of rational-emotive therapy*. San Francisco, CA: Jossey-Bass.

Wessler, R.L. and Ellis, A. (1980) Supervision in rational-emotive therapy. In A.K. Hess (ed.) *Psychotherapy supervision*. New York: Wiley.

Wessler, R.L. and Ellis, A. (1983) Supervision in counseling: Rational-emotive therapy. *The Counseling Psychologist, 11(1)*, 43–49.

Young, H.S. (1974) *A rational counseling primer*. New York: Institute for Rational-Emotive Therapy.

Young, H.S. (1977) Counseling strategies with working class adolescents. In J.L.

Wolfe and E. Brand (eds) *Twenty years of rational therapy: Proceedings of the first national conference on rational psychotherapy*. New York: Institute for Rational-Emotive Therapy.

Young, H.S. (1984a) Practising RET with lower-class clients. *British Journal of Cognitive Psychotherapy, 2(2)*, 33–59.

Young, H.S. (1984b) Practising RET with bible-belt christians. *British Journal of Cognitive Psychotherapy, 2(2)*, 60–76.

Young, H.S. (1984c). Teaching rational self-value concepts to tough customers. *British Journal of Cognitive Psychotherapy, 2(2)*, 77–97.

# CHAPTER SIX  **Rational Behaviour Therapy**
*Maxie C. Maultsby Jr and Tony A. Gore*

## Introduction

Let us begin with the most important unique feature of RBT. To our knowledge, RBT is the only technique of psychotherapy that bases its therapeutic concepts and techniques on the well established neuro-psychophysiological facts described by Bogen (1969a, 1969b), Gazzaniga (1970), Luria (1966a, 1966b, 1973) and others about the unique specialized functions of the right and left human brains in emotional and behavioural control.

Although the next feature of RBT is not unique, it is relatively rare and highly valuable. RBT has the six main characteristics of all ideal psychotherapies. RBT is: (a) comprehensive, (b) short-term, (c) cross-cultural, (d) drug-free, (e) it produces long-term results, and (f) the behaviour concepts and emotional self-help techniques used in RBT (Maultsby 1984) enable state schools and community groups to offer interested people effective, yet economical, mass mental health improvement programmes.

At this point readers may wonder: 'What is the evidence that RBT actually has the six features of an ideal psychotherapy?'

(a)  RBT is comprehensive because it deals directly with all three groups of human behaviours: the cognitive, emotive and physical.
(b)  RBT is short-term psychotherapy because it routinely teaches patients the research-tested, drug-free, emotional self-help technique called Rational Self-Counselling (Maultsby 1975a). This emphasis on scientific emotional self-help enables people to help themselves at will, between therapy sessions. This greatly speeds up therapeutic progress while making it as comprehensive as possible.
(c)  RBT is a cross-cultural psychotherapy because it is acceptable to and effective for people whose ages, races, cultural values and lifestyles differ widely from those of their psychotherapists (Brandsma, Maultsby and Welsh 1979; Fowler 1980; Maultsby 1975a, 1980; Patton 1976; Ross 1978; Ruhnow 1977; Schwager 1975; Werito 1981). This fact makes RBT ideal for treating both the traditionally 'good' psychotherapy candidates, as well as treating adolescents, the elderly, the poor,

members of racial and ethnic minorities and other traditionally 'poor' psychotherapy candidates.

(d) Medical science has not yet been able to improve on nature at its best. That is why RBT therapists believe that healthy, undrugged brains are the safest and most reliable therapeutic aids. Consequently RBT is drug-free psychotherapy for people with physically healthy brains.

(e) RBT produces long-term results because adequately treated people learn proven, effective emotional self-help skills. Such people are better able than ever before to cope successfully with future problems in daily living (Maultsby 1982).

## History and underpinnings of rational behaviour therapy

*Historical development of RBT*

Rational behaviour therapy is the outgrowth of four major influences in the first author's professional career. After completing his medical education as a physician, he spent fifteen years conducting an in-depth study of the well-established scientific approaches to understanding and helping people help themselves emotionally. That knowledge, combined with the influence of the neuropsychology of Luria (1960, 1966a, 1966b, 1973), the behavioural learning theory of Skinner (Holland and Skinner 1961; Mowrer 1960; Skinner 1957), and the rational-emotive psychotherapy techniques of Ellis (1962) resulted in the first author creating rational behaviour therapy (Maultsby 1984).

Dr Albert Ellis (1962) had, by far, the single most important influence on the first author as he developed RBT as a comprehensive technique of psychotherapy (Maultsby 1977). However, unlike Ellis's technique (Ellis 1977a, 1977b, 1978), RBT leaves philosophical issues to the individual preference of patients. In addition, RBT eschews technical eclecticism in favour of therapeutic techniques derived exclusively from RBT's psychosomatic learning theory of healthy human behaviour (Maultsby 1984).

*Major theoretical concepts*

The ten basic theoretical concepts in RBT theory are listed below:

1. The brain is the main organ of survival, learning and control of both

healthy and unhealthy cognitive, emotive and physical habits.

2. There are no significant differences between the brains of members of different races (Tobias 1970).

3. Effective psychotherapy and counselling will accurately reflect the established facts about human right and left brain neuropsychophysiology as described by: Bogen (1969a, 1969b), Gazzaniga (1970) Luria (1966a, 1966b, 19732) and other modern neuropsychophysiologists.

4. In physically healthy people, words (especially nouns, verbs, and adjectives) are the most common, learned stimuli for the neuropsychological activities that produce and maintain healthy and unhealthy emotional and physical habits (Hudgins 1933; Luria 1960; Mowrer 1966; Pavlov as quoted by Volgyesi 1954, Staats and Staats 1957, 1958; Watzlawick 1978).

5. Human emotions are inner urges (i.e. specific motivations) for actions, caused by learned emotive or visceral responses which are elicted and controlled by semi-permanent neuropsychological units called attitudes and beliefs (Adams and Victor 1977; Grace and Graham 1952; Maultsby 1975a, 1978, 1984).

6. The neuropsychophysiological mechanisms of learning are the same for healthy and unhealthy emotional and physical habits (DiCara 1970; Maultsby 1984; Miller 1969; Olds 1969; Rotter 1954, 1966, 1971).

7. People react to two worlds: the world of objective reality outside their minds and the world of subjective reality, created and recorded by their minds. The world of subjective reality is the only reality people can experience directly. But emotionally healthy living most consistently occurs when a person's world of subjective reality accurately reflects the world of objective reality (Eaton, Peterson and Davis 1976; Maultsby 1984; Watzlawick 1978).

8. Successful psychotherapy without drugs or electric shock is an experience in therapeutic cognitive, and emotive re-education that requires patients to learn the emotionally healthy use of their brains.

9. For patients to achieve permanent psychotherapeutic change, they must have and follow a specific therapeutic treatment plan at least as diligently and for as long as they would if they were trying to learn any complex new skill, for example, speaking a foreign language, driving a car or typing (Maultsby 1984).

10. There are three major groups of human behavioural problems: learned behaviour problems due to unhealthy learning and conditioning of psychoemotional responses; not learned (or organically caused) behavioural problems (Smythies 1966); and psychosomatic problems.

Learned problems respond best to RBT alone; psychosomatic problems respond best to a combination of RBT and medication; not learned problems respond best to medication treatment.

## How client problems are conceptualized

The RBT therapist conceptualizes patients' problems as based on the ABC model of life experience. This model is a theoretical extension of the research-supported original ABC model of human emotions described by Ellis (1962), Grace and Graham (1952), Graham, Stern and Winokur (1958), and Graham, Kabler and Graham (1962).

### THE ABC MODEL OF LIFE EXPERIENCES

A.   Perceptions, or what people notice; plus
B.   People's sincere evaluative thoughts about their perceptions; plus
C-1. People's 'gut' or emotional feelings, triggered and maintained by the evaluative thoughts at B.
C-2. People's physical behaviours, also triggered and maintained by the evaluative thoughts at B.

The ABC model makes this clear. It is a popular overgeneralization to think that external events alone cause either human emotional feelings or physical reactions. The hypothesis of RBT is: people tend to cause their own emotional and physical reactions by the ideas they have come to believe.

At first, many people resist accepting the ABC model of life experiences. It does not seem right to them to think that they cause their own emotions, especially the painful ones that they have always angrily blamed on others or their situation. RBT therapists help patients quickly get past that initial therapeutic resistance by pointing out that all new ideas initially feel wrong when they conflict with old beliefs. For example, most people laughed when the first person said that the world was round, but the only people who laugh at that fact now are naive children and equally uninformed adults.

After reflecting on this, patients almost always begin to make the self-discovery that before they (and all other people) have a new emotional feeling three things happen. First they notice something; they perceive some real event or they imagine or remember one. Second, they have sincere evaluative thoughts about what their perceptions mean to them and about them.

There are only three major types of evaluative thoughts: relatively positive, relatively negative and relatively neutral. That is why the third thing that generally happens when people have a new emotion is that their sincere evaluative thoughts trigger and maintain both the relatively positive, relatively negative or relatively neutral emotional feelings and physical actions people have in response to their perceptions at A.

This psychoemotional hypothesis takes the magical 'IT' (which supposedly upsets people) out of human emotional control. We help patients discover its truth for themselves as follows. We say: 'Imagine that there were three people looking at the same bottle of whisky in a shop window, but that each person had different emotional feelings about it. However, could they each have different emotions, if IT, the bottle of whisky, controlled their emotional feelings? Obviously the bottle could not do anything to anyone but would merely be an object of each person's awareness. Then each person would choose his or her emotional reaction with his or her choice of beliefs about the bottle.

One person could have positive thoughts about how nice a cool cocktail would taste. Another person could have negative thoughts about his last drunken driving conviction. The third person could have neutral thoughts that enabled her quickly to ignore the bottle and admire the sterling silver place setting it occupied.

But what would have happened if each of those people had taken a drink of coffee while it was still too hot to drink? Each person's mouth would have felt the same type of physical pain. That is because physical feelings do not work like emotional feelings. IT, a stimulus in the outside world (e.g. hot coffee), can and will cause physical feelings. But only the person who feels emotional feelings can cause them.

After learning their emotional ABCs, people most often ask: 'Isn't there more to my emotions than ABC? Are human emotions really that simple?' The hypothesis of RBT is: yes, before people's emotional reactions become habitual, they are just that simple. But after people with normally functioning brains think the same sincere evaluative thoughts at B, about the same perceptions at A, and get the same emotive and behavioural Cs enough times, the following extremely important thing happens. Their left brains convert those repeatedly paired perceptions and sincere thoughts into semipermanent, personally meaningful, conscious, appreciative units, or mental programmes, called *beliefs* (Maultsby 1975a pp. 34–40).

*From ABC to a–BC: belief-controlled reactions*

| | | |
|---|---|---|
| A  Perceptions | after enough repeated pairings | No external perceptions at A |
| B  Evaluative thoughts | | a–B Only beliefs (that is, habitual evaluative thoughts) |
| C  Emotive and physical reactions | | C  Emotive and physical reactions |

In RBT, the a-B apperceptive unit represents a belief. The capital B in the a-B unit indicates that spoken or conscious self-talk is the controlling cue in the apperceptive unit. Neuropsychologically, the words at B (in the a-B apperceptive unit) trigger in right brains holistic mental images of old, real, as well as imagined A-events. Therefore, the a-B apperceptive unit triggers the same habitual emotional and physical reactions at C as the real As and Bs triggered in the original ABC pairing.

After people form beliefs, their left brains no longer need to process old A-stimuli as single mental events. At this point, their left brain's words elicit internally stored a-B apperceptive units, which then trigger right brain controlled habitual emotional and physical reactions at C. Every repetition of that a-BC sequence is an instance of practising those habitual C-reactions.

**The role of beliefs in self-control**   RBT maintains that beliefs free people from subhuman, animal-like dependence on the external world for appropriate emotional, physical and behavioural cues.

Neuropsychophysiologically, imagination is all that healthy brains need to trigger the appropriate mental images necessary for both physical and emotional learning. Those same mental mechanisms enable people to practise daily – purposefully or unwittingly – all their emotional habits. Unfortunately, though, people rarely see their daily emotional reactions as emotional practice. Why? Simply because most people don't use the word 'practice' when they think about their emotions. Yet, whether or not people realize it or admit it, every time they repeat any specific emotional reaction in specific situations, they are practising having that emotion in those situations.

In RBT, the A-b perception represents attitude. The small 'b' in the A-b units indicates that attitudes are wordless, and therefore unspoken, 'superconscious'[1] forms of belief. Beliefs are the spoken or conscious form of attitudes. That important clinical insight enables an individual to help patients take the magical ITs out of their emotional understanding.

Neuropsychologically, attitudes index or code every habitual thought, cognitive map and mental image of the objects, events and actions we perceive. That is why after people form attitudes, their right brains no longer perceive old external stimuli at A as single mental events. Instead, right brains then perceive those old 'A' stimuli as conditioned cues, coded with A-b attitudes that trigger holistic brain programmes for habitual emotional and physical reactions at 'C'. Therefore, with minimal or no conscious thought, people can react with instant, seemingly involuntary but correct emotional and physical reactions to their old attitude-coded perceptions of old external activating events.

Those instant, involuntary, yet correct reactions indicate that patients have reached the advanced stage of habit learning called 'emotional insight'. Emotional insight indicates that these specific A-perceptions and B-thoughts have been paired enough times with the same emotive response for the right brain to have taken that emotive response and used it as an 'emotive rope' to tie those separate ABC components into a behavioural gestalt. During practice (stage two of habit learning), the left brain used those separate As and Bs to direct and control the early learning process. But the right brain's behavioural gestalts indicate that behavioural habits have formed. People commonly describe that new behavioural state with ideas like: 'Now I've got the feel of it; now I see it; now I feel I know how to do it.' The 'emotive ropes' or 'emotive bindings' (commonly described as 'feeling right') that hold behavioural gestalts together are probably the main bases of prosody and dysprosody. Prosody and dysprosody are the nonverbal affective components of vocal and so-called body language. Monrad-Krohn (1947) and Ross and Mesulam (1979) discuss in instructive detail the essential role prosody plays in effective interpersonal communication and the severe emotional problems dysprosody causes. We mention those concepts merely as examples of the essential contribution that the silent right brain makes to effective linguistic communication.

An important therapeutic insight is that people's wordless, 'superconscious' attitudes create the impression that magical, external HEs, SHEs, ITs and THEYs are in control of their emotions. Fortunately, though, these impressions are, in many cases, illusions. Otherwise, psychotherapy would be a waste of time and money.

Another way the patient's problems are conceptualized in RBT is in terms of how 'rational' or 'irrational' the beliefs and attitudes associated with the problem seem to be. We teach the patient how to make this decision about 'rationality' versus 'irrationality' on the basis of whether or not the thought, emotional feeling or physical behaviour of concern is based on three or more of the five rules for 'rational' behaviour, as it is used in rational behaviour therapy.

Before we describe those rules, however, we will first discuss what the word 'rational', as used in RBT, does NOT mean. It does not mean what most people mean when they use the word.

Most people (including most traditional psychotherapists) use the word 'rational' to describe their carefully thought-out, logically coherent ideas and actions, and use the word 'irrational' to describe the illogical, unreasonable or contrary ideas and actions of other people. There is also a universal tendency to consider one's own ideas and actions as more rational, or more frequently rational, than other people's.

When you tell people that their ideas or actions are irrational (or they tell you that yours are), are you and they usually in agreement or disagreement? Most probably you and they are in disagreement almost every time that happens. That fact applies to most other people who have healthy, undrugged brains.

People with healthy, undrugged brains rarely feel that their most sincere, deeply held beliefs are wrong or irrational. So, if people's pretherapy beliefs and disbeliefs were all they needed to solve their emotional problems, they wouldn't need psychotherapy. RBT holds that to be healthy and therapeutic, therefore, the meaning of 'rational' has to go beyond personal beliefs and disbeliefs and refer to an optimal level of mental health. This explains why, when RBT therapists use the word 'rational', they mean cognitive, emotive and physical behaviours that simultaneously obey at least three of:

### The five rules for optimal mental health

1. Healthy behaviour is based on obvious fact.
2. Healthy behaviour best helps you protect your life and health.
3. Healthy behaviour best helps you achieve your short-term and long-term goals.
4. Healthy behaviour best helps you avoid your most undesirable conflicts with other people.
5. Healthy behaviour best helps you feel the emotions you want to feel, without alcohol or other drugs.

Now change the word 'healthy' to 'rational' in those rules, and you will have the five rules used in RBT to describe 'rational' thoughts, beliefs, attitudes, emotional feelings and physical actions.

Remember though, it is not enough for cognitive, emotive and physical behaviours to obey one or two of those rules. To be 'rational', behaviours must obey at least three of the five rules at the same time.

The five rules for 'rational' behaviour make it easy to recognize 'irrational' behaviours. In RBT, 'irrational' behaviours mean cognitive, emotive and physical behaviours that simultaneously disobey three or more of these five rules.

You may wonder: 'What about a behaviour that obeys one or two of the rational rules, disobeys one or two and is irrelevant to the others?' The behaviour cannot be 'rational' in the RBT meaning of the word; at best, it will be 'nonrational'. But 'nonrational' behaviour is not good enough to produce optimal mental health, so RBT therapists reject it as readily as they reject clearly 'irrational' behaviour.

## Practical applications

### The therapeutic relationship

Our research on the therapeutic relationship in RBT (Maultsby 1975b) indicated an interesting fact.[2] There is good reason to doubt that there is an objective thing in RBT that can be reliably recognized as a specific 'therapeutic relationship'. Instead, it seems more logical to talk about therapeutic interactions; that means interactions between therapists and patients that help patients to help themselves.

That research finding led us to conclude that consistent therapeutic interactions in RBT have three essential features: (a) efficient teaching of effective self-help concepts and techniques to patients; (b) a friendly competent therapist; and (c) a co-operative patient. For a detailed discussion of this topic, see chapter 9 in *Rational Behavior Therapy* (Maultsby 1984).

### Strategies of treatment

Some therapists or counsellors might ask: 'But if attitudes are wordless and "superconscious", how can you get people to change them?'

The answer is: 'Easily! Just show them how to convert their wordless attitudes back to their belief forms.' Here's how: first, point out that attitudes and beliefs are simply different forms of the results of the same A-perceptions and B-thoughts, having been processed differently by the right and left brains. Once people understand this, they usually have no trouble seeing that beliefs are simply the word forms of attitudes, and that attitudes are simply the wordless forms of beliefs. Long before their therapy, most patients have learned that their attitudes and beliefs are intimately related. So they are already well prepared for the next step in converting an attitude to its spoken belief form.

Second, tell patients to ask themselves and then honestly answer this question: 'By reacting as I did, what ideas did I imply that I sincerely believed?'

Third, give patients a common yet instructive example of their attitudes in action. A good example is: suppose you were driving a car and a child suddenly ran across the road in front of you. You would immediately slam on the brakes and feel afraid, all without taking time to think anything first. By reacting that way, you would have behaved as if you had sincerely thought: 'I'm about to have a terrible accident; I'd better stop immediately.' Well, those ideas would have been your attitudes. They are the appropriate ideas that would have come in to your head if you had had the time to think anything before you slammed on the brakes; so that these ideas express the wordless or unspoken forms of your safe-driving beliefs.

Your wordless or unspoken beliefs exist in your 'superconscious' mind as attitudes. 'Superconscious' attitudes enable a person to react to external situations instantly and seemingly involuntarily, but with appropriate, learned reactions (such as fearful auto-braking) without the person needing to think conscious thoughts about the situation beforehand.

Now suppose that while driving, you see two children running down the pavement parallel to the street. You would probably maintain your speed and continue to feel calm about doing it. Again, you would react without consciously thinking anything. Why? Because your controlling attitudes then would be the unspoken mental equivalent of beliefs such as, 'There is no danger, I have no reason to slow down or feel afraid.' Those personal examples show you clearly the essential role that attitudes play in rapid, logical, appropriate emotional and physical reactions.

**The normal therapeutic sequence in RBT**   First do the intake. We almost always complete the intake in an hour. On rare occasions, however, unusually distressed patients with unusually complicated problems will require as many as three hours of intake ventilating before they are ready to get involved in therapy. Here's the two-part rule: when we have heard all we want to hear about a new patient's problem AND the patient seems ready to start looking for therapeutic solutions, that ends the intake. Then formal RBT immediately begins.

Normally, the first step in formal RBT is introducing patients to their emotional ABCs. If you are also using the recommended 'rational bibliotherapy',[3] you would assign your patients chapter 1 in *You and Your Emotions* (Maultsby and Hendricks 1974); or for alcoholics or other drug abusers, you would assign Booklet One in the rational bibliotherapeutic series, *Freedom from Alcohol and Tranquilizers* (Maultsby 1979). Depending on how co-operative your patients are, you might spend one to two sessions on the emotional ABCs.

Next you would cover the five rules for optimal emotional health – i.e. the five rules for rational behaviour. The bibliotherapy assignments would then be chapter 2 in *You and Your Emotions* or Booklet Two in the bibliotherapeutic series for alcoholics and other drug abusers.

Again, depending on your patients' co-operativeness, you might spend one, two or maybe even three sessions on getting them used to thinking of and applying the 'five rational rules' to their problem-related thinking and behaviour.

Next, you would explain to your patients 'cognitive-emotive dissonance.'[4] Then you would introduce your patients to the idea of doing regular, written rational self-analysis (RSA) (chapter 3 in *You and Your Emotions*, and Booklet Three in the bibliotherapeutic series for alcoholics and other drug abusers). For the 80 per cent of patients who will bring at least one written RSA per week to therapy, you would structure the therapy sessions around discussing those RSAs.[5].

After your patients discuss with you a well-done RSA, they are then ready to start doing daily rational-emotive imagery, or REI (chapter 4 in *You and Your Emotions* and Booklet Four in the bibliotherapeutic series for alcoholics and other drugs abusers).

After patients begin doing REIs, they are still given weekly bibliotherapy assignments until they complete the six chapters in *You and Your Emotions* or the five booklets in the bibliotherapeutic series for alcoholics and other drug abusers. Then, only if patients request further reading materials (about 25 per cent do), we refer them to one of the more advanced self-help books: *Help Yourself to Happiness* (Maultsby 1975a), *Your Guide to Emotional Well Being* (Maultsby 1980), or *A Million Dollars for Your Hangover* (Maultsby 1978).

*Major treatment techniques*

Major treatment techniques included in RBT include rational self-analysis (RSA) and rational-emotive imagery (REI). As stated in the section on the normal sequence of RTB, a patient is first taught the ABCs of life experience and the five rules for rational thinking. Once that is accomplished, the patient can perform rational self-analysis and rational-emotive imagery. Below is further explanation of RSA and REI.

**Written rational self-analysis (RSA)**   Written rational self-analysis is the first major therapeutic technique in RBT. A written RSA between therapy sessions is a structured way for patients to discover the cause–effect relationships between the cognitive, emotive and physical components of their personal problems, and also the rational changes they must, and can, make at will to start helping themselves to happiness immediately.

For the best results with written RSAs have your patients use the standard RSA format and their own everyday language. They should write down their experiences as soon as possible after they occur; that way they will get the fastest, most lasting results possible. Emphasize that people are never too upset to do an RSA, and that actually an RSA is faster and safer than minor tranquillizers for calming people down.

*The standard RSA format*

A.   ACTIVATING EVENT: What you perceive happened.

Da.   CAMERA CHECK: If you perceived anything a video camera would not show, correct that to what a video camera would have shown.

B.   YOUR BELIEFS: Your sincere thoughts about A, plus your attitudes about each B sentence.

Db.   RATIONAL DEBATE OF B: Answer 'yes' or 'no' for each 'rational question' about each B sentence. Then write rational alternative self-talk for each irrational B idea. For ideas that prove to be rational write: 'That's rational' in the Db section for that idea.

B-1                               Db-1
B-2                               Db-2
C.  CONSEQUENCES OF B:      E.  EXPECTED NEW
                                    BEHAVIOURS
   1. Emotional feelings        1. New emotional feelings
   2. Actions                   2. New actions

The correct RSA sequence is as follows:

FIRST STEP: Have patients describe A, the activating event, on the left side of an imaginary line down the centre of their paper. In their usual language, patients are simply to state the facts as they saw and experienced them. For example: 'For a month now, I have had three letters of recommendation hanging over my head and it is driving me crazy.' That was the A section of a real RSA, done by Dr F., an English professor whose RSA will be used in this chapter as a teaching example.

SECOND STEP: Immediately under their A section, patients are to write B, their beliefs. As best they remember, they are to state word for word their sincere thoughts, self-talk, or inner speech about the A event.

Have patients number each B section idea. Then they are to show whether they had a positive, negative or neutral attitude about each idea by writing '(positive or good)', '(negative or bad)', or '(neutral)' in parentheses following each idea. Dr F.'s first two B section ideas were: B-1: 'What can I say?' (negative); and B-2: 'Why should I have to write letters I do not want to write?' (negative).

Both of those B items were unanswered questions. In the B section, patients are to label all unanswered questions as 'rhetorical questions'. Next, patients are to state the personal beliefs that are hidden in those questions; then, in the Db section, patients are to debate rationally each of those stated beliefs.

Normally, it takes about six times as much space to correct irrational thinking as it does to write it. So advise patients to leave six times as many blank lines under each B section idea as it took to write it. That way, they will probably have enough space on the opposite side of the page to debate that idea rationally in the Db section. Of course, patients can always use the back of the page if they need more space for their rational debate.

After patients complete their B section, they are to count up their positives, negatives, and neutrals. Their totals will show them the main types of attitudes that helped trigger their emotional feelings and the other reactions they put in their C section about A, the activating event. This manoeuvre makes clear how and why patients' 'superconscious', wordless attitudes can be more important than their conscious, verbal thoughts in some of their reactions.

THIRD STEP: In the C section, have your patients write the behavioural consequences of their B ideas. The C section has two parts: emotional feelings and actions. In the appropriate section, patients are to state simply how they felt emotionally and what they did physically. In Dr F.'s RSA (given later in this chapter) the C section lists these consequences: *Emotional feelings*: anger, anxiety, and shame. *Action*: procrastination.

FOURTH STEP: Immediately under the C section, have patients write the 'five rational questions'. In reality, questions are neither rational nor irrational. The label 'the five rational questions' is just a shorthand way of saying, 'the five questions that help ensure that your cognitions, emotional feelings, and physical actions will be rational'.

## The five rational questions

1. Is my thinking here based on obvious fact?
2. Will my thinking here help me protect my life and health?
3. Will my thinking here best help me achieve my short-term and long-term goals?
4. Will my thinking here best help me avoid my most unwanted conflicts with others?
5. Will my thinking here best help me habitually feel the emotions I want to feel?

FIFTH STEP: Opposite the C section, have your patients write the E section; it contains the new emotional feelings and actions they want to have in similar future A-type events.

Advise patients not to put wishes of the 'Oh, if I only had . . .' type in their E section. The E section is for wants that they have already decided to make their habits. So they are to list only emotions and actions for which they can honestly say: 'The next time I shall . . .' Remind patients that the E section describes only their own choices of new emotional and physical actions for similar future A events. They are to ignore completely behaviours that others (including their therapist) may want them to learn, but which they are not yet convinced are right for them.

Initially, in RSAs of negative emotions, the most rational new emotional goal will be to feel less negative or more calm in similar future A events. 'But what', you may wonder, 'if patients want to enjoy an event they now hate or fear?' That is okay; they have that emotional choice, too. But the most rational emotional goals will usually be those that patients are most likely to achieve most quickly. This brings us to an important insight: to replace a strong, negative emotion with a positive emotion, people must first pass through the calm or neutral emotional state first. That is why it is important to remember that calm or neutral emotions are real emotions too, and that the opposite of negative emotions are not necessarily positive emotions but can also be neutral emotions.

If, for example, patients want to stop having pre-exam anxiety, they must first get rid of the fearful attitudes that maintain their anxious responses. If they at once require themselves to love taking exams, they will probably fail, for they will be demanding too much immediate emotional change; and permanent new emotional learning does not occur in such an extreme, dramatic way. That is why their most rational first emotional goal would probably be to fear taking exams less and less until they can take them calmly. That's enough for most people. But after that, if patients still want to, they can learn to love taking exams.

Common examples of hated behaviours patients often want to learn to like doing are studying; doing certain types of work; having sex or certain types of sex; writing; speaking in public; refusing to overeat, drink too much, or smoke anymore. Usually though, your patients will not want to like the things they hate or are depressed about. They will just want calmly to forget them.

Sometimes your patients will not be sure what emotions or actions they want to have in future A events. Tell those patients to leave the E section blank; but they are to make sure they put their most sincerely rational thoughts in their Db section. Their sincere rational thoughts will often point them directly to the most rational emotional and behavioural goals to adopt. When they discover these goals, they are to write them in their E sections.

Remind your patients that rational E sections will be logically related to their rationally chosen Db section ideas. So it will be a waste of time to write 'to feel calm' at E if they have Db ideas like, 'It really is awful. No one in their right mind would stand for it. I will just die if it happens again.'

At this point patients often ask: 'Isn't it unhealthy for people to stop having emotions?' Yes; to stop having emotions completely would be most unhealthy. Fortunately, though, doing RSAs cannot stop people from having emotions completely. The minds of physically healthy people force their brains to trigger and maintain some type of emotional state every second they are awake. So if people are conscious and have healthy, undrugged brains, they will always have some type of emotion. It may not be the emotion they want; it may even be the one they hate the most; but they will definitely have some emotion.

There are only two things that RSAs do: first, without alcohol or other drugs, RSAs help people have fewer undesirable emotions and physical reactions; and second, RSAs help people have more desirable emotions and physical reactions, also without alcohol or other drugs. So, correct meaningless E section statements such as: 'I want to have no feelings at all.' No one can achieve that emotional goal and remain healthy and awake.

SIXTH STEP: The sixth step in doing an RSA is Da, the camera check of A. Patients are to ask themselves: 'Would a video camera have recorded the A events as I described them?' If their answer is 'yes' for each A section sentence, patients are to write 'factual' or 'all facts' in the Da section and go on to the Db section. But if patients have 'no' answers, that means they have mistaken one or more personal opinions for a statement of fact. In the Da section, patients are to correct any such statements to reflect what a video camera would have recorded. For example, you would correct, 'I cried my heart out all the way home,' to 'I cried intensely until I got home, but my heart did not leave my body, not even for a second.'

Do camera images always accurately describe facts? No, for just like the human brain, cameras can misrepresent obvious facts. But the value of the camera check is *not* based on what a video camera might have recorded, but on what a video camera could *not* have recorded. For example, take the self-perception 'I cried my heart out.' No video camera could have recorded a person's heart leaving, or being out of, his or her body. So that A section statement could not pass the camera check of A, as it would not fit the obvious facts of the person's situation. But to have the most emotionally healthy self-control, people's perceptions must accurately fit the obvious facts of their situations.

Sometimes patients are concerned about how to write the A section of an RSA for an emotional feeling that is not in response to some specific external event. They point out that one cannot do a camera check of an emotional feeling. But emotional feelings are neuropsychophysiological facts; patients either have them, and describe them accurately, or they do not. So they can put simple statements of emotional facts, such as 'I was sad' or 'I felt depressed' in the A section though they would still write 'sad' or 'depressed' in the emotion part of their C section). Then, in their Da section, they would simply write 'factual' for their camera check of an A section about feelings.

Remember, though, that in RBT, feelings are almost always one-word nouns. If at A patients say, 'I just died from embarrassment,' in the Da section they would correct that to: 'I did not die, but I did feel more embarrassed than I wanted to feel.' Then in their C section they would also write 'embarrassed'.

SEVENTH STEP: The seventh step in doing an RSA is Db, the rational check and debate of each B section idea using the 'five rational questions'. Then, as needed, patients are to replace irrational B ideas with rational ideas in the Db section.

First, patients are to read over their B-1 idea; next, see if they can give three or more honest 'yes' answers to the 'five rational questions' about it: if they can, they write 'That's rational' at Db-1 and go on to B-2. But if they cannot give at least three honest 'yes' answers to the 'five rational questions', patients write 'That idea is irrational' at Db-1. Then they think of different ideas about their situation that have these two features:

(a) The patient can give at least three honest 'yes' answers to the 'five rational questions' about the new ideas.
(b) The patient is willing to make the new ideas into personal beliefs by acting them out in future A situations.

Then, patients are to write those ideas in their Db section. However, remind your patients that it does not matter how rational an idea may be in itself; if they are not willing to make that idea their personal belief by habitually acting it out, it will not help them.


**Rational-emotive imagery (REI)** Rational-emotive imagery (REI) is the second therapeutic technique in RBT. It is the rational technique for healthy emotional practice. Its basis is the neuropsychological fact that imagining (i.e. mentally practising emotional or physical reactions) produces the same quality of rapid learning as real life experience produces (Beritoff 1965; Eccles 1958; Luria 1966a, 1966b, 1973; Maultsby 1984; Mowrer 1966; Razran 1961). Consequently, every time people mentally picture themselves thinking, emotionally feeling, and physically acting the way they want to, they are using REI, the most efficient form of emotional practice. REI is also helpful for enhancing physical practice. When patients practise REI daily, they teach themselves new emotional habits in the safest and fastest way possible. See Table 6.1 for the standard instructions for REI.

**Table 6.1**  Standardized instructions for REI

1. Read the Da, Db, and E section of a well-done RSA.
2. Get relaxed using the instant better feeling manoeuvre (IBFM) (Maultsby 1984).
3. When you are noticeably relaxed, mentally picture yourself as vividly as possible back in the Da situation described in you RSA.
4. As you vividly picture yourself back in the Da situation, thinking your rational Db thoughts, imagine yourself having your E section emotional feelings and physical behaviour. Make the experience as vivid and realistic as possible.
5. Maintain that image and rethink your rational Db thoughts. If B section thoughts pop into your mind, calmly challenge them with your Db thoughts, and calmly ignore all non-RSA thoughts.
6. Repeat step 5 over and over for ten minutes. If you have two RSAs to practise, spend five minutes on each. But do not do REI on more than two RSAs during one ten-minute REI session.

Tell your patients not to expect an emotional miracle after just two or three REI sessions. It takes both time and repeated practice to extinguish and autocondition new emotional habits. Patients should be advised to practise REI daily using the same RSA until they start experiencing the type of C section responses they want to have in everyday life. A suggested daily REI routine is outlined in Table 6.2.

**Table 6.2**  Daily REI routine

1. Advise your patients to put themselves to sleep every night with REI. It is cheaper, safer and quicker than most sleeping pills.
2. Ten minutes before patients get out of bed each morning is the next time for REI. It will help them start their day with the pleasantly powerful emotional feelings associated with confidence of success.
3. Ten minutes before lunch, or instead of their cigarette break and/or tea or coffee break, patients are to do REI again. Then they will be fighting irrational emotions, lung cancer, heart disease, and bad breath all at the same time!
4. Especially before their first afternoon cocktail, have your patients do ten minutes of REI. If they do, they will be most likely to stop after only two cocktails, then remember eating and enjoying their evening meal.

In addition to the REI routine in Table 6.2 patients can also do REI with their eyes open: while driving or riding to work, waiting in queues, waiting in traffic jams, or waiting for someone who is late. At those times REI helps keep blood pressure down and prevent other stress-related difficulties such as tension headaches. Having a daily REI schedule enables patients to autocondition their new, healthier cognitions (which are essential for their new, healthier behaviours) in the shortest time possible. In addition, daily REIs reinforce patients' other self-help efforts and increase their commitment to therapeutic change.

## *Overcoming obstacles to client progress*

One way of overcoming the obstacles to a client's progress is to follow the normal therapeutic sequence in RBT, as outlined in the strategies of treatment section.

Another method used is 'rational bibliotherapy'. Rational bibliotherapy means systematic reading of easy-to-understand self-help reading materials that are based on RBT theory. This is a simple yet highly effective way to overcome therapeutic resistance and get patients quickly involved in therapeutic emotional self-help. But as with any self-help manoeuvre, the therapeutic results vary directly with the amount of structured, goal-orientated instructions patient receive. In our experience, the most effective instructions for bibliotherapy include daily reading goals.

Immediately after the intake evaluation, we tell patients to read chapter 1 in *You and Your Emotions* (Maultsby and Hendricks 1974) once a day, every day until the next appointment. Even if patients read slowly, they can probably read the chapter in twenty minutes. We emphasize that if patients are not willing to invest twenty minutes a day in solving their problems, they are dooming themselves to slow therapeutic progress, but we also point out that patients have the right to progress as rapidly or slowly as they choose.

The reading on the first day is merely to give patients a clear understanding of the material. The second day's reading is to help patients discover ideas with which they disagree. We ask patients to write those ideas down and bring them to the next session for discussion. At first, most patients tend to disagree with almost anything that will require them to change their habitual behaviour; thus, showing immediate interest in patients' possible disagreements is an important treatment strategy. It quickly gets those potential therapeutic barriers out in the open where they can be speedily eliminated.

The third day's reading is for patients to find and briefly write down the ideas with which they agree and why they agree with them. Having patients record these ideas aids therapeutic progress in two ways. First, it increases the probability that patients will put those ideas into daily use, and second, it increases the probability that patients will avoid the antitherapeutic game of 'fool-the-therapist'.

For the fourth day's reading, we tell patients to look for and write notes about events described in the book which they have seen in the daily lives of others. This exercise helps patients quickly get over the self-defeating idea that their lives are uniquely complicated or difficult.

For the fifth day's reading, we have patients look for examples of events in their daily lives in which they applied the insights gained from their bibliotherapeutic reading and the results they achieved. The standard RBT bibliotherapeutic reading *You and Your Emotions* (Maultsby and Hendricks 1974), describes *only* basic principles of normal human behaviour. Therefore, once people start thinking about them, they readily see those basic principles in action in their own and in the daily lives of other people.

Since repetition is usually the royal road to the most rapid learning, for the seventh day's reading we ask patients to review their notes as preparation for discussing them in their next therapy session.

After these instructions, 80 to 90 per cent of our patients will return to therapy having read their assignment at least once; of those, 40 to 60 per cent will have read it twice; between 10 and 30 per cent will have read the assignment three to five times; and about 0.1 per cent will have read it six or more times. Many of these latter patients will have moderate to severe problems with obsessive-compulsive behaviour. They are usually the most worrisome and difficult patients to treat, but calm persistence usually yields good therapeutic results.[6]

No, rational bibliotherapy is *not* essential for successful RBT; neither are rational self-analysis (RSA) and rational-emotive imagery. But these techniques make RBT ideally effective and most enjoyable for both therapists and patients. Still, if psychotherapists merely discuss their patients' problems, using the emotional ABCs and the five rules for rational behaviour, their patients will still make appropriate therapeutic progress. On the average, however, therapeutic progress will be slower than it would have been, had patients used these techniques. Still 10 to 20 per cent of our patients seem to prefer to let us do all the work.

## Case example

A case is treated according to the normal sequence of rational behaviour therapy outlined earlier. The intake would be obtained as outlined and the patient would be given the recommended rational bibliotherapy. The patient would be taught the emotional ABCs and the five rules for rational thinking. The concept of cognitive-emotive dissonance would be explained to the patient as appropriate. After the intake and up to the rational self-analysis phase, therapy is primarily a directive educational process with the therapist serving as the educator. It is only when you get to the RSA phase that the patient is doing most of the work.

You will find in this example a patient who has already learned her ABCs and the five rules for rational thinking, and is currently doing an RSA, which represents the backbone of the work done by patients in a RBT session.

One of the features of RBT is that when you learn how to apply the concepts to one problem you can easily apply it to another, as this case will demonstrate.

Dr F., a widowed English professor, and her teenage daughter had received RBT to learn how to interact more rationally with each other. About a year after therapy Dr F. decided to use her skill in doing RSAs to solve her problem with procrastination. When Dr F. later described her success, we asked her to let us present her RSA here as a teaching example. Let's now examine each section of her complete RSA. It demonstrates well how and why getting patients to learn to do rational self-analysis helps make RBT a comprehensive, short-term psychotherapy that produces long-term results.

### Dr F.'s RSA

A. ACTIVATING EVENT

For a month now, I have had three letters of recommendation hanging over my head and it's driving me crazy.

Da. THE CAMERA CHECK OF A

Nothing is hanging over my head and I am the only IT that can drive me crazy. But since I don't like the idea of being crazy, I refuse to drive myself there. A month ago, I promised three students I would write letters of recommendation for them. But instead of writing the letters, I'm making myself miserable while I put off doing it.

B.    BELIEFS

Db.    RATIONAL DEBATE OF B

B-1   What can I say? (negative) That's a rhetorical question hiding the belief that I don't know what to say.

Db-1 My belief gets a 'No' for RQs ('rational questions') 1, 3, 4, and 5. Rational thinking is: I can say anything I want to say. I don't have to be effusive or dishonest. I can simply say I believe the students have whatever potential I believe they have to do graduate work in English. Then I can describe what they have done in my classes.

B-2   Why should I have to write letters when I don't want to? (negative) That's another rhetorical question hiding the belief that it's unfair that they should expect me to write letters I don't want to write.

Db-2 The belief gets 'no' for RQs, 1, 3, 4 and 5. Rational thinking is: Writing letters of recommendation is part of my job. Therefore, I am obliged to write letters for students if they request them. Three letters is a reasonable number. So to say that I shouldn't be expected to write them is absurd. And it's even more absurd for me to feel angry about it. I'm just trying to justify avoiding my responsibilities. I agreed to work for the university; writing these letters is a part of my job. So I calmly choose to write them.

B-3   I hardly know these students. (negative)

Db-3 That idea gets 'no' for RQs 1, 3, 4 and 5. Rational thinking is: If I want to know these students better than I do, I can easily schedule conferences with them and get better acquainted.

B-4   I'll be forced to say things about these students that I

Db-4 My thinking here gets 'no' for RQs 1, 3, 4 and 5. Rational

don't believe. (negative)

thinking is: I won't be forced to say anything I don't believe. I alone will write the letters. I alone will decide what I say in them and I alone will mail them. My belief just doesn't make rational sense, so I'll give it up and write the letters.

B-5 I don't want to write letters when I don't know the facts. (negative)

Db-5 That idea gets 'no' for RQs 3, 4, and 5. My thought is a fact, but it's irrelevant. If I want more facts than I already have about my students, all I have to do is study their files.

B-6 I don't like being forced to do anything I don't want to do. (negative)

Db-6 That idea gets 'no' for RQs 3, 4 and 5. My thought is a fact, but it's irrelevant to this situation. No one is going to overpower me and force me to write the letters. So I don't and won't have to write them. But because it is part of my job and I choose to do my job well, I will write them.

B-7 I know I shouldn't be procrastinating like this. (negative)

Db-7 That idea gets 'no' for RQs 1, 3, and 5. I should be procrastinating, exactly as I am doing.[7] But since I don't like this experience, I'll change it immediately.

C. CONSEQUENCES OF B
  1. Emotional feelings
     (a) Anger.
     (b) Anxiety.
     (c) Shame.
  2. Actions
     (a) Procrastination.

E. EXPECTED NEW BEHAVIOURS
  1. New emotional feelings
     (a) Calm, if not positive feelings.
  2. New actions
     (a) Immediately write these and future letters of recommendation.

Well done RSAs immediately decrease negative emotions and immediately reinforce rational, positive emotions. Whether patients analyze positive or negative emotions, therefore, well done RSAs cause them to feel better immediately. What if patients don't get that immediate (not necessarily pleasant but) better feeling? Advise them beforehand that in such cases it's best to check their RSA immediately for (a) accuracy of their camera check of A, and (b) sincerity of Db–rational debates of their B section beliefs. If no improvements in the RSA seem indicated, that RSA is to be a priority discussion topic in the next RBT session.

Why have patients analyze their positive emotions? Analyzing their positive emotions helps patients become aware of their essential contribution to their happiness. That awareness makes patients more appropriately dependent on themselves and less irrationally dependent upon their therapists or on other people or on 'fate' for their happiness. But as we encourage patients to do an RSA on every troublesome negative emotion, we suggest RSAs on positive emotions *only* occasionally, for instance when patients seem to be inappropriately ignoring their own contributions to their happiness, and/or when patients seem to be inappropriately exaggerating the perceived contribution of others or of fate.

Dr F.'s well done RSA is typical of the type of RSAs co-operative patients start doing after eight to ten RBT sessions. Skill in doing RSAs makes patients rapidly and happily self-confident in the healthiest sense. That's why therapy terminations in RBT are usually both smooth and mutually pleasant.

## Notes

1 'Superconscious' refers to psychological phenomena which can be operative with minimal or no conscious thought.
2 Upon request, the first author will send to interested therapists and counsellors a report of that clinical study.
3 Bibliotherapy is a therapeutic aid; it's not essential.
4 'Cognitive-emotive dissonance' is the unavoidable state in therapeutic change where ill-prepared patients (regardless of the therapeutic technique being used) are most likely to want to give up their therapeutic efforts. However, adequate rational patient preparation enables patients to move rapidly through this state to the advanced therapeutic change called emotional insight. (See chapter 13 in *Rational Behavior Therapy* (Maultsby 1984).)
5 Up to 20 per cent of your educated patients will not diligently do either bibliotherapy or written rational self-analysis; but they will still benefit from RBT if they

keep regular appointments and if you discuss their problems using the ABC format and the five rules for rational thinking. In our opinion, these patients learn most comfortably from vocal as opposed to written communications. They especially like and benefit from listening to recordings of their RBT sessions.

6 Upon request, the first author will send to interested therapists and counsellors a copy of our printed reading instructions, which is free to be reproduced at will for their patients' use.

7 'Should' here refers to the 'should of existence': 'If I am procrastinating, I should be procrastinating' (see section 2 of chapter 14 in *Rational Behavior Therapy* (Maultsby 1984) for a more detailed explanation of this concept).

# References

Adams, R.D. and Victor, M. (1977) *Principles of neurology*. New York: McGraw-Hill.

Beritoff, J.S. (1965) *Neural mechanisms of higher vertebrate behavior*, trans. W.T. Liberson. Boston: Little, Brown.

Bogen, J.F. (1969a) The other side of the brain, 1: Dysgraphia and dyscopia following cerebral commissurotomy. *Bulletin of the Los Angeles Neurological Society, 34(2)*, 73–105.

Bogen, J.F. (1969b) The other side of the brain, 2: An appositional mind. *Bulletin of the Los Angeles Neurological Society, 34(3)*, 135–162.

Brandsma, J.M., Maultsby, M.C. and Welsh, R. (1979) *Outpatient treatment of alcoholism*. Baltimore, MD: University Park Press.

DiCara, L.V. (1970) Learning in the autonomic nervous system. *Scientific American, 222*, 31–39.

Eaton, M.T., Peterson, M.H. and Davis, J. (1976) *Psychiatry flushing*, New York: Medical Examination Publishing Company.

Eccles, J.C. (1958) The physiology of imagination. *Scientific American, 199*, 135.

Ellis, A. (1962) *Reason and emotion in psychotherapy*. New York: Lyle Stuart.

Ellis, A. (1977a) RET as a personality theory, therapy approach and philosophy of life. In J.L. Wolfe and E. Brand (eds) *Twenty years of rational therapy*. New York: Institute for Rational-Emotive Therapy.

Ellis, A. (1977b) Similarities and differences between RET and RBT. Personal communication.

Ellis, A. (1978) The problem of achieving scientific cognitive-behavior therapy. *Counseling Psychologist, 7(3)*, 21–23.

Fowler, J. (1980) Personal communication,

Gazzaniga, M.S. (1970) *The bisected brain*. Englewood Cliffs, NJ: Prentice-Hall.

Grace, W.J. and Graham, D.T. (1952) Relationship of specific attitudes and emotions to certain bodily diseases. *Psychosomatic Medicine, 14*, 243–251.

Graham, D.T., Kabler, J.D. and Graham, F.K. Physiological response to the suggestion of attitudes specific for hives and hypertension. *Psychosomatic Medicine*, *24*, 159–169.

Graham, D.T., Stern, J.A. and Winokur, G. (1958) Experimental investigation of the specificity of attitude hypothesis in psychosomatic disease. *Psychosomatic Medicine*, *20*, 446–457.

Holland, J.G. and Skinner, B.F. (1961) *The analysis of behavior*. New York: McGraw-Hill.

Hudgins, C.V. (1933) Conditioning and voluntary control of the pupillary light reflex. *Journal of General Psychology*, *8*, 38–48.

Luria, A.R. (1960) *The role of speech in the regulation of normal and abnormal behavior*. Bethesda, MD: US Department of Health, Education and Welfare, Russian Scientific Translation Program.

Luria, A.R. (1966a) *Human brain and psychological processes*. New York: Harper and Row.

Luria, A.R. (1966b) *Higher cortical function in man*. New York: Basic Books.

Luria, A.R. (1973) *The working brain*. New York: Basic Books.

Maultsby, M.C. (1975a) *Help yourself to happiness: Through rational self-counseling*. New York: Institute for Rational-Emotive Therapy.

Maultsby, M.C. (1975b) Patients' opinion of the therapeutic relationship in rational behavior psychotherapy. *Psychological Reports*, *37*, 795–798.

Maultsby, M.C. (1977) The evolutions of rational behavior therapy. In J.L. Wolfe and E. Brand (eds) *Twenty years of rational therapy*. New York: Institute for Rational-Emotive Therapy.

Maultsby, M.C. (1978) A million dollars for your hangover. Lexington, KY: Rational Self-Help Books.

Maultsby, M.D. (1979) *Freedom from alcohol and tranquilizers* (a series of five rational bibliotherapeutic booklets). Lexington, KY: Rational Self-Help Aids.

Maultsby, M.C. (1980) *Your guide to emotional well being*. Lexington, KY: Rational Self-Help Aids.

Maultsby, M.C. (1982) Rational behavior therapy. In S.M. Turner and R.T. Jones (eds) *Behavior modification in black populations: Empirical findings and psychosocial issues*. New York: Plenum Publishing.

Maultsby, M.C. (1984) *Rational behavior therapy*. New Jersey: Prentice-Hall.

Maultsby, M.C. and Hendricks, A. (1974) *You and Your Emotions*. Lexington, KY: Rational Self-Help Books.

Miller, N.E. (1969) Learning of visceral and glandular responses. *Science*, *163*, 436–445.

Monrad-Krohn, G.H. (1947) Dysprosody, or altered melody of language. *Brain*, *70*, 405–415.

Mowrer, O.H. (1960) *Learning theory and behavior*. New York: Wiley.

Mowrer, O.H. (1966) *Learning theory and the symbolic process*. New York: Wiley.

Olds, J. (1969) The central nervous system and the reinforcement of behavior. *American Psychologist*, *24*, 114–132.

Patton, L.P. (1976) The effects of rational behavior training on emotionally disturbed adolescents in alternative school settings. Doctoral dissertation, North Texas State University.

Razran, G.H.S. (1961) The observable unconscious and the inferable conscious in current Soviet psychophysiology. *Psychological Review*, *68*, 81–147.

Ross, E.D. and Mesulam, M. (1979) Dominant language functions of the right hemisphere: Prosody and emotional gesturing. *Archives of Neurology*, *36*. 144–148.

Ross, G. (1978) Reducing irrational personality traits, trait anxiety and intra-interpersonal needs in high school students. *Journal of Measurements and Evaluation in Guidance*. *11*, 44–50.

Rotter, J.B. (1954) *Social learning and clinical psychology*. New York: Prentice-Hall.

Rotter, J.B. (1966) Generalized expectancies of internal versus external control of reinforcement. *Psychological Monographs*, *80*, 1–28.

Rotter, J.B. (1971) External control and internal control. *Psychology Today*, 37–59.

Ruhnow, M. (Federal probation officer, North District of Texas) (1977). Personal communication.

Schwager, H.A. (1975) Effects of applying rational behavior training in a group counseling situation with disadvantaged adults. Counseling Services Report 22. Glassgo AFB, Montana: Mountain-Plains Education, Economic Development Programs.

Skinner, B.F. (1957) *Verbal behavior*. New York: Appleton-Century-Crofts.

Smythies, J.R. (1966) *The neurological foundations of psychiatry: An outline of the mechanism of emotions, memory, learning and the organization of behavior with particular regard to the limbic system*. New York: Academic Press.

Staats, A.W. and Staats, C.K. (1958) Attitudes established by classical conditioning. *Journal of Abnormal and Social Psychology*, *57*, 187–191.

Staats, C.K. and Staats, A.W. (1957) Meaning established by classical conditioning. *Journal of Experimental Psychology*, *54*, 74–80.

Tobias, P.V. (1970) Brain size, grey matter and race – fact or fiction? *American Journal of Physical Anthropology*, *32*, 3–26.

Volgyesi, F.A. (1954) School for patients: Hypnosis, therapy and psychoprophylaxis. *British Journal of Medical Hypnosis*, *5*, 10–17.

Watzlawick, P. (1978) *The language of change*. New York: Basic Books.

Werito, L. (1981) Personal communication.

# CHAPTER SEVEN    Cognitive Appraisal Therapy (CAT)
*Richard L. Wessler and Sheenah W.R. Hankin-Wessler*

## History and underpinnings of cognitive appraisal therapy

*Historical development of CAT*

Cognitive appraisal therapy (CAT) is the phrase the authors adopted to identify their work and to distinguish it from rational-emotive therapy (RET) and cognitive therapy (CT), its sources. Because we have been involved in RET training programmes in both North America and Europe for several years, we believed that it was appropriate to adopt a new phrase to avoid or reduce any confusion that might result from our past work. We developed CAT from our clinical and counselling experiences, and it should be regarded as a set of clinical hypotheses about certain disorders and of interventions we have found effective with our clients.

The need for modifications in RET and CT became apparent to us as we attempted to use these approaches in their pure form. RET seemed too theoretically dogmatic to us, and CT is limited in that it does not pertain to enough of our clientele, many of whom had disturbances that did not fit precisely into the category of neurotic depression for which CT was initially devised. Subsequently, we discovered that many of our theoretical notions, particularly our hypothesis about the developmental history of the individual, were discussed by Guidano and Liotti (1983), but their publication was not available when we began to modify our principles and practices.

We believe that most practitioners who advocate the practice of RET do not fully understand the theoretical and philosophical assumptions of RET. Though RET reportedly is widely practised, the version that is practised may not include the very assumptions that make orthodox RET distinctive within the cognitive-behavioural approaches. Our purpose in developing CAT is more to call attention to these assumptions than to promote a new approach to therapy. The field of psychological therapy is fragmented enough; integration rather than fragmentation seems more desirable to us.

We agree with Ellis and Beck about the role of cognitions in disturbance, but disagree on the importance of exploring developmental history; neither Ellis nor Beck gives sufficient attention to history in their writings and their practice. We disagree with Ellis on some fundamental theoretical issues, and with both Beck and Ellis on therapeutic methods. These differences are reported below and at various other points in this chapter.

Differences between Ellis's RET and the first author's version of RET are apparent. A sampling of differences can be detected in a close reading of the basic RET text he co-authored (Wessler and Wessler 1980). Among the differences on theoretical points are the explicit separation of evaluative, inferential, and descriptive cognitions. (Descriptive cognitions are thoughts and reports about what a perceiver has actually witnessed, while inferential cognitions are statements that go well beyond the readily observable and verifiable. Inferences include conclusions, attributions, and other logical and illogical operations on observations. Evaluative cognitions add a dimension of appraisal or judgment to observations.) We reject what has become the cornerstone of RET, the primacy of absolute imperatives (must-statements) in the creation of psychological disturbances; we find no evidence that must-statements of any sort inevitably and necessarily create disturbance, as Ellis has claimed (Wessler 1984a). We also differ with respect to Ellis's anti-religious statements, and seek to work with not against religious values (Wessler 1984b).

Our therapeutic methods also differed, as one can discover by listening to audio- and videotape recordings of therapy sessions made by Richard Wessler. (These demonstration tapes continue, at the time of writing, to be offered for sale by the Institute for Rational-Emotive Therapy.) Wessler makes no reference in these tapes to Ellis's ABC model, irrational beliefs, the disputing of cognitions, rational-emotive imagery, the self-imposed contingency management procedure Ellis calls 'operant conditioning', or other interventions typically used in RET. These tapes, then, represent an early version of CAT. The style of interaction is more collaborative and less confrontational than that usually associated with RET.

We differ less with Beck's CT, but while we retain much of Beck's (1976) account of the cognitive contents of the emotional disorders, we add a fourth dimension to the cognitive triad of negative thoughts about the self, the world, and the future. We add negative thoughts about the past, and direct a large minority of our therapeutic effort to understanding and modifying clients' views of their past personal history.

We are more concerned with developmental history as reconstructed by clients than are most other cognitive-behavioural approaches. Further, we seek a more comprehensive, holistic view of our clients than practitioners of RET and CT do. We are less concerned with target behaviours, which are of prime concern to behaviour therapists, and we do not use the forms and schedules typically employed in CT.

The phrase that came closest to stating our position was 'cognitive appraisal', taken from R.S. Lazarus's writings about stress and emotions (Lazarus and Folkman 1984). Lazarus holds that the phrase 'cognitive appraisal' is in the public domain, and neither endorses nor rejects our use of the term. What we say is that cognitions (or knowledge) and appraisals (or evaluations) of self and situations are important factors in emotions and actions, and in their disturbance.

CAT is both insight- and action-orientated. In working with clients, we attempt to produce both understanding and change, and emphasize flexibility in interventions. Further, due to our familiarity with psychopharmacology, we recognize that there can be significant biochemical factors in psychological disturbance. Thus, accurate diagnosis is essential.

Finally, CAT assumes an interdependence of cognitive, emotive, and behavioural events, and the importance of assessing these. We favour the comprehensive approach to assessment proposed by A.A. Lazarus (1981), multimodal therapy, due to its practice of assessing clients on multiple dimensions and its rejection of overly-inclusive theories of psychopathology. Multimodal therapy is primarily an assessment system and a conviction that lasting therapeutic changes result from working with clients in as many modalities as possible. CAT, by contrast, focuses on interventions and specification of cognitive targets for change.

## Major theoretical concepts

**Personal rules of living**   We see people as rule-governed creatures who apply their rules to specific large and small life situations, as they understand those situations (cf. Hogan 1973). People use their rules to adapt to situations, although they may apply their rules mindlessly (i.e. without awareness), and the results they obtain are usually mixed (i.e. less than totally satisfactory). In a sense, we are our rules. Our purpose in CAT is to bring rules into awareness, to point out the results of following specific rules, and to find ways to obtain better (though often still less than totally satisfactory) results. Often such self-examination leads to a modification of one's rules, while at other times it involves accepting one's rules and reordering the results sought.

We call these rules by which people live, Personal Rules of Living (PRLs). These cognititons are crucial in understanding a person's decisions, actions and affect. The notion of rules come from Beck's (1976) writings. 'The person uses a kind of mental rule book to guide his actions and evaluate himself and others. He applies the rules in judging whether his own behaviour or that of others is "right" or "wrong" . . . We use rules not only as a guide for conduct but also to provide a framework for understanding life situations' (p. 42).

A Personal Rule of Living is a cognitive structure that represents an individual's version of lawful relationships among psychological and social events, and the moral and ethical prescriptions held by the individual. A PRL states what is or what should be or both. PRLs are laws, both in the sense of natural law that describes regularities, and in the sense of value-based law intended to regulate human affairs.

Personal Rules of Living are both explicit, in that the person may be phenomenologically aware of them, and implicit, in that some are mindlessly followed without conscious awareness. They are neither 'rational' nor 'irrational'; indeed, these terms have become meaningless to us. They are the principles and values by which people make inferences and evaluations about events in their lives.

PRLs, when held with rigidity and great conviction, may produce seemingly maladaptive actions. For example, one may sacrifice personal pleasure in order to make a better life for one's children, or actually give up one's own life in order to save others. Such actions are neither hedonistic nor aimed at personal survival, but are understandable in terms of one's personal philosophy.

Because personal philosophies state what one should or ought to do, they may be thought of as moral statements. PRLs, then, are involved in the so-called moral emotions (Sommers 1981): anger, social anxiety, some forms of depression, shame, guilt, jealousy, envy, and other emotions pertaining to moral statements about what people in general, or oneself, ought to do in certain situations. We agree with the assumption that 'morality is a natural phenomenon, an adaptive response to evolutionary pressures' (Hogan 1973, p. 218). The relationships between PRLs and emotions are described in greater detail in a later section of this chapter.

Of special significance are PRLs that result in self-appraisal. Judgments about oneself stem from one's principles and values. Self-esteem is a matter of seeing oneself as acting consistently with one's PRLs. Guilt and shame are assumed to result from failing to fulfil one's PRLs, and anxiety from the anticipation of acting inconsistently, when negative self-appraisal accompanies the knowledge of past, present, or future failure. Unlike RET, which holds that unconditional self-acceptance (i.e. neutral self-appraisal) is both possible and desirable, CAT assumes that people are unwilling and unable to suspend self-judgment. CAT does not advocate the surrendering of

PRLs and self-judgments, but the modifying of PRLs when necessary in order to reach more workable conclusions and satisfying outcomes. PRLs that are more functional and adaptive, rather than no PRLs at all, are sought in CAT. Some PRLs are peripheral while others are more central; the more central ones are assumed to be more firmly entrenched and less open to change.

PRLs may conflict with each other. For example, the PRL, 'I must perform as well as possible,' may conflict with another PRL which says, 'I must not get too involved in any one pursuit, for variety is the spice of life.' In this example, the work ethic conflicts with the value of personal enjoyment. The clash of PRLs is often a focus in CAT, for rules seldom exist in neat, consistent sets. The failure to recognize and reconcile conflicting PRLs leads to psychological anguish. For example, a client reported feeling very depressed following a business trip, but could not understand the source of his depression. Upon listening to his narrative account of the trip, the therapist discovered that the client had gone reluctantly because he was required to sell a service he disapproved of, but went in order to avoid self-accusations of irresponsibility. His conflict centred on the ethics of selling something he considered ill-advised and his belief that it is irresponsible to avoid unpleasant tasks identified by his supervisor as necessary for the job.

**Phenomenological developmental history**   We believe that people's current lives and PRLs are shaped by their past experiences as they recall them. The origins of one's PRLs are often, in our experience, crucial in their reassessment and revision. A person will find it a more difficult task to modify a PRL if significant figures from his/her past taught, advocated, or implied it. We enquire into and investigate the phenomenological developmental history in order to create opportunities for cognitive, affective, and behavioural change, especially when the client shows few indications of change.

Further, humans seems to have a need to understand themselves in cause-and-effect terms. We are innate storytellers for whom a personal narrative must make historical sense (Landau 1984). Self-understanding is incomplete without an explanation in historical sequence of how we became the way we think we are. It is not important that the personal story of our lives is accurate; understanding, not facts, is the goal. Our personal history, then, is developmental and phenomenological. We may not know the end of our story, but we want very much to know the beginning.

Although we have emphasized *personal* rules of living, it should be noted that personal rules may be shared with others in our community, especially within one's family. We share Hogan's assumptions that 'all purposive behavior occurs within matrices of overlapping rule systems . . . associated with every human rule system is an ethic . . . [and] individual differences . . . must be accounted for in terms of the differing fashions in which persons think about and use rules' (Hogan 1973, p. 218). We acquire our moral principles and social values from society through mass media, family, teachers and peer groups. These are highly influential sources of information, and a client is not going to reject or even modify a PRL simply because a therapist says to do so. Too many people in the client's past have said otherwise, and too many mixed adaptive/maladaptive results have been obtained for him/her to change his/her mind so easily.

Phenomenological developmental history, then, we view as essential (a) for self-understanding, and (b) for working with clients who do not easily change.

**Holistic emphasis**   A third major theoretical consideration in CAT is not a concept but an emphasis. It is a holistic emphasis on the person as an open system that exists in a social, economic, political, and interpersonal context, and that interacts with his psychological representation of his enviromental context. Two of our dissatisfactions with RET and CT are their overemphasis on here-and-now thoughts and events with little consideration of the past, and on specific thoughts or beliefs in specific situations. The what-were-you-telling-yourself-in-that-situation  or  what-were-your-automatic-thoughts approaches seem piecemeal to us. This is not to say that they are wrong and should never be used, but that they address situation-specific cognitions rather than fundamental PRLs.

In CAT we seek a more holistic view of the client and attempt not only to understand what cognitions and appraisals were activated in a particular episode, but to try to create a more coherent picture of the client so that we can help him/her to forecast how he/she will act in new situations. To this end, self-understanding seems essential, and a person's guiding, salient PRLs seem to us to be the best form self-understanding can take.

**Biochemical factors**   Another emphasis is on biochemical factors that might be implicated in a client's disturbance. When they are, we make an appropriate referral for medication. Biochemical factors are further emphasized in that we assume that a selection has occurred throughout human evolutionary history to produce a species susceptible to rules governing behaviour. In order to acquire rules given by other people, nature requires an organism that will readily accept the directions and teachings of parents and other persons in authority. In order to live in groups, nature requires an organism that will to a large extent replace external authority with self-authority (Hogan 1973). We assume that people have a biological tendency to acquire PRLs and to take them seriously enough to use them as a foundation for conduct and self-judgment. Finally we emphasize biological factors so that we can de-emphasize an overly psychological account of people. Unlike radical behaviourists for whom all behaviour is acquired through experience, we think that certain dispositions, for instance emotional reactance, are biologically based.

**Psychological model**   A theoretical model seems necessary for therapists to guide their assessments and interventions. We have developed a model of emoting and behaving that in most points resembles Plutchik's (1980) theory of emotion. It is essentially the model of the 'emotional episode' described in Wessler and Wessler (1980), with some refinements and extensions. Plutchik's theory fits nicely into a cognitive framework, and avoids the controversy of whether cognition or affect is primary in emotional processes (Plutchik 1985). The components of this model are: stimulus, cognition, feeling state and physiological arousal, impulses to action, overt behaviour, and effects of action.

Plutchik casts his theory in an evolutionary perspective and defends it with sound research and scholarship. He hypothesizes that anxiety is aroused when a person conceives of a threat or danger. When the threat is posed to the person's self-image, ego defences, especially mental defences, are activated. Depression is said to result from subjectively conceived or actual loss. Ego defences are activated when the conceived loss is to the self. A.A. Lazarus (1981) has made virtually identical use of Plutchik's theory as we have.

The model of the 'emotional episode' differs in that cognition is subdivided into four steps: detection of stimulus, descriptions of stimulus, inferences about one's descriptions, and appraisals of one's descriptions and inferences. Cognition also appears in the emotional episode, in that decisions are interposed as a step between emotional response (feeling state and physiological arousal in Plutchik's model) and behavioural response, and corresponds roughly to Plutchik's 'impulses to action' (Wessler 1984a). Without decisions, action seems mechanistically determined.

The usefulness of this model is that any segment of it can become a target for therapeutic interventions: (a) the stimulus, either internal or external, e.g. another person's action, a phobic situation, or one's own emotion; (b) cognitions (observations about the stimulus, inferences, and appraisals); (c) affective state; (d) physiological arousal; (e) decisions to act or respond; (f) overt action; (g) feedback from the consequences of selecting and performing one action pattern rather than another (Wessler 1984a).

## How client problems are conceptualized

**Three types of emotions** The various types of cognitions are featured in minimodels of emotional responses we have devised, drawing upon the theoretical and empirical work of Plutchik and R.S. Lazarus, and the clinical writings of Beck, Ellis, and Wessler. These minimodels illustrate the cognitive and evaluative components in emotional processes. In CAT, we use three families of troublesome emotions: anger, anxiety, and depression.

1. *Anger*. The nonevaluative cognitions in anger focus on transgressions against one's PRLs about proper conduct. As Beck (1976) has pointed out, the transgressions may be either real or imagined, factual or anticipated. The appraisal is one of condemnation and damning.

   In anger, there are PRLs about how the offended party shall react to transgressions (with at least mental condemnation, and with overt condemnation and aggression if the transgressor is a safe target; if not the anger may be displaced). We assume that the degree of anger (ranging, say, from irritation to rage) correlates with degree of condemnation. The expressing of anger, as contrasted with the subjective experience of anger, depends on other PRLs the person holds, and upon his/her expectations about the interpersonal consequences. The expressing of anger can have powerful effects, and remains one of the most heavily relied upon methods of interpersonal influence. Power depends on a dependent other, so anger is directly expressed by people in secure or powerful positions, and indirectly expressed by those who see themselves as weak or who feel guilty when acknowledging feelings forbidden by PRLs.

   We see guilt as a special kind of anger, directed at oneself for violating PRLs. Guilt involves private self-denigration for 'crimes' or 'sins' of omission or commission, and does not necessarily require the public exposure of one's wrongdoing. We urge clients who report guilty feelings to look for the violated PRL, to reduce self-condemnation by graciously forgiving themselves, if possible to make amends for their 'crimes' or 'sins', and to effect plans to avoid future occurrences.

2. *Anxiety*. In assuming that anxiety underlies neurotic disorders, CAT is in the mainstream of tradition that extends back to Freud. Overt and covert manoeuvres to avoid anxiety are defences. (We recognize that some forms of anxiety, and especially monophobias, may not have cognitive bases, that is, they might be due to noncognitive conditioning alone, but this theoretical issue involves subtle interpretations of data.) We work in CAT *as if* there is a cognitive component in all forms of anxiety, and simultaneously attend to corrective experiences that can be seen as reconditionings.

The minimodel of anxiety assumes that people conceive of threats to their self-image and/or wellbeing, become fearful when they think they cannot cope with the threats, and take some overt action or mental activity to reduce or avoid anxiety. The cognitive (knowledge) component consists of thoughts which anticipate the occurrence of the threatening or dangerous event, and appraisals (evaluations) of how the event is, and/or what about the event is, threatening or dangerous (extreme negative appraisal). For example, anxiety about seeking a new relationship, reported by one client, was due to her anticipation of ultimate rejection. Social anxiety is a moral emotion in that one fears being regarded by others as weak, inadequate, or unworthy; the PRL is that one must do what is right in order to win the approval of other people. Their rejection or criticism is evaluated in a highly negative way.

In this example, the anticipation of ultimate rejection is a cognitive forecast or expectation, and the extreme negative evaluation is the appraisal. Both the probability that her expectation will be fulfilled and the degree of negative appraisal of the possible outcome are targets for intervention in CAT. The forecast as well as the appraisal are thought to come from PRLs which define people as not trustworthy, herself as easily rejectable, and the experience of rejection as 'awful' and proof of her inadequacy and/or worthlessness.

Shame may be seen as a special form of anxiety about the prospect or actuality of one's weaknesses or shortcomings or wrongdoings being discovered by other people. Unlike guilt, shame requires public exposure, or at least the threat of public exposure. Shame also implies weakness or inadequacy, and thus there is an anxious tendency to escape or avoid public exposure rather than to attack the threat as in anger.

3. *Depression*. Depression involves cognitions of loss or devaluation, and

themes of frustration and deprivation. Appraisals typically concern the enormity of the loss, and self-critical thoughts about one's inadequacy and/or moral worthlessness. These negative self-appraisals often thwart people's efforts to reduce deprivation and frustration. A typical PRL goes like this, 'I can't be much good because I have been deprived of so much; people get what they deserve.' We generally follow Beck's findings about the cognitive aspects of depression, with his emphasis on identifying negative forecasts and appraisals. However, we emphasize past personal history in our conceptions of clients' problems, and direct attention to the reappraising of past events. We do this because we have found that clients often do not alter their views of present and future events due to their appraisals of past events. Cognitive themes of helplessness and hopelessness are frequently due to (accurate or inaccurate) perceptions of lack of success and/or effectiveness in the past, and the extrapolation that the future will be no better.

**Inappropriate affect**   There are two ways to determine whether affect should be considered a 'disorder'. One is to use DSM-III criteria. A second way is to use the notion of subjective disturbance. Since anger and anxiety are not particularly easy to diagnose with DSM-III, the extent to which the individual subjectively reports distress is a good guide. A variant of the second approach is to use the reactions of other people as a guide, especially in cases of anger which can disrupt interpersonal relations.

Subjective criteria should be used with care. Some people seem not to want to feel anything. Others have no vocabulary in which to speak of their emotional feelings, while still others do not share a vocabulary with their therapists. Some people mislabel their feelings, or use psychiatric terms to refer to nonpsychiatric conditions. An example is the person who reports feeling anxious when it is clear from a therapeutic interview that the person experiences the agitation of anger. A second example is the person who reports feeling depressed when he/she simply means sad. Yet another example is the person who reports feeling anxious and goes on to recite a textbook checklist of depressive symptoms but who does not realize that depression rather than anxiety is the proper diagnosis. (We hasten to add that there is no reason why the person should know the accepted medical vocabulary, but, of course, the therapist must.)

We do not believe that the absence of anxiety, anger, or depression is necessarily psychologically healthy, nor that the elimination of these conditions is the appropriate target for change. We hold that there is some evolutionary significance to these emotions, but that they may be troublesome to the person who experiences them, and hence well worth working on. The key word is 'troublesome', for then and only then can we justify taking them as targets of change.

It seems inappropriate to us to speak of 'inappropriate' emotions, except in the sense that a social norm may be violated either by feeling a certain emotion or by expressing it. Thus, to experience anger when one has not been offended seems 'inappropriate' according to social criteria; to feel afraid when there is no danger seems likewise 'inappropriate'. However, in neither of these examples would we treat the client unless DSM-III or the subjective 'troublesome' criterion were met.

**Expression of affect**   In addition to the phenomenological experience of affect, there is its expression. All emotional expressions are governed by social norms, some of which may be inconsistent or mixed. The injunction never to show anger, which might be adopted as a PRL, ignores situations in which anger may be safely, justifiably and usefully expressed. Sex-linked prescriptions, for instance that men should not cry, may be accepted by some people and rejected by others of a different subculture or family culture. Its opposite, that men should cry and that everyone should 'get their feelings out', is a minority social norm that cannot therefore be universally applied. To speak of 'inappropriate' affect and its expression requires a great deal of specification of norms and circumstances.

The expression of affect within therapy sessions is sought in order to elicit PRLs and details of phenomenological developmental history. Corrective emotional experiences are more likely when affect is aroused. Cognitive change is less likely, in our experience, in the absence of affective arousal; and arousal must be expressed, reported, or displayed in some manner in order for the therapist to detect it.

**Troublesome behaviours**   In speaking of behaviours as (dys)functional or (mal)adaptive, the cognitive-behaviour therapies implicitly make evolutionary assumptions about human action. A basic concept in evolution theory is the adaptation of species or of organisms to environments. In identifying dysfunctional or maladaptive behaviours as targets of change, the cognitive-behaviour therapies are no different from most current thinking about psychopathology. However, 'maladaptive' behaviours can most easily be identified when a single criterion is used. The issue becomes significantly more complicated when one considers behaviour that is maladaptive by one criterion but not by another.

The martyr, to take an extreme example, displays 'maladaptive' behaviour when the single criterion of pleasure or survival is applied, as in RET. When other criteria are introduced the picture becomes more complex, and whether to call the behaviour 'maladaptive' becomes less clear. Another example is the man who works long hours to earn as much money as he thinks he needs to provide for his family, but in so doing neglects the very family he intends to provide for. His behaviour is maladaptive according to the family closeness criterion, but adaptive when the income criterion is applied.

To classify behaviours as 'disturbed' is similarly challenging. Certain habits are damaging to one's health, or to close relationships, or to leading a 'productive' life. When labelling certain behaviours as disturbed, one should specify in what ways, and according to what values, they are disturbed, to whom they are disturbing, and what other behaviours can be considered less disturbed.

Because we see behaviours as determined by one's PRLs, we see them as stemming from the desire to fulfil one's principles and values. Avoidance patterns of behaviour may be seen as fulfilling a PRL to avoid subjective feelings of tension, or as based on a belief that there is danger or threat imminent, rather than as purposeless rituals or phobic manoeuvres. The results of one's actions, then, are often quite mixed – anxiety gets reduced at a price to the individual; familiar interactions bring both reassurance and conflict.

Few behaviours are unambiguously adaptive or maladaptive. They are mixed, and should be understood according to the PRLs that form the various criteria for judging them. Reinforcement has its costs. Our purpose in CAT is to help people strike a balance between the rewards and costs of their actions so that they are less troubled by them.

**Disturbing thoughts**　We do not believe that so-called 'irrational beliefs' or negative thoughts should be targets for change simply because they can be so identified. The only justification for targeting them for change is their role in producing troublesome affect and action. A thought may be unrealistic and yet remain more adaptive than not. In this instance, we disagree with Raimy (1975), whose misconception hypothesis states that more accurate mental representations of reality will result in better adjustment to reality. For instance, a person may judge him/herself as more competent than peers do; such self-confidence may not be justified in reality, but may serve to move him/her to attempt and perhaps accomplish what he/she would not otherwise achieve.


**Acquisition of psychological disturbance**  CAT assumes that PRLs are learned through experience and from the teachings – both intended and unintended – of parents, teachers, peers, mass media and other sources about (a) proper conduct, (b) the nature of people and the world, and (c) oneself. Further, CAT assumes that people learn from examples furnished by others (vicarious learning via modelling) as well as from explicit messages furnished by agents of socialization.

Early childhood is especially important. Through immaturity, the child may distort the example or message, or assimilate it in ways not intended by the adult; or lessons may simply be understood in childish ways rather than as an adult would understand them. (The first author recalls his grandmother telling him that the length of his second toe indicated that he would never be wealthy. Although he later reinterpreted her message as an adult would – by disregarding it – the ends of his feet serve as constant reminders of the old message.)

PRLs acquired in childhood may serve the child well within the family, but may not work effectively outside it. One of our clients got along with an authoritarian father by following the rule to avoid conflict at all times, but then found that he was unable to express any disagreement with his boss without extraordinary justification of his argument, and even then only with a sense of guilt and fear.

In general, we believe, the less critical one is of one's own PRLs and the less discriminating one is in applying them, the more likely it is that they will result in costly behaviours. Adults find it easier to socialize children who are not very critical of their messages, and understandably parents do not encourage critical or independent thinking about principles and values until the children are much older; even then, we are more likely to encourage critical thinking in other people's children than in our own. Very often children make mistakes in learning that are never corrected. For example, in acquiring grammar, children make mistakes of overgeneralization of rules; they have difficulty in learning irregular verbs, and some people never learn to correct such mistakes despite the efforts of educators. Likewise, some people overgeneralize their PRLs and fail to correct their misapplications of them.

The phenomenological developmental history is important in understanding one's own acquisition of PRLs. The revision of PRLs may depend, in some cases, on one's capacity for changing one's mind about the wisdom of childhood's elders. Self-reported history, of course, is not necessarily reality, but we assume that history as one symbolizes and recalls it (and thereby reconstructs it) is more influential than what actually occurred.

**Perpetuation of psychological disturbance**   We assume that people perpetuate their disturbances because their thoughts, actions, and affects are not totally maladaptive. They will not adopt a less costly adaptive pattern unless they can test out and experience a superior one. There seem to be two reasons for this: (a) the threat of losing the familiar, and (b) the need to learn from self-demonstration. Any two-fingered typist will agree that touch-typing is faster; but old habits die hard, in part because new habits are initially less efficient. Further, two-fingered virtuosi may believe, perhaps correctly, that their system is better for them, regardless of what is better for other people. As applied to disturbance, people continue their costly mixed-adaptive patterns because new ones are not self-evidently superior. For this reason, we reject the educational model of therapy. Relearning-by-doing rather than being educated seems like a more accurate way to speak of therapeutic change. Education implies that a therapist who knows teaches a client who does not know.

Finally, people seem motivated to remain faithful to old PRLs, especially to rules that relate to self-esteem. The rewards for acting in ways that are deemed disturbed may be self-administered. Furthermore, people may behave in ways designed to elicit predictable reactions from others or to interpret others' reactions in familiar ways (Carson 1969; Guidano and Liotti 1983; Wachtel 1977), thus perpetuating the subjective validity of their PRLs and self-concepts. Without the familarity of the predictable, they might not know who they are, and fear the void and the loss of personal control. Worse, by relinquishing some cherished beliefs, they might find that their fears about themselves are confirmed. We find it useful, therefore, to speak with clients about modifying their rules rather than surrendering them, and about adding to their view of themselves rather than eliminating ideas that have long formed part of their views of self and the world.

# Practical applications

## *The therapeutic relationship*

We attempt to develop a relationship of trust and strong therapeutic alliance with clients. Without a good working relationship, the work of therapy cannot be done. The therapist has responsibility for promoting this relationship. To do so, we express a caring attitude toward clients, acceptance of them, and respect for them as people who struggle with their problems. Most clients, in addition to whatever other difficulties they might have, feel demoralized. By recognizing this, and offering realistic hope, we contribute to the collaboration needed for therapy.

We see the relationship as a collaborative one, in which both parties are equal. Thus, we avoid the I-am-going-to-do-something-for/to-you attitude. Toward this end, we ask clients for their opinions about therapy, about us as therapists, and about the extent to which we have fulfilled their expectations. Our usual procedure is to ask clients for their views of us, and also for their view of our views of them. We do this at the end of the initial session, a practice recommended by Janis (1983), as well as at times during later sessions.

The expression of empathy is important in building relationships. We take empathy to include the understanding of both feelings and cognitions. We often anticipate what clients will say about themselves, their thoughts and feelings. Such anticipations communicate empathetic understanding.

Self-disclosure is an important ingredient in creating a good working relationship. We do not pour out personal problems to clients, but we do speak of our lives, our families, the crises of the past, and at times current crises, for instance a death in the family. Pictures of us and our families appear in our offices (nonverbal self-disclosure), and we may refer to one or another of the people pictured while discussing some point. These and other disclosures say, in effect, that we are very much alike in many respects, have had experiences not unlike yours, and so understand you.

Consistent with our holistic emphasis, we do not regard the client as a mere set of symptoms or target behaviours to be treated with techniques learned from textbooks. Nor do we see them as collections of cognitions and emotions to be dealt with in a molecular fashion. Thus, we freely discuss matters that do not seem directly relevant to therapy, for example political elections and current movies, because all intimate social relationships contain such trivia – the trivia that builds solidarity.

We consider flexibility an important part of the therapist's actions, and try to adopt a style of interaction that fits the client and promotes change. While most of this is done by noting the client's style of interpersonal behaviour, some of it results from answers to direct questions about clients' expectations of therapy and of therapists. An item on the Multimodal Life History Questionnaire (Lazarus 1981) asks for such expectations, along with other information that affects the conduct of therapy. We routinely use this questionnaire, and often use the written responses as bases for discussion with clients.

As examples of flexibility of interpersonal style, with anxious clients we remain calm; with depressed clients we become more lively; with passive, self-effacing clients we avoid strong, wise teaching postures; with clients who expect traditional therapy, we are prepared to listen more than talk; for clients who lack information, we are prepared to furnish it when possible. In all cases, we adopt language that is appropriate for the client. We dislike psychological jargon and avoid it in speaking with clients, and when clients themselves engage in psychobabble, we ask for clarifications or 'translations' into human language. We give particular attention to nuances of language, and, of course, listen for clients' meanings rather than respond to the surface structure of their words.

Like it or not, therapists often serve as models for clients. 'I stopped and asked myself, "What would my therapist think and do in this situation?", and that is what I did.' Clients who make this or similar statements have come to regard their therapists as people to respect, admire, and emulate. Clients vicariously absorb information, wisdom, and turns of phrases from therapists.

Therapists have responsibilities not only to know therapeutic methods, but to present a model of confidence and competence. Personal problems should not interfere with the process of therapy, but therapists need not be perfect. People who pose as perfect cannot build good relationships. We recall an incident when a client made progress only after the therapist admitted a mistake, and the client in Zen-like fashion concluded that others may furnish guidance but change must come from within.

Once again, self-disclosure – or simply being honest with clients – lets us become known as people. We admit our squabbles with each other, our difficulties with the children, and acknowledge past events and decisions we regretfully wish we could do over. We reveal our imperfect moments with confidence, and try to show that we practise what we advocate. We have had, and are still solving problems, and any advice we can give we base on our own experiences. The more we can show that we are or have been like the client, the greater the chances that the client will accept us as a model and identify with us.

Aspects of the therapeutic relationship affect client motivation.

Motivation to change is counterbalanced for many clients by anxiety about acting differently and becoming someone unknown and possibly unlikeable. The motivation for change and the motivation to avoid fear promote the status quo. By being supportive and encouraging, we strengthen the motivation for change. We remain optimistic about the client's future, and promote realistic expectations for change. Through understanding and empathy, we attempt to overcome demoralization and fear of change.

## Strategies of treatment

The goals of CAT are to help clients change troublesome patterns of affect and action, while realizing that no adaptive behaviour is entirely without cost. A successful outcome is one that the client deems successful. Thus, we try to know the client's goals, to discuss and question when these goals are not apparent, and to negotiate new goals when explicitly stated ones are not realistic or are outside the realm of CAT.

Strictly speaking, we use CAT for problems of anxiety (including shame), anger (including guilt), and depression. We use other forms of intervention for other problems. These include referral for medication for endogenous anxiety and depression, behavioural methods (e.g. exposure and avoidance prevention) for phobias, and combinations of the foregoing where indicated (e.g. medication, behavioural methods and problem-solving for obsessive-compulsive patterns). We give advice, even if it is not asked for, about topics ranging from financial to romantic, from dealing with parents to dealing with children. We are not prepared, with CAT alone, to help people break habits, lose weight, or give up alcohol or other drugs. However, even problems as seemingly circumscribed as weight loss or sexual dysfunction may involve (and in our experience usually do involve) PRLs and other issues that no isolated behavioural or other regimen can treat.

We also take as goals, self-understanding and the reappraisal of one's phenomenological developmental history. Insight is desirable, although we do not subscribe to the notion that insight alone produces change, nor that it is always a necessary condition for change to occur. Insight is an important process goal, but it is a means to therapeutic outcome goals and not an end in itself. The same can be said for the process goal of building an effective working relationship with clients.

In planning a course of treatment, we rely on careful assessment of goals and find the Multimodal Life History Questionnaire very helpful in this task. The process of assessment continues throughout the course of therapy, as we explore problems in greater detail. Progress and change yield new problems and new challenges.

Our purpose in initial and later assessment is to discover and lay out in our minds a network of cognitions, emotions, and actions, and to formulate with the client which problems to deal with first. Because we do not think of clients' problems as isolated sequences of irrational beliefs or negative thoughts, we do not start with the first or most obvious problem the client presents. For example, if a client wants help with anger about her child's misbehaviour, we investigate further to discover whether she has a PRL that states that the child must obey her or else she cannot be much of a mother, and then generates anger toward her child due to her own feelings of anxiety and guilt.

Further, in assessing cognitions, we do not stop at the most convenient cognition, but look and listen for chains of ideas linked one to another. There may be appraisals at each link, but particularly at the end of the chain. Ideas, for example, that one must be perfect, may be linked to other ideas – e.g. that one will only get taken care of and avoid deprivation if one is perfect. A PRL about perfection links with a PRL about survival.

Self-appraisals receive special attention. Self-image or self-concept is a theory about oneself or a hypothesis about one's personality. Appraisals are evident in such terms as self-esteem and self-worth.

We continually assess PRLs. One unexpected but very positive discovery in using the 'rules' approach with clients is the ease with which the notion is understood. Children, particularly in the pre-teen years, are very concerned about rules; while observing their play it often seems as though the rules are more important than actually playing the game. As adults, we are surrounded by rules, regulations, laws, and (at times unspoken) social norms. In practice, we ask clients to state their rules when discussing a particular incident, or we may infer the rules ourselves and share our inferences for verification by clients.

We base our inferences on what clients say and do, and by noting their regularities. Therapists' inferences are necessary, as some key PRLs may be held without awareness – that is, they are nonconscious. At least for purposes of assessing PRLs, we try to make the nonconscious conscious.

Finally, since we have defined disturbance in terms of subjective 'troublesomeness', we are concerned with assessing how troublesome the emotions and behaviours are that clients describe in discussing their problems. By knowing approximately how disruptive the affect and actions are, we can choose what issues to put first and avoid giving the impression that *all* anger, anxiety, disordered affect, bad habits, and the like should be examined and changed.

## Major treatment techniques

CAT is a person-orientated approach to treatment, as opposed to a theory-orientated approach wherein clients are fitted to therapists' theories about them. It is a problem-orientated approach, as opposed to a technique-orientated one in which a standard list of techniques are used with every client with little or no concern for the individual. The term 'technique' is a simple mechanistic one, and is not complex enough to deal with human experience. In CAT, we try to avoid theory-bound and technique-bound therapy. For these reasons, our discussion of techniques in CAT is illustrative rather than exhaustive. We advocate using any form of intervention with a client, provided it is ethical and might benefit the individual. As in Lazurus's multimodal therapy, we are concerned with the effectiveness of techniques not their pedigree.

**Cognitive change methods**   Therapeutic discussion not only provides opportunities for assessment but for interventions as well. The simple act of putting a PRL into words is helpful for some clients. After working with a client for some time, merely expressing a PRL in the client's or therapist's words may stimulate ideas about how to modify the rule or what more adaptive rule might replace it.

A simple way to elicit PRLs is to ask the 'Where is the evidence?' question found in RET and CT. There are different answers sought by this question in Ellis's and Beck's approaches. Ellis asks the rhetorical question, 'Where is the evidence?' to prove one's 'irrational beliefs' (must-statements), and, of course, none can be cited as proof, for they are statements of personal values not of facts. Personal values are largely matters of tradition or faith, and are not subject to scrutiny for evidence. Beck's use of the question is more truly empirical: where is the evidence that your descriptions and inferences about reality are true, is the intent of his usage.

We find 'Where is the evidence?' questions useful, for they invite people to share their versions of reality with us – and these are fundamental phenomenological data. Even unanswerable questions about one's values can make one stop and think. In CAT, we ask the 'Where is the evidence?' question with a different intent; we are really asking, 'Where is the evidence that your PRL is working for you the way it should?' In other words, we emphasize the functional outcomes of living by a certain rule, although we sometimes ask for a rule's rationale as well.

The evidence question also pulls information about the phenomenologic al developmental history of the individual. The mere identification of the source of a PRL is often enough to cause cognitive change. We prefer to ask, 'Where did you get that rule?' rather than 'Where's the evidence?' because it elicits information about a client's personal story more efficiently.

Thirdly, we have found it helpful to point out discrepancies or conflicts between or among the identified PRLs. People's values are rarely consistently or tightly organized. Instead, they might be described as loosely disorganized. In a pluralistic society, particularly in the highly ethnically diverse northeastern part of the USA where we work, it is not surprising to find competing sets of values. Even within a family, father and mother may send (or may have sent in the past) significantly different messages about proper conduct. For example, a young man's deceased mother nurtured his artistic ambitions which his father downgraded in favour of a survive-at-any-cost business philosophy. As he gained insight about the internal conflict, he declared it to be an issue of trying to serve two masters (both of whom he had internalized), and knew that he must choose between them. Marital conflicts are often due to clashing expectations about the proper conduct of husband and wife. Such conflicts arise from different family backgrounds and values, as well as differences between families' beliefs and the latest fashionable messages from contemporary urban society. By showing clients how their rules clash, we create some degree of cognitive dissonance. We urge clients to rethink their rules, modify them, and reorder or prioritize them.

Other primarily cognitive methods include anecdotes and parables, humour, and discussions of existential or spiritual questions. The latter are especially important with very religious clients; we have found that CAT is particularly helpful with such clients, and we neither assume spiritual matters to be cognitive phenomena, as Lazarus (1981) does, nor scorn the beliefs of the devout as we were taught to do in RET (Wessler 1984b). We make frequent use of imagery (Lazarus 1981; Plutchik 1984) and cognitive rehearsal (Raimy 1975), on the assumption that one is unlikely to think or act differently unless one can picture oneself doing so outside the therapy session.

Decision-making represents a special type of cognitive intervention. The making of personal decisions is integral to CAT. Decisions include the goals of therapy, but also encompass how to reach those goals. We are very active in helping clients make decisions, to anticipate the outcomes of their decisions, and to formulate plans for implementing their decisions. Decision-making requires problem identification, the consideration of alternative solutions, and various means for implementing solutions (Janis

1983). Personal decisions must be realistic, but of equal importance is that they must not conflict with PRLs or they will not be acted on.

Finally, our view is that verbal methods of producing changes are less effective than experiential ones. Verbal interventions are among the weakest forms of persuasion. Insight must be followed by plans, and plans must be put into action. Our sessions are for insight and strategy; change occurs both in and between sessions. Hence, we have discussed cognitive techniques primarily for their value in assessment and not as robust treatment interventions.

To the foregoing we can add those statements therapists make about the client to the client, using as data therapists' observations made within the session as well as reports from clients about their everyday life. Such direct feedback from the therapists is one of two strategies Goldfried (1980) identifies as common to most if not all legitimate approaches to therapy. By reporting what we see and hear, and by adding our comments and tentative interpretations, we accomplish the direct feedback mission. Upon such information clients build plans for change.

**Experiential-behavioural homework**   The second common therapeutic strategy Goldfried identifies is corrective emotional experiences. In order to establish new patterns of acting and thinking, clients must take a chance and act differently. If one picture is worth a thousand words, one experience is worth a thousand images.

We do not assign homework from an existing stock of such assignments. Instead we may negotiate an individual assignment with each client, an assignment that seems well-suited for the problem discussed during the session. We allocate time for thorough discussion of the experiential-behavioural assignment, and role-play or rehearse it in imagery if necessary to encourage its performance. The nature of the assignment, then, varies widely. However, we do not use the shame-attacking exercises originated in RET, nor the keeping of thought records found in CT, nor the daily log identified with some forms of behaviour therapy. We seldom assign reading as homework, for we have found that so-called 'self-help' books actually make some clients get worse; they become demoralized when they read how 'easily' their problems can be supposedly overcome, while they themselves continue to find these problems so troublesome and difficult to remedy. We do try to get clients to experiment with new behaviours, call their PRLs into question, and put their new cognitions (revised PRLs) into action. We focus on controlling actions, not on controlling emotions.

## Overcoming obstacles to client progress

Homework assignments may be brilliantly conceived, but unless they are carried out they are useless. Successful therapy requires clients to collaborate with therapists and to adopt a new philosophy and attempt new behaviours. When clients do not co-operate with therapists, do not carry out assigned tasks, or do not show the expected therapeutic changes, it may be due to a new behaviour clashing with an old PRL. PRLs may conflict with the techniques therapists use and the recommendations they make, and we hypothesize that therapists' interventions will be less effective when they do. For example, a clergyman resisted a therapist's recommendation when seeking help for penile erectile difficulties; though he was liberal among the clergy, he found that the behavioural prescription of viewing pornography in order to get sexually aroused conflicted with one of his very important rules.

Much behavioural-experiential homework may be thought of as in vivo desensitization trials. They therefore involve entering and staying in situations, or attempting behaviours, that clients find fear-provoking. People who act neurotically are hardly known for their daring or for flying in the face of their fears. It is the therapist's task to induce people to do that which they have seldom done and for which negative experiences in the form of emotional discomfort conflict with whatever positive reinforcers may await the client. Immediate relief of anxiety usually wins out over delayed and possibly uncertain, positive benefits. Clients, and indeed all people, seem to have a biologically determined PRL that says, 'I prefer not to experience discomfort.'

A challenge to therapists is to induce clients to do things that they believe are uncomfortable, anxiety-provoking, or even boring. 'Induce' is a polite word for influence and persuade, and in fact no other intervention skill is as central to CAT as the capacity to influence clients for therapeutic ends. Janis (1983) suggests that counsellors and therapists should use the legitimate power inherent in their positions to influence clients. After identifying a target for change we sometimes overtly say, and usually covertly think, 'What would I have to do to persuade you to . . .?' Since we believe that self-demonstration is a powerful cause of cognitive change, we ask no idle question of our clients. Therapists are strong agents for change. In our role as negotiator we pose questions that are designed to persuade and motivate. Examples are: 'Can you see what results you will get if you do (or do not) change?' 'Would it make sense to you to change or attempt something new?' This first question addresses potential payoffs and promotes consequential thinking. The latter checks for potential resistance by determining whether the new action is consonant with clients' values.

Reducing clients' options can be influential. This is a 'you have no choice – do this or suffer' approach. Anxiety-arousing appeals can produce change if they are accompanied by recommendations for explicit action to reduce the anxiety. It is important that this be done in a supportive manner. Asking clients, 'What would induce you to undertake this assignment?' conveys the notion of power to the client and strengthens the collaborative relationship.

Other influential tactics include the behavioural and cognitive rehearsal referred to previously, and time projection imagery (Lazarus 1981). These in-session tactics invite the client to role-play a difficult situation or to imagine his/her responses and the reactions of other people. Preparation is the key word. Preparation allows clients to develop coping strategies in advance of needing and employing them. Preparation inspires confidence. Time projection has been used effectively with clients who fearfully avoid situations and have never thought of how to cope were they not to avoid them. In public speaking anxiety, for example, sufferers may never have pictured themselves actually doing poorly or getting adverse reactions and then coping with them. Like children who look away when horror movies get scary, they fail to imagine what they will do next – their avoidance extends to their thinking as well as their (not) doing. Some depressed persons boggle their minds with the enormity of certain tasks, which are in fact not very time-consuming at all. The imagined difficulty reduces as they examine each step in the mind's eye.

Therapists' manner may be more influential than their logical arguments. We are not at all convinced that people are lay scientists, as Kelly, Beck, Ellis, Mahoney, and many others in cognitive-behaviour therapy assume. People are influenced less by fact and logic than by belief in and liking for the therapist (Janis 1983; Strong and Claiborn 1982). Therapists who try to succeed with techniques alone will not succeed, even when they have carried out a proper assessment.

Goals, relationships, and style affect motivation. Motivation to change for many clients is checked by anxiety about the steps needed for change or the results of change. We often assess clients' images about their potentials for change. If a client cannot see him/herself acting or feeling any different-ly, it is our task to show that change is indeed possible. Clients may imagine themselves acting and feeling differently, but continue to anticipate that their worse fears about themselves will be realized if they do. As an example, an obese woman could imagine herself as slim as the seven-year-old photograph she brought to her therapy session. However, she had thoughts that she did not deserve to look more attractive, and insightfully realized that without her fat to blame she would have to blame herself for the failure and rejection she anticipated. Our reply was to show that there are effective ways to cope with failure and rejection should this occur, and that even if she had to try harder to succeed than she had been used to doing, she could manage to do so. Obviously, these messages would be lost on her were it not for the relationship and trust she held for the therapist as a competent, caring, informed person.

## Case example

A thirty-five-year-old married man with two children referred himself to the Multimodal Therapy Institute in New York City. He spoke little during the first part of the initial interview, but handed the therapist a card on which he had written:

| | |
|---|---|
| Nervousness | Work (what is work?) |
| Loss of motivation Doesn't last | Being fooled by people |
| Don't sleep nights | |
| Tired early morning | |
| Worry | |
| Think about money (earning) | Unhappy (never really laugh) |
| FEAR OF LOSS | |
| Think negative thoughts Nothing positive | Mind continually races. |

When he attempted to speak, his words were choked with tears as he wept openly. After the sobbing subsided, he told his story. He had successfully run a small business for about ten years, but had sold it for a large profit a few years ago. Since then, he halfheartedly tried to sell real estate, but had lost his desire to work. He felt ashamed of his unemployment despite the fact that he had realized an extremely good return on his investment. Neither he nor his wife needed to work for income at present, and his children attended private schools. He believed that he was a poor example to his children, and could not understand how his friends and family could possibly respect him, since he neither worked nor had a formal education beyond high school.

He was referred for medication, and his biological symptoms of depression quickly responded to treatment. His sleep returned, but the psychological difficulties he had written on the card presented during the first session remained. Since he was a stranger to psychotherapy and not psychologically sophisticated, the therapist worked slowly, sharing information about himself and about the process of treatment, and generally attempting to create a warm, even friendly feeling of concern and positive regard. Indeed, the therapist found it easy to like the client, for he had built his business from nothing, had a good marriage, seemed devoted to his family, and though Catholic, obviously subscribed to the Protestant work ethic. His values seemed to be exaggerated and overly rigid, and thus CAT was appropriate for him. The therapist asked him to talk about his worries, and from the dialogue that ensued in each session, began to identify his PRLs. The major one that emerged was his rule that one must work hard to earn self-respect and the respect of other people.

However, he defined work as physical effort, long hours, and daily exhaustion. All of these conflicted with another rule, that he should spend more time with his family and thereby become a better father. He had expanded the Christian teaching of caring for other people and being kind into a PRL that resulted in his getting exploited by other people, especially by former employees with whom he had been very generous. This rule led to his having retained dishonest employees to the irritation of honest ones, and their displeasure clashed with his rule that 'In order for me to feel good I should be liked by everyone.'

His phenomenological developmental history revealed an uneventful childhood, and admiration for his father who worked at two jobs and was always tired but still had time for his son. He saw his father as too kind and generous. He reported that he obtained part-time employment at the age of fourteen, and had enlisted in the army and seen service but not combat in Vietnam. Early messages from family and church had instilled his basic values. He was deeply affected by his Catholic upbringing, although not formally religious other than keeping up routine church attendance.

It was clear that he would not (and should not) give up his basic values, but that they required some easing, and that the PRLs in conflict would have to be prioritized. Further, he needed to change the definition of work he had developed, for it presented him with a major dilemma: how to work and feel worthwhile, less guilty and anxious, without risking his newly found role in the family (no longer was he a father made absent by work) nor his nest-egg provided by sale of his business.

Each therapy session followed a format that he evolved. He spoke first of his physical symptoms and of the medication level he was on, then of the progress he had noted, and finally of the 'worry of the week', as we came to label it. Over some twenty-five sessions, his worries shifted as each was resolved. First we tackled the meaning of work, and by exploring what we knew about how other people work he came to accept that work need not be calculated in terms of physical energy and exhaustion. One behavioural result was his taking new interest in real estate sales, and he began to close deals and earn comfortable commissions. A few months prior to the termination of therapy he opened his own office where he worked part-time.

Second, one of his early worries was about buying a new retail business like the one he had sold. Though he had years of experience, he seriously doubted that he would succeed due to lack of confidence. His early retirement from business was intended to be temporary, but his depression and thoughts of unemployment, followed by panicky thoughts about lack of money at some future time, eroded his confidence. We discussed his problem in terms of retirement that led to depression which in turn led to lack of confidence to attempt the only thing that would restore his feelings of worth. He began to accept the idea that worth can be earned in many ways, not just by success in one particular business or by physically exhausting work. However, he required a great deal of reassurance that it was morally right to modify his former position on this question. He decided to postpone a decision about buying a new business, a decision that will probably be indefinitely postponed as long as the real estate sales continue to be good.

The third issue addressed was his relations with other people. He felt inferior due to his lack of education, and acted out his excessive humility by deferring to others he thought were superior. In his first real estate sales ventures he found himself intimidated by those he saw as rich and/or powerful. Our discussion took on a 'clothes do not make the man, or does education' theme. The therapist's own doubts about the value of education reinforced the client's reappraisal of his worth. He reported feeling very comfortable in later meetings with people he formerly felt inferior to, and seemed genuinely amazed that he had changed his attitude so much. He reported acting appropriately assertively with nearly everyone, even though we made no explicit attempt to do assertiveness training – he knew what to say and do, but his PRLs had kept him from doing it.

Finally, we examined his role as husband and father, and shared stories about parenting. He had a PRL about how well his children should behave. and felt inadequate when they did not behave up to his standards. He also criticized and blamed his wife for the children's conduct. The therapist shared stories about his own children, and helped the client see that his (the client's) children did not depart from the norm to any significant degree. (We compared notes on how untidy their rooms were, for example.) He began to discipline his children more effectively and to collaborate with his wife rather than criticize her, after realizing that his PRL about people liking him extended even to his own children. Further, his PRL connecting earning their respect with the right to discipline them had led him to let them have their own way in too many matters, followed by his feeling inadequate because they did not behave better. He came to see that his children were not a reflection of his feelings, nor their better conduct a panacea for his own feelings of inadequacy.

It was his own decision to reduce the frequency of sessions, and finally to terminate therapy. He reduced medication on the advice of his psychopharmacologist, after a period of six months, with no return of symptoms. The therapist continued to offer support, and asked that he remain in touch, which he has. At last report, he was doing well in both work and family life, and even began some projects he had been putting off for years. Due to a very effective therapeutic alliance, the therapist was able to exert influence on the client's thinking, and to help him overcome the discouragement and inertia that seems inevitable during the course of treatment.

## References

Beck, A.T. (1976) *Cognitive therapy and the emotional disorders*. New York: International Universities Press.

Carson, R.C. (1969) *Interaction concepts of personality*. Chicago: Aldine.

Goldfried, M.R. (1980) Toward the delineation of therapeutic change principles. *American Psychologist*, *35*, 991–999.

Guidano, V.F. and Liotti, G. (1983) *Cognitive processes and emotional disorders*. New York: Guilford Press.

Hogan, R. (1973) Moral conduct and moral character: A psychological perspective. *Psychological Bulletin*, *79*, 217–232.

Janis, I.L. (1983) *Short-term counseling: Guidelines based on recent research*. New Haven, CT: Yale University Press.

Landau, M. (1984) Human evolution as narrative. *American Scientist*, *72*, 262–268.

Lazarus, A.A. (1981) *The practice of multimodal therapy*. New York: McGraw-Hill.

Lazarus, R.S. and Folkman, S. (1984) *Stress, appraisal, and coping*. New York: Springer.

Plutchik, R. (1980) *Emotion: A psychoevolutionary synthesis*. New York: Harper and Row.

Plutchik, R. (1984) Emotions as imagery. *Journal of Mental Imagery*, *8*, 105–112.

Plutchik R. (1985) On emotions: The chicken-and-egg problem revisited. *Motivation and Emotion*, 9, 197–200.

Raimy, V. (1975). *Misunderstandings of the self*. San Francisco: Jossey-Bass.

Sommers, S. (1981) Emotionality reconsidered: The role of cognition in emotional responsiveness. *Journal of Personality and Social Psychology*, *41*, 553–561.

Strong, S.R. and Claiborn, C.D. (1982) *Change through interaction.* New York: Wiley.

Wachtel, P.L. (1977) *Psychoanalysis and behavior therapy: Toward an integration.* New York: Basic Books.

Wessler, R.A. and Wessler R.L. (1980) *The principles and practice of rational-emotive therapy.* San Francisco: Jossey-Bass.

Wessler, R.L. (1984a) Alternative conceptions of rational-emotive therapy: Toward a philosophically neutral psychotherapy. In M. Reda and M.J. Mahoney (eds) *Cognitive psychotherapies: Recent developments in theory, research, and practice.* Cambridge, MA: Ballinger.

Wessler, R.L. (1984b) A bridge too far: Incompatibilities of rational-emotive therapy and pastoral counseling. *Personnel and Guidance Journal, 63,* 264–266.

# CHAPTER EIGHT   **Personal Construct Therapy**
*Robert A. Neimeyer*

## Introduction

> The task of the therapist is to join with his client in exploring, by the only means available to man – by behavior – the implications of the constructions he has devised for understanding reality. From this point of view therapy becomes an experimental process in which constructions are devised or delineated and are then tested out. Psychotherapy is not an applied science, it is a basic science in which the scientists are the client and his therapist. (George A. Kelly 1969a)

Personal construct theory stands in a curious relation to the cognitive therapies. On the one hand, the theory's chief architect, George Kelly, has been classified as a cognitive theorist by both his contemporaries (Bruner 1956; Rogers 1956) and present-day textbook writers. On the other hand, Kelly himself strongly resisted the label. For him, as for later construct theorists (Bannister 1977; McCoy 1981), subscribing to a 'cognitive' approach implied an unfortunate bifurcation of human experience into 'thought' and 'emotion', a theoretical distinction that he believed obscured more than it revealed. In an essay written in the last year of his life, Kelly (1966, p. 15) reaffirmed his attempt to transcend the cognitive-affective dichotomy in his treatment of 'construing':

> In order to make the point, I have had to talk about constructs in such an explicit manner that I have probably given the impression that a construct is as highly articulate and cognitive as my discussion has had to be. If I had been able to say what I said in metaphor or hyperbole I might have been able to convey the impression that a construct had something to do with formless urges too fluid to be pinned down by verbal labels. But personal construct theory is no more a cognitive theory than it is an affective or conative one. There are grounds for distinction that operate in one's life that seem to elude verbal expression.

In light of Kelly's persistent efforts to disaffiliate himself from a cognitive approach to psychology, it may seem ironic that his work is nonetheless cited by such authors as Beck *et al.* (1979), Ellis (1979), Mischel (1980), Mahoney and Arnkoff (1978), and Guidano and Liotti (1983) as having influenced their own thinking. But examined more closely, this influence is not surprising. Kelly (1955) pioneered in breaking both with a psychoanalytic tradition preoccupied with unconscious dynamics, and with a behavioural school that assumed strict environmental determinism. In contrast to both models, he posited an image of the 'person as scientist', and developed a well-articulated and testable theory of personality compatible with this metaphor. Most important in the present context, he made several original contributions to clinical diagnosis, assessment, and psychotherapy, all of which stressed the active interpretive role of the client. Thus, although terminological and theoretical differences do exist between construct theory and other cognitive approaches (as will be examined below), Kelly's work gave impetus to a cognitive trend in clinical psychology, and in its broad outlines became part of the intellectual heritage of the new movement.

If personal construct theory had died with Kelly, then its coverage in this volume might be relegated to a historical footnote. But construct theory is alive and well, having gained exponentially in adherents over the last fifteen years, generating a largely empirical literature of over a thousand publications (Neimeyer 1985a). Interestingly, this evolution has proceeded virtually independently of cognitive-behavioural work in general, with most workers in each field displaying little awareness of developments in the other. I hope that the present chapter will contribute to a rapprochement of these two curiously insular traditions, and that the resulting dialogue will help foster the more integrative direction in psychotherapy research and practice that is so badly needed (Wachtel 1977).

## History and underpinnings of personal construct therapy

### Historical development of personal construct therapy

To a considerable extent, the themes that inform personal construct psychology are reflections of the themes that Kelly derived from his own life. Born in 1905 to strictly religious Presbyterian parents in the tiny farming community of Perth, Kansas, Kelly gradually transcended the limitations imposed by his environment through educational achievement (Neimeyer 1985a). While earning his BA degree in physics and mathematics, he became increasingly involved in intercollegiate debate, and in part for this reason chose to pursue work in education on an exchange scholarship at the

University of Edinburgh. He returned to the USA with a newfound interest in psychology, and enrolled as a graduate student in that field at the State University of Iowa, where he was awarded a PhD degree in 1931.

It was during his first academic position at Fort Hays Kansas State College that Kelly's unique views concerning psychotherapy and assessment began to take shape. Of course, Kelly did not approach his clinical work *de novo*, even given his bootstrap educational history. As a student he had been exposed to both stimulus–response psychology, which he had found mysterious for neglecting the hyphen in the formula, and Freudian theory, which he read with 'the mounting feeling of incredulity that anyone could write such nonsense, much less publish it' (Kelly 1969b, p. 47). But as he immersed himself in clinical practice, he began to revisit these earlier conclusions:

> The strangest thing about this period is that I went back to Freud for a second look. My recollections of Rasmussen's *Principal Nervous Pathways* and of Thorndike's electrical condenser theory of learning applied at the synapses had not proved very helpful to people who were troubled about what was to become of them. But now that I had listened to the language of distress, Freud's writings made a new kind of sense . . . He too must have listened to these same cries echoing from deep down where there were no sentences, no words, no syntax. (Kelly 1969b, pp. 50–51).

As a result of this experience, Kelly became a Freudian – at least by persuasion – and began to offer judicious and often helpful psychoanalytic interpretations to many of his clients. Eventually, however, he found himself taking these Freudian 'insights' for granted, and contrived an audacious experiment to test their role in effecting a cure:

> I began fabricating 'insights.' I deliberately offered preposterous interpretations to my clients. Some of them were about as un-Freudian as I could make them – first proposed somewhat cautiously, and then, as I began to see what was happening, more boldly. My only criteria were that the explanation account for the crucial facts as the client saw them and that it carry implications for approaching the future in a different way . . .
>
> What happened? Well, many of my preposterous explanations worked, some of them surprisingly well. . . . In those days psychology was regarded locally as a pretty far-out kind of thing anyway, and if I said that a nervous stomach was rebelling against nourishment of all kinds – parental, educational, and nutritional – most of my clients were willing to try to

make something of it. (Kelly 1969b, p. 52).

Gradually, such experiences suggested to Kelly that human beings necessarily live their lives on the basis of personal, and sometimes problematic, explanatory systems which represent the main themes of their pasts and permit them some degree of security in anticipating their future. The multiplicity of such systems devised over the course of human history – or even over the course of a single life – convinced him that 'reality' offered no simple yardstick for evaluating the absolute validity of such constructions. However disturbing it may seem, 'what we think we know is anchored only in our own assumptions, not in the bed rock of truth itself, and that world we seek to understand remains always on the horizons of our thoughts' (Kelly 1977, p. 6). This position he later identified as *constructive alternativism*, the view that 'all of our present interpretations of the universe are subject to revision or replacement' (Kelly 1955, p. 15). As Kelly stressed, this is not to say that it is a matter of indifference which set of alternative constructions one chooses to impose upon the world; but it is to say that the validation of an interpretation has less to do with gauging how well it matches an objective reality than with assessing its explanatory and predictive utility for that individual. This subtle shift away from philosophical realism differentiates personal construct theory from other cognitive approaches (cf. Neimeyer 1985b), and carries important implications for psychotherapy, as we shall see below.

A second distinctive aspect of Kelly's thought that germinated during the Fort Hays years concerned the crucial importance of *role enactment*. Specifically, he began to recognize the extent to which our interpersonal behaviour both derives from and reciprocally modifies our construction of our *core role*, that portion of our construct system that allows us to predict and control our essential interactions with other persons (Kelly 1955, p. 502). In keeping with this emphasis, Kelly and his students began to experiment with innovative new therapy techniques in the late 1930s. In these 'role therapies', clients would be prescribed carefully drafted alternative identities to practise with the therapist and then to enact for a fixed time period in daily life. Results were often dramatic, with a number of clients showing significant personality change within a few weeks (see papers by Robinson and Edwards, reprinted in Markley, Zelhart and Jackson 1982). This experience made such an impact on Kelly that he nearly labelled his nascent approach 'role theory', and reserved for the concept of roles a prominent place in his later psychology of personal constructs. This strong social-psychological emphasis – reflected in Kelly's (1955) discussion of sociality, commonality,

and interpersonal and cultural validators of construing – further distinguishes construct theory from cognitive approaches having more individualis-
tic orientations.

After World War II and his acceptance of a position at Ohio State
University, Kelly began to enunciate a comprehensive psychological theory
compatible with his earlier therapeutic experiences and philosophical com-
mitments. At the heart of his theory was his metaphor of the *person-as-
scientist*. It struck Kelly as hypocritical that psychologists would characterize their own aspirations in terms of explanation, prediction and control of
human phenomena, and then contend that their subject, 'being merely a
human organism, is obviously propelled by inexorable drives welling up
within him, or else is in gluttonous pursuit of sustenance and shelter' (Kelly
1955, p. 5). Instead, Kelly entertained the notion that it was their essential
humanity that accounted for the scientific behaviour of psychologists and
framed the question:

> what would happen if we were to reopen the question of human motiva-
> tion and use our long-range view of man to infer just what it is that sets the
> course of his behavior? Would we see his centuried progress in terms of
> appetites, tissue needs, or sex impulses? Or might he, from this perspec-
> tive, show a massive drift of quite a different sort? Might not the
> individual man, each in his own personal way, assume more the stature of
> a scientist, ever seeking to predict and control the course of events with
> which he is involved? Would he not have his theories, test his hypotheses,
> and weigh his experimental evidence? And, if so, might not the differ-
> ences between the personal viewpoints of different men correspond to the
> differences between the theoretical points of view of different scientists?
> (Kelly 1955, p. 5)

## Major theoretical concepts

Guided by this metaphor, Kelly laid down a systematic theory predicated on
the role of prediction in science, and detailed the psychological,
psychometric, and psychotherapeutic implications of this model. In this
section, I will outline the conceptual framework of personal construct
theory, enunciated formally by Kelly (1955) in terms of a 'fundamental
postulate' and eleven 'corollaries'. By attempting to state his general theory
of personality in explicit, logical form, Kelly sought to articulate the key
'presuppositions' embodied in his theory (cf. Brown 1977) in a way that

opened them to empirical scrutiny. Indeed, a great deal of research pertinent to each of the corollaries has been conducted in the last twenty-five years, and has been reviewed in an volume edited by Mancuso and Adams-Webber (1982). My coverage of the basic theory here will be quite schematic, since specialized concepts pertaining to psychotherapy will be elaborated later in the chapter.

**Starting point** In his *fundamental postulate*, Kelly held that 'a person's processes are psychologically chanellized by the way in which he anticipates events' (Kelly 1955, p. 46). In so doing, he took persons and their processes as the central concern of this theory, and built in the anticipation of the future as its primary motivational principle. Thus, from the outset, he made clear that it was human beings in their entirety that he was discussing, not lower organisms or 'parts' of persons considered in isolation (e.g. their 'cognition'). Furthermore, by concerning himself with the way our ongoing processes are channelled, he bypassed the need to devise explanations for why an 'inert' organism would become active in the first place, thereby discarding unnecessary concepts such as libidinal energy, drives, motives, and stimuli. Instead, he assumed that the person is essentially a 'form of motion', and that the direction we take with our lives depends upon the constructs we employ for anticipating our futures. He then extended the meaning of this basic position statement by means of the following corollaries, which I have categorized into those concerned with the *process* of construing, with the *structural features* of our construct systems, and with the *social embeddedness* of our anticipatory efforts.

**The construing process** Kelly hypothesized that construing entailed discerning recurring themes or regularities in events (the construction corollary), and using these as the basis for anticipating other relevant events in the future. Thus, behaviour is anchored in implicit prediction: through our actions we invest ourselves in our expectations, encounter events that bear upon them, discover evidence that validates or invalidates our anticipations, and finally revise our outlooks in light of the results (the experience corollary). Each repetition of this 'experience cycle' (Neimeyer 1985b) permits us progressively to extend and define our construct system so as to enhance its predictive and explanatory utility (the choice corollary). But at any given time there are also limits to possible change, imposed by the rigidity or 'permeability' of the constructs involved (the modulation corollary).

In essence, then, construct theory accords a very active, interpretive role to the individual: we attempt to integrate the data of our past experience into a 'personal theory', which continues to evolve as we accommodate our systems to an ever-widening field of events. Like scientific theories (Lakatos 1970), core aspects of these personal systems are highly resistant to modification, whereas peripheral aspects are more readily altered or replaced when 'falsified' by unexpected events. These systemic limitations on cognitive change imply an intimate connection between the process of construing and the structure of our conceptual frameworks, the topic of the next section.

**Construct system structure**     Perhaps the most distinctive of Kelly's contributions was his discussion of cognitive structure. At a molecular level of analysis, he contended that meaning was essentially a matter of *contrast*, as reflected in the 'bipolar' structure of individual construct dimensions. For example, a client might construe herself and her mother as 'caring', and contrast both with her husband, who is 'distant'. Thus, a single construct functions both to attribute similarities to some elements of experience, and to differentiate these from others (the dichotomy corollary). Although some constructs are quite general while others are very specific, there are limits to the applicability of any given dimension (the range corollary). At a more molar level of analysis, Kelly also outlined the way in which individual constructs are linked by lines of implication to form the individual's *construct system*, with more abstract 'superordinate' constructs serving to cross-reference more concrete 'subordinate' dimensions (the organization corollary). In general, it is these superordinate structures (particularly those bearing on our self-identity, cf. Guidano and Liotti 1983) that are most stable and resistant to change, since to modify them would require sweeping changes in subordinate constructs that are implicatively linked to them. For example, upon her first encounter with a secular college atmosphere, a devoutly Christian young woman might successfully revise her self-construction of herself in subordinate roles (e.g. as a participant in certain social organizations), but be far more threatened by challenges to her (superordinate) religious identity. Finally, Kelly contends that the individual's construct system typically forms a meaningful whole when fully understood, though the person may in some cases employ a variety of construct subsystems that are incompatible with each other (the fragmentation corollary). These structural features of the construct system can be assessed by means of the Role Construct Repertory Test or Reptest (Fransella and Bannister 1977; Neimeyer and Neimeyer 1981), the clinical application of which will be illustrated below.

**The social embeddedness of construing** Finally, Kelly acknowledged the importance of the social dimension in our construction of reality. Although individuals ultimately are unique in the content and structure of their interpretive frameworks (the individuality corollary), this does not preclude the significant overlap in their construing which arises from membership in a particular family or culture (the commonality corollary). Equally important, our behaviour in relation to other people is regulated by our attempt to 'subsume' or understand their construction processes (the sociality corollary), an effort that provides a psychosocial basis for the definition of *role*. Thus, by addressing social experience within his basic theory, Kelly was emphasizing that psychological functioning, whether 'normal' or 'disordered', has an important interpersonal component. Thus, the origins of emotional disturbance can be traced not only to 'faulty logical inference' or the failure of the cognitive system to square with 'empirical reality', but also to disruptions in the social construction of reality, some of which will be discussed and illustrated below.

## How client problems are conceptualized

A further distinction between personal construct theory and most current cognitive therapeutic approaches derives from its refined discussion of *psychological disorder*. At the most general level, a disorder can be identified with the inability of the construct system to accommodate to changing events; it occurs when a particular construction 'is used repeatedly in spite of consistent invalidation' (Kelly 1955, p. 831). At a more fine-grained level of analysis, however, construct theory offers numerous potential explanations for client problems. In rough outline, these correspond to the facets of the theory discussed above. At a *process* level, an individual may habitually abort the experience cycle at any of its five stages, thereby failing to modify his or her outlook in the light of disconfirmatory events (Neimeyer 1985b). For instance, the depressed client may 'constrict' her world in an effort to minimize her contact with anxiety-provoking events that are not easily anticipated within her current construct system. Unfortunately, this attempt to shrink the world to a manageable size often precludes the client from encountering those events that would challenge the validity of her current, predominantly negative, constructions (Neimeyer 1985c). Alternatively, a client may push others to behave in accordance with his already invalidated predictions of their behaviour, in a 'hostile' effort to shore up his own construction of their motives (Kelly 1955, pp. 874 ff). Thus, while the depressed person may fail to encounter the events that would prompt a revision of her construing, the 'hostile' person may confront the fact that others do not conform to his predictions but then attempt to force them to act in accordance with his expectations. In both cases, movement through the full experience cycle is blocked, and no further elaboration of the construct system takes place.

Other disorders can be linked to *structural* properties of the client's construct system. A number of dysfunctional behaviours may be maintained largely because the implications of alternative, more adaptive behaviours are so poorly elaborated within the client's current system. For example, — Fransella (1972) found that stutterers at the beginning of therapy had very coherent, meaningful construct systems concerning 'being a stutterer', but had far sketchier constructions of 'being fluent'. Using repertory grid technique, she also demonstrated that those clients whose identities were most bound up with their symptoms were least likely to reduce the number of disfluencies they displayed over the course of therapy. Although such tightly organized systems centring around one's symptoms may be maladaptive, the total disruption of construct system structure may be still worse. Excessive conceptual loosening or fragmentation has been linked to such serious conditions as schizophrenia (Bannister 1962) and imminent suicide risk (Landfield 1976; Neimeyer 1984). From this perspective, optimal functioning is associated with construct systems that are hierarchically organized around core constructs that are both comprehensive and relatively stable (Epting and Amerikaner 1980).

Finally, problems may result from inadequacies or disruptions in our *social* construction of reality. For example, intimate relationships typically provide 'consensual validation' for both partners' construing of social experience – including the nature of their relationship (Duck 1977). For this reason, an individual may experience relationship disruption when he discovers that his own outlook is far less congruent with that of his friend or spouse than he initially expected (Neimeyer and Neimeyer 1985). Just as this breakdown in 'commonality' can occasion relationship problems, so can the failure to engage in adequate 'sociality' or social perspective-taking. Deficiencies in being able to 'take the role of the other' have been linked to antisocial personality problems or sociopathy (Widom 1976).

While this synoptic discussion necessarily oversimplifies construct theory's approach to diagnosis (Bannister 1975; Button 1985; Epting 1984; Kelly 1955), it does suggest how a multifaceted theory can yield a variegated depiction of psychological problems and disorders. Such diagnostic considerations are intimately interwoven with the clinician's intervention strategies, as we shall see below.

## Practical applications

Personal construct therapy can be usefully compared to other cognitive approaches at three main levels: (a) the kind of therapeutic relationship that each establishes, (b) the treatment strategies that follow from their respective theoretical orientations, and (c) the particular techniques that each favours to encourage client change. Each of these progressively more concrete levels will be discussed below, along with the special problem of client 'resistance' to the therapist's efforts.

### The therapeutic relationship

With the eye-catching armamentarium of techniques utilized by cognitive therapists, it is tempting to lose sight of a basic fact – that all effective therapies rely on the development of a constructive relationship between the client and therapist (Strupp 1977). Within the cognitive therapies, there is general assent that such a relationship entails the therapist's 'acceptance' of the client (e.g. Arnkoff 1983; Beck *et al.* 1979; Ellis 1979). Kelly (1955) concurs on this general point, but adds that in personal construct therapy acceptance has a very specific meaning:

> 'Acceptance' as it appears in most current psychological and psychiatric writings seems to be a pretty vague concept. We have attempted to make it communicable by defining it as a willingness to see the world through the other person's eyes. It thus becomes a precondition for the intentional adoption of role relationships.
>
> . . . Acceptance does not mean seeking mere commonality of ideas between clinician and client, it means seeking a way of *subsuming* the construct system of the client. (Kelly 1955, pp. 373–374).

On a practical level, the personal construct therapist conveys his or her acceptance of the client by carefully examining and trying to utilize the client's idiosyncratic images and figures of speech. The goal of this effort is twofold: to maximize the impact and precision of therapeutic communication, and to begin to assess deficiencies in the client's construing processes. Although the importance of taking up the client's outlook is usually conveyed implicitly in therapy by the therapist's line of questioning, there are times when it is useful to clarify this overarching goal in a more explicit way. For example, in his treatment of one particularly passive client who simply waited to respond to the therapist's direct 'probes', Kelly noted that:

> I don't see therapy as simply a matter of probing, my probing. I see it more as a matter of my coming first to understand your outlook as well as possible, and for that, you see, you have to take quite a bit of initiative and educate me. And once we've got the pattern, the way you handle things, the way you do things, then we can start to inquire whether these are effective, to see whether they're working, to see what the gaps seem to be. And we can join with each other in a series of inquiries, but it . . . isn't quite probing. (Kelly, in Neimeyer 1980, pp. 83–84)

Thus, in personal construct therapy, the first task of the therapist is to view the world at least temporarily through the client's experiential spectacles. Kelly (1955) referred to this fundamental attitude as the *credulous approach*, the assumption that the client's 'words and symbolic behavior possess an intrinsic truth which the clinician should not ignore' (p. 322). The clinician utilizing a credulous approach would explore in detail the implications of the client's version of an event – even if it appeared to depart from the 'objective reality' of the situation. As Epting (1984) points out, the initial concern of the personal construct therapist 'is not with being taken in by the client, but rather with being left out by the client so that no real view of [his or her] personal world is ever gained' (p. 9). This phenomenological orientation contrasts with that of other cognitive therapists whose immediate efforts to criticize the logic and validity of a client's statements may impede their arriving at a more comprehensive and personal assessment of his or her problematic world view.

Despite this difference, personal construct therapy, together with other cognitive approaches, emphasizes *collaborative empiricism* in the role relationship between client and therapist (Arnkoff 1983). In keeping with his model of the person as scientist, Kelly (1955) stressed that:

> the psychotherapist helps the client design and implement experiments. He pays attention to controls. He helps the client define hypotheses. He

helps the client avoid abortive undertakings. He uses the psychotherapy room as a laboratory. . . . Finally, he recognizes that in the inevitable scheme of things he is himself a part of the validating evidence which the client must take into account in reckoning the outcome of his psychotherapeutic experiment. (p. 941)

From this perspective, the therapist/client relationship resembles that between a research supervisor and a student researcher: the former may have expertise in ways of testing theories and evaluating evidence, but the latter is clearly more familiar with the 'content area' of his or her own life (Bannister 1975). This guiding metaphor influences the personal construct therapist's choice of strategies and technical procedures, as we shall see below.

But there is one important feature of the therapist's role that deserves special emphasis, since few cognitively-orientated clinicians outside construct theory discuss it in detail – the *validational* function of the therapist's behaviour. Kelly (1955) notes that: 'As in the case of all constructions, we see the client viewing the clinician through a series of templets accumulated from the past and "tried on for size." Stated another way, the client applies certain hypotheses to the therapist and subsequently verifies them or abandons them after having tried them out with varying degrees of persistence' (pp. 575–576). Thus, Kelly agrees with psychodynamic theorists that the client typically perceives the therapist initially through the filter of *transference*, but disagrees with the implication that this necessarily represents a 'pathological' reaction. Indeed, Kelly (1955) regards it as both natural and healthy when a client is able to apply to the therapist 'a varying sequence of constructs from the figures of his past,' as when he is seen as gentle like mother, organized like father, formal like Professor Muchmore, and so on. In this form of *secondary transference*, the client attempts to interpret the therapist's behaviour in terms of constructions that are both permeable (applicable to a range of other figures) and corrigible (capable of being invalidated, revised and refined). What is more problematic is the phenomenon of *primary transference*, in which the client 'types' the therapist 'preemptively' as *nothing but* a 'cold and remote authority', 'my best friend', and the like. Rather than representing tentative hypotheses about the therapist's behaviour, such constructions tend to be applied to the therapist as a whole figure, and are resistant to modification through gentle disconfirmation during the therapy hour. Although the constructs the client imposes on the therapist may cast the therapist in a parental role, they may also cast him or her in a variety of alternative roles (as a possession, a foil, an absolver of guilt, etc.), the implications of which Kelly (1955, chapter 11) discusses in detail. By attending to the hypotheses the client is testing in relation to the clinician, it is possible to understand more deeply the way in which the client construes role relationships with significant others (Soldz 1984).

Aside from these diagnostic implications, Kelly contends that the transference relationship can be used for therapeutic ends. As a representative of the social world, the therapist must respond in such a way as to invalidate the client's more global and outmoded role constructs, and help the client elaborate a more flexible and functional fund of constructions that can be applied to the contemporary figures in his or her life. This aspect of personal construct therapy has much in common with Gustafson's (1981) conception of brief psychodynamic treatment, in which the therapist 'must show that he is different' – through behaviour more than interpretation – from the 'transference expectations' of the client. Kelly agrees with Wachtel (1977) that these diagnostic and therapeutic goals require a flexible response style on the part of the therapist – if the clinician acts only as a 'blank slate' then the only role constructs being assessed and validated concern the construction of the other as a detached and impassive observer! Instead, Kelly (1955) enjoins the therapist to 'play a part as a reasonably faithful example of natural human reactions, rather than one which is superhuman or divested of all human spontaneity' (p. 593). At a technical level, this may entail the use of *enactment techniques*, in which the clinician 'enacts a series of carefully chosen parts and seeks to have the client develop adequate role relationships to the figures portrayed' (Kelly 1955, p. 664). In summary, the therapeutic relationship in personal construct therapy provides not only a context for client change, but also one of the major mechanisms by which such change is fostered. Although the versatility of this relationship makes it difficult to characterize it in general terms, it tends to be less disputational and directive than other forms of cognitive therapy, and is instead more invitational and exploratory (Neimeyer 1985b).

## Strategies of treatment

In personal construct therapy, the strategies employed by the client and therapist are essentially refinements of 'the ways that, on one occasion or another, man has always employed for dealing with perplexities' (Kelly 1969c, p. 231). Stated differently, therapy is a form of *accelerated living* in which the client undertakes revisions and extensions of his construct system that would take much longer to accomplish in his daily life. To aid the clinician in formulating the changes required in the client's system, Kelly (1969c) provides a synopsis of eight therapeutic strategies in the language of his theory. A readable elaboration of these same strategies has been provided by Kenny (1985).

At the most superficial level, the therapist can encourage *slot change*, the client's reversal of position with respect to one of the more obvious constructs already in his or her system. For example, a client may describe herself as quite 'critical' of her teenage daughter, even though she is 'understanding' in relation to other members of the family. A therapist interested in helping her improve her relationship with her daughter might advise her to be similarly understanding in that relationship. Although such advice – usually transmitted implicitly rather than explicitly – may produce dramatic changes in a client's behaviour, they are typically shortlived, since no real elaboration of the pre-existing problematic construct system has taken place. A further hazard of slot movement may befall the therapist who is unaware of the contrast poles of the client's relevant constructs. This is illustrated by the case of the husband who refrains from showing any emotion in discussions with his wife in an effort to 'protect' her. If the client construes this as the only alternative to 'exploding', the unwitting therapist who prods him to be more emotional in his marital communication may risk precipitating a reaction he or she did not anticipate. From a construct theory standpoint, such slot change occurs because 'the system of constructs which one establishes for himself represents the network of pathways along which he is free to move. Each pathway is a two-way street, he can move either up or down the street, but he cannot strike out across country without building new conceptual routes to follow' (Kelly 1955, p. 128).

A second strategy entails helping the client *select another construct* from his or her system and apply it to the matters at hand. This strategy is formalized in Kelly's (1955, pp. 515–517) description of the *C-P-C cycle*. In this process, the client is encouraged first to engage in 'circumspection', to generate a number of alternative ways of construing or behaving in a problem situation. This is followed by the critical assessment of each of these alternatives, leading to 'pre-emption', or the selection of one among the available field of alternatives that seems especially relevant or useful. Finally, the client makes a 'choice' to act on the basis of the most viable alternative, behaving in a way that appears most elaborative in the light of his or her system. A similar strategy has been popularized by Goldfried (1980) in his use of problem-solving approaches to therapy.

A third and more ambitious goal that may be appropriate to longer-term therapy concerns the *articulation of preverbal constructs* in the client's system. Like Meichenbaum and Gilmore (1984), construct theorists recognize that many of the most superordinate schemata by which we organize our experience are difficult to verbalize, and may be symbolized by an especially 'prototypical' element in their context (Kelly 1955; cf. Crockett 1982). Thus, at critical junctures in therapy, a client may be at a loss to describe verbally exactly why his wife's behaviour angers him so, except to say that she is 'just like his mother' in the way she treat him. Such 'tacit construing' (Neimeyer 1981) often concerns our dependency relationships with others, since it is based on images of our early caregivers which were formulated before we had command of symbolic speech (Guidano and Liotti 1983). Kelly (1955) assumes that articulating these preverbal constructions in therapy facilitates a client's experimenting with them, and eventually revising them in light of current experience. A detailed example of this process can be found in transcripts of Kelly's therapy with a difficult client (Neimeyer 1980).

A fourth strategy entails *testing the system's internal consistency*. As suggested in the fragmentation corollary, individuals sometimes operate with apparently contradictory subsystems, and one goal of therapy might be to promote their integration. For instance, my early therapy sessions with a highly successful woman executive centred around her extraordinary ability to control not only people and events, but also her own display of emotions, all qualities she highly prized. At work, she single-handedly co-ordinated the efforts of dozens of people to ensure that major trade shows and conferences took place exactly as she had planned. In contrast, her personal life was a shambles of disorganization. She would literally forget children's birthdays, stand up her friends for mutual activities, and even neglect to notify family members of her change of address. The emergence of this latter material in our discussions prompted me to ask, 'How does all this fit with your description of yourself as "in control"?' Hesitantly, she responded, 'It doesn't . . . I guess my word isn't worth much in my personal life.' This led us to formulate her 'loss of control' in her personal life and her 'overcontrol' in her work as the extreme ends of the same basic construct dimension, both of which had significant disadvantages. As a consequence, therapy turned toward integrating these disparate subsystems, by importing into her personal life some of the organizational skills she used so effectively in business, and into her work some of the sharing of responsibility she accepted in other areas.

The fifth major strategy, *testing a construction for its predictive validity*, is directly implied by the personal science paradigm that originated with construct theory. It involves helping the client derive a clear prediction from his or her current problematic construing of a situation, and then devise a means of testing it for accuracy by using his own behaviour as the 'independent variable' in an experiment (Kelly 1970). This is illustrated by the case of a group therapy client who was immobilized for months by the dilemma of whether or not to plant a tall hedge in his backyard: if he did so, he worried that he would estrange his neighbours, but if he did not, he would never be able to get the privacy he desired. He saw the obvious solution – asking his neighbours' opinion about the project – as unworkable, since he was convinced they would disapprove and force him to scuttle the project. With the support of group members, he was able to reconstrue consulting the neighbours simply as an experiment, a way of testing his prediction that they would be opposed. The members and therapist also helped him examine the implications of the possible outcomes to this experiment, and role-played with him a comfortable way of broaching the topic with his neighbours. As a result, he was able to carry out the assignment and gather information that helped invalidate his characteristically negative construing of others. In recent years similar empirical methods have been adopted by many of the cognitive therapies (e.g. Beck *et al.* 1979; Guidano and Liotti 1983; Mahoney 1977).

A sixth aim of therapy may be to *increase or decrease the range of convenience of certain constructs* in the person's system. This amounts to encouraging a client to apply a given construct to more or fewer events in his or her life, as the case may be. The former strategy is often useful in helping a client 'stretch' a well-established construct to interpret a new, anxiety-provoking domain of experience. Thus, a mechanic with little interpersonal insight might be invited to think of his wife's anger as a 'pressure gauge' which indicates that something is wrong 'under the hood' and requires attention. Training in listening skills in therapy could then be presented as a 'tool' to help 'repair' a problem that could lead to marital 'breakdown'. Especially when presented in a humorous manner, such metaphoric use of constructs can be an invaluable therapeutic aid. The alternative strategy of 'shrinking' certain constructs to a kind of obsolescence will be illustrated in the sample therapy described below.

A seventh kind of strategic move in therapy consists of *altering the meaning of a construct*. This is exemplified in the case of a husband, Ron, whose frequent 'suggestions' to his wife (e.g. 'You'd better take your coat; it's cold outside') were a source of constant marital friction. In the course of marital therapy, I used the 'laddering' technique (Hinkle, in Bannister and Mair 1968) to elicit the superordinate implications of this behaviour from Ron's standpoint. I first asked him what the opposite of 'making suggestions' was to him, and he replied, 'keeping quiet'. I then asked him whether he would prefer to have someone make suggestions to him or keep quiet. He responded that he preferred getting suggestions. When I asked him *why* he preferred that alternative, he indicated that it 'showed that you care', whereas keeping quiet 'showed that it didn't matter'. Repeating this cycle of questioning, I discovered that 'caring' made Ron 'feel good', whereas someone acting as if it 'didn't matter' left him 'feeling in limbo'. This aspect of Ron's construct system is depicted in Figure 8.1, along with the results of a similar ladder elicited from his wife Pam.

Comparing these two construct systems, it become clear that the same advice-giving behaviour (connoting 'mothering' to Pam) carried dramatically different implications for the two spouses. For Ron it seemed to imply involvement and caring, things he highly valued, whereas for Pam it seemed to cast her in a dependent, childlike role that she was struggling to outgrow. Although this exercise was not a panacea for their problems, it did help Ron see 'suggestion-making' as less strongly aligned with superordinate constructs implying caring and feeling good. This was a first step toward Ron's constructing a new role relationship with Pam, one predicated on a clearer understanding of her own frame of reference.

Finally, the client and therapist can work to *form new construct dimensions*. This is the most ambitious undertaking of all, since it requires the client not merely to modify, but partially to replace, his or her habitual outlook. Kelly (1955, pp. 161 ff.) discusses a number of conditions that facilitate this therapeutic goal, including presenting the client with fresh elements or experiences that are less bound by old constructs, using experimentation, and avoiding direct, threatening challenges to the old construct system. These conditions are nicely met by the various *enactment techniques* to be described in the next section.

## Major treatment techniques

There is a strong temptation for various schools of psychotherapy to argue for their distinctiveness on the basis of their unique treatment procedures. Thus, psychoanalysis distinguished itself from the dominant medical model in part through its novel 'talk therapy' relying on free association and interpretation; and early behaviour therapy staked its claim in part by repudiating such verbal procedures in favour of more action-orientated conditioning techniques. Similarly, with the advent of the cognitive therapies, new therapeutic and assessment techniques have grown in 'awesome

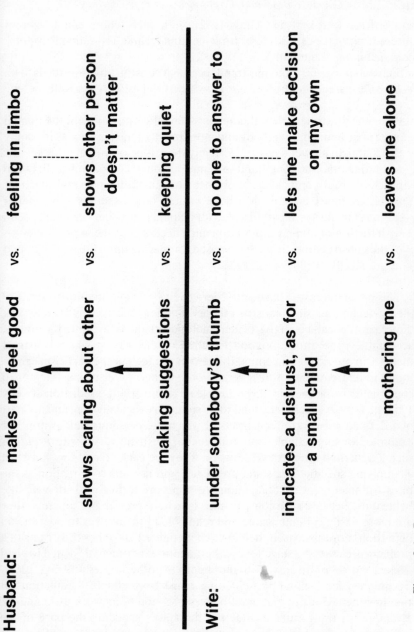

**Husband:**

makes me feel good     vs.     feeling in limbo

shows caring about other     vs.     shows other person doesn't matter

making suggestions     vs.     keeping quiet

**Wife:**

under somebody's thumb     vs.     no one to answer to

indicates a distrust, as for a small child     vs.     lets me make decision on my own

mothering me     vs.     leaves me alone

**Figure 8.1** Personal construct 'ladders' showing implications of husband's advice-giving behaviour for both members of the couple

proportions' (Arnkoff and Glass 1982), with each school emphasizing a different set of procedures (e.g. triple-column techniques, rational disputation, self-control methods).

Somewhat in contrast to this trend, personal construct therapy tends to be *technically eclectic but theoretically consistent* (Karst 1980). As Kelly noted:

> Personal construct psychotherapy is a way of getting on with the human enterprise and it may embody and mobilize all of the techniques for doing this that man has yet devised. Certainly there is no one psychotherapeutic technique and no one kind of interpersonal compatibility between psychotherapist and client. . . .Hence one may find a personal construct psychotherapist employing a huge variety of procedures – not helter skelter, but always as part of a plan for helping himself and his client get on with the job of human exploration and checking out the appropriateness of the constructions they have devised for placing upon the world around them. (Kelly 1969b, pp. 221–222)

This being the case, I have opted here to give greater attention to strategy than to technique, since construct theory is better conceived as a framework directing the choice of particular methods than as a limited menu of acceptable procedures. A good example of the way in which construct theory can provide a conceptual framework for technical eclecticism can be found in its treatment of *tight* versus *loose* forms of construing. Tightened constructs are defined as those that lead to unvarying predictions (Kelly 1955, p. 483). As such, they tend to be stated in exact language and are part of a defined network of constructs of which the person is well aware. For example, for some couples, the construct of 'husband versus wife' is part of such a tightened interpretive network. They see each pole of this construct as implying specific duties and privileges, and use this construction as the basis for unequivocal anticipations of appropriate husband- or wife-like behaviour. Because such constructions tend to be precise and concrete, they are more easily communicated and readily lend themselves to operational definition. For this reason, helping a client tighten his or her construing of a problem area sets the stage for the therapeutic experiment designed to yield a 'clear-cut yes or no answer' to the client's hypothesis (Kelly 1955 p. 1063). Techniques for facilitating tightening range from simple modulations of therapist behaviour to elaborate between-session homework assignments. Examples of the former include the therapist's speeding the pace of the interview, raising his or her voice slightly, using precise, 'objective' language, taking notes during the session, and asking the client to compare and contrast different experiences, clarify a point, or summarize what has been said. Homework assignments compatible with this goal include a large array of self-monitoring techniques that require the client to record specific dysfunctional thoughts, quantify emotional reactions, examine the logic or rationality of his beliefs, or formulate and test explicit predictions that derive from them. Thus, from a personal construct standpoint, the broad armamentarium of cognitive-behavioural procedures described elsewhere in this volume represent sophisticated examples of tightening techniques.

But as important as tightened construing is, it can also be hazardous, leading to the development of constructs that are too incidental, brittle and impermeable to encompass many of life's complexities. For this reason, healthy functioning (and successful psychotherapy) entails a delicate tacking back and forth between tight and loose forms of construing. In contrast to tight constructs, loose constructs lead to varying predictions (Kelly 1955, p. 484) and hence are more speculative, shifting, and resilient. Predictions formulated on the basis of such construing tend to be more ambiguous, leading to constructions that are seen as being 'approximately true' or making 'a general kind of sense'. Kelly (1955, p. 855) likens loose construing to making 'rough sketches' of the world in contrast to having to draw in each precise line. As such, it is the first step in the *creativity cycle*, which starts with vague, hard-to-articulate and sometimes apparently preposterous attempts to interpret a new and elusive aspect of experience, and terminates in a tightened form of construing that yields a well-planned, but novel, experiment. Thus, loosening serves a vital function: it 'releases facts, long taken as self-evident, from their rigid conceptual moorings' (Kelly 1955, p. 1031), so that they can be seen in a new and often unsuspected light. Personal construct therapy involves a series of creativity cycles, some occurring within a single session, others spanning several weeks of contact.

As with tightening, several procedures can be utilized to promote loosening in the client's construing. At a process level, the therapist can slow the pace of the interview, judiciously using silence and evocative, metaphoric language to elicit expression of new and inexact discriminations from the client. At a more technical level, the therapist can use chain association, progressive relaxation, guided fantasy, and even the recording of dream activity, which Kelly (1955) regards as 'the most loosened construction one can put into words' (p. 1037). Although the loosening fostered by these techniques frequently brings to light material that helps a client 'shuffle some of his ideas into new combinations' (Kelly 1955, p. 1033), it also has its hazards. In particular, it can become an addictive and circular refuge from anxiety unless it eventually is tightened into behavioural experimentation.

Therefore, the exclusive use of *either* tightening *or* loosening techniques is contraindicated in most therapies. Instead, therapy – and creative living – require 'steering between Scylla and Charybdis. If construing is tight, one runs the risk of being shattered on the uncompromising rocks of reality. If it is loose, one may be spun around endlessly in the whirlpool of fantasy' (Kelly 1955, p. 849). From this perspective, both the preoccupation of psychoanalysts with loosening techniques and that of cognitive-behaviourists with tightening procedures represent unfortunate tendencies to get 'stuck' in one phase or the other of the creativity cycle. As a consequence, the former risks losing its way in diffuse speculation, while the latter risks bogging down in concrete particulars incidental to a client's core problem.

Despite the technical versatility of personal construct therapy, certain procedures have a special congruence with the basic theory, and deserve attention for that reason. The two illustrative techniques I will consider here include *controlled elaboration* and *enactment*.

As a primarily verbal technique, *controlled elaboration* can take the form of helping a client considering a radical new behaviour to 'think through how this would be done and how it would turn out in the end' (Kelly 1955, p. 585). In addition to making the constructs governing the choice more internally consistent and communicable, such a procedure can also 'help the client delineate his construct system in such a manner that it can be tested verbally against reality on a laboratory basis in the conference room' (Kelly 1955, p. 886).

Elaborative techniques can be especially useful in facilitating a client's reconstruing of negative past events. In line with the basic philosophy of constructive alternativism, an individual's biography is, for Kelly (1955), 'a present structure which is documented by selected memories of the past and is in part a viewing screen upon which the events of the past seem to have form and consequence' (p. 989; cf. Mancuso and Ceely 1980). Thus, in listening to the recounting of a client's past, the clinician attends to the vibrant themes which the client discerns in his or her experience, rather than hearing the fateful march of a sequence of events that have 'determined' the client's current personality. For example, after listening to an adult client's story of how all of his close relationships with women had been failures since his mother ridiculed him in his childhood, the therapist might ask, 'As you look back on it now, how would you have wanted your mother to respond to you?' They might then examine an alternative biographical trajectory which might be further elaborated in response to questions like, 'What would have happened *if* she had only behaved differently?' 'How would your childhood have been different? your adolescence? your current relationships?' Thus, 'the more the client elaborates how he would behave differently if all of this had not happened to him, the clearer the alternative pattern becomes' (Kelly, 1955, p. 949). With the alternative ways of behaving within easier conceptual reach, the client can then be encouraged to give them a behavioural trial.

Elaborative procedures can also be assigned as homework to prime a client to begin moving toward a more hopeful future. This can be illustrated by the case of a severely depressed woman who would daily study the obituary column in the newspaper, carefully noting the ages of the young people who had died, and imagining the content of an obituary reporting her own death by suicide. After taking appropriate precautions to prevent her acting on her suicidal impulses, I formulated her obituary reading as 'an extremely creative way of convincing herself that death was her clearest option'. I then asked her to consider using the same 'creative imagination' to spell out an alternative outcome, by composing instead a 'human interest story' that documented her struggle against and triumph over the hardship of her life. Experimental and clinical research consistent with this approach has been reviewed elsewhere (Neimeyer 1985c).

The second major technique, *enactment*, is equally consonant with the underlying philosophy of personal construct theory. As with the above techniques, these role-play procedures range in complexity from spontaneous in-session *casual enactments* in which the therapist and client(s) play the parts, to carefully planned *fixed role therapies* in which the client generalizes the role being enacted to his or her day-to-day life.

Casual enactment procedures are frequently used to help a client elaborate on an incident presented during the therapy hour. For example, after hearing a client report on a falling out with her boyfriend, the therapist might suggest, 'Let's see if we can get a better idea how this talk with him went. Suppose I'm your boyfriend. . .' and then speak a few lines taken from the encounter. By replaying the altercation in the therapy room, the therapist and client ensure that they have a common perceptual ground for later discussion of the incident. It also helps 'turn the client's attention toward the reality outside the therapy room' (Kelly 1955, p. 1027), a factor that is crucial if the therapy is time-limited.

Kelly (1955, pp. 1026 ff.) provides four guidelines for the use of casual enactment procedures. He cautions first against prefacing it with a long intellectualized discussion, and instead advocates that the therapist assume his role almost immediately after suggesting the role-play topic. He also suggests that the enactment be kept brief – typically only a few minutes – and that it include the exchange of parts, so that both therapist and client have a chance to play each role. A major advantage of this procedure is that it helps introduce the client to genuine role relationships, since in reversing roles the client must make some effort to take up the other person's point of view. This feature of enactment makes it particularly useful in marital therapy, where spouses can be asked to portray not only their own, but also their partner's perspective in conflict situations. Finally, Kelly warns the therapist against caricaturing the client in the reverse role-play situation in a misguided effort to force upon him or her an 'insight' into his/her behaviour with others. Such exaggerations only arouse predictable defensiveness, a topic that will be examined further below.

Casual enactments can be used in therapy for a variety of purposes. At the most immediate level, they can provide the therapist with some first-hand information on the client's interactive style with different kinds of figures. Of course, one cannot make the naive assumption that the client's role-play with the therapist precisely replicates his or her behaviour with significant others. But the variation in the client's reaction to different figures enacted by the therapist is often revealing, especially if the therapist is able to relinquish his or her own self-consciousness and play the part with some vividness. A second advantage of enactment is that it can help circumvent a client's defensiveness by allowing him or her to wear the protective mask of make-believe. Thus, a client might be invited to play the part of a close friend who has come to talk to the therapist about the client. In such a scene, the clinician may be better able to ask difficult questions, such as 'Do you know whether Martha is secretly afraid that her husband will leave her, or has she confided in you to that extent?' The 'as-if' quality of enactment also suits it to the exploration of hypothetical situations directly pertinent to the client's presenting problem. For example, a scene could be constructed in which the client spoke from the perspective of someone who had 'already suffered all the terrible things that he has been apprehensive about' (Kelly 1955, p. 1150). Role-plays of this kind can be used to help a person reflect on how he might 'pick up the pieces' and go on living even if his worst fears were actualized. Finally, enactment may provide a useful means of elucidating the client–therapist relationship itself. Transcripts of Kelly's therapy sessions (in Neimeyer 1980) illustrate how inviting the client temporarily to portray the therapist's perspective can shed considerable light on what the client expects from therapy and the role in which he or she is casting the therapist.

A more intensive use of role-playing is represented by *fixed role therapy* in which enactment becomes the central psychotherapeutic technique. The starting point for this procedure is a *self-characterization* written by the client, in which he/she is asked to describe him/herself from the standpoint of an imaginary friend 'who knows him/her intimately and sympathetically, perhaps better than anyone could ever really know him/her.' To help promote perspective taking, this 'character sketch' is written in the third person, starting with a phrase like 'Joni Jackson is. . .'. Kelly (1955, p. 334) notes that such homework tends to elicit the client's descriptions of areas of his or her life which contain 'enough uncertainty to make exploration interesting and enough structure to make it meaningful'. Although in fixed role therapy the self-characterization is preliminary to other techniques, it can be a potent treatment procedure in its own right (cf. Fransella 1981).

The second phase of treatment entails the careful analysis of the client's self-characterization by the clinician, usually in consultation with a group of professional colleagues. Together they consider the sequence, organization and content of the sketch, and particularly attempt to tease out the underlying role constructs that are implicit in the client's protocol. They then creatively formulate an alternative *enactment sketch*, which the client will be asked to portray in his or her day-to-day interactions with others for a fixed period of time, typically two to three weeks. To be successful, this new role must contain different – though not necessarily 'better' – ways of constructing role relations with others. For example, a client's self-characterization might suggest a constant vigilance concerning whether others are 'deceitful versus truthful', and accordingly describe her own behaviour in terms of needing either to remain 'in control' of interpersonal situations or to risk being 'taken advantage of' in them. The enactment sketch for such a client should be organized along construct dimensions that are in a sense orthogonal to his/her operative constructs. Thus the new role might describe a hypothetical character (e.g. Frieda Choose) who views people as puzzles to be solved, and who tends to be spontaneous and inquisitive in social settings.

Next, the clinician presents the client with a one- or two-page description of this new role, and together they modify the sketch until it depicts a plausible kind of person, not necessarily someone the client would admire or try to emulate, but someone whom she might like to get to know. The client is then asked to make-believe that Joni, her real self, has gone on a brief vacation, during which Frieda will be living in her home, performing her work, and so on. The client is then given the enactment sketch, and asked to refer to it several times a day with the goal of trying to think, feel and behave in different situations as Frieda would – not in an effort to become her permanently, but as a social experiment in discovering the implications of looking at life differently. The client and therapist meet frequently over the enactment period to rehearse Frieda's part, with the therapist playing the role of progressively more intimate figures over the sequence of interviews (e.g. fellow workers, friends, parents, husband). At the end of the fixed enactment period, the make-believe role is laid aside, the client resumes being Joni, and the therapeutic team discusses any lessons that have been learned from their undertaking. The power of this technique lies not in its prescribing concrete changes in the client's outlook, but in underscoring the philosophy of constructive alternativism: that we have the freedom – and the responsibility – to invent and reinvent our outlooks across the course of our lives. Extended presentations of this novel procedure have been provided by Kelly (1955, 1973) and Adams-Webber (1981), and applications discussed by Bonarius (1970), Karst and Trexler (1970), and Kremsdorf (1985).

## Overcoming obstacles to client progress

Since personal construct theory does not assume a defensive basis to human motivation, the notion of 'resistance' loses much of the importance it has within psychodynamic circles (Kelly 1955, p. 1101). Reflecting on a slow-moving and difficult therapy case of his own, Kelly once noted:

> When we talk about defenses within personal construct theory, we are saying essentially that the construct system does not support the kinds of insights we think the person should be able to see . . . Construct theory, then, is concerned with these defenses, not just as kinds of perversity toward the therapist, but as genuinely vulnerable points in the [client's] construct system. (in Neimeyer 1980, p. 80)

Viewed in this light, labelling a client 'resistant' can be more destructive than clarifying, insofar as it offers a pseudoexplanation for his failure to show therapeutic movement and implies an adversarial relationship between client and therapist. An example is provided by a recent case in which I was consulted by a graduate student therapist. The client in question was a middle-aged woman, newly separated from her abusive husband of eleven years. Despite the client's professed intention to end the marriage, she balked at the therapist's advice – offered with increasing insistence over their six sessions of contact – to file for divorce. Frustrated by this obvious 'resistance', the therapist's faculty supervisor had begun advocating that she should threaten to terminate therapy unless the client consulted a lawyer. The therapist, uncomfortable with this ultimatum, was looking for an alternative means of restoring movement to a stalled therapy.

Rather than attempt to motivate the client by coercion, I counselled the student to take seriously the possibility that the client's behaviour represented an *elaborative choice* within her construct system. That is, despite her avowed dissatisfaction with her marriage, the role of 'being married' still carried more tangible, or less problematic, implications than its contrast, 'being divorced'. I suggested that little resolution of the client's impasse could be expected until these implications were understood and taken into consideration. In this particular case, it seemed likely that the client was experiencing both *anxiety* and *threat* at the prospect of divorce. Anxiety is 'the recognition that the events with which one is confronted lie outside the range of convenience of one's construct system' (Kelly 1955, p. 495). That is, the client may simply have had few means of anticipating what life outside marriage might be like, and so might have been reluctant to relinquish a status whose implications she had explored for over a decade! Additionally, she may have experienced threat, defined as 'the awareness of imminent comprehensive change in one's core structures' (Kelly 1955, p. 489). In this case, the slot movement from 'being married' to 'being divorced' might have implied numerous changes on other constructs in her system, for example, from being 'successful' to being a 'failure', from being 'taken care of' to being 'alone', and so on. If these hypotheses were valid, therapy might be conducted along very different lines. For example, encouraging her to read self-help books on being single and to attend divorced persons' support groups could assist her in elaborating a more adequate set of constructs for predicting the transition she was about to make. Moreover, enactment might be used as a means of helping her to behave 'as if' she were single, before any additional formal steps in that direction were taken. This might take the form of small-scale behavioural experiments in which she might test whether divorce carried the sweeping implications for her core role that she at first imagined. In summary, the phenomenon of 'resistance' is more often the construction of the therapist than of the client. Impediments to therapeutic progress can be minimized if the therapist maintains conditions favourable to the development of new constructs (Kelly 1955, pp. 166 ff.). When such impasses occur, they can typically be traced to genuine shortcomings in the client's existing construct system, and so yield more readily to elaborative and enactment techniques than to direct assault. This tendency for personal construct therapists 'to protect the client from involving core structures before he is ready to consider abandoning them' (Kelly 1955, p. 1146) distinguishes them from cognitive therapists who directly assail the validity or logic of a client's defensive cognitions without first helping him/her explore more adequate alternative constructions.

## Case example

In recent years a post-Kellian personal construct therapy has begun to take shape, incorporating many of Kelly's basic insights while trying to surmount some of the limitations imposed by his particular sociohistorical context. Perhaps the most important of these new directions is the growing tendency of construct therapists to move beyond the traditional one-to-one treatment setting. Kelly himself advocated individual treatment for most disorders because it maximized the number of ways the therapist could be construed by the client, and circumvented difficult issues of therapist collusion with one individual against another. In contemporary perspective this view is somewhat outdated and confining, given the power of spouses, family and group members to validate one another's construing. A review of personal construct contributions to therapy with couples (e.g. G. Neimeyer 1985; Neimeyer and Hudson 1985), families (e.g. Mancuso and Handin 1984; Procter 1981), and groups (Morris 1977; Winter 1985) is beyond the scope of this chapter. In the space available, however, I will try to illustrate the application of construct theory to the treatment of a distressed couple, since working with a system of intermediate size requires a consideration of both intrapersonal and interpersonal conceptualizations and change strategies. Case studies of individual therapy have been provided by Leitner (1980) and Neimeyer (1980).

Jeremy and Lynda were a couple in their late twenties who sought therapy at Jeremy's insistence after three years of marriage. In the initial phone contact with me, Jeremy alluded to an undefined 'crisis' that had erupted in their relationship, and disclosed that he did not know if he could continue in the marriage given these developments. He suggested that I arrange a session with his wife alone, but accepted my recommendation that he accompany her to the session.

In our first contact, I introduced the structure for our sessions, emphasizing that we would try to formulate some concrete goals for therapy that we would work toward for a specified period of time. Thus, I attempted to establish realistic expectations for the course of therapy, in light of the fact that most marital therapy (regardless of orientation) is short-term, requiring the specification of 'targets that are often more circumscribed than one might wish' (Follette and Jacobson 1985). Both Jeremy and Lynda seemed relieved by the prospect of a time-limited intervention, and contracted to meet with me for six weekly sessions, at which time we would negotiate whether further treatment would be useful.

As both spouses discussed the problems that precipitated therapy, it became clear that Lynda had experienced long-standing dissatisfaction regarding her husband's being controlling in the relationship. For example, she vividly related how he tightly regulated household expenditures, indirectly criticizing her 'frivolous' purchase of shoes and other personal items. In addition, he seemed terse and unexpressive, especially in conflict situations, which she described as 'like fighting with a brick wall'. Her failure to 'get through to him' led to her visiting her parents in another city a few weeks prior to therapy, and phoning Jeremy with the message that she didn't want to return.

Interestingly, in Jeremy's view his wife's threat to leave was not his greatest concern. Instead, he regarded the precipitating problem as her disclosure – in the same telephone conversation – that she and a group of friends had casually visited one of her old boyfriends from five years before. This had led to his 'interrogating' her about the nature of the relationship, and his discovery that she had had sex with this boyfriend prior to her meeting Jeremy. Despite Lynda's willingness to return to Jeremy and work on their relationship, and her assurance that she had remained faithful to him throughout their courtship and marriage, this disclosure left Jeremy deeply depressed, angry, and 'physically sick', reactions that had remained intense in the weeks prior to therapy. In fact, the distress that Jeremy continued to experience was so incapacitating that it had threatened the couple's own subsequent (and partially successful) efforts to re-establish their relationship on more egalitarian and emotionally expressive grounds.

In personal construct terms, what seemed required of successful therapy in this case was not simply the development of positive behavioural exchanges between spouses, or even coaching in communication skills, although both strategies were incorporated into therapy as useful ancillary interventions. Instead, what seemed crucial was an understanding and modification of those *role constructs* concerning their relationship that had been challenged by Lynda's disclosure. Specifically, since construct theorists conceptualize negative emotions as indicators of 'unsuccessful' construing (McCoy 1981, p. 96), pinpointing Jeremy's invalidated constructions of the marital relationship (signalled by his emotional upheaval) became a primary goal of treatment.

Some indication of the nature of these dysfunctional role constructs emerged in the first session. In giving his version of their relationship history, Jeremy remarked that he was first attracted to Lynda because in his eyes she was 'shy and sweet . . . the kind of girl that you see in fairy tales'. In keeping with this pristine image, he 'never touched her' until they were engaged, just as he had never touched any of the girls he 'cared about', even though 'they wanted it'. At the same time, Jeremy made it clear that he was not always a 'Prince Charming' in relation to women, since he had had numerous premarital affairs 'just for sex'. This suggested that Jeremy operated with a pre-emptive construction of 'marriagable' women as virginal 'princesses', rather than a more permeable construction of womanhood capable of including normal autonomous sexual behaviour. For her own part, Lynda initially validated his construction of her in the 'princess' role, both by responding positively to his 'romantic' overtures (e.g. proposing to her in a horsedrawn carriage, 'proving his love' by pursuing her despite geographic separation), and by selectively hiding those aspects of her past that were inconsistent with his construction of their reciprocal roles. This relational pattern had been shattered, however, by the disclosure of Lynda's sexuality; and Jeremy reacted in the only way his undifferentiated construction of women permitted: by 'slot-rattling' her to the unverbalized contrast end of his 'princess' construction. According to a personal construct conceptualization of relationship problems (Neimeyer and Neimeyer 1985), this pattern reflects a *disrupted relationship*, which forces both partners to modify their construction of their roles to accommodate new relational realities.

As a homework assignment, I asked each member of the couple to specify three 'target goals' that he or she would like to work toward in the therapy. Both spouses specified problems that gave them 'a great deal' of discomfort. For Lynda, these included 'learning to control her moodiness', and 'gaining more independence' from her husband, whereas for Jeremy, they included 'being more honest about feelings' and 'showing more affection'. Interestingly, both parters also noted sexual dissatisfactions, with Lynda hoping to become 'less sexually inhibited' and Jeremy attempting to become 'less demanding'. An Areas of Change Questionnaire (Weiss and Margolin 1977) completed by both spouses pointed up similar sources of dissatisfaction with their behaviour as a couple.

At the outset of our second session I administered a Relationship Grid (G. Neimeyer and Hudson 1985) in recognition of the fact that couples have their own 'idiosyncratic cognitive sets and schemata' and that 'a formal component of therapy that examines these . . . is needed' (Follette and Jacobson 1985, p. 20). In brief, the grid requires each partner independently to rate ten different reciprocal relationships (e.g. husband to wife, wife to husband) on a standard list of ten construct scales (e.g. affectionate versus distant, forgiving versus holds a grudge). Relationships to be rated include not only the couple's own marriage, but also those of both sets of parents, friends, and an 'ideal' couple (see G. Neimeyer and Hudson 1985, for details of administration and scoring). By performing a principal components analysis on each set of ratings (cf. Neimeyer and Neimeyer 1981), I was able to form some hypotheses not only about the way in which Jeremy and Lynda viewed their own marriage, but also about the fundamental construct hierarchies that each partner used to understand intimate relationships in general.

Significantly, the relational construct systems of the two spouses differed in several respects. At a general level, Jeremy rated only 59 per cent of the entire sample of relationships under the evaluatively 'positive' poles of the constructs, and fully 32 per cent under the 'neutral' zero rating, whereas his wife construed the same marriages as 77 per cent 'positive', and *none* as indeterminate. This suggested that Jeremy was both less optimistic and considerably more uncertain about relationships than Lynda. In particular, Jeremy was unable to construe the marriage of Lynda's parents under *either* pole of *any* of the constructs, suggesting that it was a complete mystery to him. Lynda, on the other hand, had no difficulty in rating her husband's parents, viewing his father as 'withholding' and 'controlling', but as 'taking care of' Jeremy's mother, a pattern Lynda also reported in Jeremy's relationship to her. Both partners construed Jeremy as extremely 'distrustful' of Lynda, and perceived Lynda as 'respectful', 'trusting', and 'supportive' toward him.

Despite this degree of consensus about the nature of their own present relationship, the two spouses seemed to be operating with quite different implicit 'theories' regarding intimacy. Some clues concerning such divergence were provided by examining the intercorrelations among the constructs each used to construe the common set of relationships. For example, Lynda regarded being 'affectionate' as virtually synonymous with 'expressing emotions' ($r=.91$), whereas Jeremy saw the two behaviours as *inversely* related ($r=-.34$). This might be interpreted as reflecting Lynda's belief that emotional exchanges were quite central to a caring relationship, whereas for Jeremy, affection implied suppressing (and perhaps protecting the spouse from) vivid displays of (negative?) feeling. Further differences of this type were evident on several other dimensions (including the relationship between 'support' and 'control', which Jeremy saw as highly correlated and Lynda viewed as diametrically opposed). In light of their target goals, it was also revealing that Jeremy construed 'respect' for others as automatically implying that one 'looked after' them ($r=.96$), while Lynda saw no such implication (r=.00). Finally, the principal component of each grid identified the most 'superordinate' relationship construct for each partner: for Jeremy, this concerned taking care of the spouse, whereas for Lynda, it involved not blaming the partner.

These assessment results prompted several subsequent interventions. These began at a behavioural level, in line with Kelly's (1955) recognition that 'sometimes it is more feasible to try to produce personality readjustments by attacking the symptoms rather than by going directly after the basically faulty structures' (pp. 995–996). Thus, in session two we discussed the couple's angry deadlock regarding sexuality: Lynda wanted to have sex two or three times a week, but Jeremy wanted it seven or eight. As a result, simple physical displays of affection had become fraught with anxiety for both partners, since Lynda inevitably interpreted them as sexual overtures and Jeremy anticipated rejection. I spontaneously suggested a way out of this dilemma by contracting with them to observe four 'sex-free days' in the coming week (two days to be chosen by each spouse), with the provision that Lynda was to 'surprise' her husband by initiating sex on one of them. Both partners laughingly agreed that it sounded 'crazy but fun'. I supplemented this assignment with bibliotherapy using the popular self-help book by Barbach (1984). The following week the two reported that the assignment had gone 'very well indeed', and Lynda noted that Jeremy seemed to be becoming generally more expressive of affection.

As therapy progressed, I began to supplement behavioural experiments of this kind with increasingly cognitive interventions. For example, in our third session I brought up Jeremy's apparent inability to construe the nature of Lynda's parents' marriage. His explanation that he 'didn't want to speculate about something that wasn't his business' was met by Lynda's rejoinder that his in-laws 'should be his business'. This led to a spirited discussion of the marital relationship of her parents, and the recognition that in their own marriage, Jeremy and Lynda seemed to recapitulate her father's tendency to 'always control the family' and her mother's tendency to 'drift to the sidelines'. This enabled me to formulate Lynda's 'sensitivity' to Jeremy's unilaterally making many of their joint decisions partly as a (transference) reaction to the power relations in her family of origin, an interpretation that helped Jeremy appreciate her point of view more fully. In later sessions, we frequently used casual enactment procedures to foster more adequate 'sociality', or perspective-taking, by asking each spouse to enact the other's role in a 'replay' of a recent argument or discussion. We also jointly designed homework deriving from our previous repertory grid assessment of their relational construct systems. In one assignment, for example, each spouse suggested a 'difference of opinion' that 'made them curious' in their grid results. For her part, Lynda chose to examine 'the place of emotional expression' in affectionate relationships, whereas Jeremy wanted to follow up their relation to their parents by talking further about their similarities to and differences from *both* sets of parents. These then formed the 'agenda' for controlled and time-limited between-session conversations that were tape-recorded and discussed in subsequent sessions.

In the later stages of therapy Jeremy reported important gains in the overall quality of his marriage, but continued to feel 'deeply depressed' about Lynda's premarital sexual involvements, especially when he was alone. For this reason, I relaxed the fairly high degree of structure in our earlier sessions, in order to promote exploration of the 'looser', more preverbal relational constructs that apparently had been invalidated. In the fifth session Jeremy articulated this superordinate construction, referring to it as a 'madonna-prostitute complex'. He admitted that in his mind, 'there were no shades of grey': women were either one or the other, with nothing in between. In light of this, Jeremy's susceptibility to depression was under-standable, since reliance upon such highly polarized constructions may leave one vulnerable to severe invalidation in the face of ambiguous realities. Thus, dichotomous construing has been linked to depression proneness in both cognitive (Beck *et al.* 1979) and personal construct (R. Neimeyer 1984, 1985c) models of this problem. Interestingly, Lynda's construction of men was much more differentiated: she categorized them as 'cowboys and Californians . . . all of them different'. This suggested that it was Jeremy's, and not Lynda's, construction of the opposite sex that most needed elabora-tion, and led me to make special efforts to promote a more complex understanding of his wife's perspective. In one such intervention, I asked him to 'put himself in a woman's position' and tell me why he (as Lynda) might withhold from a fiancé something as important as details of previous sexual activity. Jeremy answered, 'Well, because she thought I wouldn't marry her otherwise,' then paused and added, 'because she loved me.' The next session he explained that he had decided 'not to ask her any more questions' about other lovers, and to 'try to accept' what had happened as something in the past. Drawing on his remark that he 'felt he had lost something', I formulated his sadness as 'grieving for a lost image of their relationship'. We also examined the way in which Lynda's behaviour had served temporarily to validate his inflexible view of her. As she remarked, 'I did everything I could to be that madonna.' In this way we framed their dysfunctional role relationship as a reciprocal one, and suggested that elaborating it was a responsibility both shared.

Lynda and Jeremy came to our last contracted session reporting that they were 'getting along better than they had in three years'. They noted that they were 'fighting fairer now', and had initiated a spontaneous quid pro quo contract: that Jeremy would cut back one cigarette per day for every pound that Lynda lost on her new diet plan. They requested extending therapy by one session to 'fine tune' their relationship and troubleshoot any difficulties that arose in implementing their self-initiated contract. In that subsequent session, Lynda reported that she had 'messed up' the diet once, but had got 'right back on it'. Post-therapy assessment on their personalized target goals questionnaires indicated that they had made 'a great deal of improvement' to 'total improvement' on five out of the six relational problems that had brought them into therapy (for Jeremy, becoming more open with his feelings and showing more affection; for Lynda, controlling her moodiness; and for both spouses, developing better sexual relations). They also reported that they had continued their sexual bibliotherapy, and that Lynda felt the 'pressure had been taken off of her' as Jeremy had become more playful and less insistent. The one residual area of conflict concerned Jeremy's tendency to subtly control their joint decision-making. A follow-up 'booster' session three months later confirmed that their marriage had remained 'better than average' since therapy, though they continued to work on their own on equalizing power in the relationship. Lynda agreed with Jeremy's assessment that with the help of therapy, they had 'climbed a number of stairs. When we first came in, we were in the basement. Now we're near the top.'

## Conclusion

In this chapter I have tried to sketch the history and theoretical outlines of personal construct therapy, illustrating its application at both a strategic and technical level. In doing this, I have had to omit much – particularly the extensive empirical literature on personal constructs in clinical practice that is reviewed elsewhere (Neimeyer 1985b). But I hope that this chapter has conveyed some of the spirit and substance of a personal construct approach, and hinted at the contribution it can make to the eventual integration of psychotherapeutic practice. As one of the original wellsprings of cognitive therapy, construct theory remains remarkably contemporary, and may help shape the future – as well as the past – of our discipline.

# References

Adams-Webber, J.R. (1979) *Personal construct theory: Concepts and applications*. New York: Wiley.

Adams-Webber, J.R. (1981) Fixed role therapy. In R.L. Corsini (ed.) *Handbook of innovative psychotherapies*. New York: Wiley.

Arnkoff, D.B. (1983) Common and specific factors in cognitive therapy. In M.J. Lambert (ed.) *Psychotherapy and patient relationships*. Homewood IL: Dorsey.

Arnkoff, D.B. and Glass, C. (1982) Cognitive clinical constructs. In P. Kendall (ed.) *Advances in cognitive-behavioral research and therapy*, vol. 1. New York: Academic Press.

Bannister, D. (1962) The nature and measurement of schizophrenic thought disorder. *Journal of Mental Science*, *108*, 825–842.

Bannister, D. (1975) Personal construct theory psychotherapy. In D. Bannister (ed.) *Issues and approaches in the psychological therapies*. New York: Wiley.

Bannister, D. (1977) The logic of passion. In D. Bannister (ed.) *New perspectives in personal construct theory*. London: Academic Press.

Bannister, D. and Mair, J.M.M. (1968) *The evaluation of personal constructs*. New York: Academic Press.

Barbach, L. (1984) *For each other*. New York: Signet.

Beck, A.T., Rush, A.J., Shaw, B.F. and Emery, G. (1979). *Cognitive therapy of depression*. New York: Guilford Press.

Bonarius, H. (1970) Fixed role therapy: A double paradox. *British Journal of Medical Psychology*, *43*, 213–219.

Brown, H.I. (1977) *Perception, theory, and commitment*. Chicago: University of Chicago Press.

Bruner, J.S. (1956) A cognitive theory of personality. *Contemporary Psychology*, *1*, 355–357.

Button, E. (ed.) (1985) *Personal construct theory and mental health*. Beckenham, Kent: Croom Helm.

Crockett, W.H. (1982) The organization of construct systems. In J.C. Mancuso and J.R. Adams-Webber (eds) *The construing person*. New York: Praeger.

Duck, S.W. (1977) Inquiry, hypothesis, and the quest for validation. In S.W. Duck (ed.) *Theories of interpersonal attraction*. London: Academic Press.

Ellis, A. (1979) Toward a new theory of personality. In A. Ellis and J.M. Whiteley (eds) *Theoretical and empirical foundations of Rational-Emotive Therapy*. Monterey, CA: Brooks/Cole.

Epting, F.R. (1984) *Personal construct counseling and psychotherapy*. New York: Wiley.

Epting, F.R. and Amerikaner, M. (1980) Optimal functioning: A personal construct approach. In A.W. Landfield and L. Leitner (eds) *Personal construct psychology*. New York: Wiley.

Follette, W. and Jacobson, N. (1985) Assessment and treatment of incompatible marital relationships. In W. Ickes (ed.) *Compatible and incompatible relationships*. New York: Springer-Verlag.

Fransella, F. (1972) *Personal change and reconstruction*. New York: Academic Press.

Fransella, F. (1981) Nature babbling to herself: The self-characterization as a therapeutic tool. In H. Bonarius, R. Holland and S. Rosenberg (eds) *Personal construct psychology: Recent advances in theory and practice*. New York: St Martins.

Fransella, F. and Bannister, D. (1977) *A manual for repertory grid technique*. London: Academic Press.

Goldfried, M.R. (1980) Psychotherapy as coping skills training. In M.J. Mahoney (ed.) *Psychotherapy process*. New York: Plenum.

Guidano, V.F. and Liotti, G. (1983) *Cognitive processes and emotional disorders*. New York: Guilford Press.

Gustafson, J. (1981) The complex secret of brief psychotherapy in the works of Malan and Balint. In S. Budman (ed.) *Forms of brief therapy*. New York: Guilford Press.

Karst, T.O. (1980) The relationship between personal construct theory and psychotherapeutic techniques. In A.W. Landfield and L.M. Leitner (eds) *Personal construct psychology: Psychotherapy and personality*. New York: Wiley.

Karst, T.O. and Trexler, L.D. (1970) Initial study using fixed role therapy and rational-emotive therapy in treating public speaking anxiety. *Journal of Consulting and Clinical Psychology*, *34*, 360–366.

Kelly, G.A. (1955) *The psychology of personal constructs*. New York: Norton.

Kelly, G.A. (1966) A brief introduction to personal construct theory. In D. Bannister (ed.) *Perspectives in personal construct theory*. London: Academic Press.

Kelly, G.A. (1969a) The psychotherapeutic relationship. In B. Maher (ed.) *Clinical psychology and personality: The selected papers of George Kelly*. New York: Wiley.

Kelly, G.A. (1969b) The autobiography of a theory. In B. Maher (ed.) *Clinical psychology and personality: The selected papers of George Kelly*. New York: Wiley.

Kelly, G.A. (1969c) Personal construct theory and the psychotherapeutic interview. In B. Maher (ed.) *Clinical psychology and personality: The selected papers of George Kelly*. New York: Wiley.

Kelly, G.A. (1970) Behavior is an experiment. In D. Bannister (ed.) *Perspectives in personal construct theory*. London: Academic Press.

Kelly, G.A. (1973) Fixed role therapy. In R.M. Jurjevich (ed.) *Direct psychotherapy*. Coral Gables, Fla.: University of Miami Press.

Kelly, G.A. (1977) The psychology of the unknown. In D. Bannister (ed.) *New perspectives in personal construct theory*. London: Academic Press.

Kenny, V. (1985) The psychological reconstruction of life. *Irish Journal of Psychotherapy*, *13*, 2.

Kremsdorf, R.B. (1985) An extension of fixed-role therapy with a couple. In F.R.

Epting and A.W. Landfield (eds) *Anticipating personal construct theory*. Lincoln: University of Nebraska Press.

Lakatos, I. (1970) Falsification and the methodology of scientific research programmes. In I. Lakatos and A. Musgrave (eds) *Criticism and the growth of knowledge*. Cambridge: Cambridge University Press.

Landfield, A.W. (1976) A personal construct approach to suicidal behavior. In P. Slater (ed.) *Explorations of intrapersonal space*. New York: Wiley.

Leitner, L.M. (1980) Personal construct treatment of a severely disturbed woman. In A.W. Landfield and L.M. Leitner (eds) *Personal construct psychology: Psychotherapy and personality*. New York: Wiley.

McCoy, M. (1977) A reconstruction of emotion. In D. Bannister (ed.) *New perspectives in personal constraint theory*. London: Academic Press.

McCoy, M. (1981) Positive and negative emotion. In H. Bonarius, R. Holland and S. Rosenberg (eds) *Personal construct psychology: Recent advances in theory and practice*. New York: St Martins.

Mahoney, M.J. (1977) Personal science. In A . Ellis and R. Grieger (eds) *Handbook of rational-emotive therapy*. New York: Springer.

Mahoney, M.J. and Arnkoff, D. (1978) Cognitive and self-control therapies. In S. Garfield and A. Bergin (eds) *Handbook of psychotherapy and behavior change*. New York: Wiley.

Mancuso, J.C. and Adams-Webber, J.R. (1982) *The construing person*. New York: Praeger.

Mancuso, J.C. and Ceely, S.G. (1980) The self as memory processing. *Cognitive Therapy and Research*, *4*, 1–25.

Mancuso, J.C. and Handin, K.H. (1984) Prompting parents toward constructivist caregiving practices. In I. Sigel and L. Laosa (eds) *Changing families*. New York: Plenum.

Markley, R.P., Zelhart, P.F. and Jackson, T.T. (1982) Explorations in fixed role therapy. *Fort Hays Studies*, *3*. 2.

Meichenbaum, D. and Gilmore, J.B. (1984) The nature of unconscious processes: A cognitive-behavioral perspective. In K. Bowers and D. Meichenbaum (eds) *The unconscious reconsidered*. New York: Wiley.

Mischel, W. (1980) George Kelly's anticipation of psychology: A personal tribute. In M.J. Mahoney (ed.) *Psychotherapy process*. New York: Plenum.

Morris, J.B. (1977) The prediction and measurement of change in a psychotherapy group using the repertory grid. In F. Fransella and D. Bannister (eds) *A manual for repertory grid technique*. New York: Academic Press.

Neimeyer, G.J. (1985) A personal construct approach to the counseling of couples. In F.R. Epting and A.W. Landfield (eds) *Anticipating personal construct theory*. Lincoln: Nebraska Press.

Neimeyer, G.J. and Hudson, J.E. (1985) Couple's constructs: Personal systems in marital satisfaction. In D. Bannister (ed.) *Issues and approaches in personal construct theory*. New York: Academic Press.

Neimeyer, G.J. and Neimeyer, R.A. (1981) Personal construct perspectives on cognitive assessment. In T. Merluzzi, C. Glass and M. Genest (eds) *Cognitive assessment*. New York: Guilford Press.

Neimeyer, R.A. (1980) George Kelly as therapist: A review of his tapes. In A.W. Landfield and L.M. Leitner (eds) *Personal construct psychology: Psychotherapy and personality*. New York: Academic Press.

Neimeyer, R.A. (1981) The structure of meaningfulness of tacit construing. In H. Bonarius, R. Holland and S. Rosenberg (eds) *Personal construct psychology: Recent advances in theory and practice*. New York: St Martins.

Neimeyer, R.A. (1984) Toward a personal construct conceptualization of depression and suicide. In F.R. Epting and R.A. Neimeyer (eds) *Personal meanings of death: Applications of personal construct theory to clinical practice*. New York: Hemisphere/McGraw-Hill.

Neimeyer, R.A. (1985a) *The development of personal construct psychology*. Lincoln: Nebraska Press.

Neimeyer, R.A. (1985b) Personal constructs in clinical practice. In P. Kendall (ed.) *Advances in cognitive-behavioral research and therapy*, vol. 4. New York: Academic Press.

Neimeyer, R.A. (1985c) Personal constructs in depression: Research and clinical implications. In E. Button (ed.) *Personal construct theory and mental health*. Beckenham, Kent: Croom Helm.

Neimeyer, R.A. and Neimeyer, G.J. (1985) Disturbed relationships. In E. Button (ed.) *Personal construct theory and mental health*. Beckenham, Kent: Croom Helm.

Procter, H. (1981) Family construct psychology. In S. Walrond-Skinner (ed.) *Developments in family therapy*. London: Routledge.

Rogers, C.R. (1956) Intellectualized psychotherapy. *Contemporary Psychology*, *1*, 337–338.

Soldz, S. (1984) Hostility in the severely disturbed personality. Paper presented at the Fifth International Congress on Personal Construct Psychology, Boston.

Strupp, H.H. (1977) A reformulation of the dynamics of the therapist's contribution. In A.S. Gurman and A.M. Razin (eds) *Effective psychotherapy*. New York: Pergamon.

Wachtel, P. (1977) *Psychoanalysis and behavior therapy: Toward an integration*. New York: Basic Books.

Weiss, R. and Margolin, G. (1977) Marital conflict and accord. In A. Ciminero, K. Calhoun and H. Adams (eds) *Handbook for behavioral assessment*. New York: Wiley.

Widom, C.S. (1976) Interpersonal and personal construct systems in psychopaths. *Journal of Consulting and Clinical Psychology*, *44*, 614–623.

Winter, D. (1985) Group therapy with depressives: A personal construct theory perspective. *International Journal of Mental Health*, *13*, 67–85.

CHAPTER NINE   **Interpersonal Cognitive Problem-Solving Therapy (ICPS)**
*Jerome J. Platt, Maurice F. Prout and David S. Metzger*

**History and underpinnings of interpersonal cognitive problem-solving therapy**

*Historical development of ICPS*

Psychotherapy, including dynamically-orientated psychology, has long been conceptualized as including some focus upon an internal 'problem-solving' process. In the course of traditional treatment, problem-solving was assumed to become enhanced in some unspecified (non-operationally defined) manner. Yet, serious attention to a definition of problem-solving, in terms of the *capacity to problem-solve in real life situations*, only appears to date from Jahoda (1953). Jahoda, in contrast to earlier writers, directly identified the capacity to problem-solve as a criterion defining positive mental health. Until recently, however, this suggestion was not taken seriously by clinicians or clinical researchers, for whom the primary focus remained those processes (e.g. motives, conflicts) which interfered with the ability to face and resolve problems. Problem-solving has, however, come to occupy an important role in cognitive-behaviour therapy.

The study of problem-solving has a long and respected history in psychology. Until about fifteen years ago, however, the focus of studies was only upon the measurement of cognitive abilities when the person was confronted with impersonal tasks, such as solving a puzzle or syllogism. As part of the study of problem-solving, tests were developed to measure such variables as general reasoning ability, concept formation, and intellectual creativity.

Davis (1966) prepared a review of the research and theory in human problem-solving which summarized three areas of problem-solving theory: traditional learning, a cognitive *gestalt* approach, and a computer/ mathematical model. He stated:

recent empirical studies are categorized according to the type of behavior elicited by the particular problem solving tasks: anagram, 'insight', water-jar, and arithmetic problems are considered to be solved by covert trial-and-error behavior, switch-light classification, probability learning, and numerous 'miscellaneous' tasks are approached by overt trial-and-error behavior.' (Davis 1966, p. 36)

Simon and Newell (1971) reviewed cognitive problem-solving thinking in 1971, yet never mentioned anything related to interpersonal functioning. They stated that 'a theory of problem solving should predict the performance of a problem solver handling specified tasks' (Simon and Newell 1971, p.145).

Meichenbaum and Goodman (1971) made one of the first attempts to relate problem-solving to human adjustment in children. However, again, the problems presented to the children were impersonal in nature: the Porteus Maze Test and performance IQ on the WISC. They hypothesized that children act impulsively because prior to taking action they do not think through the problem. The study employed an individual training procedure which required the impulsive child to talk to himself, at first overtly and later covertly, in an attempt to increase self-control. As a consequence, the impulsive handling of other paper and pencil tasks was reduced but there was no significant change in the child's impulsive behaviour while in the classroom; in other words, reducing the child's impulsive behaviours while handling impersonal paper and pencil tasks did not generalize to the child's interpersonal behaviours. It was not until the early 1970s that the focus of research in problem-solving skills began to shift from impersonal to interpersonal problems.

## Major theoretical concepts

The initial writings in the area of interpersonal problem-solving are represented by the works of D'Zurilla and Goldfried (1971); Goldfried and D'Zurilla (1969); Goldfried and Davison (1976). These authors suggested that a person's effectiveness in coping with the world is determined largely by the ability to utilize problem-solving skills. Problem-solving was defined as both a cognitive and behavioural process that (a) makes available a variety of potentially effective response alternatives, and (b) increases the probability of selecting the most effective response from among these various alternatives (Goldfried and D'Zurilla 1971, p. 180). According to these authors the concept of 'effectiveness' is analogous to the solution of a problem. Not only will effective solutions allow for the management of the problem at hand, but perhaps equally important is the concept that additional positive consequences may result from newfound ways of managing the difficult situation.

In order to become an effective problem-solver, Goldfried and D'Zurilla outlined five components to the process: (a) general orientation to problem-solving and problematic situations; (b) problem definition and formulation; (c) generation of alternatives; (d) decision-making; and finally (e) verification. They emphasized that these steps were developed as a guide for training and that modifications of emphasis and sequence would be necessary, contingent upon the client and/or problem situation.

To Goldfried and D'Zurilla's credit, 'problems' were defined not as representative of a psychopathological state, but rather conceptualized as the normal ebb and flow of living life. Hence, difficulties were portrayed to the client as normal, and it was emphasized that the development and implementation of skills were needed in the management of both minor and major life events. In addition, the notion of brainstorming was underscored in negotiating problems, with the intent of generating a large number of alternative solutions. The task at hand during this second stage was quantity, later to be followed by determining the quality and 'fit' of each alternative solution to a particular problem area. In order to render an assessment of each solution, the client was urged to consider the various consequences if that strategy was employed. While this component is a subjective enterprise, it allowed the person access to a stage of assessment and safe exploration prior to carrying out activity in vivo. Finally, verification enabled assessment of actual behaviour to determine whether the attempted solution was successful or whether it required modification.

Central to their proposal was the notion that many life events which are problematic are not amenable to a fixed and static process. Rather, most problematic situations are in a constant state of flux requiring new strategies and alternatives to be developed as the situation transforms itself. Hence perception of the situation may change, initial goals and desires may be modified, and the original anticipated consequences may also alter. Thus, according to Kanfer and Busenmeyer (1982), in order to be an effective problem-solver the client must recognize that the situation may require a number of interdependent solutions whereby the feedback process becomes a critical element in guiding later decisions in an evolving process. According to the authors, 'dynamic decisions are like a sequence of small moves that are guided by feedback to a moving target' (Kanfer and Busenmeyer 1982, p. 246). Some problems that would require an ongoing process would be: entering the job market, divorce/marriage, changing jobs or career, ageing, and chronic illness.

In modifying the five-step model proposed by Goldfried and D'Zurilla, Kanfer and Busenmeyer suggested that: (a) it might be better to conceptualize the original goal not as a simple entity but rather as a series of discrete goals; (b) the brainstorming technique may not be appropriate for situations which require ongoing modification – hence, while the generation of alternatives is essential to effective problem-solving, it must be done within the context of an ongoing process, so that alternatives are always being generated and altered depending upon the changing circumstances; and (c) verification should not be viewed as the final outcome of a stepwise process, but rather should continue as the problem evolves and changes.

While the original model proposed by Goldfried and Davison is of major importance in the management of many real life problems, the modifications generated by Kanfer and Busenmeyer may allow for a process-orientated model and has wider utility in the management of stressful life events.

Perhaps one of the most intensive studies of the problem-solving process as it relates to human adjustment has been carried out by the senior author and his associates at Hahnemann University School of Medicine – George Spivack, Myrna Shure, Jerome M. Siegel, and Marshall Swift. Over a period of some fifteen years, these researchers have investigated the role of problem-solving in the development of social competence and the adjustment process overall. In particular, research has been directed towards the identification of the thinking processes that underlie the successful resolution of personal or interpersonal problems, and the development of remedial programmes for individuals who have demonstrated difficulty in coping with problems of daily living. Among the groups studied have been pre-school children, latency age children, adolescents, youthful offenders, heroin addicts, pregnant teenagers, adolescent and adult psychiatric patients, and the elderly.

The basic assumption underlying this research has been that when a person is confronted with an immediate need or interpersonal conflict situation, it is reasonable to assume he stands a good chance of resolving his problems if he is characteristically sensitive and knowledgeable about how to solve them. Such problem-solving may encompass an ability to articulate the problem and conceive of options available for actions, the ability to see the necessary means and potential obstacles that comprise any one plan of actions and the tendency to weigh consequences relative to actions. The approach itself has come to be known as interpersonal cognitive problem-solving (ICPS).

The body of work that has evolved at Hahnemann University has been enriched by the work of others around the country, all of which taken together provides at this point a substantial data base to support the theory and its particular social competence model. To date it has resulted in a number of validated prevention and therapeutic intervention programmes for high-risk groups of various ages, from children to teenagers and adults.

## How client problems are conceptualized

The theory as originally proposed by Spivack presents a set of related axioms: that a key element in *any* explanation of interpersonal adjustment or psychopathology is the quality of social relationships; that experiencing interpersonal problems is a natural consequence of being human; and that the centrality and ubiquitousness of interpersonal problems points to the significance of the ability to learn and employ means of solving problems.

The theory postulates the hypothetical construct of an ability to recognize and think through or 'problem-solve' interpersonal problem situations. This 'process' construct is offered to explain significant individual differences in the efficiency with which we navigate through our worlds of everyday problems with significant others throughout our lives.

Finally, the theory hypothesizes that: (a) interpersonal cognitive problem-solving skills are learned (e.g. probably reflecting early childrearing interactions and specific parental problem-solving styles; (b) different interpersonal cognitive problem-solving skills may have different significance for the social adjustment and mental health of individuals depending upon age; (c) manifest deficiency in interpersonal cognitive problem-solving in an individual at any point in time may reflect (i) insufficient learning of such skills to begin with (e.g. due to deficient childrearing or neurological defects), (ii) blockage of such thinking due to interfering emotions (e.g. irrational or defensive thinking), or (iii) deterioration in such thinking (e.g. with advanced age or brain damage); and finally (d) therapeutic or educational programmes that enhance the operation of interpersonal cognitive problem-solving skills or remove barriers to their exercise will enhance social adjustment, and/or prevent the development of psychological dysfunction.

The theory proposes (and a growing body of research data supports the assertion) that at the psychological level there evolves with normal growth a grouping of interpersonal cognitive problem-solving skills that mediate the capacity with which we cope with the everyday interpersonal problems that confront us. If the growing child is brought up in a familial, school and community environment which teaches and supports the exercise of such cognitive processes, the child will grow in effectiveness. If, on the other hand, this does not occur, the growing person will begin to manifest the various emotional and interpersonal stresses and symptoms of psychological dysfunction. In a parallel fashion, circumstances that inhibit the exercise of these social skills, or cause a deterioration in their operation, will also cause such dysfunction. Conversely, programmes or experiences which enhance these skills in at-risk (i.e. low problem-solving or likely deterioration) groups will decrease the likelihood of the occurrence of dysfunction. Details of this social competence theory, its research development, its implications for psychopathology, and its derivative intervention programmes have been reviewed elsewhere (Platt and Spivack 1975; Shure and Spivack 1978; Spivack and Shure 1974; Spivack, Platt and Shure 1976; Spivack and Shure 1982).

The correlational evidence validating the relevance of interpersonal cognitive problem-solving skills to dysfunction throughout the life span is extensive. The skills appearing to be necessary for successful resolution of problematic interpersonal situations include: (a) sensitivity to interpersonal problems, (b) causal thinking, (c) consequential thinking, (d) alternative thinking, (e) means–ends thinking, and (f) perspective-taking. Some of these, and the research supporting them, will be described below.

**Alternative thinking**     The capacity to generate alternative solutions to everyday interpersonal problems has been related to indices of adjustment across the full life span, in pre-school children through eighth graders (e.g. Schiller 1978; Shure and Spivack 1978, 1980; Arend, Gove and Sroufe 1979; Elias 1978; Johnson, Yu and Roopnarine 1980; Richard and Dodge 1981; Shure 1980; Marsh, Serafica and Barenboim 1981), in adolescents (Platt *et al*. 1974), in adults (Platt and Spivack 1972a, 1972b, 1973, 1974), and in the elderly (Spivack *et al*. 1978).

**Consequential thinking**     This is defined as considering the consequences of one's social acts, in terms of their impact both on other people and on oneself. There may be two features to this competence. One concerns the possible consequences which spontaneously arise in the mind of the person in a problem situation, and the other relates to the immediacy of these anticipated consequences. Research to date suggests that this capacity begins to play a significant role in social adjustment from adolescence (see Spivack and Levine 1963; Spivack, Platt and Shure 1976). One study

(Spivack and Levine 1963) further indicates that the absence of such considerations among disturbed, impulsive teenagers involves the ignoring not only of possible negative consequences of punishable acts, but also of the possible positive consequences of rewardable acts. Thus, the deficiency in such thinking is not specific in its implications for transgression (i.e. failing to be deterred by consideration of negative consequences) but has broader implications (i.e. failing to reach beyond the present and into the future when contemplating *all* action).

**Means–ends thinking** This is defined as articulating the sequences of step-by-step means that may be necessary to carry out a particular solution to an interpersonal problem. It requires an ordering of steps that might be taken, some recognition that such planning takes time, and an acknowledge-ment that there may be obstacles to any plan that will require attention. The process of means–end thinking probably requires the capacity to consider a complex series of possible events, including how more than one person may interact in a given situation. Such is suggested by the intimate relationship the process bears to perspective-taking (see Platt and Spivack 1973; Spivack, Platt and Shure 1976; Shure 1980), which is the ability to appreciate the different points of view different people may have when they jointly confront the same situation.

**Social-causal thinking** This reflects the degree to which the individual spontaneously understands that how one feels or acts, or what has occurred by way of a problem, has been determined by prior events. In a general sense, this skill also reflects an awareness of the existence of motives in human behaviour, an understanding of which may often help one appreciate the reasonableness or likely success of a solution. Here we find an interest-ing parallel with consequential thinking, one that is perhaps more than coincidental. Both spontaneous causal and spontaneous consequential thinking involve the temporal dimension. In one case the person appreciates a current problem in terms of future consequences, and in the other in terms of previous causes. A factor analytic study of interpersonal cognitive problem-solving in adults (Platt and Spivack 1973) found that measures of these two processes defined the same factor. The suggestion is that these two skills may represent a quality of temporal sequential thinking that bears directly on human adjustment. The better-adjusted individual not only weighs alternatives but sees a problem in the light of prior causes and later effects.

Having briefly described several interpersonal cognitive problem-solving skills, it is important to emphasize the process quality of such cognition. Interpersonal cognitive problem-solving skills define how people think in the area of interpersonal problems, specifically in appreciating and coping with problems. The working assumption underlying this orientation is that although the success with which a problem is solved on any given occasion may be determined by what the person thinks, in the long term the person will come up with the right solution when interpersonal cognitive problem-solving processes have been learned and applied (i.e. the person knows how to think problems through when they arise).

## Practical applications

### *The therapeutic relationship*

Since the major emphasis in this approach to problem-solving is interpersonal, considerable weight is placed upon the interaction between client and therapist. The therapist will often function in a variety of capacities depending upon where the client is in the problem-solving process. Hence the therapist may function as a clarifier of misconceptions – for example, 'The degree of stress you experience appears related to the way you manage situations with your (wife, boss, father, neighbour, etc.). The stress frequently can be anchored to an interpersonal event.' The therapist may serve in the role of an educator, instructing the client in the various stages of problem-solving. Within this role the therapist may help structure with the client 'safe' situational difficulties that can be simulated and role-played for assessment purposes. Also, the therapist usually functions as an active provider of feedback and as a facilitator to the client – for example, 'Let me share with you my reaction if I were the other party,' or 'How might you approach him differently, knowing how defensive he usually is around that issue?' Above all, the relationship is founded upon trust whereby the client can learn interpersonal skills in an atmosphere that is nonthreatening. The relationship is often active; specific problems are delineated, alternatives are worked on, potential consequences that the client may not see are brought to light, and role-playing is often utilized.

In many ways the therapist functions as an active consultant to the client. The assessment of the problem(s), investigation of old ineffectual solutions, the development and teaching of new alternatives, and the exposure within the 'safe' environment of the therapist's office all require the active and involved participation by both parties.

The therapist must be aware of his own reactions to the client. Frequently, the manner in which the client interacts with the therapist represents how he is perceived by others – aggressive, unassertive, passive-aggressive, and so on. At appropriate times providing active feedback to the client as to how he comes across, what he does and does not do, is most helpful in beginning to manage problem situations. While the role of the therapist is active, it should not be overbearing nor foster a clinging dependency. The ultimate goal of therapy is the development of an effective interpersonal problem-solving strategy on the part of the client. The result is that the therapist gradually fades to the background and the client takes more control over defining and solving problems.

## Strategies of treatment

The particular format and length of problem-solving therapy is in many ways contingent upon the patient and the skills he/she brings with him/her to the treatment situation. Some patients begin with fairly well-developed skills in the interpersonal area and require relatively few sessions devoted to the elucidation of the essential concepts of interpersonal cognitive problem-solving. Others come with a much more limited repertoire of effective problem-solving skills and thus require a more intensive (in both time and content) sequence of training in the basic skills and their application.

The therapist is consequently placed initially, and indeed throughout the treatment process, in the role of assessing current skills and planning for the introduction of new learning tasks which will add incrementally to the existing skills repertoire of the patient. The therapist must, therefore, not only be highly proficient in the techniques of skill assessment and training, but must also be flexible in the implementation of the various programme elements.

Certain general principles are emphasized throughout (ICPS) treatment programmes. These include an attitude that: (a) problems of daily living almost always involve interpersonal issues, even if they do not appear to be interpersonal on the surface; (b) such problems are common, normal and to be expected in everyday life; (c) the effective management of interpersonal problems is best learned by focusing on the here and now rather than on the historical events and issues which have combined to produce the problem; and (d) many interpersonal problems can be avoided or resolved more effectively following the acquisition of appropriate problem-solving skills.

Structured psychotherapy programmes which include both treatment manuals and client workbooks exist. Platt, Spivack and Swift (1974) originally designed, and Platt and Spivack (1976) further developed, a highly structured programme for adolescents and adults entitled 'Interpersonal Problem-Solving Group Therapy'. This programme was designed to train individuals in interpersonal problem-solving skills. Platt and Duome (1980) later developed a structured programme specifically designed to meet the needs of drug abuse clients (see Platt *et al.* 1982).

## *Major treatment techniques*

The first set of skills typically focused upon in ICPS therapy are those subsumed under the general heading of problem clarification. How do you know when you have a problem? This particular question relates to the observation that many patients are unaware of the problem(s) they may be facing at a particular point in time.

In initial sessions, patients are encouraged to generate lists of problems – common problem situations they encounter in daily living. In doing so, the patient presents the therapist with what is typically a wealth of opportunity to highlight some common aspects of problem situations. These include the fact that most problems of consequence are interpersonal in nature, and that even if not primarily interpersonal, they often do have an interpersonal aspect. Furthermore, these problems often have an identifiable subjective impact – they produce discomfort, confusion, or anger and often lead to social withdrawal. While it is always preferable that these 'symptoms' of existing problems emanate from patients themselves, the degree to which this occurs will again depend upon the level of ICPS skills which the patient brings to the initial session – in this case, the specific skills associated with recognition of the existence of a problem.

The subjective impact of problem situations is identified to the patient as a cue signalling the presence of problems and the necessity for the initiation of a thoughtful process of resolution. One of the most critical aspects of the therapy is this focus upon process. Both patients and therapists must be acutely aware of this focus. The purpose of ICPS therapy is not to solve a specific problem or even a set of problems, but rather to learn a process which has broad application to the patient in a variety of interpersonal situations.

Other sessions in the early stages of therapy may, depending upon the level of the patient's skill repertoire as noted above, focus on more basic skills involved in the clarification of problem situations. These might include exercises designed to help patients separate facts from opinions, techniques for collecting relevant information about the problem situation, or learning to collect information about how others view the problem situation. The major emphasis of these sessions is that in order to deal with problems effectively a substantial amount of information from the environment must be collected and considered. Patients must become sensitive not only to their internal cues but to external ones as well.

It is this environmental context of problem situations to which the next several sessions are directed. In these sessions patients are directed to focus upon skills involving developing awareness of, and sensitivity to, the emotional states (feelings) of others, and methods for communicating their own emotional states (feelings). Through the use of role-playing exercises, discussion, and homework assignments, patients gain expertise in learning how others are feeling and what effects these feelings may have upon the existence and resolution of the problem. This requires sensitivity not only to verbal but also to nonverbal communication. Patients are taught to look for and recognize facial expressions, gestures and other bodily cues. Additional time is spent in practising their own skills in communicating feelings effectively. While much of this work takes place within the session, there is increasing emphasis placed upon the application of these skills by the patient outside of therapy. Consequently, as therapy progresses, a greater portion of time is spent discussing the success with which the skills are being applied by the patient in the course of their daily lives outside of the therapy sessions. Although the emphasis throughout the programme is upon cognitive skill development, it is important that patients realize that behavioural change is the criterion through which attainment of therapeutic goals is determined. Thus, the increasing employment by the patient of ICPS skills in actual life situations is not only part of the training process, it is an end-goal of training itself.

It is this emphasis upon taking appropriate action to which the final series of sessions is directed. The underlying theme of these sessions is that for actions to lead to desired results, the thinking skills learned earlier in therapy must be applied. Problems must be recognized, clearly defined and articulated, the involvement of others must be acknowledged and understood, and lines of communication must be established. This sequence of problem-solving thought processes may itself become the focus of several sessions, the point of which is to emphasize the destructive nature of impulsive behaviour and the absolute necessity to think before acting. To highlight this point patients may be encouraged to think aloud, to examine the manner in which they decide on courses of action, and to consider appropriate alternative 'styles' of action.

A variety of artificial and real life problems may be used in the subsequent series of sessions. These problems are used initially to provide patients with opportunities to practise skills in defining problem situations and yet move fairly quickly toward the development of 'plans' and strategies for actions. This is facilitated by the introduction of work devoted to the generation of alternative thinking. Patients at this stage are encouraged to think of a variety of potential actions which could achieve more effective control or resolution of their problems. The ability to generate a number of alternative actions is introduced as a critical skill in the light of the intractability of many interpersonal problems. Some well-planned actions may not produce the effect anticipated; some simply do not work, and patients must be prepared to sustain action over an extended period of time. Thus there is an absolute necessity to have a variety of alternate courses of action readily available.

Closely linked to the notion of alternative thinking is the consideration of consequences. In generating alternative actions available in a given situation, potential consequences should be anticipated and can provide guidance in the selection of actions to be implemented. Patients are encouraged to look at their alternative actions and to generate possible consequences for each. This requires the patient to consider the fact that interpersonal actions often have reactions which are not always desirable. Therefore, in anticipating the consequences of actions, patients learn to be selective in the choice of alternatives and to prepare for possible consequences which may necessitate further effort.

## Outline of the ICPS programme

As originally developed, implemented and assessed, ICPS therapy has been most frequently conducted in a small group format. Given the primary objective of cognitive skills acquisition, the group provides an important opportunity for concrete behavioural exercises and feedback generally unavailable in the individual session. This is not meant to suggest that the material cannot be implemented by the therapist with patients individually. In fact, for some patients, as in the case study which follows, group involvement may be contraindicated and in some cases appropriate groups may not be readily available. Generally, group approaches work most efficiently within a programmatic environment where similarities in patient characteristics tend to be greater.

The programme structure consists of nineteen units roughly divided into two major groupings. The first half of the nineteen-unit programme comprises a sequenced series of prerequisite skills deemed to be necessary for an individual to be able to implement the specific problem-solving skills contained in the second half of the programme. The units and their topics are as follows:

**Unit 1** Unit 1 attempts to establish a noncritical and productive group atmosphere in which problems can be recognized and discussed. The first task is designed to help the group in defining problems by focusing on the feelings associated with having problems. The second task requires the group to generate a list of common problems people have, with a focus on those of an interpersonal nature.

**Unit 2** The second unit attempts to delineate the essential differences between facts and opinions in human interactions as an important element in problem-solving. The first task, involving TAT cards, requires the group to decide what constitutes facts or opinions in a description of the scene. The second task emphasizes the distinction between facts and feelings in a posed TAT scene. The third task emphasizes observational skills by requiring the group to listen to a skit and then to answer certain 'factual' questions about what they have seen.

**Unit 3** This unit deals with the importance of being observant in discovering facts about the environment. The necessity for paying attention to details is introduced in the first task. TAT cards are flashed at the group, which is then required to describe as much of the scene as they can remember. The second task focuses on the kinds of cues which could be used in remembering faces.

**Unit 4** This unit focuses on ways of obtaining more information about interpersonal situations than that which is available through observation. A tape is presented in the first task which illustrates the principle of asking direct questions. A second tape, of fragmented sentences, requires the group to ask questions designed to obtain the missing information. The essential characteristics of good questions are discussed in the context of obtaining information efficiently.

**Unit 5**   The tasks in this unit illustrate the fact that people often have different points of view and that understanding this is important to solving problems. The first task is simply to list favourite foods and TV programmes to show that within the group not everyone shares the same likes and dislikes. The principle is reinforced in the second task of interpreting a TAT card scene where individual differences in interpretations are pointed out.

**Unit 6**   Unit 6 deals with recognizing how other people feel as an important guide in solving problems. The first task encourages the group to distinguish between verbal and nonverbal methods of communicating. The second provides group members with practice in nonverbal communication in structured situations, with the group evaluating the individual effectiveness of members.

**Unit 7**   Unit 7 concentrates on recognizing and generating facial express-ions as an important mode of communication. The first two tasks require the group to identify feelings from facial expressions on slides and to imitate these expressions. In the third task the group members role-play situations in which one member must communicate his response to a request solely through facial expressions.

**Unit 8**   This unit concentrates on specific methods that may be used to aid one's memory. In the unit tasks the group members describe various techniques they have used to remember specific conversations while a list is made of all their suggestions. The group members draw on this list in obtaining information over the telephone.

**Unit 9**   Unit 9 emphasizes the importance of remembering faces and introduces the technique of self-directed language as a mediating mechan-ism in problem-solving. The two exercises require the group to pick a familiar face out of a crowd of people in a photograph. Attention to detail is stressed as a necessary part of a self-directed verbal statement.

**Unit 10**   Unit 10 introduces the concept that taking time to think before coming to a decision is necessary in order to reach the right decision. This is illustrated in the first exercise where the group must correctly match a figure with two identical ones from a group of very similar figures. The similarity of the figures requires careful attention to detail. The use of self-directed statements is reiterated here as a guide in making the correct choice.

**Unit 11** Unit 11 further emphasizes the principle of thinking out loud as one of the ways to define a problem clearly. Several stories are presented as exercises in which the group must state the problem facing the protagonist. Defining the problem is shown to be the first step in arriving at a solution.

**Unit 12** This unit focuses on the second step in solving problems: generating alternative solutions to interpersonal problem situations. The group discusses the possible ways of solving the problems they face, focusing exclusively on the generation of alternatives rather than on evaluation of their appropriateness.

**Unit 13** Building upon Unit 12, this unit orientates the group towards evaluating alternative courses of action. The first task involves careful consideration of the possible consequences of each alternative that was suggested in the preceding unit. The second exercise presents three series of slides depicting people caught in situations where they have to make a choice between two alternatives. The group practises considering the advantages and disadvantages of the two choices.

**Unit 14** Three central concepts have been introduced in Units 11, 12 and 13: defining the problem, thinking of alternatives, and considering consequences. Unit 14 serves as a review of these problem-solving principles, and introduces the idea of defining a goal. Individual group members' problems serve as focal points for discussion at this point.

**Unit 15** Unit 15 deals with the ability to see a situation from another person's viewpoint. As an illustrative exercise the group members write several stories based on TAT cards. The differences in points of view evidenced in these stories are discussed by the group. The second exercise involves a careful analysis of a taped argument between husband and wife regarding their respective viewpoints.

**Unit 16** This unit attempts to deal with the problems associated with presenting one's own viewpoint. A skit is enacted by the group to serve as a focal point in discussion regarding the best way to present a point of view and to deal with the feelings associated with changing one's mind.

**Unit 17** The importance of keeping to the point is emphasized in Unit 17. The exercises involve acting out skits illustrating the problem of digression. The discussion centres on ways of keeping a conversation focused on the problem at hand.

**Unit 18** Unit 18 attempts to consolidate the principles of problem-solving into a series of logical consecutive steps. To emphasize the importance of thinking in terms of specific and detailed steps, the group is asked to relate exactly what they will do upon leaving for the evening. The second task requires them to detail a series of step-by-step actions to be taken in solving three problems.

**Unit 19** The final structured unit deals with organizing all the principles of problem-solving and applying them to various problem situations. In the first two tasks, the group is provided with a problem situation in the form of a story and several skits. They are then required to use each stage of problem-solving in reaching the stated goal. In the third task, the group members are on their own in bringing what they have learned to bear on solving given interpersonal problems. From this point on, the group becomes involved in the ongoing real life problems of its individual members.

## *Overcoming obstacles to client progress*

Within the traditional framework of therapy, impasses or obstacles to progress are labelled 'resistances'. While maintaining this descriptive word, a caution is offered: the resistance presented by the client need not be limited to the interaction between therapist and client, but often includes other issues as well. The following represent some typical obstacles found in conducting interpersonal problem-solving therapy.

It is critical that the therapist recognizes that while one part of the client wishes to change, another part desires to remain within the same patterns of interaction. Precisely because the client continues to employ the same strategies, despite their painful outcomes, one must ask why – what maintains this behaviour? Several reasons may perpetuate what at first glance appears to be an unreasonable behaviour pattern.

1. Anxiety – the client may possess the requisite behavioural skills for interpersonal transaction but is inhibited by anxiety. Therefore, exploration about looking foolish, being uncomfortable with a new style, doubts about whether he/she can 'carry it off', etc. are fruitful themes to explore. Also the client may be anxious about the general process of change and moving on. Some feel comfortable with the familiar and are willing to pay the price of inefficiency rather than risk venturing into unknown territory. In the above cases a thorough review of the programme and how it is likely to benefit the client, as well as a detailed review of how painful and/or ineffective his/her current strategies are, would be helpful. Also, a thorough exploration of the client's worst imagined consequences resulting from changing his style is often beneficial. Here the anxiety is not anchored to the fear of performing the new behaviour but rather to its fantasized punitive consequences. In this case, exploration needs to be given to the probability of catastrophe as well as to strategies for managing painful consequences if these should occur. Finally, if the client's anxiety cannot be anchored to the process of change, or to imagined negative consequences, or to discomfort about another style, relaxation techniques may be employed as a general attempt to reduce anxiety.
2. Another frequently encountered resistance stems from an often hidden resentment concerning the issue of 'Why do I have to change?' When this has arisen, it is often responded to with the notion that if the client does not change he/she will continue to be ineffective and experience pain in his/her relationships. In addition, it is emphasized that the structured relearning is mainly for his or her own benefit, and the anticipated positive consequences are again reviewed. Clients essentially need to be reminded that there are anticipated benefits to change.
3. The client's anticipation of outcome must be assessed initially and continuously throughout therapy. If the client's perception of outcome as a result of therapy is idealized, the therapy will encounter an impasse as it

becomes apparent to him that the results of therapy are not what he thought he bargained for. Hence, the therapist needs to determine whether the client's hoped-for outcome is reasonable.

4. Frequently clients, especially those treated previously with a more traditional therapy, enter interpersonal problem-solving therapy with an assumption that they need only talk about the past as a means of altering the present and future. In this case, the client must be made thoroughly aware of the structure, process, and demands that will be entailed in this type of therapy.

5. Often, clients demand of themselves and the therapist immediate, wide-ranging results. This demand is bound to end in disappointment and resentment and, therefore, requires an orientation to the therapy as a gradual skill-building process that requires time to practise the skills being learned.

6. If the client is referred to therapy by someone else in order that he or she may be 'therapeutized', a level of resistance is usually present from the beginning. The task here is to attempt to convince the client of the benefits that he or she should gain by proceeding through the training. The critical issue, of course, is who is motivated, the referral party or the client.

7. At times clients present for therapy with good motivation and an understanding that the therapy is a gradual experience, but demand of themselves and the therapist a 100 per cent guarantee that they will never encounter failure in interpersonal situations. When this occurs, the client can frequently be successful during the therapy only to become radically dissatisfied sometime after termination. It is suggested that concepts of probability rather than guarantees characterize the real world, and that if negative consequences occur they can also be problem-solved.

8. Almost always clients encounter some level of resistance around home-work. It is easier to manage one hour a week in an office visit than to struggle with perhaps ten to fifteen hours a week of interpersonal tasks outside the therapy hour. This resistance is natural and should be expected. However, the theme to be emphasized is that the client is moving to a more independent position, and that this requires constant practice and exposure.

9. Many clients present with a 'mastery' rather than a 'coping' 'set'. The client demands perfection of himself and if he doesn't achieve it he attributes failure to himself or the therapist. Again, it needs to be emphasized that problem-solving is a skill to be learned; it will take some time and mistakes are to be expected.

The above cited obstacles are meant to acquaint the reader with those difficulties most often experienced during the course of ICPS therapy. Resistances are to be accepted as quite normal and constitute one more area of work to be managed in the interpersonal problem-solving model.

## Case example

The case to be used as an example involves the adaptation of the original interpersonal cognitive problem-solving programme, originally designed for small group application, to an individual case. This form of presentation best serves to illustrate the use of the interpersonal cognitive problem-solving approach with specific client problems.

In the small group therapy format, as we have seen, the programme structure consists of nineteen units roughly divided into two major groupings, the first half of which comprises a sequenced series of prerequisite skills considered necessary for an individual to be able to implement the specific problem-solving skills contained in the second half. The case presented here follows this format, a detailed outline of which can be found in Platt, Spivack and Swift (1974).

This case presents the treatment of a young woman, Jean, who presented with anxiety and depression as her chief complaints but, in addition, was found to be almost devoid of interpersonal competency. The treatment approach as outlined in the case follows the interpersonal problem-solving therapy approach of the therapist and his colleagues (Platt, Spivack and Swift 1974; Spivack, Platt and Shure 1976) as well as the behavioural training approach of Wolpe (1969).

An in-depth intake interview suggested that much of Jean's distress could well be the end product of a lack of interpersonal skill. As a consequence, most personal transactions, especially those dealing with her husband or mother, left Jean feeling overpowered, confused, misunderstood, angry and finally depressed. A significant event, the contemplation of having a child, heightened a sense of depression along with concomitant thoughts as to whether Jean might possibly harm the child. Jean was receiving considerable pressure from her mother and husband to have a child.

A review of history revealed the following: the patient was twenty-eight, had been married for five years and was employed as a legal secretary. She and her husband were pleased with the marriage and Jean questioned whether altering the family unit (having a child) would 'spoil things'. As a child she described always acquiescing to her parents' wishes, indeed calling herself a 'pleaser' who did not make waves. She could not recall ever rebelling in a direct manner. She described feeling uncomfortable in social situations if they required more effort than superficial niceties. She stated that she really did not think that at the age of twenty-eight she knew how the world operated. In essence she was saying she did not possess a language or skill for interpersonal processes.

Regarding psychological illness, the family history was negative for depressive illness (unipolar or bipolar), chemical addictions, psychotic illness, and general anxiety disorders. Although there was a maternal aunt who suffered from agoraphobia with panic attacks, Jean herself did not experience any panic or agoraphobic symptoms. Her primary complaint was one of anxiety limited to social situations and a general feeling of being depressed.

The treatment as outlined below describes assessment devices utilized to estimate interpersonal skill, as well as specific interventions. Clearly a linkage was made between her lack of interpersonal skill and her feelings. It was decided that a positive enhancement of her ability to manage interpersonal processes would yield an improvement in her affect as well as her self-esteem.

## Course of therapy

During the first two sessions, which were intended as orientation and information-gathering meetings, the aims of therapy were explained. Jean was told that the purpose for which we would be meeting would be to help her develop her problem-solving skills in order to enable her to cope successfully with interpersonal problem situations. It was further explained that interpersonal problems were a part of everyday life for all people and that almost everyone could profit from learning how to recognize and solve such problems, but that she was particularly in need of this training. The therapist explained a number of important points about the programme, including (a) the therapist's experience that the kinds of skills which we were working on could be learned, but only through active participation in the treatment on her part; (b) that the focus of the programme was upon problems of an interpersonal nature which included the development of her own skills at recognizing emotional states in herself and in others; (c) that our sessions were to be a place for her to bring the problems which she was now facing and would be facing later during the course of therapy; and (d) that the proper focus of the therapy sessions was upon the present and future, not the past. In this regard, the therapist explained that this approach to therapy was different from her previous therapy experiences in that the focus was primarily upon how to solve her problems and not upon understanding events that had already occurred and which may have led to the development of her current problem.

The therapist then explained that a thorough knowledge of her present situation was necessary in order to assess the extent of her present level of skills in the interpersonal sphere in order to help him decide which areas should be given major emphasis. This assessment was based upon administration of a structured interview designed to evaluate current deficiencies in problem-solving ability. Information gathered in the structured interview was supplemented by other information, including performance on the Means–Ends Problem-Solving Measure (Platt and Spivack 1975) as well as measures of ability in interpersonal situations: recognizing problems, generating alternatives, considering consequences, and thinking in terms of cause and effect relationships (Platt and Spivack 1977). Not surprisingly, Jean was found to have very low scores on almost all of these measures – scores which generally placed her in the range obtained by psychiatric patients who were only capable of making borderline adjustments to their life situations. For the purposes of brevity, a detailed analysis of her profile of problem-solving scores is not included here. However, it was clear that her greatest deficiencies lay in the following areas: recognition of problem situations, generation of alternatives, thinking through the solution to an interpersonal problem in a stepwise fashion, and ability to role-take or to recognize the role of motivations on the part of significant others in interpersonal situations. Jean did, however, fall in the low normal range in the areas of being able to think in cause-and-effect terms in interpersonal situations, and of being able to consider consequences of interpersonal events. These latter scores perhaps reflect some specific environmental learning in her relationship with her husband, Michael. In addition to these measures, a careful history was taken of Jean's interactions with her husband, and particularly the circumstances under which her fears of hurting him during sexual acts arose. A similar analysis was done for the situations involved in Jean's fears about hurting her baby. The results of this assessment clearly underlined the clinical impressions gained by the therapist. Jean was seen to be an individual who, while giving the initial impression of intellectual brightness, was significantly impaired in the area of social-interpersonal skills.

From a discussion with Jean, it was clear that when faced with a problem involving other people a great deal of difficulty in controlling her anxiety arose because of the fact that she did not completely comprehend just how to meet the expectations others had of her, and in addition she had no idea of how significant others were responding to her in a given situation unless their response was very obvious. As if to underline this deficiency, during the second session Jean asked the therapist at the point of discussing this issue, 'How do you feel now?' The therapist responded in terms of such statements as 'pleased' (at her interest), and 'relaxed'. He praised her for asking this question and assured her that she should feel free to ask such questions of him whenever she wished, and that she should do the same in situations with other persons, such as when she was with her husband and friends.

Jean was seen on a weekly basis for fifty-minute sessions. The therapist intended to set a pace whereby each week would be devoted to a specific issue. Thus, the topics covered in each session would have a maximum interest value and Jean would have to attend to her 'homework' assignments to keep up.

Session 3 focused on two issues: (a) establishment by the therapist of a noncritical and productive atmosphere in which Jean could focus upon the problems she was facing, and (b) having Jean begin to learn about how to recognize the existence of problem situations by becoming aware of and labelling the feelings associated with having a problem. Jean was encouraged to begin to develop a list of her interpersonal problems so that an ordering of treatment priorities could be undertaken. At the conclusion of this session, Jean was told that we would be devoting part of each following therapy session to learning a specific set of tasks designed to help her improve her problem-solving skills, and another part to a discussion of the problems she was then facing in her life and the application of her problem-solving skills to their resolution.

Session 4 focused on an attempt to delineate the essential differences between fact and opinion in interpersonal situations. Jean was handed a set of TAT cards and asked to describe them. Then she was asked to identify which parts of her description were fact and which were opinion as well as the basis for each of her decisions. The distinction made for her was that facts in interpersonal situations are facts because we can actually see them or can verify them with information obtained from others. Opinion, however, reflects what we feel, imagine or believe while not actually seeing it or being able to confirm it readily; we infer it from what we actually do see. Jean was not very clear about this distinction and some time was spent in discussing it. The point was somewhat clarified for her when we discussed how Jean communicated with her husband, Michael. She came to see that she could ask him 'how he felt', rather than only depending upon her judgment of his internal state, which was at this time not accurate.

Sessions 5 and 6 dealt with the importance of being observant of facts about the interpersonal environment; the necessity and means of obtaining all the facts one needs in order to solve a problem before actually attempting to solve it; and the necessity of inhibiting the first impulse to do something immediately in a situation when faced with a new problem. The major point of discussion was about the need, when faced with a problem, to 'Stop! Look! and Ask!' before proceeding to take a course of action. Jean was asked for examples of situations in which she had made a hasty or impulsive decision because of her need to do something immediately. A task involving a series of previously prepared audio tapes was introduced at this point. This task required Jean to listen to fragmented sentences and to formulate questions which would best obtain the missing information. This task led to a discussion of the properties of 'good' questions and their relevance to effective communication and problem-solving.

Session 7, with Michael, focused on the issue of recognition and accept-ance of the fact that individuals have different interpretations as well as points of view about interpersonal events. To illustrate this, the patient and her husband were given TAT cards and asked to describe the characters. The quite different descriptions presented by Jean and Michael gave rise to a discussion of how the 'facts' in a given situation may be different to each of us, and furthermore, how even when we do tend to agree on them we may still wish, as a result, to take quite different courses of action. The session concluded with a discussion of Jean's and Michael's plans for a vacation. The therapist suggested that they continue, at home, their discussion of this issue upon which they held different views, applying the problem-solving approach.

Sessions 8, 9, and 10 dealt with recognizing and communicating feelings as an important guide to recognizing and resolving interpersonal problems. Jean was asked to indicate how she would transmit the message of displea-sure in a non-verbal fashion to another person. She had some difficulty in doing this, as was expected by the therapist, and he spent a substantial portion of session 8 modelling modes of transmitting displeasure, such as by acting bored, fidgeting, frowning, etc. Actual situations in which she could practise this ability were identified and she was asked to practise. She also was told to watch for the employment of such cues by other persons with whom she came in contact.

Session 9 began with a review of Jean's experiences in practising and being alert for the use of nonverbal cues. This review took up the entire session. It was suggested that she practise at home in front of a mirror before doing so with her husband because of her concern about looking 'foolish'.

Session 10: Jean was very pleased with her success in transmitting cues to her husband over the last week. She felt for the first time that she was 'really making progress'. This session was then concerned with (a) recognizing and identifying facial expressions from photographs in *People* magazine and other sources, and (b) practising imitating some of the expressions which were portrayed. Jean had now got into the habit of doing her practise assignments at home and was looking forward to doing them.

Session 11: Jean was quite concerned about what she perceived to be Michael's displeasure with her during the last week. Possible reasons for this were discussed and what emerged was the fact that Michael apparently had been 'teasing' her by not giving her accurate feedback on questions she had asked or on the identification of facial expressions when she had attempted to implement them in their interactions. Some supportive action on the part of the therapist seemed called for and Jean was reassured that (a) she had been making good progress, and (b) Michael was probably not deliberately attempting to undermine her efforts, but rather was most likely not aware of what he was doing. When it was suggested that Jean confront Michael directly about this, she was rather hesitant to do so. This incident suggested the need on Jean's part for some assertiveness training, which had been originally planned for a later point in the course of therapy, and it was introduced at this time by means of role-playing and behavioural rehearsal.

Session 12: during this session Jean blurted out a most significant statement regarding her self-esteem: 'I'm not so dumb any more.' Upon being asked to reflect upon that statement, she said, 'For the first time I feel that I have some control over what's happening to me – before this, I always felt that everyone seemed to know something I didn't – and that I was stupid in some way – well, I guess I was.' The therapist reported his pleasure at Jean's statement and suggested that she continue her efforts at practising, in her daily life, the skills which she was learning.

Session 13: at this point, the therapist felt that it was necessary to refrain from introducing any new material into the sessions but rather to spend some time reviewing the progress which had been made to date (which in his opinion had been significant) so that Jean could begin to solidify the gains she had made and which had led to increased self-esteem. To do this it seemed necessary to discuss what self-esteem meant to Jean. When asked, she had a general definition of self-esteem in terms of 'feeling good about herself' but was not able really to define it much further. In order to assist her in defining her opinion of herself, it was suggested that she might, additionally, consider defining self-esteem in terms of her feelings about the extent to which she was able to be successful in doing what was important to her. When asked about developing an 'importance hierarchy', Jean defined herself in terms of her fulfilling roles defined by others, including 'a good daughter, wife, employee, etc.' She seemed truly surprised when the therapist suggested that these were roles defined by others and that perhaps she had never given any thought to developing her own definition of how 'feeling good about herself' could be defined in terms of her own values. We agreed to return to this issue as soon as she had given it some further thought.

Session 14: since Jean did not seem ready to continue our discussion of the last session concerning what self-esteem meant to her, and as her home life seemed to be creating no major issues, this session was devoted to a review of what had been covered to date in terms of problem-solving skills. By now Jean had incorporated some skills into her repertoire and could report some positive experiences, a fact which she seemed pleased about. Other skill areas in which she had not yet gained proficiency (such as recognition of emotional states) were identified, and some of the principles involved in using them were reviewed, along with specific exercises for her to use outside the therapy sessions. She seemed to be increasingly receptive to the approach being used by the therapist and now had incorporated some of the language of problem-solving into her speech.

Session 15: during this session, Jean reported that she had been giving some thought to what self-esteem meant to her and now felt that it really meant 'doing well what she wanted to do'. This involved (a) having greater control in any interactions with her husband, boss, and mother – as reflected in the statement, 'not feeling down after I talk to them, particularly my mother' (she reported that this was not as much of a problem for her as it had been, but still existed); and (b) knowing better who she was in terms of 'having goals . . . a purpose . . . a meaning to life, instead of just existing and responding'. The therapist reported his pleasure at the obvious thought she had been giving to this question, and urged her to continue doing so. The therapist decided at this point not to provide any further structure for her so that she could further evolve her own ideas about this important issue.

Session 17: after reviewing the past week's progress, the discussion was directed by the therapist to the issue of how not to leap to conclusions when faced with a demanding situation, a problem which Jean had reported. As a teaching tool, Jean was given Kagan's Matching Familiar Task, which requires the respondent correctly to match a figure with an identical one from a group of very similar figures. This task requires great attention to detail because of the similarity of the figures. In general, the length of time spent in coming to a decision is very directly related to the percentage of successful responses, and has been found by the therapist to be an excellent tool in demonstrating that impulsive, in contrast to carefully thought-out, decisions are less effective in terms of arriving at the correct course of action in a given situation. Jean completed the task seemingly without paying a great deal of attention to it, and was quite surprised to find that she had made most of the choices incorrectly. This exercise served as the basis for a discussion of (a) how impulsively arrived at decisions are often incorrect, and (b) the advantage of thinking before acting. Having agreed to the correctness of (a) and the need for (b), the therapist then introduced the concept of using overt self-directed statements to guide one's decision-making. After modelling how this was done, the therapist got Jean to practise doing so. When the obvious question arose as to how she would look talking to herself, it was suggested that she could talk to herself covertly. However, she was not to do this until she had practised with overt self-directed speech at home for several days.

Session 18: Jean arrived as a confirmed advocate of problem-solving! She had found the idea of self-directed speech of value to her in coping with the problem of controlling her impulsive behaviour, although she had not really yet been faced with a situation in which to test it.

Sessions 19, 20 and 21: using the technique of self-directed speech, Jean was given practice in working through several problem situations in which she was faced with making a decision. The therapist role-played Michael and presented her with situations in which she was to respond. During these sessions the therapist introduced the concept of thinking through a problem in imagination in advance of actually carrying out a course of action.

Sessions 22 and 23 were focused on the generating of alternatives to interpersonal problem situations which the therapist presented. The goal here was to think of as many different ways of solving the problem as possible.

During this time, Jean and her mother began having increasing difficulties centred around Jean's not yet having any children. Jean was, both in her opinion and in that of the therapist, able to cope somewhat better with her mother than she thought she could have done before therapy, but still had a need for a moderate amount of support. Approximately one and a half sessions were specifically directed towards behavioural rehearsal in preparation for an anticipated visit by her mother. This actual problem situation provided a good opportunity for introducing the concepts of alternative thinking and the evaluation of the various outcomes they could produce in terms of the advantages and disadvantages of each.

Session 24 centred around a review of the events of her mother's visit.

Jean had employed several of the tactics she had learned, seemingly with a moderate amount of success, but felt somewhat guilty about having done so. The therapist focused the discussion on what had gone well, and afterwards Jean seemed reasonably satisfied with her performance.

Sessions 25 to 28: with the departure of her mother, Jean did not seem to have any pressing problems and the therapist decided to return to Jean's fears of emotional involvement. The remainder of this session and the next three were spent on inducing deep muscle relaxation, and getting the patient to imagine herself in successively more emotionally close, and therefore anxiety-producing, situations involving her husband and a baby (Wolpe 1969). During this time, the reported anxiety level that the patient experienced decreased moderately.

Sessions 29 and 30: during session 29, the therapist and Jean reviewed progress to date. Jean stated that she felt that the primary goals had been reached and that she now felt better able to cope with previously stressful situations. She felt, in particular, that she was able to recognize and understand better her own internal states and to successfully resolve interpersonal problems. Self-esteem was clearly perceived by both of us to be at a significantly higher level than it had been at the beginning of treatment. The therapist suggested, and Jean agreed to, a retest using the battery of interpersonal cognitive problem-solving measures administered at the beginning of treatment.

Following the readministration, Jean was found to have gained significantly in her interpersonal cognitive problem-solving skills. She essentially moved into the normal range of interpersonal cognitive problem-solving scores in all areas. With no immediate pressing problems in Jean's life, she felt that she would like to have an opportunity to attempt to cope on her own for a while, with the understanding that she would contact the therapist if she felt overwhelmed.

Months later, the therapist received a letter from Jean in which she described how pleased she was with her ability to handle problem situations in her life. She described her life situation as not problem-free, but as one she could cope with and feel competent about her ability to do so.

# References

Arend, R., Gove, F.L. and Sroufe, A.L. (1970). Continuity of individual adaptation from infancy to kindergarten: A predictive study of ego-resiliency and curiosity in pre-schoolers. *Child Development, 50,* 950–959.

Davis, G.A. (1966) Current status of research and theory in human problem solving. *Psychological Bulletin*, *66*, 36–54.

D'Zurilla, T.J. and Goldfried, M.R (1971). Problem solving and behavior modification. *Journal of Abnormal Psychology*, *78*, 107–126.

Elias, M.J. (1978). The development of a theory-based measure of how children understand and attempt to resolve problematic social situations. Unpublished master's thesis, University of Connecticut, Storrs.

Goldfried, M.R. and Davison, G.C. (1976) *Clinical Behavior Therapy*, New York: Holt, Rinehart and Winston.

Goldfried, M.R. and D'Zurilla, T.J. (1969) A behavioral-analytic model for assessing competence. In C.D. Spielberger (ed.) *Current topics in clinical psychology*, vol. 1. New York: Academic Press.

Jahoda, M. (1953) The meaning of psychological health. *Social Casework, 34*, 349.

Johnson, J.E., Yu, S. and Roopnarine, J. (1980) *Social cognitive ability, interpersonal behaviors, and peer status within a mixed age group*. Paper presented at the meeting of the Southwestern Society for Research in Human Development, Lawrence, K.S., March.

Kanfer, F.H. and Busenmeyer, J. (1982) The use of problem solving and decision making in behavior therapy. *Clinical Psychology Review*, *2*, 239–266.

Marsh, D.T., Serafica, F.C. and Barenboim, C. (1981) Interrelationships among perspective-taking, interpersonal problem solving, and interpersonal functioning. *Journal of Genetic Psychology*, *138*, 37–48.

Meichenbaum, D. and Goodman, J. (1971) Training impulsive children to talk to themselves: A means of developing self-control. *Journal of Abnormal Psychology*, *77*, 115–126.

Platt, J.J. and Duome, M. (1980) *Training in interpersonal problem solving (TIPS)*, Philadelphia, Department of Mental Health Sciences, Hahnemann University.

Platt, J.J., Morell, J., Flaherty, E. and Metzger, D. (1982) *Controlled study of methadone rehabilitation process*. Final report no. R01-DA01929. Washington, DC: National Institute on Drug Abuse.

Platt, J.J., Siegel, J.M. and Spivack, G. (1975) Do psychiatric patients and normals see the same solutions as effective in solving interpersonal problems? *Journal of Consulting and Clinical Psychology*, *43*, 279.

Platt, J.J. and Spivack, G. (1972a) Problem-solving thinking of psychiatric patients. *Journal of Consulting and Clinical Psychology*, *39*, 148–151.

Platt, J.J. and Spivack, G. (1972b) Social competence and effective problem-solving thinking in psychiatric patients. *Journal of Clinical Psychology*, *28*, 3–5.

Platt, J.J. and Spivack, G. (1973) Studies in problem solving thinking of psychiatric patients: Patient-control differences and factorial structure of problem-solving thinking. *Proceedings of the 81st Annual Convention of the American Psychological Association*, *8*, 461–462.

Platt, J.J. and Spivack, G. (1974) Means of solving real-life problems: I. Psychiatric patients vs. controls, and cross-cultural comparisons of normal females. *Journal of Community Psychology*, *2*, 45–48.

Platt, J.J. and Spivack, G. (1975) *Means–end problem-solving procedure (MEPS): Manual.* Philadelphia, Department of Mental Health Sciences, Hahnemann Medical College and Hospital.

Platt, J.J. and Spivack, G. (1976) *Workbook for training in interpersonal problem solving thinking.* Philadelphia, Department of Mental Health Sciences, Hahnemann Medical College and Hospital.

Platt, J.J. and Spivack, G. (1977) *Measures of interpersonal cognitive problem-solving for adults and adolescents.* Philadelphia: Department of Mental Health Sciences, Hahnemann Medical College and Hospital.

Platt, J.J., Spivack, G., Altman, N., Altman, D., and Peizer, S.B. (1974) Adolescent problem-solving thinking. *Journal of Consulting and Clinical Psychology, 42,* 787–793.

Platt, J.J., Spivack, G., and Swift, M. (1974) *Problem solving therapy with maladjusted groups.* Research and evaluation report no. 28. Philadelphia, Department of Mental Health Sciences, Hahnemann Medical College and Hospital.

Richard, B.A. and Dodge, K.A. (1982) Social maladjustment and problem-solving in school-aged children. *Journal of Consulting and Clinical Psychology, 50,* 226–233.

Schiller, J.D. (1978) Child care arrangements and ego functioning. The effects of stability and entry age on young children. Unpublished doctoral dissertation, University of California, Berkeley.

Shure, M.B. (1980) *Interpersonal problem solving in ten-year-olds.* Final report no. MH-27741. Washington, DC: National Institute of Mental Health.

Shure, M.B. and Spivack, G. (1978) *Problem solving techniques in childrearing.* San Francisco: Jossey–Bass.

Shure, M.B. and Spivack, G. (1980) Interpersonal problem solving as a mediator of behavioral adjustment in pre-school and kindergarten children. *Journal of Applied Developmental Psychology, 1,* 29–43.

Simon, H.A. and Newell, A. (1971) Human problem-solving: The state of the theory in 1970. *American Psychologist, 26,* 145–159.

Spivack, G. and Levine, M. (1963) *Self-regulation in acting-out and normal adolescents.* Report no. M-4531, Washington, DC: National Institute of Health.

Spivack, G., Platt, J.J. and Shure, M.B. (1976) *The problem solving approach to adjustment.* San Francisco: Jossey-Bass.

Spivack, G. and Shure, M.B. (1974) *Social adjustment of young children.* San Francisco: Jossey–Bass.

Spivack, G. and Shure, M.B. (1982) Interpersonal cognitive problem solving and clinical theory. In B. Lahey and A.E. Kazdin (eds), *Advances in child clinical psychology,* vol. 5. New York: Plenum.

Spivack, G., Standen, C.H., Bryson, J. and Garrett, L. (1978) *Interpersonal problem-solving thinking in an elderly group.* Presented at a poster session of the American Psychological Association, Toronto.

Wolpe, J. (1969) *The practice of behavior therapy.* New York: Pergamon Press.

# CHAPTER TEN   Cognitive-Behavioural Hypnotherapy
*William L. Golden and Fred Friedberg*

## Cognitive-behavioural hypnotherapy and other approaches to hypnosis*

### Non-cognitive-behavioural approaches to hypnosis

In this section we will consider four leading approaches to hypnosis and intend to show how these differ from CBH.

Cognitive-behavioural hypnotherapy (CBH) is a therapeutic approach that combines various cognitive, behavioural, and hypnotic strategies. CBH differs from other contemporary hypnotherapeutic approaches in several significant ways.

According to traditional notions, hypnosis is an altered state of consciousness and hypnotic responsiveness is considered an innate, unmodifiable characteristic referred to as hypnotic susceptibility. The therapist practising traditional hypnosis assumes responsibility for inducing hypnosis and therapeutic change, while encouraging passivity, dependency, and expectations for external control in the subject.

In contrast, cognitive-behavioural hypnotherapists are more likely to view hypnosis as a learnable skill, based on the principles of social learning and cognitive theory. Furthermore, the client's role involves active and conscious participation in the development and utilization of hypnotic skills. Therapeutic change is attributed to the client via specific change strategies rather than merely to the skills of the hypnotist. Instead of explaining hypnosis in terms of a vaguely defined altered state of consciousness, most

---

* **Editors' Note.**   As Golden and Friedberg note, CBH is *not* a distinctive theoretical approach in its own right, but is 'a generic term for cognitive-behavioural approaches to hypnosis'. Since CBH has neither its own set of major theoretical concepts nor unique ways of conceptualizing clients' problems, the authors were asked to use a modified version of the chapter structure. They were asked to devote more space to discussing how CBH relates to other non-cognitive-behavioural approaches to hypnosis and to outlining specific approaches that fall under the general rubric of CBH.

cognitive-behavioural hypnotherapists define hypnosis in terms of specific antecedent conditions such as the precise wording of the suggestions, the subject's pre-hypnosis attitudes and expectations, and the degree of client involvement in the actual hypnotic process.

**Traditional hypnotherapy**   CBH is not to be confused with the traditional approach of providing symptom relief through direct suggestion (Bernheim 1895). For example, a traditional hypnotist might give a hypnotized client the following suggestion for pain control: 'By the time I count to ten your pain will completely disappear.' Sometimes, special techniques such as imagery are used: the hypnotist might suggest that the client imagines receiving some type of anaesthesia that creates a feeling of numbness and a reduction in pain. Although self-hypnosis is occasionally taught, clients are not encouraged to take an active role in their treatment. Furthermore, efforts are usually not made to provide the client with an understanding of the factors that cause or maintain the problem, nor is there an attempt to alter these causal factors.

However, several of the traditional hypnotherapists (Bernheim 1895; Prince and Coriat 1907) have described insight-orientated methods that resemble rational-emotive hypnotherapy (described later in this chapter). These hypnotherapists discovered that it was sometimes necessary to persuade, reason with, and re-educate their clients in order to achieve symptom removal. As part of their 'rational' approach, suggestions to change attitudes rather than merely the presenting symptoms were given to the hypnotized client. Unfortunately, hypnotherapists during the early part of the twentieth century showed a greater interest in the treatment of symptoms through direct suggestion, and so rational hypnotherapy was not developed until recently (Boutin 1978; Boutin and Tosi 1983; Golden 1983a; Tosi and Baisden 1984).

Traditional hypnosis is effective in treating some conditions, such as clinical pain, asthma, and insomnia, but not others, such as obesity, cigarette smoking, and alcoholism.

**Hypnoanalysis**   Freud (1920) was very critical of hypnotic treatment based on direct suggestion. On the basis of his experience with traditional hypnotherapy, he concluded that:

It could be employed in certain cases only and not in others; with some much could be achieved by it, and with others very little, one never knew why. But worse than its capricious nature was the lack of permanence in the results; after a time, if one heard from the patient again, the old malady had reappeared or had been replaced by another. (Freud 1920, p. 157)

Nevertheless, some of Freud's followers maintained interest in hypnosis and its integration with psychoanalysis. In hypnoanalysis, as it is called, the therapist combines the methods of hypnosis with psychoanalysis. The main purpose of hypnoanalysis is to shorten the duration of psychoanalytic treatment. Otherwise, it is similar to most psychoanalytic approaches in that interpretation of defences, resistances, dreams, and transference are integral parts of the treatment.

According to Fromm (1984), the rationale for employing hypnosis in hypnoanalysis is that it enables the therapist to communicate directly with the unconscious mind of the client. Retrieval of unconscious material is accomplished through techniques such as age regression and heightened recall. Free association and dream interpretation are facilitated through hypnotic procedures. For example, the hypnotist can use hypnotic suggestion to induce dreams as well as to increase the client's recall and understanding of dreams.

Both hypnoanalytic and cognitive-behavioural approaches are insight-orientated. However, there is disagreement about what type of insight is of therapeutic value. According to hypnoanalysts (Brenman and Gill 1947; Fromm 1984), permanent change will not occur unless the client's unconscious conflicts are uncovered and 'worked through'. On the other hand, clients in CBH treatment are taught how to become aware of maladaptive cognitions, such as negative self-suggestions and their effects on emotions and behaviour. These self-defeating cognitions are either conscious or what Freud might have referred to as 'preconscious' (i.e. thoughts capable of becoming conscious).

Although hypnoanalytic techniques can be used to identify maladaptive thoughts, attitudes, and beliefs (see Golden 1983a), most of the conventional cognitive-behavioural self-monitoring procedures can be employed for this purpose. Furthermore, cognitive-behavioural therapists maintain that insight alone is not sufficient for therapeutic change. It is also important to modify maladaptive cognitions through some type of cognitive restructuring procedure.

**Ericksonian hypnotherapy** CBH can also be distinguished from the Ericksonian approach (Erickson and Rossi 1979). The treatment methods in CBH are direct and didactic. Success depends on the willingness of the client to collaborate with the therapist by learning, practising, and applying self-hypnotic strategies. Although Ericksonian hypnotherapists talk about unconscious experiential learning, they do not directly teach coping skills to their clients. Erickson preferred indirect suggestions because he believed that efforts to influence clients directly typically mobilize resistance. Therefore, indirect suggestions such as paradoxical instructions and embedded commands are given in an attempt to circumvent client awareness of suggestions and possible resistance to them.

Ericksonian hypnotherapy is not insight-orientated. The focus is on symptom relief. There is no attempt to overcome unconscious conflicts nor to alter directly the client's maladaptive cognitions. Unconscious conflicts and resistances are utilized rather than analyzed. For example, the Ericksonian therapist is likely to instruct the oppositional client to continue to resist as a strategy to obtain compliance. Such strategies may be appropriate with clients who cannot or will not co-operate with direct interventions. Ericksonian methods have been integrated with CBH (see Golden, 1985).

**The hypnobehavioural model** Pavlov (1941) was the first to explain hypnosis in terms of conditioning, while Salter (1949) hypothesized that words are classically conditioned stimuli that elicit the conditioned response of hypnosis. Salter used hypnosis to countercondition fears and phobias, and to train clients in the use of positive self-suggestions (just to name a few of his applications). Salter's methods are very similar to modern cognitive and behavioural techniques such as relaxation training, desensitization and cognitive restructuring.

More recently, Kroger and Fezler (1976) have expanded the hypnobehavioural model, integrating hypnosis with a number of covert conditioning procedures. Furthermore, Weitzenhoffer (1972) noted that many hypnotherapeutic techniques resemble behaviour therapy procedures. Spanos and Barber (1976) have more specifically pointed out that cognitive strategies are found in both hypnosis and behaviour therapy. Each method directs the individual to think and imagine in response to the therapeutic instructions or suggestions.

*Specific approaches within CBH*

We will now outline specific existing approaches to hypnosis that fall under the generic rubric of CBH.

**Rational-emotive hypnotherapy**   The basic premise of rational-emotive therapy (RET) (see chapter by Dryden and Ellis) it that emotional disturbance is largely the result of 'irrational' thinking (Ellis 1962). The fundamental principle of therapeutic change in RET is that one can directly modify irrational thoughts and misperceptions, and thereby produce constructive emotional and behavioural change.

Rational-emotive hypnotherapy (REH) is a combination of hypnosis and RET. As in RET, REH is based on the similar assumption that emotional distress arises from a negative or 'irrational' type of self-hypnosis (Ellis 1962; Golden 1983a). In therapy sessions, irrational beliefs are disputed and replaced with rational alternatives while the client is hypnotized. In addition, clients are taught to give themselves rational suggestions during self-hypnosis.

Within the REH framework, hypnosis is therapeutic when it interrupts the negative self-hypnotic process. Ellis (1962) writes, 'All hypnotic suggestion that is therapeutically successful probably works through autosuggestion – since unless the patient himself takes over the suggestions of the hypnotherapist and consciously keeps thinking about them when the therapist is no longer present, only the most short-lived kind of results are likely to follow' (p. 276). Barber (1978) and Ruch (1975) have similarly hypothesized that hypnotic suggestions are only effective if individuals accept them as their own suggestions.

**Rational stage-directed hypnotherapy**   Tosi's Rational Stage-Directed Hypnotherapy (RSDH) is an amalgam of trance model hypnosis and cognitive restructuring procedures, especially RET (Boutin 1978; Tosi and Baisden 1984). Boutin (1978) has postulated that therapeutic change in RSDH is a result of cognitive restructuring facilitated by a hypnotic induction procedure. Specifically, a hypnotic state of relaxation is assumed to allow the client to be more receptive to suggestions; therefore in RSDH an hypnotic induction procedure is used as a preparation for cognitive restructuring.

In RSDH, the client is guided through six stages or levels of therapy.

The first stage involves identification of self-defeating ideas, emotions, and behaviours connected to problem situations; then the client is taught more 'rational' modes of thinking consistent with RET. In the second stage the client imagines, under hypnosis, trying out new thoughts and constructive behaviours in the problem situation. During the third stage the client is encouraged to make a commitment to change. The fourth stage involves the client applying rational thinking and other self-management skills in vivo. During the fifth stage, the client internalizes rational modes of thinking and acting. Finally, in the sixth stage, significant therapeutic changes become more frequent and permanent.

**Barber's cognitive-behavioural model of hypnosis** Barber and his associates (Barber, Spanos and Chaves 1974; Spanos and Barber 1976) view hypnotic phenomena as the result of cognitive processes such as attitudes, expectations, and imagery. In several controlled studies (see Barber 1979; Barber *et al.* 1974; Spanos and Barber 1976 for reviews), suggestions and 'task-motivated' instructions alone were found to be as effective as hypnotic induction procedures in producing classical hypnotic phenomena such as age regression, amnesia, hallucinations, catalepsy, arm levitation, and analgesia. The Barber research group have interpreted these findings as evidence that induction procedures are not necessary to experience phenomena usually attributed to the hypnotic trance state. Spanos and Barber (1976) have proposed a cognitive-behavioural explanation of hypnosis as an alternative to the traditional model. In their model, hypnotic responsiveness depends on four variables:

(a) The motivation and co-operation of the individual receiving the treatment or suggestions.
(b) The attitudes and expectations of the individual toward the treatment.
(c) The wording of the instructions or suggestions.
(d) The individual's involvement or 'absorption' in suggestion-related thoughts and imagery.

The literature reviews of Spanos and Barber (1974, 1976) concluded that (a) positive attitudes and expectations about treatment increase the effectiveness of behaviour therapy and hypnotic procedures, and (b) suggestions that provide an individual with cognitive strategies are more likely to be experienced. For example, anaesthesia is more likely to be experienced when the subject is given a strategy such as instructions to imagine receiving an injection of Novocain.

Although Barber and his associates have provided compelling evidence for the influence of the above variables in generating hypnotic phenomena, they have not proved that all forms of hypnosis can be explained by these factors. Barber's research examined cognitive-behavioural hypnosis. Perhaps alternative clinical strategies such as those devised by Erickson and his followers (Erickson and Rossi 1979) involve different types of hypnotic phenomena that, for instance, may not depend on the conscious co-operation of the client. In the use of paradoxical suggestions, for example, clients may think they are rebelling when, in fact, they are co-operating.

**The hypnotic skills training approach**   Several cognitive-behavioural hypnotherapists (Diamond 1974, 1977; Katz 1979) argue that hypnotic suggestibility is a learnable skill rather than an unmodifiable trait, as most traditional hypnotists would maintain. Diamond and Katz have developed a skills training approach to enhance the hypnotic responsiveness of clients. Their programme is based on Barber's research and includes cognitive-behavioural procedures such as modelling, instruction in how to think and imagine along with suggestions, thought-stopping techniques to block out distracting thoughts such as 'I can't do it,' and successive approximations whereby clients are reinforced for incremental improvements in hypnotic responsiveness.

Diamond, in his literature reviews (1974, 1977) concluded that hypnotic responsiveness can be increased with cognitive-behavioural methods. In two subsequent studies (Gargiulo 1983; Katz 1979), hypnotic skills training was found to be more effective than traditional methods in enhancing hypnotic susceptibility. More specifically, Gargiulo reported that skills training was more effective than a traditional hypnotic procedure in helping subjects cope with pain as measured by a cold pressor test. However, Gargiulo found that hypnotic susceptibility scores were also related to hypnotic responsiveness. These findings suggest that hypnotic suggestibility is possessed by some individuals more than others, but it can also be modified through cognitive-behavioural training.

## Major theoretical concepts

CBH is a generic term for cognitive-behavioural approaches to hypnosis such as rational-emotive hypnotherapy, rational stage-directed hypnotherapy, and hypnotic skills training. CBH is not based on a single unified theory of personality or psychopathology. However, CBH methods are compatible with a general ABC theory of emotion, wherein As are stimuli or activating events, Bs are thoughts, images, beliefs, or attitudes that produce Cs, which are emotional, sensory, physiological, or behavioural responses.

CBH therapists differ in how they view hypnosis. For example, RSDH therapists (Boutin 1978; Tosi and Baisden 1984) subscribe to a traditional trance model. We, on the other hand, prefer Spanos and Barber's (1976) cognitive-behavioural model of hypnosis.

## How client problems are conceptualized

Hypnosis involves sensory, emotional, physiological and behavioural changes produced through suggestion and imagination. CBH is based on the assumption that much emotional distress arises from a negative type of self-hypnosis. Araoz (1981, 1982) has coined the term 'negative self-hypnosis' to describe this process. He explains that negative thinking and imagining are hypnotic-like when they are accepted without critical evaluation.

The concept of 'negative self-hypnosis' can further be used to help the client understand how self-defeating thoughts and images can be changed through the corrective process of positive self-hypnosis (Araoz 1981, 1982). The client is thus shown how to control the self-hypnotic process.

**Why CBH is used with clients** CBH methods are selected and applied on a strictly utilitarian basis, i.e., whenever the clinician adjudges CBH to have therapeutic potential for a particular problem or client.

There are a number of reasons why CBH may be the preferred intervention: (a) the use of client-controlled hypnotic procedures, i.e. hypnotic skills training, allows the therapist to succeed with clients who might have failed to respond to traditional methods of hypnosis; (b) certain clinical problems, e.g. clinical pain and anxiety, may be more effectively treated with CBH than by cognitive restructuring procedures alone; (c) clients who request and then receive hypnosis are more likely to succeed in therapy because their expectations have been met; (d) some clients, especially those seeking smoking cessation or weight loss, may want a dramatic form of intervention that they believe will abruptly change their habit patterns. Although hypnosis alone is not effective in treating habit or withdrawal problems, CBH provides the clinician with an approach that satisfies clients' expectations for hypnosis while at the same time teaching them cognitive and behavioural strategies for effective habit control or withdrawal endurance.

The use of cognitive and behavioural strategies within a hypnotic context greatly broadens the range of short-term effective interventions available to the therapist. Hypnosis and cognitive-behavioural therapies can be easily integrated for therapeutic interventions.


## Practical applications

### The therapeutic relationship

In cognitive-behavioural hypnotherapy, the therapeutic relationship is interactive and co-operative. As mentioned earlier, Barber and his research group have emphasized that the individual receiving the treatment or suggestions must be motivated and willing to co-operate. Araoz (1982) has coined the acronym 'TEAM' to describe the type of relationship which he believes is necessary for successful hypnosis: the client should *Trust* the therapist, have positive *Expectations* and *Attitudes* about hypnosis, and be *Motivated*.

Cognitive-behavioural hypnotherapy is client-centred in that it focuses on the goals of the client. These goals are clearly defined at the beginning of treatment and the client participates in the selection of techniques that are likely to achieve the desired results. For example, if pain alleviation is sought, the cognitive-behavioural hypnotherapist would get the client to sample a variety of hypnotic, cognitive, and behavioural strategies; the therapist would then direct the client to employ those strategies that were successful in controlling pain.

The client is also involved in selecting the hypnotic induction procedure. Instead of using only standardized inductions such as those described by Kroger and Fezler (1976), clients can participate in constructing individualized procedures. Also, the client can learn how to formulate suggestions for treatment. The development of self-hypnotic skills is facilitated by such active client involvement.


### Strategies of treatment

**Clinical application of the hypnotic skills approach**     Prior to a formal hypnotic induction, we provide clients with hypnotic skills training to show them *how* to respond to suggestion, rather than merely testing them for hypnotic susceptibility. For example, instead of testing their response to lightness and hand levitation, we teach them how to produce these reactions. Thus, we present traditionally hypnotic susceptability tests as practice exercises to develop hypnotic skills. The client thus learns self-initiation and control of hypnotic phenomena prior to experiencing hetero-hypnosis (i.e. hypnosis induced through the suggestions of a hypnotist). Clients who are shown that hypnosis not only requires their co-operation but is also under their control are more likely to (a) develop realistic expectations about hypnosis, and (b) attribute success to themselves rather than the hypnotist. In support of our self-control emphasis in hypnotherapy, Davison, Tsujimoto and Glaros (1973) found that self-relaxation treatment of insomnia is more likely to show sustained improvements when subjects attribute successful therapeutic outcomes to themselves rather than to an externally controlled medication treatment.

In our clinical experience, skills training is more effective in establishing therapeutic rapport than the traditional method of testing for hypnotic susceptibility. When tested, clients may feel pressured or challenged; if they respond 'poorly' to the testing they may feel defeated, while if they respond 'well' they may feel threatened by the prospect of external control. A traditional hypnotist would categorize an initially unresponsive individual as a 'poor' hypnotic subject and, therefore, unsuitable for hypnotherapy. To the contrary, the authors have found that almost all individuals can learn to become adequate hypnotic subjects with skills training, and we have therefore succeeded with a wider group of individuals than would have been predicted by susceptibility tests alone.

**A transcript for hypnotic skills training**   The following is a transcript of the hypnotic skills training procedure that one of the authors (W. G.) has used (from Golden 1982):

In order for you to learn to respond to complex suggestions that involve changes in your feelings and behaviour, it is important that you first learn to respond to simple suggestions. Therefore we are going to go through a series of exercises that are designed to help you learn how to respond to simple hypnotic suggestions.

Hypnosis is not magical, nor is it something that happens to you. It requires your co-operation and participation. Hypnosis is a skill. Therefore, everyone can learn to respond and with practice you can get better at it.

The skill is in being able to think and imagine along with a suggestion. Hypnosis involves concentrating on thoughts and images that are consistent with the goals of a suggestion. For example, if your goal is relaxation, imagining a pleasant fantasy such as a country, mountain or beach scene would help you to become relaxed. Likewise you can also create relaxation with your thoughts or what can be called self-suggestions. In the case of relaxation, you could give yourself suggestions such as 'My whole body is beginning to relax. My arms and legs are relaxing . . . beginning to relax more and more. The relaxation is spreading, etc.' Using pain control as another example, if you wanted to create anaesthesia you would use thoughts and fantasies that would produce numbness. You could imagine that you were receiving an injection of Novocain and suggest to yourself, 'My hand is becoming numb, I'm feeling less and less sensation. I'm starting to feel a rubbery feeling.' You would continue the imaging and repeat these suggestions until you got the desired effect.

Not only is it important to concentrate on the thoughts and fantasies that will produce the desired result, but it is also important to block out negative thoughts and fantasies that might interfere with your ability to respond to suggestion. If a person who is attempting to create a feeling of numbness focuses on thoughts that are incompatible with anaesthesia (such as concentrating on the pain and thinking, 'This will never work; I really didn't receive an injection of Novocain') he or she will not obtain the desired results. There are several techniques you can use to block out these negative thoughts.

*Focusing* – Simply focusing your attention and concentrating on thoughts and fantasies that are consistent with your goals will usually be sufficient to obtain a successful response to suggestion. This method allows you to distract your attention from negative thoughts that would otherwise interfere with your concentration.

*Thought stopping* – There are several thought-stopping techniques. First, think to yourself the word 'Stop!' whenever negative thoughts intrude into your consciousness. Second, after thinking the word 'Stop!' focus again on the thoughts and fantasies that are related to your goal. Each time a negative thought 'pops' into your 'mind' repeat the procedure. Some people find thought-stoppage to be most effective when they imagine a traffic stop sign while thinking the word 'Stop!'.

*'Letting go' of negative thoughts and fantasies* – Some people are able to 'let go' of negative thoughts and do not need to use thought-stoppage. 'Letting go' refers to letting a thought pass through your 'mind' instead of holding onto it and dwelling upon it. Occasionally, we all have negative

and bizarre thoughts. If we are not alarmed by the presence of these thoughts and fantasies and, hence, do not focus on them, our 'stream of consciousness' will eventually flow to other thoughts. So if negative thoughts intrude, just let them pass and return to the thoughts and fantasies that will produce the desired results.

Now you are ready to apply these strategies to several exercises, so that you can discover which techniques work for you. You do not have to respond to all of the suggestions in these exercises in order to be a good hypnotic subject. As long as you are able to respond in some way to some suggestions, you will be capable of experiencing hypnosis.

*Exercise no. 1. Hand heaviness* – The goal of the hand heaviness exercise is to create a feeling of heaviness in your arm. Before you begin, think of something that would be so heavy that you would eventually be forced to put it down. Make use of relevant experiences from your life. Some images that others have found helpful include: (a) holding a shopping bag full of heavy books or groceries, (b) lifting a barbell weight, (c) trying to lift a piece of furniture, (d) holding a bowling ball, and (e) holding a huge book, like a dictionary, in the palm of your hand. You want to imagine holding something heavy which, if real, would make your arm tired and cause you to lower it.

Once you have selected your fantasy for producing hand heaviness, sit back in your chair and close your eyes. Most people can image better with their eyes closed. Hold both arms out in front of you, palms up. Keep your arms straight and parallel to one another. Imagine that you are supporting something very heavy with your dominant hand and arm.

Whatever you choose as your fantasy for heaviness, use as many of your senses as possible to imagine it. See it, its shape, its colour, and its size. Feel it. Recall the feeling of heaviness you experienced when you actually held or lifted the object.

In addition to using imagery, give yourself suggestions such as, 'My arm is feeling heavy, the muscles are getting tired, fatigued. I feel the strain in the muscles. The —— is so heavy that I can't keep my arm up. I feel the weight pulling my arm down, down.' Use your own words to suggest heaviness and lowering of the arm. It is most important that you work with the suggestion by imagining an appropriate fantasy and thinking the appropriate thoughts. Block out any thoughts that are incompatible with the suggestion. Use focusing, thought-stoppage, or the 'letting go' technique on any negative, competing thoughts. Imagine your arm getting so tired that it begins to drop lower and lower, until you can no longer keep the arm up, and you let it drop.

*Exercise no. 2. Hand levitation* – This exercise is a little more difficult, and requires more concentration and involvement than the preceding one. Think of something that would be consistent with developing a feeling of lightness in one of your hands. Some common images are: (a) a large helium balloon under the palm of your hand, (b) several helium balloons tied around your wrist, (c) your hand is a balloon being pumped up with helium, (d) your hand is a piece of metal being drawn upward by the magnetic force of your head, which is a huge electromagnet, and (e) your arm is being lifted by a series of ropes and pulleys that are being manipulated by you or someone else. Feel free to use your imagination in creating your own fantasies and suggestions. Since the goal is hand levitation, use strategies that result in such strong feelings of lightness that your hand and arm lift up.

When you are ready to begin, close your eyes, and extend your arms straight out in front of you. Use as many senses as possible to imagine your fantasy. If you are using a balloon image, picture its shape, size, and colour. Feel its texture and buoyancy. Recall how balloons have felt to you in the past.

In order to make one of your hands feel lighter than the other, give yourself suggestions of lightness, such as, 'I feel the lightness in the palm of my hand and throughout my arm. That arm is feeling lighter than the other. I feel slight movement in my fingers. I feel my hand lifting. The arm is becoming lighter and is starting to lift. My whole arm is lifting higher and higher, lifting up . . .' Create your own suggestions in your own words. Imagine the balloon lifting up, rising into the air, and finally moving upward toward your face. Repeat the suggestions as many times as needed in order to create feelings of lightness and hand levitation. Give yourself time to respond. Remember to block out any intrusive thoughts that would interfere with the goals of the exercise.

*Exercise no. 3. Chevreul's pendulum* – Chevreul's pendulum can be constructed by tying a string, seven to eight inches long, to a finger ring, a washer, or some other weight. Hold the string between your index finger and thumb. Extend your arm out in front of you so that the elbow does not rest against your body or anything else. Stare at the pendulum and imagine it moving clockwise, or back and forth. Wait long enough for the pendulum to move in the imagined direction. Then, imagine the pendulum changing direction and wait for it to actually change direction.

The movement of the pendulum, like the movement on a ouija board, occurs for a simple reason. There is nothing magical about either one. They do not predict the future nor do they have anything to do with extrasensory perception as some people claim. The activity of the pendulum and the ouija board is the result of tiny movements in your fingers, hand, and arm. Although unnoticeable to you, these movements are consistent with the imagined movements. This is an example of how your thinking affects your behaviour.

*Exercise no. 4. Arm catalepsy* – The arm catalepsy task provides you with another opportunity to practise self-hypnotic skills. The goal of this exercise is to temporarily make your arm stiff and rigid. Think of something that would be consistent with your arm becoming rigid and immobile. Some people imagine their arm in a cast or a splint. Others imagine that their arms are bars of steel or are made of wood. Use your imagination and feel free to create your own fantasy.

First, make a tight fist and hold your arm out straight, stiff, and rigid. Close your eyes and imagine your fantasy. Block out any interfering thoughts. While you continue to fantasize that your arm is immobile, and you tell yourself that it is immobile and cannot be bent, try to bend it. As long as you are absorbed in fantasies and thoughts consistent with arm rigidity, you will have difficulty bending your arm. Once you stop imagining your arm as rigid, and you tell yourself you can bend it, you will, in fact, be able to move your arm easily.

**Basic strategy in cognitive-behavioural hypnotherapy**   The principal goal of cognitive-behavioural hypnotherapy is to reverse the effects of negative and unproductive self-suggestions through a combination of hypnotic, cognitive, and behavioural strategies. Initially, the therapist explains the cognitive-behavioural model to the client and corrects misconceptions about hypnosis. Then the client learns to respond to suggestion through the hypnotic skills training procedure. After the skills training phase, hypnotic induction procedures are employed.

Although Barber and his associates have pointed out that induction procedures are not necessary for hypnotic suggestions to be effective, it is still what clients expect to receive in hypnotherapy. Since expectations have been shown to be important in determining hypnotic responsiveness (Spanos and Barber 1976), the use of hypnotic inductions in the clinical setting is consistent with a cognitive-behavioural approach. Barber (1984) himself reports that, in his clinical practice, he now uses 'hypnosis' in the form of deep relaxation prior to offering therapeutic suggestions.

There are a number of hypnotic induction procedures (see Kroger and Fezler 1976). We prefer to make our decision about which induction procedure will be employed on the basis of the client's preferences as well as his/her responses to the skills training exercises described earlier. For example, if a client were very responsive to suggestions of lightness, then a hand levitation induction procedure would be recommended. Alternatively, if the client were more receptive to suggestions of heaviness, eye fixation and closure would be more appropriate.

In cognitive-behavioural hypnosis, clients are taught about 'negative self-hypnosis', that is, how maladaptive emotions and self-defeating behaviours stem from an uncritical acceptance of one's negative self-statements (Araoz 1981, 1982). For example, self-statements such as, 'I'm too weak to lose weight, I'll always be a fat person,' are suggestions that prevent an individual from losing weight. Other self-suggestions such as, 'I failed; therefore, I'm worthless,' lead to feelings of depression. Clients learn how to replace these negative self-suggestions with more constructive suggestions, such as 'I *can* still accept myself, even if I fail.' They are further instructed to incorporate these therapeutic suggestions during self-hypnosis practice and in the actual problematic situations. The therapist also explains that constructive self-suggestions can be effectively used without a prior hypnotic induction whenever the client needs immediate help, such as when feeling anxiety, or experiencing cravings to smoke.

## Major treatment techniques

**Self-monitoring**  In cognitive-behaviour therapy, clients are instructed to monitor and record the frequency, intensity, and duration of their symptoms, maladaptive feelings and behaviour. In addition, they are taught to recognize the connection between their thoughts and their emotions and behaviour. Similarly, in cognitive-behavioural hypnotherapy, clients monitor associations between negative self-suggestions and their emotional and behavioural consequences. As in RET, clients learn to counteract their self-defeating thoughts by replacing them with more 'rational' and constructive suggestions.

**Evocative imagery**  Imagery can be used to evoke thoughts, fantasies, and feelings which may not be revealed with self-monitoring or other methods. By visualizing a personally stressful situation, the client may discover the same thoughts and emotions that are, or would be, experienced in the real situation. Such imagery heightens awareness and thus facilitates the ability of the client to pinpoint disturbing thoughts and feelings that are elicited by each activating event. For example, evocative imagery helped Mr V.

become aware of thoughts and feelings that interfered with his ability to take reasonable risks in business. Although Mr V. easily generated ideas for increasing his income, he avoided acting on them and sought hypnosis to overcome his aversion to risk-taking.

After hypnotic induction, the therapist (W.G.) instructed Mr V. to imagine taking appropriate risks in business. Mr V. reported feeling anxious and thinking that he should not take risks unless he was absolutely certain he would succeed. The imagery also elicited a childhood memory wherein another boy bullied him, while his father, refusing to intervene, said, 'Son, hit him!' The client further remembered saying, 'I will if you hold his hands, Dad. I want to make sure I don't lose.' Mr V. also recalled how he avoided risks throughout his life because he was horrified by the prospect of failure. The successful evocative imagery exercise allowed therapy to proceed to the next step: overcoming Mr V.'s exaggerated fear of failure and encouraging behavioural risk-taking.

**Disputing irrational beliefs** Ellis's (1962) method of disputing 'irrational' beliefs shows clients how to re-evaluate and correct their misperceptions and misconceptions. As a hypnotic tool, the disputation (either didactic or Socratic) begins after the hypnotic induction. Within the didactic method, the therapist offers direct, instructive suggestions to the client. The therapist corrects misconceptions (such as 'I must be liked by everyone') and suggests more rational attitudes.

In contrast, the Socratic method entails self-discovery. Clients are encouraged to examine their faulty assumptions without the assistance of didactic suggestions. For example, Mr V., the previously mentioned client who feared taking business risks, was highly receptive to the Socratic method. After Mr V. received hypnotic suggestions for deep relaxation, the following dialogue between therapist and client took place:

Mr V.: I guess I always had to be sure I would succeed.
Therapist (W.G.): And why do you have to be sure?
Mr V.: Because I might fail.
Therapist: And if you did?
Mr V.: Well, I don't want to fail.
Therapist: Of course not, no one wants to fail. But what is so frightening about failure that it paralyzes you and prevents you from doing things that could make you more successful?

Mr V.: I guess I couldn't live with failure.

Therapist: Why not?

Mr V.: Because I couldn't face other people, my family, my friends.

Therapist: Why, would they condemn you?

Mr V.: No, I guess not. In fact, I've screwed up before, and everyone was really quite supportive. I guess it's me. *I'm* condemning me.

Therapist: Then what does it mean to you to make mistakes and fail?

Mr V.: That I'm a failure and I guess, well, it looks like, I'd rather not try than possibly fail, like when I was a kid. I'd rather take a beating than try and fight and lose.

Therapist: Do you really think you'd be a failure if you took some risks and failed?

Mr V.: No, that's ridiculous, especially when I hear it said out loud. Of course not. I've been very successful in many ways. I have a terrific marriage and two lovely grown-up kids, and I'm quite successful in business. We're living very comfortably. I'm just coming to you to be *more* successful. I guess I've got to start to take some of those risks instead of avoiding each opportunity as if it were going to be the ruin of me.

Therapist: That's right. Now are you ready to work on changing some of those self-defeating attitudes and patterns?

Mr V.: Yes.

A therapist may combine or alternate between the Socratic and didactic approaches. For example, once the client learns rational re-evaluation through didactic means, the therapist may then switch to a more Socratic style to place more responsibility on the client. However, it is important to keep in mind that clients seeking hypnosis often expect the therapist to be directive at all times, telling the client what to think and do. Even these individuals can be gradually encouraged toward more active participation in hypnotherapy, for example through self-hypnosis training.

**Mood induction**     Clients can better understand how they contribute to their disturbances through the method of mood induction. This technique is particularly useful with clients who either do not believe or cannot understand the connection between their thoughts and emotions. Following a hypnotic induction procedure, the client is instructed to think the negative thoughts that appear to engender his or her symptoms. As the client's distressing emotions are induced, he or she experiences how specific thoughts produce symptoms. Finally, the client is asked to practise more rational points of view and observe the actions of rational thinking in reducing stress.

**Rational-emotive imagery (REI)** Through REI, clients practise coping with difficult situations. Although there are different ways of conducting REI (see Ellis and Harper 1975; Maultsby 1975), we prefer to guide the client through the imagery first, and then allow him/her to practise REI as a self-control or self-hypnotic technique. A relaxation or hypnotic induction can be used prior to the imagery, during which the client imagines him or herself in the stressful situation – for example, asking for a raise. The therapist then provides rational-emotive suggestions[1] which are either formulated collaboratively with the client or by the therapist alone. For example, in John's case, REI was the principal method used to alleviate his test anxiety. John requested that the therapist offer the suggestions while he (John) was hypnotized and passively listening. In accordance with his preference, John was asked during the REI to imagine himself taking an exam as he listened to suggestions such as, 'You can do well on your exams as long as you study; but no matter how you do, you are still worthwhile, and can treat yourself well.' In a similar hypnotic procedure for studying, John imagined himself using various study skills (e.g. mentally rehearsing important facts). He was then given rational suggestions about studying (such as 'No one can remember everything they read; you can do well even if you forget some important information') and suggestions for improved concentration. Finally, John incorporated these exercises into self-hypnosis home practice.

Another client, Wendy, who requested hypnosis for weight control, preferred a more active role in constructing rational-emotive suggestions for REI. On one occasion her resistance to physical exercising was examined. After a hypnotic induction, Wendy imagined that she was at her spa, and reported feeling embarrassed about what others might think of her. The following dialogue between Wendy and her therapist (W.G.) took place while she was hypnotized;

Wendy: They'll see how fat I am and think, what business does that fat pig have parading around here in that gym suit?
Therapist: And do you think that people would really think that of you?
Wendy: Probably not, I guess I could remind myself of that.
Therapist: But if someone did think that of you, why would that be awful?
Wendy: I guess that has to do with my self-worth. If they dislike me because I'm less attractive than them, I'm no good. I'm not as good as them.

Therapist: Now, Wendy, I want you to consider what you have just said.

Wendy: I know that's irrational. My self-worth isn't based on what others think of me or whether I'm fat or not.

Therapist: That's right. Now what I want you to do is imagine being at the health spa and I want you to give yourself rational suggestions to counteract your negative self-hypnosis that is causing you to feel ashamed and avoid the spa.

Wendy: OK.

Therapist: How are you feeling?

Wendy: Fine, like I belong there.

Therapist: And what are you suggesting to yourself to feel better about being there?

Wendy: I have a right to be there. It doesn't matter what others think. Probably no one is going to pay me any mind. They're probably all wrapped up in what they're doing. They don't care about me being there. But, if they did, tough shit. It has nothing to do with my worth. I'm OK whether I'm overweight or not, whether I'm accepted or not.

Therapist: Very good. And just as you can exercise your body at the spa, you can use going to the spa as an opportunity to exercise your self-hypnotic skills and repeat these suggestions to yourself when you're there. Now you may open your eyes feeling more relaxed and comfortable about going to the spa. Feeling wide awake and alert. Now do you feel ready to take that risk?

Wendy: Why not?

**Self-hypnosis training** Self-hypnosis, a very important element in cognitive-behavioural hypnotherapy, can be used by clients to rehearse or prepare for difficult situations. During home sessions, clients practise self-hypnotic skills, including relaxation, REI, and mental rehearsal of rational thoughts and constructive self-suggestions. In subsequent in vivo exposures they apply what they have practised mentally.

**Coping desensitization** The coping skills approach to desensitization (Goldfried 1971; Meichenbaum 1972) is similar to REI. Both methods direct clients to rehearse coping strategies, such as self-suggestion and relaxation procedures, while visualizing personally stressful events. In contrast to REI, a hierarchy is constructed for coping desensitization consisting of graded exposures to the situations in which clients experience anxiety. Although more time-consuming, graduated exposures are more likely to benefit extremely anxious and phobic clients who are resistant to more direct interventions.

To incorporate coping desensitization with hypnosis, a hypnotic induction procedure is given before presentation of items from the client's hierarchy. During visualization of scenes, the therapist suggests rational thoughts to replace maladaptive cognitions. Clients are then encouraged to practise relaxation techniques as well as rational suggestions during the procedure, and between sessions during in vivo exposure.

**Flooding**  In flooding, the client receives a sustained encounter with an anxiety-provoking situation or image until the anxiety is no longer elicited. Behaviour therapists have selectively invoked the principles of counterconditioning, extinction, or habituation to explain the efficacy of flooding. Cognitive-behaviour therapists explain these procedures as opportunities for clients to re-evaluate their fears and develop coping strategies. For example, during exposure to a feared situation, an individual may have a 'corrective experience' and realize that no real danger exists. Recent experimental research has confirmed that desensitization and flooding are more effective when subjects are assigned specific rational self-statements and relaxation techniques to cope with exposure to anxiety-provoking situations (see Golden, Geller and Hendricks 1981; Meichenbaum 1972).

When flooding is used in hypnotherapy, the hypnotic induction procedure precedes presentation of the stressful stimulus. Clients may also be encouraged to use rational suggestions and relaxation techniques to reduce their anxiety during flooding.

## Overcoming obstacles to client progress

Resistance can be defined operationally as the failure of the client to comply with therapeutic procedures. A practical point at which to intervene would then be when the clinician actually observes the client's failure to comply with therapeutic instructions or homework assignments. The therapist could then begin to explore with the client the possible reasons for the resistance. Three main sources of resistance have been identified by Golden (1983b): (a) therapy and therapist factors, such as absence of rapport between therapist and client; (b) environmental and other external factors, such as deliberate sabotage from others in the client's social milieu, and (c) factors operating within the client such as self-defeating cognitions and insufficient motivation.

The inclusion of cognitions as possible causes of resistance does pose several potential problems. It is important to avoid inventing new 'explanatory fictions' such as 'lack of motivation' or 'low frustration tolerance', after throwing out more traditional ones such as 'unconscious Oedipal conflicts'. However, if our concepts allow prediction and control, they are useful. Therapists can then plan potentially effective interventions to overcome resistance, rather than merely analyzing it, or rationalizing failure as due to the resistance of the client. Therefore, the cognitive-behavioural approach to resistance can include a search for self-defeating cognitions, 'hidden agendas', motivational problems, and reinforcing consequences.

Given the above formulation, two basic approaches for dealing with resistance are possible: (a) overcoming resistance when it occurs, and (b) preventing resistance from occurring. As will be shown later, there are indirect interventions as well as direct ones for preventing and overcoming resistance. First we will examine the direct methods.

**Avoiding the development of resistance: suggestions from behavioural medicine**   Certain recommendations from the field of behavioural medicine (Pomerleau 1979) can be applied to cognitive-behavioural hypnotherapy. (a) Educate the client from the onset of therapy about treatment and its rationale. Cognitive-behavioural hypnosis is consistent with such full disclosure, in that it shows the client directly how to achieve the desired hypnotic results and therapy goals. (b) Tailor the treatment so that it fits into the client's daily routine. For example, programme self-hypnotic home practice according to the client's preferences as well as therapeutic requirements. (c) Use 'shaping', or successive approximations, with clients receiving complex treatments. For example, with a pain control client, teach only one or two self-hypnotic strategies for pain reduction, instead of possibly overwhelming the client with several strategies at once.

In addition to the above methods, Golden (1983b) offers the following suggestions for avoiding the development of resistance. (d) Capitalize on the expectations and requests of the client. Resistance is reduced when the therapist matches the treatment methods to the client's expectations and requests. Lazarus (1973) did a clinical study on the effect of expectations on treatment that illustrates this point. Clients who requested hypnosis were assigned to a treatment that was defined as either relaxation therapy or hypnosis. Although the treatments were actually the same for both groups, the clients who received 'hypnosis' (as they requested) showed greater improvement than the group that received 'relaxation'. On the other hand, clients who did not state a preference for either type of therapy did equally well with the two differently labelled treatements.

(e) Prepare clients for difficulties and 'setbacks'. In Marlatt and Gordon's (1980) cognitive-behavioural relapse prevention programme, the therapist and client identify high-risk situations and thoughts that could lead to relapse. The client is taught to anticipate these 'triggers' in advance and to plan coping strategies for dealing with them. For example, instead of becoming discouraged and resuming smoking after 'slipping', the client wanting to quit smoking learns to expect and deal with setbacks as part of the treatment process.

**Overcoming resistance with a cognitive-behavioural problem-solving approach**  The problem-solving approach is direct in that the therapist and the client work together on the impasse as a problem to be solved. The client is taught to use the same methods that are applied in cognitive-behavioural hypnotherapy to any problem, including self-monitoring, cognitive restructuring, evocative imagery, mood induction, successive approximations, etc. For example, a client who received hypnotic treatment for interpersonal anxiety reported that the hypnotic effects were not transferring to in vivo situations. Exploring possible reasons for this failure of generalization, the client reported not practising her self-hypnosis, believing that she could not do it well in the absence of the therapist. The therapist (W.G.) recommended successive approximations whereby the client first practised self-hypnosis in the therapist's office alone, then at home, and finally with success in vivo.

**Indirect methods for dealing with resistance**  As discussed earlier, the distinguishing characteristics of cognitive-behavioural hypnotherapy are its direct and didactic treatment methods. Clients are taught self-hypnotic and other self-control procedures to be used as coping skills. Success in cognitive-behavioural hypnotherapy depends on the willingness of the client to co-operate with the therapist, and the client's conscious and persistent application of the treatment procedures. As described in the preceding section of this chapter, a collaborative problem-solving approach can overcome some client resistance. Nevertheless, there are a number of clients who are unwilling or unable to co-operate – who resist, at least initially, any and all attempts to help them. Indirect methods, such as paradoxical suggestions, may facilitate treatment of these individuals. Since an exposition of indirect interventions is beyond the scope of this chapter, readers are advised to consult the sources which describe the indirect methods of Milton Erickson (Erickson and Rossi 1979; Haley 1973). Recently, Golden (1985) has proposed in integration of cognitive-behavioural and Ericksonian methods.

**Indications for cognitive-behavioural hypnotherapy**   In our clinical experience, we have found that hypnosis is generally indicated for clients who request it. As discussed earlier, Lazarus (1973) has shown that clients are more likely to respond to treatment when the therapist honours their stated preferences for hypnosis, rather than offering an alternative treatment. Likewise, we do not recommend hypnosis for clients who are opposed to it. Conducting any hypnotic treatment on a reluctant client is likely to undermine therapeutic rapport and progress. We further advise caution with individuals exhibiting severe paranoid ideation. Even when such clients request hypnosis, they may become paranoid about the therapist controlling their mind. However, this pitfall is less likely to occur within a cognitive-behavioural approach emphasizing *self*-control of the hypnotic process.

Wadden and Anderton (1982), in their review of the controlled research on the clinical uses of hypnosis, concluded that traditional hypnosis is particularly effective in the treatment of asthma, clinical pain, and warts. In a subsequent literature review of clinical hypnosis and relaxation therapy, Barber (1984) concluded that hypnosuggestive procedures are effective in the treatment of migraine and tension headaches, insomnia, and hypertension.

On the other hand, the results of traditional hypnotic treatment for 'habit' problems such as obesity, cigarette smoking, and alcoholism have been disappointing. For example, Wadden and Anderton (1982) report that the success rate of hypnotherapy for stopping cigarette smoking, observed at one-year post-treatment, is only about 20 per cent. However, our clinical data suggest that the integration of hypnosis with hypnotic skills training and cognitive-behaviour therapy is more effective for smoking cessation than the traditional approaches to hypnosis reviewed by Wadden and Anderton. We found that 8 out of 12 clients (67 per cent) stopped smoking for at least four weeks after completion of a four-session cognitive-behavioural hypnotic (CBH) treatment (see case example, next section). The first author (W.G.) served as the therapist. After a one-year follow-up interval, 7 out of 12 (58 per cent) remained abstinent. The second author (F.F.) treated 9 smoking clients with an abbreviated one-session version of this CBH procedure. 5 out of 9 (56 per cent) stopped smoking for at least four weeks immediately following treatment, and 43 per cent (4/9) remained non-smoking at a one-year follow-up. Of course, these preliminary clinical results need to be replicated in controlled outcome studies of CBH for smoking.

Other investigators have also found that the integration of cognitive-behavioural methods with hypnosis increases the effectiveness of hypnotherapy. Boutin and Tosi (1983) found that Rational Stage-Directed Hypnotherapy (RSDH), a CBH procedure described earlier, was more effective than hypnosis alone in reducing test anxiety. Furthermore, Fuller (1981) found RSDH to be more effective than cognitive restructuring alone or hypnosis alone in alleviating depression in a geriatric population. Finally, Araoz (1982, 1984) reported, on the basis of clinical data, that his CBH procedure for sexual dysfunction was more effective than traditional sex therapy.

To summarize, these initial findings on cognitive-behavioural-hypnotic approaches are encouraging. Such results suggest that CBH methods are indicated for the treatment of cigarette smoking, test anxiety, depression and sexual dysfunction. Replication of these positive outcomes and the application of CBH approaches to other clinical problems await further research.

## Case example

As an illustration of cognitive-behavioural hypnotherapy, we will present a somewhat standardized four-session procedure for smoking cessation that was used with Sally. We have found this time-limited treatment to be an effective way to integrate cognitive-behavioural procedures and hypnosis.

### Session no.1

The therapist (W.G) explained how hypnosis and cognitive-behavioural therapy can be used to stop smoking. Then Sally's misconceptions about hypnosis – for example, her belief in magical effortless cures – were examined and corrected. It was explained that hypnosis is a function of thinking, imagining, and concentrating, and that successful treatment would require her active participation.

As in other cognitive-behavioural approaches, Sally's smoking history was taken. Like most clients, Sally was able to identify only a few of her antecedent smoking conditions. Therefore she was instructed, as homework, to monitor her frequency of smoking, the situations in which she smoked, and the thoughts and feelings that preceded each cigarette. Her reasons for wanting to quit were discussed and any negatively worded reasons, such as, 'I don't want to die of cancer,' were rephrased with positive wording, such as 'I want to live longer; I want to be healthier.' Later, her reasons for wanting to quit provided motivating suggestions during self-hypnosis. Generally speaking, most hypnotists construct hypnotic suggestions with positive wording.

Finally, Sally received hypnosis skills training, as described in detail at the beginning of the chapter. She was most responsive to the hand lightness and levitation exercise which was assigned as home practice.

## Session no.2

During the second session, the client's smoking record was reviewed, and these antecedents to smoking were pinpointed: job stress, social anxiety, boredom, and frustration. Some of the thoughts that served as triggers to smoking were in the form of perfectionist demands, while other thoughts, such as, 'I can't stand feeling tense; I've got to have a cigarette,' showed poor tolerance of frustration. Alternative ways of thinking and acting in each situation were discussed. For instance, a constructive hypnotic suggestion, such as 'I will have more and more control over my desire to smoke as I learn to relax and enjoy breathing clean fresh air,' was developed as a replacement for, 'I've just got to have a cigarette.' Furthermore, relaxation techniques were recommended as an alternative method to reduce anxiety and stress.

Then hypnosis was induced via hand levitation – the strategy found to be most effective in prior hypnotic skills training with Sally. Relaxation procedures were also part of the hypnotic induction. Sally was instructed to focus on her breathing and allow the process to slow down and deepen. It was suggested that, as her breathing slowed, feelings of relaxation would spread throughout her body. To deepen relaxation further, Sally was asked to imagine the pleasant calming scene which had been constructed with the therapist prior to the induction. She was then given instructions for initiating self-hypnosis by taking five long, slow deep breaths while focusing on an increasing sense of relaxation every time she exhaled. In addition, she was given hypnotic suggestions to delay acting on the impulse to smoke long enough to use breathing and other self-hypnotic techniques to reduce her anxiety and cravings for nicotine.

Sally's next assignment was to continue to monitor and record every cigarette smoked, but to delay smoking for fifteen minutes after the onset of a craving, and practise self-hypnosis during the interval. The fifteen-minute delay shows the client that he or she does not have to smoke immediately in response to either a smoking urge or a negative emotion. Clients such as Sally often decide not to smoke after the interval, which further reinforces their increasing sense of self-control.

## Session no.3

During the third session, Sally's smoking record was again reviewed and all successful smoking delays were verbally praised. The therapist asked for a description of all techniques that were effective in reducing anxiety and the craving for nicotine. Problem areas were examined, and additional coping strategies for controlling anxiety and cravings were developed.

Next, the client was hypnotized with the induction procedure of session 2. During the hypnosis, the therapist suggested that Sally (a) imagine herself in each smoking situation, (b) experience the negative thoughts and feelings associated with each situation, and (c) imagine herself coping with each situation.

After the hypnosis, Sally set a cut-off date for stopping smoking, and the therapist presented the choice of reducing smoking frequency gradually or immediately. Sally selected immediate cessation, and was therefore asked to stop smoking twenty-four hours before the next session. Twenty-four hours of cigarette deprivation prior to the fourth session allows the therapist to target the client's coping difficulties as they are happening.

## Session no.4

Like most clients who have been treated with this four-session approach, Sally arrived at the fourth session in a state of discomfort resulting from twenty-four hours of nicotine deprivation.

After hypnosis was induced through hand levitation and relaxation techniques, the client was reminded of her reasons for wanting to stop smoking. Then she was again asked to imagine herself in smoking situations, and signal by raising her right index finger whenever the imagery elicited anxiety or cravings. The therapist then suggested that the client should use the previously learned cognitive, behavioural, and hypnotic strategies, and finally lower her finger when she was successful in reducing anxiety and cravings. This procedure is similar to Goldfried's (1971) and Meichenbaum's (1972) coping desensitization procedures.

After Sally succeeded in reducing anxiety and cravings, relapse prevention, as described earlier, was implemented. She imagined herself 'slipping' but, rather than giving up, was instructed to give herself suggestions such as 'Even if I slip, I am basically moving forward and can control my smoking; just because I slipped, it doesn't mean I will fail; I will continue to succeed.' In addition, Sally imagined situations where she could not reduce the craving, but coped with the discomfort through self-suggestions such as, 'I can stand this discomfort; eventually, it will pass.'

After successfully completing the above programme, Sally provided the following evaluation of her experience with hypnotherapy:

> Despite all of Dr Golden's warnings to the contrary, I had persisted in believing that hypnosis was magic, that it would cure me without any real effort on my part. Now I realize that hypnosis just gives you something to fall back on when the going gets tough. Since I recognized this, I feel reassured and confident again. There was no magic spell, only a little help when you needed it. The rest – including making the effort at self-hypnosis – was up to me. And, as I kept telling myself when I was in a trance, I could do it.

## Note

1  Rational or rational-emotive suggestions are self-statements formulated on the basis of RET principles and offered as hypnotic suggestions.

## References

Araoz, D.L. (1981) Negative self-hypnosis. *Journal of Contemporary Psychotherapy*, *12*, 45–52.

Araoz, D.L. (1982) *Hypnosis and sex therapy*. New York: Brunner/Mazel.

Araoz, D.L. (1984) Hypnosis in the treatment of sexual dysfunctions. In W.C. Webster II and A.H. Smith Jr (eds) *Clinical hypnosis: A multidisciplinary approach*. Philadelphia: Lippincott.

Barber, T.X. (1978) Hypnosis, suggestions, and psychosomatic phenomena: A new look from the standpoint of recent experimental studies. *The American Journal of Clinical Hypnosis*, *21*, 13–27.

Barber, T.X. (1979) Suggested (hypnotic) behavior: The trance paradigm versus an alternative paradigm. In E. Fromm and R.E. Shor (eds) *Hypnosis: Developments in research and new perspectives* (2nd rev. edn). New York: Aldine.

Barber, T.X. (1984) Hypnosis, deep relaxation, and active relaxation: Data theory and clinical applications. In R.L. Woolfolk and P.M. Lehrer (eds) *Principles and practice of stress management*. New York: Guilford Press.

Barber, T.X., Spanos, N.P. and Chaves, J.F. (1984) *Hypnosis, imagination and human potentialities*. New York: Pergamon Press.

Bernheim, H. (1895) *Suggestive therapeutics*. New York: G.P. Putnam's Sons.

Boutin, G.E. (1978) Treatment of test anxiety by rational stage-directed hypnotherapy: A case study. *American Journal of Clinical Hypnosis, 81*, 180–198.

Boutin, G.E. and Tosi, D.J. (1983) The modification of irrational ideas and test anxiety through rational stage-directed hypnotherapy. *Journal of Clinical Psychology, 39*, 382–391.

Brenman, M. and Gill M.M. (1947) *Hypnotherapy: A survey of the literature*. New York: International Universities Press.

Davison, G.C., Tsujimato, R.N. and Glaros, A.G. (1973) Attribution and the maintenance of behavior change in falling asleep. *Journal of Abnormal Psychology, 82*, 124–133.

Diamond, M.J. (1974) Modification of hypnotizability: A review. *Psychological Bulletin, 81*, 180–198.

Diamond, M.J. (1977) Hypnotizability is modifiable: An alternative approach. *International Journal of Clinical and Experimental Hypnosis, 25*, 147–166.

Ellis, A. (1962) *Reason and emotion in psychotherapy*. New York: Lyle Stuart.

Ellis, A. and Harper, R.A. (1975) *A new guide to rational living*. Englewood Cliffs, NJ: Prentice Hall.

Erickson, M.H. and Rossi, E.L. (1979) *Hypnotherapy: An exploratory casebook*. New York: Irvington.

Freud, S. (1920) *A general introduction to psychoanalysis*. New York: Washington Square Press.

Fromm, E. (1984) The theory and practice of hypnoanalysis. In W.C. Webster II and A.H. Smith Jr (eds) *Clinical hypnosis: A multidisciplinary approach*. Philadelphia: Lippincott.

Fuller, J. (1981) Rational stage-directed hypnotherapy in the treatment of self-concept and depression in a geriatric nursing home population: A cognitive experimental approach. Unpublished PhD dissertation. Ohio State University.

Gargiulo, T. (1983) Influence of training in hypnotic responsivity on hypnotically suggested analgesia. Unpublished PhD dissertation, California Coast University.

Golden, W.L. (1982) *Self-hypnosis: The rational-emotive approach* (cassette recording). New York: Institute for Rational-Emotive Therapy.

Golden, W.L. (1983a) Rational-emotive hypnotherapy: Principles and techniques. *British Journal of Cognitive Psychotherapy, 1(1)*, 47–56.

Golden, W.L. (1983b) Resistance in cognitive-behaviour therapy, *British Journal of Cognitive Psychotherapy. 1(2)*, 33–42.

Golden, W.L. (1985) An integration of Ericksonian and cognitive-behavioural hypnotherapy in the treatment of anxiety disorders. In E.T. Dowd and J.M. Healy (eds) *Case studies in hypnotherapy*. New York: Guilford Press.

Golden, W.L., Geller, E. and Hendricks, C.A. (1981) A coping skills approach to flooding therapy in the treatment of test anxiety. *Rational Living, 16(2)*, 17–20.

Goldfried, M.R. (1971) Systematic desensitization as training in self-control. *Journal of Consulting and Clinical Psychology*, *34*, 228–238.

Haley, J. (1973) *Uncommon therapy: The psychiatric techniques of Milton Erickson, M.D.* New York: Ballantine Books.

Katz, N.W. (1979) Comparative efficacy of behavioral training, training plus relaxation, and sleep/trance hypnotic induction in increasing hypnotic susceptibility. *Journal of Consulting and Clinical Psychology*, *47*, 119–127.

Kroger, W.S. and Fezler, W.D. (1976) *Hypnosis and behavior modification: Imagery conditioning*. Philadelphia: Lippincott.

Lazarus, A.A. (1973) 'Hypnosis' as a facilitator in behavior therapy. *International Journal of Clinical and Experimental Hypnosis*, *21*, 25–31.

Marlatt, G.A. and Gordon, J.R. (1980) Determinants of relapse: Implications for the maintenance of behaviour change. In F.C. Davidson and S.M. Davidson (eds) *Behavioral medicine: Changing health life styles*. New York: Brunner/Mazel.

Maultsby, M.C., Jr (1975) *Help yourself to happiness: Through rational self-counseling*. Boston: Marlborough House.

Meichenbaum, D.H. (1972) Cognitive modification of test anxious college students. *Journal of Consulting and Clinical Psychology*, *39*, 370–380.

Pavlov, I.P. (1941) *Conditioned reflexes and psychiatry*. New York: International Publishers.

Pomerleau, O.F. (1979) Behavioral medicine: The contribution of the experimental analysis of behavior to medical care. *American Psychologist*, *34*, 654–663.

Prince, M. and Coriat, I. (1907) Cases illustrating the educational treatment of the psycho-neuroses. *Journal of Abnormal Psychology*, *2*, 166–177.

Ruch, J.C. (1975) Self-hypnosis: The result of heterohypnosis or vice versa? *International Journal of Clinical and Experimental Hypnosis*, *23*, 282–304.

Salter, A. (1949) *Conditioned reflex therapy*. New York: Capricorn Books.

Spanos, N.P. and Barber, T.X. (1972) Cognitive activity during 'hypnotic' suggestibility: Goal-directed fantasy and experience of non-volition. *Journal of Personality*, *40*, 520–524.

Spanos, N.P. and Barber, T.X. (1974) Toward a convergence in hypnosis research. *American Psychologist*, *29*, 500–511.

Spanos, N.P. and Barber, T.X. (1976) Behavior modification and hypnosis. In M. Hersen, R.M. Eisler and P.M. Miller (eds) *Progress in behavior modification*. New York: Academic Press.

Tosi, D.J. and Baisden, B.S. (1984) Cognitive-experiential therapy and hypnosis. In W.C. Webster II and A.H. Smith Jr (eds) *Clinical hypnosis: A multidisciplinary approach*. Philadelphia: Lippincott.

Wadden, T.A. and Anderton, C.H. (1982) The clinical use of hypnosis. *Psychological Bulletin, 91*, 215–243.

Weitzenhoffer, A.M. (1972) Behavior therapeutic techniques and hypnotherapeutic methods. *American Journal of Clinical Hypnosis, 15*, 71–82.

## CHAPTER ELEVEN

**Multimodal Therapy: The Cognitive-Behavioural Tradition and Beyond**
*Maurits G.T. Kwee and Arnold A. Lazarus*

## History and underpinnings of multimodal therapy

*Historical development of multimodal therapy*

Multimodal therapy (MMT) is a multifaceted approach that has evolved from a 'unimodal' (strictly behavioural) and later a 'bimodal' (cognitive-behavioural) tradition (Kwee 1981). Recently, general systems theory has provided a unifying transdisciplinary structure for multimodal thinking (cf. De Rosnay 1979).

In the late 1950s and early 1960s A.A. Lazarus pioneered, together with J. Wolpe and S. Rachman, the unimodal behavioural approach. It was Lazarus (1958) who coined the term 'behaviour therapy' to refer to objective and laboratory-derived techniques, and who instigated several innovative studies. These included: (a) the first empirical study on systematic desensitization (Lazarus and Rachman 1957); (b) the application of aversive imagery (Lazarus 1958); (c) the behavioural treatment of phobias in children (Lazarus 1960); (d) the practice of systematic desensitization in groups (Lazarus 1961); (e) the use of emotive imagery (Lazarus and Abramovitz 1962); and (f) an evaluation of treatment outcomes in 126 cases of severe neurosis (Lazarus 1963). At that time learning theory, and more specifically conditioning theory according to the neo-Hullian paradigm (Wolpe and Lazarus 1966), formed the exclusive basis for behaviour therapy.

When Lazarus argued for a broad spectrum or bimodal behaviour therapy in the mid-1960s, he anticipated the conceptual shift that took place in the 1970s, when behaviour therapy 'went cognitive'. In a paper on technical eclecticism, Lazarus (1967) encouraged practitioners of behaviour therapy to use any technique that had been empirically proven to be effective, such as Ellis's (1962) cognitive techniques. His classic text, *Behavior Therapy and Beyond* (Lazarus 1971), may be considered the first book on what has come to be called 'cognitive-behavioural therapy'.

With the introduction of multimodal behaviour therapy, Lazarus (1973) extended this approach to also include affect and other modalities. Equal coverage of the following modalities is emphasized: Behaviour (B), Affect (A), Sensation (S), Imagery (I), Cognition (C), Interpersonal relationships

(I.) and biological and Drug-related issues (D.), the BASIC I.D. These modalities represent the major fields of general experimental psychology, and are also thought of as a reflection of personality. Since most therapeutic approaches have a conceptualization of human conduct that is unimodal, bimodal or at best trimodal – behaviour, cognition and affect – it seems to us that behaviour therapy lags far behind MMT, if Wilson's (1982) statement is corroborated: 'If we began with overt behavior in the 1950s and 1960s, then added cognition in the 1970s, can affect be far behind? In looking for a new emphasis in behavior therapy, it might be "affect in the eighties" ' (p. 298).

This conception of human functioning still strikes us as an incomplete statement of MMT. By covering the entire BASIC I.D., it seems to us that MMT transcends the usual cognitive-behaviour therapy framework (Lazarus 1977).

In trying to look at the BASIC I.D. from a general systems theory perspective (Von Bertalanffy 1974), MMT goes beyond 'affective-cognitive-behaviour therapy', and might prompt far-reaching changes in the 1980s for the behavioural approach (cf. Schwartz 1982). Franks (1982) points out:

> While still speculative, the merging of . . . [systems theory] with the precepts of behavior therapy offers considerable promise . . . it is data-based, sympathetic to learning principles . . . [it] could enable us to bring together diverse fields in such a manner as to solve problems that are inherently complex, multiprocessed, and multileveled in nature. (p. 5)

As a broad framework with more inclusive premises, systems theory, being compatible with social learning theory, might function as a unifying conceptual umbrella for MMT. Systems theory is a metatheory, a theory about theories, that tries to organize the findings in some or all of the sciences of life and behaviour into a single conceptual structure (Miller 1978). The assumption is made that the world is made up of a population of objects called systems. A system is a set of interacting elements that forms a constituting integrated whole that can be observed at different levels of organization (e.g. cell, organ, organism, group, organization, and society). Systems at all these levels are open and composed of subsystems which process inputs, throughputs, and outputs of various forms of matter, energy, and information.[1] As Durkin (1981) explained, a system has four major properties: (a) it is hierarchically arrayed, and is as such both a part (subsystem) and a whole (suprasystem); (b) it has an isomorphy common to all systems and common organizing processes; (c) it maintains wholeness and achieves self-regulation as well as progressive self-transformation to higher levels of adaptation; and (d) it exchanges matter, energy, and information with the environment by (selectively) opening and closing its boundaries of input and output.

Systems thinking is important in the development of MMT because it provides a synthesis of explanations of clinical events in a way that is complementary to earlier MMT concepts. Futhermore, it helps illuminate how the distinct modalities of the BASIC I.D. interrelate by providing a comprehensible and clear arrangement of complex client material, particularly by means of a *blueprint* for functional analyses. As the 'avant gardists' of the cognitive-behavioural tradition, MMT, by incorporating systems theory, might be on the verge of a general theory for psychotherapy, in which the wealth of research data will be organized and synthesized in the next few decades.

## Major theoretical concepts

In our pursuit of clinical effectiveness we endorse a flexible, versatile and systematic eclectic stance. This development remains in accordance with the cognitive-behavioural tradition, with its appreciation of careful observation, formulation and testing of hypotheses, and ongoing self-correction based on empirical data. MMT provides a specifiable and operational framework. It conforms to the prevailing norms of scientific specificity for answering the essential question: what specific techniques, administered by whom, are effective for what types of clients, with what kind of problems, under which conditions, and for which reasons?

**Basic concepts** The choice of any therapeutic intervention will depend largely on the clinician's theory of causality. The notion that maladaptive behaviours stem from conditioning calls for deconditioning techniques. The view that dysfunctional cognitions form the basis of psychological disturbances leads to cognitive disputation as the mainstay of therapy. In the same vein, evocative techniques are indicated if one subscribes to a person-centred outlook of emotional disturbance. What specific theoretical constructs, concepts, principles and terms form the *substratum* for MMT? When accounting for the vagaries of human conduct we need to heed Occam's Razor and respect the principle of parsimony (Lazarus 1981).

Our personalities are shaped and maintained by classical, operant and vicarious learning. Respondent and instrumental conditioning can account for a wide range of human experiences and encounters. For instance, *classical conditioning* plays an important role as an explanatory concept in the case of a woman who, after having experienced significant losses, avoided contacts, and developed a depression. *Operant conditioning* is useful in explaining how the same woman reinforces her depression by locking herself up in the bedroom and by manipulating her social environment. However, as Bandura (1977) explained, most conditioning in humans is cognitively mediated. In mastering problem-solving skills, trial and error or successive approximation methods are definitely insufficient. Positive results are facilitated by learning via observation, imitation and identification, which can be subsumed under the heading of *modelling and vicarious processes*.

Because people do not react automatically to external events it is necessary to add *private events* to our pool of basic concepts. Idiosyncratic sensations, thoughts, images, and feelings often override the best-laid plans of contiguity, contingency, and example. Thoughts and images about stimuli determine which of them are noticed, how they are evaluated, and what will be remembered. One does not respond to some real environment, but rather to a perceived environment. The cognitive domain addresses the idiosyncratic use of selective attention, expectancies, semantics, and encoding, as well as the specific impact of values, beliefs, and attitudes on overt behaviour. Having entered the realm of private events, it also becomes clear (a) that different people display different degrees of self-awareness, and (b) that subliminal stimuli can influence people's conscious thoughts, feelings, and behaviours. People are not necessarily aware of certain connections between present events and past experiences. During altered states of consciousness one may have access to memories or skills not amenable to conscious recall. A striking example was given by Wachtel (1977) who recounts the experience of a woman, born in Hungary and emigrated to America at an early age, who knew no Hungarian when awake but who could speak Hungarian during anaesthesia.

*Nonconscious processes* as well as *defensive reactions* are capable of influencing behaviour. As emphasized by Shevrin and Dickman (1980) empirical evidence suggests that 'nonconscious psychological processes' are a conceptual necessity for understanding how human beings know, learn, or act. While integrating thoughts, feelings, and behaviours, people are often unaware of motivating factors and tend to avoid unpleasant stimuli through a variety of defensive reactions.

Whereas psychodynamic theory views 'defense mechanisms' as

perceptual, attitudinal, or attentional shifts that aid the ego in neutralizing overbearing id impulses, our use of the term 'defensive reactions' is a simple and direct acknowledgement of the empirical fact that people are capable of truncating their own awareness, of beguiling themselves, of mislabeling their affective responses, and of losing touch with themselves (and others) in a variety of ways. (Lazarus 1981, p. 37).

We are apt to defend against pain, discomfort, and negative emotions like anxiety, anger, depression, guilt, and shame. Thus, in our attempt to reduce dissonance, people will readily succumb to devices such as repression,

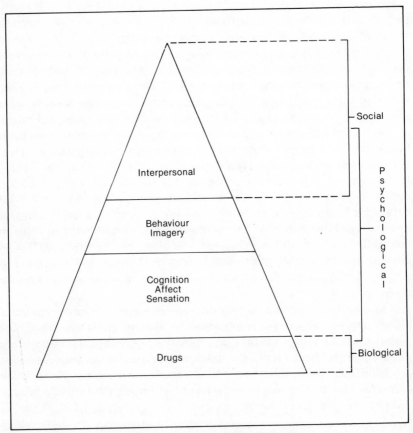

**Figure 11.1** The hierarchical ordering of the BASIC I.D.

sublimation, reaction-formation, regression, rationalization, projection, displacement, or denial.

When dealing with dyadic and other complex interactions we add explanatory concepts from *communication and systems theory*. Interpersonal relationships can be better understood when we also look at the whole, which is more than the sum of its parts (e.g. the family), instead of only at the separate parts (the individuals). In MMT, the focus of attention swings back and forth from the person to the social system of which the individual forms a part. The person who wants to change is the client. When family members are concerned about an individual, we regard them too as clients. When dealing with relationships it is important to identify communications and metacommunications. One can examine the content-level and process-level of a communication and identify the relational meaning of a message as to improve the quality of the client's relationships.

The multimodal framework as expressed by the BASIC I.D. conceptualizes personality as a living system for providing a biopsychosocial organization and synthesis. General systems theory offers a broad view of human functioning within which one can understand the interrelatedness of seemingly disparate modalities. In the cognitive-behavioural approaches the model of the human mind is usually presented as a static linear paradigm. A dynamic circular paradigm implies that a strong emotion influences perception by selecting, anticipating, and remembering the emotional event. To paraphrase Rabkin (1983):

> The alternative to a mentalistic notion that blames faulty ideas for symptoms would be a concept that recognizes that there is a failure of a corrective process to sweep aside the dysfunctional thoughts that we all have. A hierarchical model allows that one can have thoughts about thoughts and even thoughts about feelings, creating layer upon layer of a tangled web of circular loops. (p. 1101).

We discard linear causality as an explanatory concept in favour of *circular causality*. By adopting the latter it is impossible to say whether 'cause' (as defined) precedes 'effect' or whether 'effect' precedes 'cause'. Emphasis is on the multiplicity of causes and a functional relatedness of modalities in reciprocal interaction.

**General systems theory**    The BASIC I.D. as a psychological system has the properties of open living structures by being in a constant relationship with its environment. It is further described as a complex of components in dynamic and mutual interaction organized for adaptation. The components are interconnected in a causally connected sequence, and are related to each other in a stable manner over time. According to the principle of circular causality, not a single modality exists in isolation. Therefore if one induces homeostasis in a certain modality, one creates *ipso facto* disequilibrium in other modalities. How can systems theory offer guidelines in choosing the most appropriate modalities and techniques for intervention? In order to find an answer, some properties of the BASIC I.D. as a circular, open, self-regulating, and goal-directed system need to be explained (Miller 1978).

First of all, the hierarchical ordering of the BASIC I.D. shown in Figure 11.1 has been proposed (cf. Lazarus, Kreitzberg and Sassenrath 1981).

In Figure 11.1 the psychological system is presented in the form of a pyramid in order of organizational complexity of levels. The modalities vary from relatively simple to complex. As the prime factor it is important to mention the biological substrate first. Because all sensations are experienced physically, this 'input' modality is closely linked to D. Affect is linked to Sensation but includes Cognition and Imagery as well as expressive Behavioural components. Together they constitute the 'throughput' modalities. While Behaviour is influenced by the modalities preceding it, Interpersonal relationships form the culmination of the interplay of modalities, involving more than one person. Influenced by the other six modalities the latter may be considered the 'output' modality, as it is the most outwardly focused aspect of human functioning in terms of the BASIC I.D.

Other properties of the BASIC I.D. as a system are:

1. *Wholeness*: The BASIC I.D. is a *gestalt* that consists of distinct but inseparable modalities that are more than the sum of their parts. A given modality cannot be understood unless its interrelatedness and connections to the other modalities are understood.
2. *Relationship*: Relationships keep the BASIC I.D. together. The central question is *what* is going on, rather than why things are going on, between the modalities. Instead of looking at the separate modalities, a systems perspective examines significant interactions between and across the BASIC I.D. in terms of function.
3. *Equifinality*: An end result is determined not only by past experiences but also by the character of the process or the parameters of the system itself. The BASIC I.D. may attain the same (maladaptive) final state

independent of different initial conditions. Instead of looking exclusively for historical factors, the emphasis is on the here-and-now situation, particularly on the existing, self-perpetuating mechanisms.

4. *Homeostasis*: Homeostasis is a function of the BASIC I.D. in which it maintains psychological equilibrium in the face of external and internal disturbances. It keeps the modalities of a dynamic balance, staying within the same range, yet subject to a variety of influences. Balance is maintained by feedback processes at each hierarchical level of the system.

5. *Feedback*: The BASIC I.D. is held stable and helps the person to reach adaptation by means of feedback mechanisms. Feedback is defined by Wiener (1948) as 'The property of being able to adjust future conduct by past experience.' Whereas negative feedback (decrease of output) is a process that maintains homeostasis of the old system, positive feedback (increase of output) is directed toward change, i.e. disruption (loss of homeostasis of the system) and readjustment.[2]

By incorporating systems theory, MMT has a parsimonious framework of explanatory concepts that are capable of organizing the BASIC I.D. and that lend themselves to empirical research.

## How client problems are conceptualized

In order to conceptualize client problems, a modality profile – a specific list of problems (and proposed techniques) in each area of the BASIC I.D. – is devised. The BASIC I.D. represents the fundamental vectors of the psychological system. Learning to think and speak in BASIC I.D. terms opens new vistas for solving clinical problems.

**Problem assessment by modality**  In assessing the 'anatomy' of psychological disturbances, multimodal therapists consistently probe a large 'body' of salient issues before making 'incisions'. The following checklist may be helpful to pinpoint excesses and deficits of modalities according to the canons of scientific specificity.[3]

1. *Behaviour*: What are the client's main behavioural strengths or assets? What behaviours are getting in the way of reaching personal goals?

Attention is paid to differentiating between fight versus flight reactions (Cannon 1939). Anticipation of problem situations leads to approach and/or avoidance behaviours. Clients avoid situations actively or passively with their symptomatic behaviours. Following Miller (1944), 'approach-approach', 'avoidance-avoidance', 'approach-avoidance' and 'double approach-avoidance' tendencies may be distinguished.

2. *Affect*: What 'makes' the client feel glad, mad, sad, scared, or guilty? How does he or she then behave? One enquires about the client's sympathy, love, jealousy and hatred, as well as areas of shame and guilt. How and when does the client experience maladaptive feelings of anxiety, anger, or depression, and what tends to result in a reduction of emotional strains? Does the client tend to express affect in functional (sensory or somatic) terms, e.g. 'tired' instead of depressed, or 'pain' instead of sadness?

3. *Sensation*: What does the client especially like or dislike to see, hear, taste, touch, and smell? Is he/she sensitive to temperature, equilibrium kinesthetics or proprioceptives? Are there any persistent unpleasant sensations such as aches, pains, dizziness or tremors? Through which senses does the client organize his or her world? What are the client's sensual and sexual turn-ons and turn-offs?

4. *Imagery*: Is the client able to form clear mental images? Which positive or negative pictures about the past, present or future arouse any significant mood? How would the client describe his or her self-image? What does the client like or dislike about the way he or she perceives himself or herself? What are the client's projections about the world? Are there any recurrent fantasies or dreams that may be troublesome? Do these images appear to have a symbolic meaning? (Lazarus 1978).

5. *Cognition*: What are the client's most cherished beliefs, values and intellectual interests? Are the client's attributions external or internal? Is the client a victim of the 'tyranny of shoulds' (Ellis 1962). Is the client abstracting correctly: i.e. can he or she distinguish between descriptions, inferences and evaluations? (Kwee 1982). What are the client's absolutisms? Does he or she overgeneralize, oversocialize, catastrophize or personalize? Does he or she infer arbitrarily or reason dichotomously (Lazarus and Fay 1975)?

6. *Interpersonal relationships*: Who are the most important people in the client's life? What do significant others expect from or do to the client? What does the client expect from or do to them? How skilled is the client in communicating? Is the client a non-assertive or aggressive responder? Does the client suffer from interpersonal clashes, authority or rivalry

conflicts, marital distress or family disharmony? Does the client live in social isolation or is he or she manipulating his or her social environment? How does the client behave during the therapeutic sessions? Is he or she taking, in Leary's (1957) terms, a dominant-hostile or a friendly-submissive position? How are the client's interpersonal relationships influenced by the ecosystem?

7. *Drugs/biological factors*: Does the client have any concerns about his or her state of health? Are there any psychosomatic disturbances?[4] What are the client's habits pertaining to nutrition, hygiene, sleep, and physical fitness? Does the client take any medication or drugs? How do biological factors influence and relate to the BASIC I.D.? Is it necessary to consult a medical practitioner?

Each target item is assessed in terms of *quality* (pleasant, unpleasant, neutral), *quantity* (frequency, intensity, duration) and *function* (who, what, where, when, how). The assessment of relevant deficits and excesses across the client's BASIC I.D. system will facilitate a thorough coverage of diverse interactive problems.

**Towards a multimodal model of emotion**  According to Lang (1969) an emotion, for instance fear, is not a 'lump' but a tripartite response pattern comprising highly interactive yet also partially independent components. These are: subjective/verbal, somatic/physiological, and motoric/behavioural categories that would seem to subsume the modalities of Imagery-Cognition, Sensation-Biology, and Behaviour-Interpersonal relationships. In an elaboration of this view, Rachman (1978) hypothesized that these response modes wax and wane almost independently of each other. He extended the model by specifying the complex interaction of the components by describing them as *discordant* and *desynchronous*. When the emotion involved is not overwhelmingly strong there is a low degree of correlation between the response systems (discordance) and a low degree of covariance as the response systems change over time (desynchrony). Also repudiating the unitary model of emotion, Bandura (1978) suggests that while the three response modes *can* be desynchronous and discordant, they are generally synchronous and concordant. We agree with his argument that:

Thought, affect, and action operate as reciprocally interacting factors rather than as loosely linked components or as conjoint events. While recognizing the role of labeling processes in emotional expressions, this approach acknowledges that thought creates physiological arousal as well as provides cognitive labels for it. Arousal can, in turn, influence thought. The relative influence exerted by these three sets of interlocking factors will vary in different individuals for different activities performed under different circumstances. (Bandura 1978 p. 257).

Our own clinical experience indicates that sometimes clients may change in the behavioural domain while remaining the same in the affective and cognitive domains. It might also occur that clients improve in the cognitive domain while showing only slight changes in the affective and behavioural domains. Another possibility is that clients change in the affective domain while showing minor improvements in the cognitive and behavioural domains. In delivering clinical services, the conscientious multimodal practitioner striving for enduring therapeutic results conducts therapy until the BASIC I.D. shows congruent improvements throughout.

An issue, raised by Hugdahl (1981) in his discussion of the treatment implications of the three-systems model, is the suggestion that different loadings on the components give an indication for tailoring the treatment to the exact patterning of the response. Considering three clients of whom the first is predominantly a 'cognitive responder', the second is largely a 'behavioural responder', and the third is mainly an 'affective responder', the treatment of choice would be respectively cognitive restructuring, in vivo exposure, and systematic desensitization. A study reported by Öst, Jerremalm and Johansson (1981) gives some support for this position. They found in a group of socially anxious clients that social skills training was better for behavioural reactors, whereas relaxation training was better for affective reactors. The idea that superior treatment effects are obtained when the techniques mesh with the client's emotional response pattern is in line with the multimodal view that a systematic perusal of the BASIC I.D. will unravel the client's preferred modalities. Nevertheless this does not imply that a person will always react in a given modality. As the BASIC I.D. is multilevelled, multilayered, and interrelated in a complex reciprocal fashion, the concept of *firing order* may bring some clarity into this matter.

The concept of sequential firing orders is in accordance with a systems theory perspective that modalities do not exist in isolation, but are in a steady state of a complex flux of interactions. Until the precise nature of these interactions is revealed by research data, firing order sequences may lend some clarity. A firing order refers to the sequential proclivities of the person's salient modalities in a given emotional episode. In any circumscribed and relevant situation, numerous combinations of modalities are possible. There are 5040 possibilities of sequential combinations in one particular situation. As a rule the client reports a series of four or five modalities during a single sequence. The prototypical firing order is SCIABI.: The person sees or hears something (S), that he or she appraises (C), followed by various images (I), that arouse affective responses (A), which may form a motive for a flight or fight reaction (B), with interpersonal repercussions, avoidance or control (I.).

Because firing orders are not fixed tendencies, someone may generate different emotions following different distinct sequences. A negative affect may follow a particular sequence on one occasion and follow a different pattern at other times. A client may discover that a BI.SA order was operative when depressed, whereas a SICA order led to anxiety. Nonetheless, in most people, reasonably stable proclivities exist much of the time. While awaiting conclusive evidence from laboratory research with regard to the primacy of one modality over the others, our view transcends seemingly contrary positions for clinical practice (cf. R.S. Lazarus 1982, 1984; Rachman 1981; Zajonc 1980, 1984).

## Practical applications

### The therapeutic relationship

MMT is *both* a clinical science *and* an art. What the therapist *does*, and who the therapist *is*, are both of the utmost importance. In addition to warmth, genuineness, empathy and unconditional acceptance of the client, the multimodal therapist needs to be a skilled 'artisan', who also practises what he or she preaches. Psychological creativity is a necessary condition for establishing rapport and solving individual problems. Ultimately it is not only scientific acumen, but also artistic skill that distinguishes the creative therapist from the mediocre technician. Credibility, flexibility, and versatility, as well as the art of persuasion, are important characteristics for dealing with 'resistance'. (See also pp. 341–342).

**Therapist's resistance**    From the multimodal stance one might enquire: 'Who is resisting whom?' It is likely that the therapist, who is inclined to resist the client's resistance, is subject to the same phenomena as the client. Resistance is frequently due to the therapist's lack of rapport-building skills.

Many novice but also some experienced therapists have trouble looking at their own in-session behaviour that may in fact be responsible for adverse reactions from the client. The therapist may refuse to take up the challenge that is posed by the client's behaviour. For example, the client may ask for a listening attitude from the therapist, whereas the latter labels this as a self-defeating avoidant activity, consuming too much therapy time. If the client's objectives do not coincide with those of the therapist, it is wise to sort out the differences of opinion, otherwise the therapist is easily misled in such cases into thinking that the client poses an insoluble problem. Minor infractions might be used by the therapist as a rationalization to terminate the treatment or to refer the client to a 'better equipped' colleague.

Therapist's resistance can be bypassed by the use of paradoxical communication, as illustrated by Lazarus's (1981) vignette:

> Mrs Smith, aged 49, had been tense and anxious since the death of her mother . . . she had always depended on her mother for advice and guidance. She was 'sad and depressed' . . . but she had recovered . . . only to become fearful and tense . . . 'Am I a schizophrenic?' she asked. I reassured her that there was nothing psychotic about her thoughts, actions, or feelings. . . . [However] she remained overly concerned about the state of her 'sanity and mental health' and I continued to offer her reassurance. I also took the position that perhaps she secretly desired to go insane, but that intervention proved unproductive. When, by the fifth or sixth session she again asked 'Are you sure I'm not a schizophrenic?' I decided to take a different tack. 'Actually, you are much worse than schizophrenic,' I said. 'In fact, you are a perfect candidate for the State Home for the Very Nervous, Bewildered, and Confused.' She giggled and said, 'I'm serious.' I answered, 'So am I.' She burst into laughter and changed the subject. (pp. 42–43).

**Client's resistance**     It is all to easy to label as 'resistance' any behaviour of the client that is unwanted by the therapist. The term often refers to the client's attitude during the therapy session as well as his or her 'refusal' to change between sessions. A client may seem to be co-operative during the sessions without observable behaviour change taking place between sessions. In such cases it is possible that goals are set too high and that minor changes are glossed over. Also, anxiety can impede a working attitude. Fear of failure, or discomfort aroused by disappointing the therapist, as well as significant others, are well known in this respect. To offset the client's disappointment about potentially slow or negligible improvements, it is good practice to predict gradual progress or even relapse, and to give an explanation for it. Resistance, then, can be prevented and overcome by avoiding unrealistic goals.

Also the metaphor of the 'authentic chameleon' is espoused, implying that the therapist makes use of the most helpful facets of his or her personality in order to establish rapport with a particular client. The goodness of fit is examined by seeing the therapist–client relationship on a continuum extending from a very close-knit, dependent bonding at the one end, to a rather formal, businesslike investment at the other. Throughout the therapy process the therapist should use the working relationship flexibly by assuming a role that fits in with the client's expectations.

Resistance is bound to occur whenever one tries to exert influence on somebody else. Otherwise therapy would be a simple job, for it would then be sufficient merely to tell the client what to do. Resistance can be experienced by a client in several ways. As soon as the client sees his or her resistive behaviours as a problem in therapy and identifies them in the hope of finding a remedy, it generally can no longer be regarded as resistance. In this case it could be defined as behaviour that coincides or is contiguous with the consciously presented problem. If resistance is part of the target problem, the handling of it does not differ from that of other problems. Lazarus and Fay (1982) advise the therapist to practise self-disclosure, to telephone the client between sessions, to make use of a cotherapist for in vivo training, or to stress the mutual interests of client and therapist, to name a few tactics they have described for overcoming resistance.

## Strategies of treatment and selection of techniques

MMT is a well-planned method of intervention which takes into account causes, concomitants, and maintaining factors of dysfunctional behaviours. Franks (1976) underscored that 'It is not so much a static theoretical product as a combination or working guide for the present and blueprint for the future' (p. viii). In essence MMT provides blueprints for modality profiles and functional analyses, and guiding principles for the selection of techniques. By making use of these blueprints and principles, the therapist will enlarge his or her understanding of the client's problems and be better able to provide the client with a well-organized treatment plan. Different therapists will thus come to make almost identical analyses of the same client, and this will lead to almost identical treatment decisions.


**Treating the BASIC I.D.**    The modality profile provides order by including each element of the BASIC I.D. Any item of the profile can be examined in greater detail by magnifying it, also in terms of the BASIC I.D. This procedure of drawing up a second-order BASIC I.D. is conducted if an impasse warrants such a re-evaluation. For instance, in a case where systematic desensitization failed to reduce emotional discomfort when the client imagined situations of past ridicule, a second-order BASIC I.D. revealed the following items: (B) withdrawn, (A) rage, (S) surging heat, (I) attack, (C) Mother was right, (I.) utter rejection, (D.) —. It became clear that the client was exceedingly angry rather than anxious about critical remarks, so that the technique of choice should have been assertion training and not desensitization.

While assessment is continuous and always multimodal, treatment may sometimes be narrowly focused, especially when the modality profile gives no indication of a significant network of interrelated problems. A fundamental assumption in treatment is that meaningful and sustained changes usually follow performance based methods. Multimodal therapists inspire, encourage and persuade their clients to take calculated emotional risks, that is, to do different things and to do things differently. Only new experiences and the client's active participation in homework assignments during 'the other 167 hours' will lead to significant changes. The following main mechanisms and change agents are identified (Lazarus 1984):

B     – Extinction, counterconditioning, positive reinforcement, punishment.
A     – Abreaction, owning and accepting feelings.
S     – Tension release, sensory pleasuring.
I     – Changes in self-image, coping images.
C     – Cognitive restructuring, awareness.
I.    – Modelling, dispersing unproductive collusions, paradoxical manoeuvres, non-judgemental acceptance.
D.    – Medical examination, pharmacotherapy.

In order to implement these various therapeutic factors, the application of any empirically useful intervention is allowed. The doctrine of technical eclecticism is espoused. This involves the orderly combination of techniques, some of which may be derived from theories of a seemingly contrary nature. The techniques selected are moulded into a harmonious system that remains open to revision. Technical eclecticism should be distinguished from the kind of eclecticism where unsystematic and uncritical combinations of explanations are derived from incompatible epistemologies. Because techniques can be effective in the absence of an adequate theoretical explanation, it is recommended that theory should be separated from technique in therapeutic practice.

An example may clarify this point. It has proven to be useful to make some depressive clients stay in bed for ten days at a stretch, allowing them to get up only for the essentials. Although the effectiveness of the regimen can be established empirically, the explanation of this phenomenon depends on the theoretical framework one adheres to. A psychoanalyst might associate freely about the symbolic significance of returning to the womb. An interactional therapist could emphasize the paradoxical impact of symptom prescription. A die-hard behaviour therapist would dwell on the value of reinforcers and sensory deprivation. Psychotherapists of all persuasions would, without doubt, similarly provide their own explanations (Lazarus 1972).

Even within one school of thought, the working principles of any technique can be explained in many different ways. For instance, the soundly demonstrated effectiveness of systematic desensitization is explained by its main innovator (Wolpe 1958) in terms of 'reciprocal inhibition'. Anxiety is eliminated by the induction of an antagonistic physiological response in the presence of arousal-provoking cues. This requires (a) a strong anxiety-antagonistic response (e.g. muscle relaxation), (b) a hierarchy of anxiety-evoking items, and (c) the continuous pairing of the two reciprocally inhibitory stimuli: anxiety and relaxation. Research evidence, however, has shown that the effectiveness of this technique does not depend on the relaxation response, the hierarchical presentation of stimuli, or the pairing of relaxation with these stimuli. Alternative explanations, including counterconditioning, habituation, extinction, exposure, problem-solving skills, and differential expectancies, have been put forward in the course of the past twenty years (Kazdin and Wilcoxon 1976). Techniques can be effective for reasons other than those the innovator had in mind, and should therefore be chosen not for their intrinsic fascination, but for their proven effectiveness. Lazarus (1981) has compiled a glossary of the most frequently used techniques in MMT, which can be found in Table 11.1.

We recommend that therapists should select and start with the most obvious and logical procedures. We also sugggest that they may avoid problem-engendering pseudosolutions by carefully observing the client's

**Table 11.1**   Compendium of major techniques

|  | General techniques | Anti-depression techniques |
|---|---|---|
| Behaviour | – Behaviour rehearsal<br>– Modelling<br>– Nonreinforcement<br>– Positive reinforcement<br>– Recording and self-monitoring<br>– Stimulus control<br>– Systematic exposure | – Gradual task assignments<br>– Activity schemes (week or day programmes)<br>– Running treatment |
| Affect | – Anger expression<br>– Anxiety management training<br>– Feeling-identification<br>– The empty chair | – Affective expression<br>– Grief therapy |
| Sensation | – Biofeedback<br>– Focusing<br>– Hypnosis<br>– Meditation<br>– Relaxation training<br>– Sensate focus training<br>– Threshold training | – Sensory deprivation and retraining<br>– Discrimination training<br>– Concentration exercises |
| Imagery | – Anti-future shock imagery<br>– Associated imagery<br>– Aversive imagery<br>– Goal-rehearsal or coping imagery<br>– Positive imagery<br>– The step-up technique<br>– Time projection (forward or backward) | – Idealized self-image<br>– Rational–emotive imagery |
| Cognition | – Bibliotherapy<br>– Correcting of misconceptions<br>– Ellis's A-B-C-D-E paradigm<br>– Problem-solving<br>– Self-instructional training<br>– Thought-blocking | – Double column technique<br>– Brochure: Coping with depression<br>– General semantics training |
| Interpersonal | – Communications training<br>– Contingency contracting<br>– Friendship training | – Creating a marital or family setting |

**Table 11.1** *contd.*

|  | General techniques | Anti-depression techniques |
|---|---|---|
|  | – Graded sexual approaches<br>– Paradoxical strategies<br>– Social skills and<br>  assertiveness training |  |
| Drugs/Biological | – Encouragement of health<br>  habits – good nutrition,<br>  exercise, recreation<br>– Referral to physician when<br>  organic problems are<br>  suspected or biological<br>  interventions are indicated | – Use of anti-depressant<br>  medication when so<br>  indicated |

previous unsuccessful attempts to solve problems. As the modality profile places specific problems within a framework and reduces vague, general and diffuse problems to discrete items, the choice of techniques usually follows logically from issues and points of emphasis. We would dissect abstract problems into concrete, specific and interactive components before providing an answer. Suppose the modality profile of the person with a 'negative self-image' yields the following items: (B) avoids taking risks, (A) feels depressed, (S) fatigue because of tenseness, (I) persistent images of failure, (C) negative and self-downing self-talk, (I.) deficits in social skills, (D.) —, the prescribed techniques will include: (B) risk-taking in vivo assignments, (A) identification of possible unexpressed anger, (S) relaxation training, (I) coping imagery, (C) rational restructuring, (I.) social skills training, (D.) —. While the selection of techniques is reasonably straightforward, the implementation of techniques requires clinical experience, acumen, and artistry. As with surgery, it is the person behind the scalpel who can wield it as an instrument of destruction or of healing (Lazarus 1981).

**Functional analysis** While many cases are mapped out sufficiently using a modality profile, in complex cases with a severe and fixed symptomatology it has proven necessary not only to analyze the *spatial* organization of the BASIC I.D., but also its *temporal* organization. As a tool for the integration of the variable space-and-time, a functional analysis offers a way of making the interrelationships between modalities manifest. Such an analysis involves processes that refer to the firing order of the BASIC I.D., and to an exchange of matter, energy, and information between the modalities. Information-processing occurs if outside stress triggers inside strain, creating a state of imbalance within the BASIC I.D. as a system. Inputs are the transmissions into the system (S), throughputs the internal events within the system (A,C,I), and outputs the transmissions from the system (B,I.) that restore homeostasis. Information inputs, throughputs and outputs are similar to the social learning theory concepts of *S*timulus, *O*rganism and *R*esponse. All reinforcements, as *C*onsequences of dysfunctional behaviours, involve feedback. The BASIC I.D. places meat on the S-O-R-C scheme when drawing up a blueprint for functional analysis that consists of five vicious cycles[5] (See Figure 11.2).

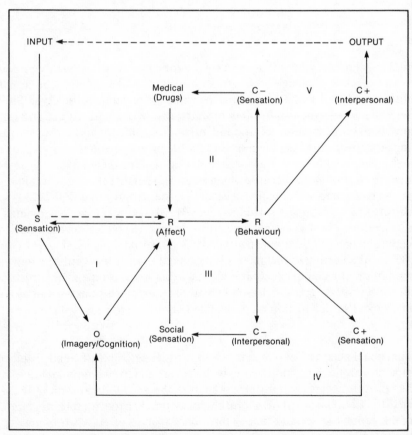

**Figure 11.2**   Blueprint for functional analysis in cognitive-behavioural (SORC) and multimodal (BASIC I.D.) terms

What we call Cycle I, *cognitive mediation*, follows the firing order configuration: SI/CA. It is not the external event (S) which causes emotional disturbance (A), but the mediating factors, images (I) and/or cognitions (C) which one has. We take a flexible stance in being aware that in the interplay between modalities other combinations are possible as well. Thus, Affect may feed back to Sensation, resulting in Cognition and/or Imagery. Also Imagery and/or Cognition may lead to Affect and eventually to Sensation. In line with classical conditioning, the mere perception (S) of a stressful situation may engender an emotional response (A), in the relative absence of cognitions (C) and/or images (I). It is important to note that S stands here for both Stimulus and Sensation: both refer to the external events that trigger symptoms. This would include, for instance, the sight of a crowd for an agoraphobic client, the touch of dirt for an obsessional client, and the beginning of the day for a depressive client.

Cycles II and III come about when the aberrant emotions give rise to avoidance behaviours, for instance depressive withdrawal, leading to *negative consequences*. The configuration of Cycle II, *intrinsic loss*, follows a BSD.A sequence. As a long-term result of the avoidant behaviours (B), the client may become chronically tense (S), and 'translates' these sensations into functional somatic complaints (e.g. dizziness, tiredness or pain), for which he or she undergoes medical examinations and is treated by pharmacotherapy (D.). Psychosomatic illnesses might also develop and become manifest depending on the client's general physical health and the presence of 'illness proclivities'. Physical dysfunctions increase the emotional disturbance (A) through feedback, whether it be anxiety, anger, dysphoria, etc.

Cycle III, *extrinsic loss*, follows a BI.SA sequence. As a result of avoidant behaviours (B), the client will also arouse negative reactions from the social environment, especially when he/she is complaining. In defence the client tries to prove that he or she is 'ill' and may end up by losing attention and drifting into social isolation and loneliness (I.). Ultimately the client is sensorily deprived and perceives (S) himself or herself in the social situation of having lost his or her job, partner and/or home, often also becoming stigmatized as a 'patient'. Feedback increases the emotional disturbance (A), etc.

Cycles IV and V are characterized by rewards that come about when *positive consequences* follow avoidant or flight behaviours. Cycle IV, *intrinsic gain*, follows the configuration of a BSI/CA sequence. The aberrant behaviour (B) leads to short-term tension reduction (S). The client might take refuge in filling a gap, concentrating on 'having a peg to hang his hat on', or turning attention away from decreasing symptoms and solving problems of living. The latter is in line with King Lear's 'Where the greater malady is fixed, the lesser is scarcely felt.' In the long term, however, the client will discover that the short-term relief does not solve any of his or her problems. The client subsequently modulates his or her cognitions (C) and/or images (I) by nursing thoughts of guilt, regret or self-reproach, that might result in desperation and suicidal ideation. Feedback makes all this lead to further emotional disregulation (A), etc.

Cycle V, *extrinsic gain*, follows the configuration of a BI.SA sequence. The dysfunctional behaviours (B) are advantageous in the short run in the interpersonal (I.) area, but in the long run they are disadvantageous and detrimental. Examples of benefits are: gaining social attention, having manipulative ploys, hiding behind facesaving devices, and being excused of responsibilities. All these manoeuvres are quasi-solutions of life problems. The end result is that generalization of perceived distressing activating events (S) takes place. Thus the client experiences his or her symptoms in even more situations than before, meaning that feedback gives rise to further emotional disregulation (A), etc.

Neurotic symptoms, then, are the result of positive feedback. The cumulative operation of uninhibited positive feedback loops, giving rise to 'wild' behaviour, is the system's attempt to maintain homeostasis (De Rosnay 1979). It leads to an indefinite expansion of emotions and a blocking of activities. In order to decrease output of affect so that new stationary states without symptoms can be attained, negative feedback loops have to be enhanced, particularly by means of various interventions. For instance, in Cycle I, the client may learn that emotions are not governed by the environment alone, and that by correcting 'irrational' ideas one can improve one's response to environmental demands and modify the accompanying feelings. In Cycle II the client may learn to see psychosomatic disturbances as a consequence of avoidant and to translate these back (e.g. through discrimination training) into emotional events. In Cycle III the client may learn to see that one's social status might improve as a long-term result of assertion training and that this will also diminish emotional overreactions and avoidance behaviours. In Cycle IV the client may learn that self-reproach precedes aberrant emotions, and that through relaxation exercises one might prevent avoidance and accept feelings of panic, rage, or sorrow. In Cycle V, finally, the client may learn that problem situations decrease when one stops using quasi-solutions and trains oneself to communicate in a more satifying way so as to make symptoms rudimentary.

## Overcoming obstacles to client progress

Obstacles might be due to lack of motivation, particularly when the client referral is involuntary, when clients experience more gains than losses from their symptoms, or when they enter therapy with unrealistic expectations. If a lack of treatment motivation is causing an impasse that cannot be worked through, multimodal therapists may refer the client to a more compatible resource or may even recommend no formal therapy. Instead of attributing lack of progress to the client, we first search our own bosoms.

Several therapist variables can be distinguished when obstacles occur – e.g. the therapeutic relationship and numerous assessment and intervention variables. We shall elaborate here on *tracking* and *bridging*, procedures that are helpful in overcoming impasses that impede therapy progress, noting that we have dealt with the issues of 'client' and 'therapist' resistance in the section entitled 'The therapeutic relationship'. (See pp. 331–333).

**Tracking**  Obstacles, if any, are handled by drawing up a second-order BASIC I.D., and if this does not suffice, by resorting to tracking and bridging.

Tracking refers to the careful scrutinizing of the BASIC I.D. to determine interactive effects across the modalities and to establish sequential firing orders of specific modalities. Different people follow different sequences, and at times the same person may display different firing orders. The identification of sequential proclivities not only enhances communication with the client, but also facilitates intervention in the relevant modalities. For instance, if an anxious client reports a CISA sequence, the following interventions are called for:

| | | |
|---|---|---|
| C: | 'What if I pass out?' | – Self-instructional training |
| I: | I see myself lying in the street | – Coping imagery |
| S: | Lightheadedness, sweaty palms | – Breathing exercises |
| A: | Anxiety and panic | – Differential relaxation |

Different sequences call for different treatments, depending also on factors that accompany and precede the emotional reaction. It is hypothesized that if one selects techniques adhering to the client's habitual sequence, the positive impact will be greater.

**Bridging**     *Bridging* refers to a procedure in which the therapist tunes in to the client's preferred representational system before branching off into other areas which seem likely to be more productive. The therapist starts deliberately where the client is before switching to other dimensions, in order to enhance communication and bypass resistance. By first entering the client's domain, he or she will feel understood, after which the therapist can more readily delve into a different modality. The therapist is likely to meet with resistance when introducing a modality different from the one the client is presenting.

> For example, instead of challenging a client that he tends to eschew the expression of feelings by erecting intellectual barriers . . . the therapist [who wanted to move into affective areas right from the start] . . . [goes] along with the client's apparent desire to dwell on cognitive components. Shortly thereafter, when the therapist again [enquires] about affective and sensory responses, the client [is] willing to reveal his sensation and then to verbalize his feelings. (Lazarus 1984, p. 493).

When the client is unable to furnish the therapist with specific problems, because the client experiences global distress without being able to pinpoint any identifiable excesses or deficits in the BASIC I.D., imagery can serve as the bridging modality. Since the nuclear family usually provides the breeding ground for emotional problems, diagnostic information is gathered by getting the client to picture his or her childhood home while taking a tour from room to room. These images can yield significant information, unlock memories and emotions that have a bearing on the client's ongoing problems, and provide clues about habitual escape and avoidance behaviours (Lazarus 1981).

## Case example

### *The client*

To illustrate our approach, the treatment of a chronic case of neurotic depression is described: Mrs R., just over fifty and the mother of a married daughter, works in a small firm together with her husband who is a few years older. She lists her complaints as: 'Dejection, dissatisfaction with myself, discontentment with life, getting little pleasure, no longer enjoying anything, despair, difficulty in making decisions, no self-confidence any more, feeling guilty in life, not daring to spend money on myself. The only thing I can still do is work.'

She had spent almost a year in a mental hospital being treated for neurotic symptoms when she was just under thirty. This rendered her incapable of doing her work properly, as she received ECT, and also tranquillizers which she continued for ten years. In this period Mrs R. was afraid of becoming pregnant and for many years her marriage remained unconsummated. When she was in her thirties her inactivity gave way to overactivity. Shortly before this, her husband had a myocardial infarction, about which she feels guilty. A year later her mother died from complications to her spine which were the result of a car accident while Mrs R. was out with her. Each weekend thereafter she went to look after her father, who reproached her with her mother's death. Two years later her husband started his own firm. Mrs R. occupied herself day and night in a perfectionistic manner with the paperwork and the housekeeping. Subsequently, when her husband was incapacitated by meningitis, she ran the firm entirely on her own for a number of years. Mrs R. herself has suffered from eye complaints, with increasing loss of sight starting in her teens.

In early middle age she underwent a cornea transplant after which she was 50 per cent blind. She was temporarily deprived of her sight almost entirely, and for about two years was unable to work. When she was nearing fifty her daughter left home. Mrs R.'s perfectionism reappeared and she became increasingly depressed. She experienced her life as empty. There were few visitors and contacts with her family. All contact with her in-laws had been broken by her husband ten years previously because he believed they did not accept her. Mrs R. described her relationship with her husband, to whom she had been married for almost thirty years, as good, despite the fact that he was basically uncommunicative and she wanted more attention from him. He was preoccupied with his work and she worked in order to be with him.

Speaking about the time before she was thirty, she recounted being the youngest member of a poor family, with an elder brother. She saw her father as dour and thrifty, and her mother as a caring woman who helped her father energetically. From adolescence to the time she was married Mrs R. worked hard in her father's business without pay. A few years before she was hospitalized Mrs R. had a miscarriage. Her daughter was born a year later and was often sick as a baby. The firm where her husband worked operated day and night, and he put in a lot of overtime. In this period she was afraid of being alone in the house and became depressed for the first time.

**Structural and modality profiles**    A 'structural profile' was first drawn up to obtain a picture of specific BASIC I.D. tendencies. The therapist asked the client to indicate her affinity for each modality on a scale of 0 to 6. These subjective ratings are easily depicted on a graph that serves as a reminder of the client's main proclivities. Mrs R.'s structural profile shows that she is essentially a 'doer' and a 'relater', rather than a 'feeler', a 'thinker' or anything else (see Table 11.2).

Subsequently a modality profile was constructed. This list of specific problems was supplemented and corrected during therapy. Knowledge of

**Table 11.2**   Modality profile of Mrs R.

Name: ........................................................

Sex:  Male/Female ........................................

Date of birth: ............................................

Address: ....................................................

........................................................

| MODALITY | Description |
|---|---|
| | B A S I C I. D. (Structural Profile) |
| Behaviour | – Avoidant behaviour in the form of an excessive amount and hours of work and repeated expansion of the business<br>– Spends no money on herself and gives herself no leisure time<br>– Behaviour characterized by inhibition and procrastination<br>– Isolates herself apathetically and frequently cries<br>– Difficulty in falling asleep and early morning awakening |
| Affect | – Feelings of worry, anxiety and panic<br>– Unassimilated grief about partial loss of sight<br>– Aggression directed at herself<br>– Increased dysphoria<br>– Depressed mood when client cannot or may not work<br>– Mood varying from sad, dejected, disheartened to usually depressed<br>– Feelings of loneliness<br>– Fears losing her job |
| Sensation | – Perception of activating events leading to depression<br>– Headaches, dizziness and light-headedness<br>– Fatigue and nausea<br>– Twitches when tense<br>– Reduction of tension when she works a lot (avoidance of |

**Table 11.2** *contd.*

| | |
|---|---|
| | confrontation with herself and filling up emptiness)<br>– 'Sensory deprivation' due to job loss and being alone |
| Imagery | – Negative self-image (stupid, dependent and 'injured')<br>– Effaces herself in favour of husband, daughter and others<br>– Sees others as better (have learned or done more)<br>– Images of deficiency with respect to others and therefore rejected and abandoned<br>– Pictures of being 'in the dumps'<br>– Negative view of the world |
| Cognition | – Personification: no self-confidence and proclaiming herself guilty<br>– Arbitrary inference: thinks she fails her husband, daughter and others<br>– Selective abstraction: personal value is dependent on performance<br>– Dichotomous reasoning: must do everything right and nothing wrong<br>– Tyranny of shoulds: frets and has difficulty making decisions<br>– Overgeneralization: failed, worthless, uncertain<br>– Catastrophization: hopeless, helpless and suicidal ideation |
| Interpersonal relationships | – Closed, indirect and somewhat suspicious posture<br>– Servile attitude towards her husband, daughters and others<br>– Unassertive in giving and demanding attention, particularly with respect to her husband<br>– Socially isolated<br>– Deficient sexual contacts<br>– Symmetrical escalation as regards getting attention and being respected (husband because of heart and client because of depression) |
| Drugs | – As a result of depression, admission into psychiatric clinic, general hospital and convalescent home (at ages 28, 29 and 50)<br>– Lived 10 years on pharmacotherapy (Librium and Nozinan)<br>– Stress-incontinence (excessive urination)<br>– Difficulty in remembering as a result of ECT |

excesses and deficiencies in the client's BASIC I.D. is necessary to determine what requires augmentation or reduction.

**Functional analysis** Because of the chronic character of the depression, a close scrutiny of Mrs R.'s modality profile is warranted. With the help of a functional analysis, it is possible to identify the nature of the relationships between the modalities. It is composed of five vicious cycles, which are kept together by feedback loops.

*Cycle I*: Cognitive mediation (SI/CA). The representation of reality is an abstraction which is not the same as objective reality. This cycle shows how, for example, at the mere perception of the beginning of the day, and feeling light-headed etc. (S), Mrs R. creates a negative self-image (I) and tends to set aside her own interests by proclaiming herself guilty for the things that went wrong (C), resulting in depression (A), which in turn leads to a negative perception of reality, etc. The following items are taken from Mrs R.'s modality profile:

| | |
|---|---|
| S | – Perception of activating events leading to depression |
| I | – Negative self-image (stupid, dependent and 'injured') |
| | – Sees others as better (having learned or done more) |
| C | – Personification: no self-confidence and proclaiming herself guilty |
| | – Dichotomous reasoning: must do everything right and nothing wrong |
| | – Tyranny of 'shoulds', frets and has difficulty making decisions |
| A | – Feelings of worry, anxiety and panic |
| | – Aggression directed toward herself. |

*Cycle II*: Intrinsic loss (BSD.A) addresses negatively experienced consequences in forms such as nervousness, tiredness, or certain physical pains. Given a particular predisposition, protracted somatizations can lead to physical dysfunctions which exert a negative influence on a person's state of mind. This cycle shows the client's intrapersonal loss as a result of depression. For instance, she endeavours to avoid feelings of depression through excessive work (B), which gives rise to tensions, headaches and fatigue (S) and finally leads to medication and a deterioration in health (D.). This in turn leads to an increase of the depression (A), etc. Items depicted from the Modality Profile:

| | |
|---|---|
| B | – Avoidant behaviour in the form of an excessive amount and duration of work and repeated expansion of the business |
| | – Spends no money on herself and gives herself no leisure time |
| S | – Headaches, dizziness, and light-headedness |
| | – Fatigue and nausea |

- Twitches when tense
D. – As a result of depression, admission into psychiatric clinic, general hospital and convalescent home (at ages 28, 29 and 50)
   - Lived ten years on pharmacotherapy (Librium and Nozinan)
   - Stress-incontinence (excessive urination)
   - Difficulty in remembering as a result of ECT
A – Depressed mood when client cannot or may not work
   - Unassimilated grief about partial loss of sight.

*Cycle III*: Extrinsic loss (BI.SA) is the negatively experienced consequences of the depression in the form of 'sensory deprivation' due to social problems, such as the loss of a job. This cycle shows the client's interpersonal loss. For instance, excessive work (B) results in social isolation (I.) and finally in 'sensory deprivation' as a consequence of having lost that work (S), which reinforces the depression (A), etc. Items depicted from the modality profile:

B – Behaviour characterized by inhibition and procrastination
   - Isolates herself apathetically and frequently cries
I. – Closed, indirect and somewhat suspicious posture
   - Servile attitude toward her husband, daughter, and others
   - Unassertive in giving and demanding attention, particularly with respect to husband
   - Socially isolated
S – 'Sensory deprivation' due to job loss and being alone
A – Increased dysphoria
   - Mood varying from sad, dejected, disheartened to usually depressed.

*Cycle IV*: Intrinsic gain (BSC/IA). The intrinsic gain from avoidant and flight behaviours is usually a reduction of tension. This cycle shows the intrapersonal gain from the client's avoidant behaviour (for instance, in the form of excessive work (B)), that is, tension reduction (S) because of avoidance of confrontation with herself and the filling up of emptiness. This confirms the idea that personal value is dependent on performance (C) and that others should be viewed as better than herself, which ties into her negative self-image (I), resulting in a strengthening of the depression (A), etc. Items depicted from the modality profile:

B – Difficulty in falling asleep and early morning awakening

S    – Reduction of tension when she works a lot (avoidance of confrontation with herself and filling up emptiness)

C    – Selective abstraction: personal value is dependent on performance
      – Overgeneralization: failed, worthless, uncertain
      – Catastrophization: hopeless, helpless, and suicidal ideation

I     – Images of deficiency with respect to others and therefore rejected and abandoned
      – Pictures of being 'in the dumps'

A    – All items listed in the modality profile.

*Cycle V*: Extrinsic gain (BI.SA). Extrinsic gain is the social advantage which the client can derive from her complaints. This cycle indicates the interpersonal gain which she secures, for instance by means of avoidance behaviour in the form of isolating herself (B). Mrs R. draws attention to herself from, and is looked after by, people of importance to her (I.), notably her husband, which feeds into various interpersonal conflicts. As a result, demoralization increases and generalizes, as do the activating events leading to depression, etc. (S), and the debilitating feelings (A) are reinforced, etc. Items selected from the modality profile:

B    – All items listed in the modality profile

I.    – Symmetrical escalation as regards getting attention and being respected (husband because of heart and client because of depression)

S    – Generalization of perceived activating events leading to depression.

A    – Depression.

## Therapy process

The change process in MMT can be broadly divided into three successive and partially overlapping segments: assessment and the formulation of hypotheses, choice and implementation of techniques, and evaluation and termination of therapy. The BASIC I.D. enables the therapist to trace the most productive route, that is, to devise a therapy plan (a strategy for therapeutic interventions) that can be evaluated and adjusted throughout treatment. While assessment is always multimodal, treatment may sometimes be trimodal, bimodal or even unimodal, depending on the network's complexity of interrelated problems.

**Strategic order** The strategic order in which the cycles are tackled is arrived at in concert with the client, so that each step in the therapy process is a planned enterprise. It is generally advisable to start with the target symptoms for which the client seeks alleviation. The therapist is best advised to start with Cycle I, so that the client learns to accept full responsibility for his or her own affect. The distress cycles can then be broken through, by which time the client should be willing to work on the gain cycles. However, as was suggested earlier, the strategic order is far from fixed. Any sequence is possible, depending on the relative importance of each cycle within the total picture.

In the case of Mrs R. it was judicious to start by working on Cycle I in order to help her become less depressed. The main object of the intervention in this cycle was for Mrs R. to believe that she herself remained responsible for her own well-being. In particular, Mrs R.'s negative self-image and her self-abnegation were addressed. Emphasis was placed upon 'parity-as-a-way-of-life' (Lazarus 1981), and the need to favour the philosophical concept of the 'fallible-human-being' (Ellis 1962). After her dysphoric mood decreased, Cycle IV (intrinsic gain) was then addressed. Mrs R. learnt to enjoy leisure time instead of always working. She started doing pleasant things for herself, such as going to a film or to the beach. Furthermore she learnt that spending time and money on herself was permissible, that she was entitled to buy clothes and makeup. An egalitarian outlook was stressed: 'Whereas some people achieve more than others, there is no evidence for the conclusion that there are intrinsically superior and inferior people.' The next indication was to proceed with Cycle V. The extrinsic gain, comprised of passively waiting for attention, fostered Mrs R.'s tendency to remain in a state of demoralization. Emphasis was placed upon securing attention by means of assertive behaviours, the abandonment of perfectionism, and direct communication with her husband and other significant people. She learnt that affective expression can elicit positive reactions from others. Next, Cycle III, extrinsic loss, especially social isolation and loneliness, was dealt with. This cycle was extinguished through the acquisition and application of social skills and the implementation of behavioural task assignments. After her loss had been alleviated somewhat, Mrs R. learnt to recognize that she perpetuated her symptoms because of their positive consequences, which in the final analysis failed to provide a satisfactory solution. Finally, Cycle II, intrinsic loss, especially somatizations and physical conditions, was dealt with. In Mrs R.'s case, efforts were made to bring about 'acceptance' and coping skills vis-à-vis her sight handicap. Furthermore, efforts were made to improve her physical

condition by means of relaxation training aimed at eliminating her headaches and fatigue.

In order to secure durable results MMT was directed not only at symptoms, but also dealt with Mrs R.'s current problems of living.


**Tactical order**    The selection of techniques within a cycle, the tactical
order, usually depends on the client's affinity for the respective modalities.
This is assessed by means of the structural profile. The therapist uses a
variety of techniques that have been proven empirically useful. For a
compendium of techniques, used in MMT, the reader is referred to Table
11.1 which contains a list of general techniques and specific measures for the
management of depression.

Techniques should be used sparingly in accordance with the individual
needs of a particular client. In the case of Mrs R. the following were applied:

B    – Activity schemes, gradual task assignments, positive reinforce-
       ments
A    – Identification of feelings, grief therapy, affective expression, anxi-
       ety management training
S    – Self-monitoring, discrimination training, relaxation training, sen-
       sate focusing
I    – Idealized self-image, time projection with positive imagery
C    – Rational self-analysis, self-instructional training
I.   – Assertiveness training, communications training (with husband)
D.   – Cessation of pharmacotherapy

Each technique was applied systematically, one at a time, within the
relevant cycle. Sometimes it was necessary to work on two or even more
cycles in the same period. When termination was at hand, Mrs R. was
provided with 'fire drills' for prevention purposes. Mrs R.'s therapy lasted
eight months and was conducted in an inpatient setting for MMT.

Progress in the therapy can be assessed at different stages of the change
process, in principle when any of the cycles have been completely covered.
Treatment can then be continued by intervening in a different cycle, or
terminated with the client's agreement.

## *Therapy evaluation*

MMT is a custom-made approach, with the only goal being that of helping clients in an effective way. Everything else, even MMT itself, can be sacrificed (Zilbergeld 1982). Ideally, therefore, each treatment should be regarded as a study, and evaluated personalistically (see Lazarus 1985).

**Results of case study**   Towards the end of the therapy Mrs R. showed clear-cut changes. She felt that she was completely over her depressive complaints, and had learned sufficient skills to solve her remaining problems and could also deal with some anticipated difficulties. By the time of her discharge she had few complaints, could talk cheerfully, laughed, had a freer walk, wore stylish clothes and had a modern hairstyle. Here is a list of changes that accrued in each area of Mrs R.'s BASIC I.D.

1. *Behaviour*: By means of activity planning Mrs R. learned to spend less time and energy at work, and acquire the capacity to enjoy leisure activities. During her residence she took part in a course whose central themes were general development and emancipation. She now receives visitors at home, an activity that she formerly avoided. She now asks others for help or support if she considers it necessary, whereas before she was primarily engaged in solving other people's problems. She is also able to spend money on herself, go out and engage in recreational activities, such as walking. In addition to taking a rest during the daytime, Mrs R. has also gradually begun to sleep better.

2. *Affect*: Mourning for and then ultimately accepting her partial loss of sight led to a decrement in Mrs R.'s despondent moods and guilt feelings and in her compulsive work urge. Anxiety management training resulted in a significant decrease in feelings of anxiety and panic. Affective expression improved her emotional life.

3. *Sensation*: Through intensive practice Mrs R.'s perception of reality has become more objective. The acquisition of a new pair of spectacles led to an improvement in sight and possibly influenced the decrease in headaches, dizziness, facial twitches, and tiredness. The client felt relaxed in general and could concentrate well in carrying out tasks.

4. *Imagery*: In combination with exercises in the idealized self-image, the carrying out of activities, and the positive view that Mrs. R finally came to take of them, she developed a positive self-image. Mrs R. discovered that she can imagine making a positive contribution in groups and establishing and maintaining contacts. These new images have acted as a self-fulfilling prophecy.

5. *Cognition*: Mrs R. has acquired greater rational self-talk to the effect that

she believes herself to be responsible for her own behaviour. Related to this is her awareness that her self-esteem is independent of performance and that she can regard herself as a fallible human being. Of crucial importance was the insight that making mistakes was not a catastrophe. She became aware that she gave herself a sense of inferiority by regarding herself as stupid and by ascribing a greater right to others than to herself. In this respect she was helped by the motto, 'Treat yourself as your best friend,' and by paying attention to what she herself wanted, rather than what others might expect.

6. *Interpersonal relationships*: A great deal of attention was paid to Mrs R.'s communication patterns and sexual relationship with her husband. He was docile and submissive in that he approved of 'everything', minded 'nothing', accepted setbacks easily, and showed few signs of joy, sorrow, or anger. Consequently Mrs R. was inclined constantly to ask him whether he felt disappointed, whether he was contented, etc., but did not believe the reassurance he usually gave her. After therapy Mrs R. was able to express her own opinions and wishes honestly, which resulted in greater satisfaction on both sides. Improved marital communication involved such matters as shared responsibility for the business, coping with setbacks, and searching for compromises. In the sexual sphere the two had been living for a long time at cross-purposes. Due to Mrs R.'s fears of pregnancy, they had been totally inactive sexually. As her husband did not voice any complaints about this, Mrs R. came to think that she was unimportant to him. Through sensate focus exercises the two partners became more open and relaxed, and finally achieved a satisfactory sexual relationship. Mrs R.'s new-found assertive skills generalized to her relationship with people other than her husband and she become socially more active. She developed more satisfying relationships with some relatives and established new contacts outside the family.

7. *Drugs*: Improved vision and complete cessation of pharmacotherapy proved to be extremely valuable for Mrs R. Progress in physical well-being was accompanied by less frequent urination and an improvement in memory.

MMT achieved its objective of bringing about specific effects by means of specific techniques. Follow-up nearly two years after the treatment had been completed showed that the effects had proved to be lasting. These results were confirmed by means of questionnaire scores.

## Notes

1 If someone kicks a stone *matter* and *energy* are transmitted from the foot to the stone. The latter will follow its course according to the laws of physics. If, however, someone kicks a dog instead of a stone, the dog may react in several ways. Its reaction depends on the *information* that is exchanged.
2 The connection between systems theory and social learning theory is exemplified by the relationship between feedback and reinforcement. Feedback and reinforcement are interrelated in as much as all reinforcements involve feedback, but not all feedbacks are necessarily reinforcing. For instance, feedback about tasks which one has learned well, or about things in which one has no interest, or to which one does not attend, or about experiences which are neither rewarding or unrewarding, will have little or no reinforcing effect (Miller 1978).
3 The Multimodal Life History Questionnaire (Lazarus 1981) covers a wide range of questions that are detailed in this section.
4 Think of nervous system, heart and vessel system, musculoskeletal system, respiratory system, gastrointestinal or genitourinary tracts, skin diseases, endocrinal disturbances and sensory dysfunctions.
5 A cycle is an infinite repetition of the same sequence of events.

## References

Bandura, A. (1977) *Social learning theory*. Englewood Cliffs, NJ: Prentice-Hall.

Bandura, A. (1978) Reflections on self-efficacy. *Advances in Behaviour Research and Therapy*, *1(4)*, 237–269.

Cannon, W.B. (1939) *The wisdom of the body* (rev. edn). New York: Norton.

De Rosnay, J. (1979) *The macroscope: A new world scientific system*. New York: Harper and Row.

Durkin, J.E. (ed.) (1981) *Living groups: Group psychotherapy and general system theory*. New York: Brunner/Mazel.

Ellis, A. (1962) *Reason and emotion in psychotherapy*. New Jersey: Lyle Stuart.

Franks, C.M. (1976) Foreword. In A.A. Lazarus, *Multimodal behavior therapy*. New York: Springer.

Franks, C.M. (1982) Behavior therapy: An overview. In C.M. Franks, G.T. Wilson, P.C. Kendall and K.D. Brownell (eds) *Annual review of behavior therapy: Theory and practice*, vol. 8. New York: Guilford Press.

Hugdahl, K. (1981) The three-systems-model of fear and emotion – A critical examination. *Behaviour Research and Therapy*, *19*, 75–85.

Kazdin, A.E. and Wilcoxon, L.A. (1976) Systematic desensitization and nonspecific treatment effects: A methodological evaluation. *Psychological Bulletin*, *83*, 729–758.

Kwee, M.G.T. (1981) Towards the clinical art and science of multimodal psychotherapy. *Current Psychological Reviews, 1,* 55–68.

Kwee, M.G.T. (1982) Psychotherapy and the practice of general semantics. *Methodology and Science, 15,* 236–256.

Lang, P.J. (1969) The mechanics of desensitization and the laboratory study of fear. In C.M. Franks (ed.) *Behavior therapy: Appraisal and status.* New York: McGraw-Hill.

Lazarus, A.A. (1958) New methods in psychotherapy: A case study. *South African Medical Journal, 33,* 660–663.

Lazarus, A.A. (1960) The elimination of children's phobias by deconditioning. In H.J. Eysenck (ed.) *Behaviour therapy and the neuroses.* Oxford: Pergamon Press.

Lazarus, A.A. (1961) Group therapy of phobic disorders by systematic desensitization. *Journal of Abnormal and Social Psychology, 63,* 505–510.

Lazarus, A.A. (1963) The results of behavior therapy in 126 cases of severe neurosis. *Behaviour Research and Therapy, 1,* 69–79.

Lazarus, A.A. (1967) In support of technical eclecticism. *Psychological Reports, 21,* 415–416.

Lazarus, A.A. (1971) *Behavior therapy and beyond.* New York: McGraw-Hill.

Lazarus, A.A. (1972) *Multimodal behavior therapy.* Fort Lee, NJ: Sigma (behavioral sciences tape library).

Lazarus, A.A. (1973) Multimodal behavior therapy: Treating the BASIC I.D. *Journal of Nervous and Mental Disease, 156,* 404–411.

Lazarus, A.A. (1977) Has behavior therapy outlived its usefulness? *American Psychologist, 32,* 550–554.

Lazarus, A.A. (1978) *In the mind's eye.* New York: Rawson.

Lazarus, A.A. (1981) *The practice of multimodal therapy.* New York: McGraw-Hill.

Lazarus, A.A. (1984) Multimodal therapy. In R.J. Corsini (ed.) *Current psychotherapies* (3rd edn). Itasca, Ill.: F.E. Peacock.

Lazarus, A.A. (ed.) (1985) *Casebook of multimodal therapy.* New York: Guilford Press.

Lazarus, A.A. and Abramovitz, A. (1962) The use of 'emotive imagery' in the treatment of children's phobias. *Journal of Mental Science, 108,* 191–195.

Lazarus, A.A. and Fay, A. (1975) *I can if I want to.* New York: Morrow.

Lazarus, A.A. and Fay, A. (1982) Resistance or rationalization. In P.L. Wachtel (ed.) *Resistance: Psychodynamic and behavioral approaches.* New York: Plenum Press.

Lazarus, A.A. and Rachman, S.J. (1957) The use of systematic desensitization in psychotherapy. *South African Medical Journal. 31,* 934–937.

Lazarus, A.A. Kreitzberg, C.B. and Sassenrath, V.J. (1981) Multimodal therapy. In R.J. Corsini (ed.) *Handbook of innovative psychotherapies.* New York: Wiley.

Lazarus, R.S. (1982) Thoughts on the relation between emotion and cognition. *American Psychologist, 37,* 1019–1024.

Lazarus, R.S. (1984) On the primacy of cognition. *American Psychologist, 39,* 124–129.

Leary, T. (1957) *The interpersonal diagnosis of personality*. New York: Ronald Press.

Miller, J.G. (1978) *Living systems*. New York: McGraw-Hill.

Miller, N.E. (1944) Experimental studies of conflict. In J.McV. Hunt (ed.) *Personality and the behavior disorders*. New York: Ronald Press.

Öst, L., Jerremalm, A. and Johansson, J. (1981) Individual response patterns and the effects of different behavioral methods in the treatment of social phobia. *Behaviour Research and Therapy*, *19*, 1–16.

Rabkin, R. (1983) Is it really as simple as ABC? *Hospital and Community Psychiatry*, *34*, 1101.

Rachman, S. (1978) *Fear and courage*. Freeman: San Francisco.

Rachman, S. (1981) The primacy of affect: Some theoretical implications. *Behaviour Research and Therapy*, *19*, 279–290.

Schwartz, G.E. (1982) Integrating psychobiology and behavior therapy: A systems perspective. In G.T. Wilson and C.M. Franks (eds) *Contemporary behavior therapy: Conceptual and empirical foundations*. New York: Guilford Press.

Shevrin, H. and Dickman, S. (1980) The psychological unconscious: A necessary assumption for all psychological theory? *American Psychologist*, *35*, 421–434.

Von Bertalanffy, L. (1974) General system theory and psychiatry. In S. Arieti (ed.) *American handbook of psychiatry*, vol. 1. New York: Basic Books.

Wachtel, P.L. (1977) *Psychoanalysis and behavior therapy: Toward an integration*. New York: Basic Books.

Wiener, N. (1948) *Cybernetics*. New York: Wiley.

Wilson, G.T. (1982) Clinical issues and strategies in the practice of behavior therapy. In C.M. Franks, G.T. Wilson, P.C. Kendall and K.D. Brownell (eds) *Annual review of behavior therapy: Theory and practice*, vol. 8. New York: Guilford Press.

Wolpe, J. (1958) *Psychotherapy by reciprocal inhibition*. Stanford: Stanford University Press.

Wolpe, J. and Lazarus, A.A. (1966) *Behavior therapy techniques*. New York: Pergamon Press.

Zajonc, R.B. (1980) Feeling and thinking: Preferences need no inferences. *American Psychologist*, *35*, 151–175.

Zajonc, R.B. (1984) On the primacy of affect. *American Psychologist*, *39*, 117–123.

Zilbergeld, B. (1982) Bespoke therapy. *Psychology Today*, *16*, 85–86.

CHAPTER TWELVE     **Cognitive-Behavioural Therapies: Commonalities, Divergences and Future Developments**
*William L. Golden and Windy Dryden*

## Commonalities and divergences

Each of the contributors to this volume has attempted to describe the distinctive features of their particular approach. However, are they really different? Are the nuances significant enough to make a real difference in terms of the treatment that a client would receive if he/she were to go to each contributor; or are the differences only theoretical? Are all of these therapists providing the same type of treatment, but are explaining it in different ways with varying nomenclature? Almost all of the authors have either directly or indirectly endorsed some form of eclecticism. If this is so and they are all eclectic, then how different would each approach be in actual practice? Are there enough real differences to justify there being different schools?

On the other hand if there are real significant differences, it is important to avoid the 'uniformity myth' (Kiesler 1966) and not treat the various cognitive-behavioural approaches as the same. If we do not acknowledge real differences among cognitive-behavioural therapies (CBTs), then we might assume CBT[1] and CBT[2] are interchangeable and are equally effective with the same kinds of clients. However CBT[1] may be superior to CBT[2] with all clients or with certain types of clients. What we need are well-controlled research studies that compare the efficacy of the various CBT methods. But according to Wessler (1983) much of the research done so far on the efficacy of CBT treatments is misleading. One reason is that researchers all too frequently employ improper labels to describe their treatment procedures. For example, Wessler notes that some researchers claiming to have conducted research on RET used improper labels and actually did not study RET, but other CBT treatments instead. Another problem, Wessler notes, is that even when the correct labels have been used the therapists, usually inexperienced graduate students, make improper use of the therapy's methods. For example, we, as well as Wessler, have observed that one of the most common errors in RET is that often when therapists believe they are challenging 'irrational' beliefs (e.g. 'I am worthless unless I am loved by others') they are often only disputing inferences (e.g. 'No one likes me'). As discussed in the chapter by Dryden and Ellis, an integral part of 'preferential' or 'pure' RET involves the disputation of 'irrational' beliefs.

One of the purposes of the present volume has been to define more clearly the various CBT approaches. We hope that therapists, as well as researchers, will now be better able to identify the major differences in technique among the various CBT approaches. Researchers could employ this information to label their treatments more accurately. While the reader will want to form his or her own opinions on the basis of reading the various chapters, we would like to attune the reader to what we think are the commonalities and differences among the approaches.

## Eclecticism

As mentioned above, most of the contributors have endorsed some form of eclecticism. Some of the contributors (e.g. Golden and Friedberg, Kwee and Lazarus, Liotti) are more liberal in their eclecticism than others (e.g. Dryden and Ellis, Neimeyer) and employ techniques from diverse therapeutic approaches such as hypnosis, behaviour therapy, family therapy, strategic therapy, etc. in addition to employing a wide variety of CBT techniques.

There are different types of eclecticism. Technical eclecticism (Lazarus 1967) as opposed to theoretical eclecticism is an approach whereby the therapist borrows techniques, not theories, from other schools. Instead of selecting techniques on the basis of what *should* work according to a particular theoretical orientation, the technically eclectic therapist is willing to employ any technique that is effective. In another form of eclecticism such as that practiced by Dryden (1984a), Ellis (1973), and Neimeyer (this volume), strategies and techniques are chosen on the basis of their being consistent with the tenets of a given theory. Neimeyer (this volume) has described this approach as 'technical but theoretically consistent eclecticism'. As an illustration of this approach to eclecticism, Dryden (1984b) has pointed out that there are certain techniques that he and some other RET therapists would not employ because the procedures would be regarded as iatrogenic (e.g. certain cathartic techniques that encourage screaming), given the view of psychological disturbance as espoused by RET theory.

## Self-monitoring

Some of the contributors routinely give clients self-monitoring forms to fill out for homework (e.g. Dryden and Ellis, Golden and Friedberg, Maultsby and Gore, Liotti, Weishaar and Beck). Others (e.g. Wessler and Hankin-Wessler) do not appear to employ specific types of record-keeping but nonetheless ask clients to engage in some type of informal monitoring of thoughts, feelings and behaviours. It would be hard to conceive of a cognitively orientated therapy that could be successful without some method of introspection that heightens clients' awareness. Where the therapists differ is in what type of cognitions they ask clients to monitor. For example, whereas Dryden and Ellis get their clients to look for and record their dogmatic 'irrational' beliefs in the form of 'musts' and 'shoulds', Weishaar and Beck get their clients to monitor and record their automatic thoughts and thinking errors. Even though Wessler and Hankin-Wessler do not ask their clients to keep formal records of thoughts, feelings, and behaviours, they do nevertheless make use of self-monitoring in that they get their clients to examine personal rules of living.

An important question for CBT theorists to consider is, to what degree do these different constructs overlap? For example a client feeling guilty over not telling his dying wife that she has cancer may be told by Dryden or Ellis that his guilt stems from the demand that 'One must never lie.' Wessler and Hankin-Wessler would explain that the client's guilt was the result of a conflict between personal rules of living: 'I should always tell the truth' and 'I should protect my wife at all times.' Weishaar and Beck would probably say the guilt was due to the overgeneralization that 'Lying is always wrong.'

Perhaps these therapists are dealing with the same basic psychological processes but are focusing on different derivatives and expressions of the same ideas. This issue will be addressed later when we discuss different levels of cognition.

## Cognitive restructuring

All of the CBT therapists employ some form of cognitive restructuring – that is, some method for producing cognitive change. Cognitive restructuring can be accomplished through different means. We would maintain that the particular method that a CBT therapist chooses is more a function of the style of the therapist than theoretical orientation. For example, the RET method of disputing 'irrational' beliefs has been criticized for being cajoling and exhortive (see chapter by Weishaar and Beck). However, the disputing of such beliefs can also be accomplished through Socratic dialogue, as well as through other cognitive restructuring procedures, by warm, empathic, soft-spoken therapists.

Cognitive restructuring may occur:

1. *Didactically* (i.e. by explanation or through bibliotherapy).
2. As a result of being engaged in *Socratic dialogue* where thought-provoking questions are asked by the therapist with the intent of getting the client to re-evaluate some of his or her self-defeating ideas and misperceptions.
3. Through *corrective experiences*; for example in vivo homework assignments which would include in vivo desensitization and Beck's method of guided discovery.
4. Through *vicarious learning* (the modelling effect) which would include the modelling of appropriate behaviours as well as self-disclosures by the therapist of how he or she overcame or dealt with problems similar to the one that the client is having.
5. By *self-analysis*, which could be accomplished with the aid of homework sheets such as those used in RET, RBT, or Beck's cognitive therapy.
6. By *self-statement modification*, that is, replacing maladaptive self-statements with more adaptive ones, as is done for instance in RET, RBT, cognitive-behavioural hypnotherapy and Meichenbaum's (1977) and Jaremko's (this volume) cognitive-behaviour modification.
7. By *mental rehearsal*, for example rational-emotive imagery, in vitro desensitization, and other imagery procedures with or without the aid of hypnosis or relaxation procedures.
8. Through *reframing*, where the event or behaviour remains the same but its meaning or 'frame' is changed. Reframing occurs when a therapist provides the client with a dramatically different (sometimes polar opposite) perspective. An example of reframing is when a socially anxious client reports that he failed at his homework assignment of approaching three women because all three refused to give him their telephone number. The event is reframed when the therapist says, 'You didn't fail, you were successful because you succeeded in approaching three women when previously you would have avoided taking such risks. I am quite pleased with your success at risk-taking.'
9. Through *storytelling, metaphors, and poetry* that encourage the client to consider alternative ways of viewing and dealing with situations. An example of this method of cognitive restructuring was used by one of the authors (W.G.) in treating a married couple who were so dependent on one another that they both felt 'trapped' and resentful. They believed that if they really loved one another they 'should' do everything together and always want to be with one another. Attempts at explaining

that this was untrue and that most married people need to have separate interests and time away from one another had little effect. What did have an impact was the following passage on marriage from Kahlil Gibran's (1923) *The Prophet*, which the therapist read to them during their therapy session:

> But let there be spaces in your togetherness,
> And let the winds of the heavens dance between you.
> Love one another, but make not a bond of love:
> Let it rather be a moving sea between the shores of your souls.
> Fill each other's cup but drink not from one cup.
> Give one another of your bread but eat not from the same loaf.
> Sing and dance together and be joyous, but let each one of you be alone,
> Even as the strings of a lute are alone though they quiver with the same music.
> Give your hearts, but not into each other's keeping.
> For only the hand of life can contain your hearts.
> And stand together yet not too near together:
> For the pillars of the temple stand apart,
> And the oak tree and the cypress grow not in each other's shadow.

The next week the wife reported that she had made a decision to begin taking guitar lessons which was one of those things that she had always wanted to do. The husband reported that he had made arrangements to get together with a friend to play racketball which he had stopped playing because his wife had no interest in sports.

10. Through *cognitive paradox*, which is different from behavioural paradox. In behavioural paradox, specific behaviours such as the client's symptoms or resistances are prescribed. Examples of behavioural paradox would include a therapist telling a client with insomnia to try to stay awake instead of trying to go to sleep, or agreeing with a negativistic oppositional client who insists that he cannot change. Cognitive paradox involves exaggeration. The therapist feeds back the 'voice of irrationality' to the client in an exaggerated form in order to get the client to re-evaluate his or her ideas. For example, one of the authors (W.G.) used cognitive paradox in treating a workaholic college teacher who spent excessive amounts of time preparing for lectures at the beginning of his teaching career. His personal rule of living or 'must', which he learned from his father, was that 'You must always work hard

and never take the easy way out.' The client rigidly applied this rule by writing out and memorizing every word of his lectures, instead of using outlines. He also refused to allow himself the leeway of ending a lecture early if he completed what he had to say. In addition, although he assigned class projects he did not allow time during class for the students to present their work. Instead he felt compelled to give a lecture at each class, or otherwise he would be taking the 'easy way out'. He sought therapy at the request of his wife because his workaholism prevented him from spending time with her and their children. Direct attempts to persuade him to ease up on his 'shoulds' by getting him to see their negative impact were used, in addition to pointing out that he was failing miserably to live according to his father's rules, because if he *really* wanted to live according to these rules he should rip up his lecture notes after each lecture and start all over again every term. Otherwise he was taking the easy way out. It was obvious to the client that this was being said in jest. The client responded by saying, 'Now you're speaking my language,' and was able that week to end his lecture four minutes before the time it was scheduled to end, and announced to the class that later in the term each student would be asked to spend a few minutes presenting his or her class project. Cognitive restructuring procedures do not necessarily operate independently of one another. This client also used coping self-statements such as, 'It is an appropriate teaching technique to have the students present their work. Actually they will probably find that more interesting than if I lectured to them all the time. That's not copping out, that's being creative.' Here the combination of paradox and reframing seems to have been involved in producing the initial change which continued as a result of the client using self-statement modification.

11. Through *teaching problem-solving skills* such as those described by Platt, Prout and Metzger.

We believe that none of the above cognitive restructuring procedures are the private domain of any of the specific CBT approaches. They are just different ways of producing cognitive change. Although a particular therapist may have a preference for one or several of these cognitive restructuring procedures, the methods themselves are atheoretical and are congruent with any CBT approach. The major difference between the various CBT approaches is in terms of what types of dysfunctional cognitions are targeted for changes. In RET, for example, although any of the cognitive restructuring procedures described above can be used, the focus is on employing them for modifying incorrect inferences and 'irrational' beliefs. In Beck's cognitive therapy these same methods can be employed for correcting automatic thoughts, underlying assumptions, and thinking errors. The same cognitive restructuring procedures can be used to modify personal rules of living, personal constructs, etc. Thus a distinction can be made between a particular cognitive technique and the purpose for which it is being used.

Another way in which cognitive restructuring differs is in terms of whether it is conducted in the context of verbal psychotherapy such as in RET, CAT and Beck's cognitive therapy, or is confined to mainly self-statement modification as a component of a behaviour therapy treatment package. In the latter approach, the cognitive treatment is integrated with traditional behaviour therapy procedures such as relaxation, desensitization, and modelling (see Meichenbaum 1977). These two approaches have been viewed as being different enough from one another to warrant separate reviews. The reader is referred to Miller and Bermans's (1983) review of the research literature examining the efficacy of cognitive restructuring in psychotherapy and Dush, Hirt and Schroeder's (1983) review of the research on self-statement modification.

## Rehearsal

The contributors all seem to prepare their clients for difficult situations through some type of mental or behavioural rehearsal. The contributors differ in terms of which particular methods they favour; imagery with relaxation, imagery with coping self-statements, imagery with hypnosis, imagery alone, behavioural rehearsal, coaching, or some combination of these methods. These techniques are all similar in that they provide clients with an opportunity to try out their new coping techniques in a safe environment prior to applying them in vivo. This allows for feedback from the therapist and a refinement of the skills that the client is developing.

## Homework

CBT approaches are also similar in that they all emphasize the importance of homework (HW) in producing change. Although some of the schools have very distinct types of assignments, there are more similarities than differences among the various CBT approaches with regard to HW. Most CBT assignments are either cognitive or behavioural:

1. *Cognitive*: As mentioned earlier, CBT approaches ask clients to engage in some type of self-monitoring of thoughts, feelings and behaviours. Some approaches such as RET, RBT, and Beck's cognitive therapy have their own special forms which are designed to help clients develop their skills at re-evaluating self-defeating thoughts and replacing them with more constructive ones.

   Bibliotherapy is another type of cognitive HW. However some cognitive therapists (e.g. Wessler and Hankin-Wessler) are less enthusiastic about bibliotherapy than others (such as Dryden and Ellis, Maultsby and Gore) who routinely assign self-help books, pamphlets and cassette recordings for HW.

2. *Behavioural*: Behavioural assignments in CBT typically involve in vivo exposure to feared and previously avoided situations in the case of anxiety, shame and embarrassment, and constructive and pleasurable activity in the case of depression. Although in vivo exposure is given different names (e.g. desensitization, flooding, risk-taking, shame-attacking, etc.) by the different CBT therapists, and may actually differ to some degree (e.g. graduated exposure versus flooding, with the aid of coping self-statements or relaxation) as well as being given different explanations (e.g. testing out hypotheses in cognitive therapy, acting against irrational beliefs in RET, extinction in cognitive behaviour modification), they all represent some variation of the exposure principle. Although behavioural in terms of involving action, they can also be considered cognitive in that they result in some type of corrective experience whereby faulty perceptions, misconceptions and erroneous beliefs may be re-evaluated. Similarly most CBT therapists assign some type of mastery and pleasure assignments (as Beck calls them) to depressed clients. Although different CBT therapists have different rationales for assigning activity, nevertheless the basic strategy (e.g. getting depressed clients to become more active) is the same.

## Dealing with resistance

Whenever HW is given, a client may offer resistance. As they describe in their sections on 'Overcoming obstacles to client progress', the contributors do differ, at least to some degree, in terms of what methods they use to deal with resistance. These differences, however, seem to be based on clinical preferences rather than theoretical differences. CBT therapists take a *problem-solving* approach, as one of the authors (Golden 1983) has described elsewhere, which is in sharp contrast to the psychodynamic approach of *interpreting* resistances. Golden has pointed out that resistance may be due to therapist factors (e.g. lack of rapport, incomplete or incorrect assessment, incorrect use of techniques, etc.) environmental factors (e.g. deliberate or inadvertent sabotage from others, such as family members), as well as client factors. After evaluating difficulties in the therapist–client relationship, CBT therapists use the same methods to deal with resistance that they use to deal with any problem (e.g. cognitive restructuring, self-management procedures, etc.). When interpersonal difficulties are involved, other methods such as family therapy can be employed (as described by Liotti, Kwee and Lazarus, this volume).

## Theoretical similarities and differences

Despite theoretical differences, one major similarity justifies grouping all the approaches in the present volume under the heading of cognitive – that is, the theories are all some variation of Woodworth's (1929) S-O-R model where 'S's are stimuli, 'O's are organismic variables which would include all types of cognitive processes and 'R's are responses (emotional, physiological, and behavioural). The theorists seem to differ mainly in the way they conceptualize 'O', the intervening variable. Depending on the particular school, the cognitive targets for change are either 'irrational' beliefs (RET, RBT), thinking errors and underlying assumptions (Beck's cognitive therapy), personal rules of living (CAT), rules in the form of self-instructions (Jaremko's cognitive-behaviour modification), personal constructs (personal construct therapy) or problem-solving deficits (ICPS). The theorists also differ over the importance of exploring and understanding the past, or phenomenological developmental history, of the individual (see chapters by Liotti on structural cognitive therapy and Wessler and Hankin-Wessler on CAT).

Another important theoretical similarity which CBT approaches share in common is the concept of levels of cognition. Most CBT theorists make a distinction between conscious cognitive activity (usually referred to as self-statements, internal dialogues, or automatic thoughts) and cognitive structures (which are usually nonconscious and more general – see chapter 1). Even Jaremko, who has taken a radical behaviouristic position, has accounted for the structuralization of cognitive activity in terms of rule-governed behaviour that becomes so habitual that it becomes automatic and reflexive, without needing explicit rule statements to reinforce it. Meichenbaum (1977) has said that internal dialogues – that is, specific self-statements and images – stem from cognitive structures which are 'a system of concepts and judgements' (1977, p. 21). Beck has made a similar distinction between automatic thoughts and images on one level, and 'schemata' – the underlying assumptions or attitudes that 'are used to classify, interpret and assign meaning to the event' (Weishaar and Beck, this volume) – on the other. In RET a similar distinction could be made between 'irrational' beliefs (the cognitive structures) and self-statements. According to Dryden and Ellis 'irrational' beliefs are often implicit or nonverbalized, whereas the client's maladaptive self-statements are the conscious expression of them.

Liotti has been the most graphic in his description of the relationship and organization of the various levels of cognition. At the core level are schemata formed during childhood that involve unconscious assumptions. At an intermediate level there are conscious constructs (such as those described by Neimeyer) about self, other people and the world. The appraisal and evaluation of events, problem-solving and planning occur at the peripheral level.

Again the major theoretical difference between the various CBT schools seems to lie in how each theorist conceives of the deeper cognitive structures or schemata. Are they 'irrational' beliefs, underlying assumptions, attitudes, superordinate personal constructs, personal rules of living, or are all of these different names for the same basic schemata?

However, agreement over the nature of the schemata would not necessarily lead to similar conclusions about their role in producing emotional disturbance. Although Meichenbaum (1977) agrees with Ellis that the schemata may consist of irrational beliefs, he disagrees with Ellis that irrational beliefs *per se* cause emotional disturbance. Meichenbaum suggests that perhaps what distinguishes nonclients from clients is that while both have irrational beliefs, better adjusted individuals cope with these beliefs better. When healthier individuals get anxious or depressed as a result of irrational thinking they then engage in coping behaviour that reduces and minimizes distress.

## Differences between theory and practice

At this point, it may be apparent to the reader that there is a difference between CBT techniques and the theories that are used to explain them. Certain techniques have become associated with specific CBT approaches, such as Ellis's disputation of 'irrational' beliefs, Maultsby's rational-emotive imagery (REI), and Kelly's fixed role enactment (see Neimeyer, this volume). However, approaches are linked with theories; techniques, on the other hand, can be explained and incorporated by any theory. Wessler (1983) has asserted that approaches cannot be evaluated on the basis of clinical outcome studies. A technique may be effective for reasons that are different from those proposed by the theorist who originally developed the technique. From a clinical viewpoint, it is more important to know which cognitive restructuring procedure is effective with which client, under what conditions, than it is to know which theory is correct in explaining why the technique is effective. Unfortunately, researchers have usually attempted to test the efficacy of *approaches*, as opposed to comparing the various CBT *techniques*. It is our opinion that the progress of CBT would be enhanced if research was directed toward the latter.

## What do CBT therapists really do in their offices?

At the beginning of the chapter the following question was raised: if a client went to a therapist from each school of CBT, would he or she receive the same treatment? The answer probably depends upon who the therapist is. There is a great deal of variation in therapist style within each school. For example, if a test-anxious college student saw Donald Meichenbaum for therapy, he or she would probably get some form of stress inoculation training or coping desensitization (Meichenbaum 1977) which would include education about the nature of stress, relaxation training, self-monitoring of negative self-statements, and training in the replacement of these negative self-statements with coping self-statements (i.e. more positive and construc- tive self-statements). The student would receive practice in applying the various cognitive and relaxation coping techniques through the use of imagery. While in a relaxed state the student would imagine himself or herself coping with study and test-taking situations. If the student became anxious during this mental rehearsal procedure he or she would be in- structed to practise reducing the anxiety by employing the cognitive and relaxation coping procedures. Finally the student would be instructed to apply these same coping tools in vivo, if needed.

The same student going to Ellis would probably get a different type of treatment. They would be instructed to read RET bibliotherapy and be taught the ABC theory. Their maladaptive self-statements and beliefs about examinations would be identified and challenged during their sessions through Socratic dialogue and didactic disputing, and between sessions, through RET HW forms. The student would be taught how to dispute anxiety-producing ideas such as 'I would be a failure if I don't succeed in school as I must,' and would be helped to develop a set of rational self-statements. Finally REI would be used as a mental rehearsal procedure to prepare the student for exam-taking.[1]

Probably a test-anxious college student would receive different treatment from Ellis than he or she would receive from Meichenbaum. But what would happen to this test-anxious student if he or she went to a second generation CBT therapist (i.e. someone trained by Ellis, Meichenbaum, Beck, etc.)? Would the treatment vary or would it be basically the same? Again it would depend upon the specific therapist this client would see. However, based on our discussions with colleagues who have been trained by different CBT theorists such as Ellis, Meichenbaum, or Beck, it seems the treatment would tend to converge rather than be as distinctive as described by the founders. For example, one of the authors (W.G.), despite an RET background, would treat the test-anxious college student with some form of coping desensitization, as described above, because it has been found to be an effective technique for treating test anxiety, and was found to be more effective than traditional desensitization (Meichenbaum 1972). My (W.G.) clinical experience has been that the combination of coping desensitization and RET is more effective than is 'pure' RET alone. Many other effective second-generation CBT therapists also vary their approach depending on the client and the nature of the presenting problems. For example, the first author (W.G.) has been one of the faculty for the cognitive-behaviour therapy fundamentals course for the Association for the Advancement of Behavior Therapy. The other faculty is Ray DiGiusseppe of the Institute for RET in New York, Arthur Freeman of Beck's Center for Cognitive Therapy and Roy Cameron who received training in CBT from Donald Meichenbaum and helped him to develop the stress inoculation training programme. Although each of us presents a purist position – Ray DiGiusseppe and myself (W.G.), RET; Arthur Freeman, cognitive therapy; and Roy Cameron, cognitive-behaviour modification – we end up explaining to the group that in actual practice that is not how we really conduct therapy. We use various CBT methods and approaches at different times depending on the client and what type of treatment seems appropriate.

An explicit set of rules for helping clinicians decide which technique to use with which client is lacking. Perhaps future research will provide us with such formulae some day. What is clear to us is that many second-generation CBT therapists are using some set of clinical decision rules, often implicitly, that seem to guide them in drawing from different CBT approaches. An ongoing forum where leading therapists from the different CBT training institutes could be usefully developed to help in the articulation of such decision rules. Of course we are not referring to rigid rules but rather guidelines. Although, at the present time, precise decision rules are lacking, we will now present a general framework which we find useful and which might be helpful to other CBT therapists in organizing and integrating some of the diverse methods and strategies in this book.

## Towards a basic framework for conducting cognitive-behaviour therapy: alliance theory perspectives

As cognitive-behaviour therapists, we have found the work of Ed Bordin (1979) on the concept of the therapeutic alliance particularly helpful in developing a basic framework for the conduct of CBT. Bordin argues that the therapeutic alliance refers to the complex of attachments and shared understandings formed and activities undertaken by therapists and clients as the former attempt to help the latter with their psychological problems.

Bordin has stressed that there are three major components of the therapeutic alliance: (a) *bonds* – which refer to the interpersonal connectedness between therapist and client; (b) *goals* – which refer to the aims of both therapist and client; and (c) *tasks* – which are activities carried out by both therapist and client in the service of the latter's goals.

We will consider each of these components separately and show that cognitive-behaviour therapists have important clinical decisions to make in each of the three alliance domains so as to individualize therapy for each client and thus maximize therapeutic benefit. In doing so therapists can take an eclectic stance and choose what appears to be the best from the diverse therapies outlined in this book for each client.

At the outset it should be noted that Bordin (1979) has speculated that effective therapy occurs when therapist and client (a) have an appropriately bonded working relationship; (b) mutually agree on the goals of the therapeutic enterprise; and (c) both understand their own and the other person's therapeutic tasks and agree to carry out these to implement the client's goals.

### Bonds

The major concern of cognitive-behaviour therapists in the bond domain should be to establish and maintain an appropriately bonded relationship that will encourage *each* individual client to implement his or her goal-directed therapeutic tasks. It should be underscored that for such practitioners there is no *single* effective bond that can be formed in the cognitive-behaviour therapies. Thus, different clients require different bonds in CBT. This observation became clear to one of us (W.D.) when on a six months' sabbatical at the Center for Cognitive Therapy in Philadelphia in 1981. As reported elsewhere (Dryden 1984b), I saw two clients on the same afternoon who benefited from a different bonded relationship with me. At 4 p.m. I saw Mrs G., a fifty-year-old married business woman, who was impressed with my British professional qualifications and whose responses to initial questions indicated that she anticipated and preferred a very formal relationship with her therapist. I provided such a relationship by using formal language, citing the research literature whenever appropriate, wearing a suit, shirt and tie and by referring to myself as Dr Dryden and to my client as Mrs G. On one occasion I inadvertently used her first name and was put firmly in my place concerning the protocol of professional relationships. On another occasion I disclosed a piece of personal information in order to make a therapeutic point and was told in no uncertain terms, 'Young man, I am not paying you good money to hear about your problems.' Here, a therapist is faced with the choice of respecting and meeting a client's bond anticipations and preferences or examining the reasons why, for example, this client was so adamantly against her therapist's informality. In our experience the latter strategy is rarely productive and cognitive-behaviour therapists are recommended to fulfil their clients' preferences for therapeutic style as long as doing so does not reinforce the client's psychological problems.

At 5 p.m. on the same afternoon I regularly saw Mr B., a forty-two-year-old male nurse who indicated that he did not respond well to his previous therapist's neutrality and formality. Our therapy sessions were thus characterized by an informal bond. Before seeing him I would remove my jacket and tie that I wore for Mrs G.; in sessions we would use our first names and would both have our feet up on my desk. We also developed the habit of taking turns to bring in cans of soda and my client referred to our meetings as 'rap' sessions while I conceptualized my work as cognitive-behaviour therapy within an informal context.

We maintain that Mrs G. would not have responded well to an informal therapeutic relationship nor would Mr B. have done as well with a highly formal mode of therapy. Thus, we argue that it is important that cognitive-behaviour therapists pay attention to the question: 'Which bond is likely to be most effective with a particular patient at a given time in the therapeutic process?' Drawing upon social psychological principles, certain writers have argued that some clients show more progress when the therapeutic bond is based on liking and trustworthiness, while others flourish more when the bond emphasizes therapist credibility and expertness (Beutler 1983; Dorn 1984; Strong and Claiborn 1982). Future research in the cognitive-behaviour therapies could fruitfully address the issue of which bond is effective with which clients. However, until we have such data, therapists could make decisions about what type of bond to foster on the basis of an early assessment of the client's anticipations and preferences in the bond domain and to try to meet such expectations at least initially. This is one reason why we would caution novice therapists against emulating the therapeutic style of leading CBT practitioners whose bond with clients may be based mainly on prestige and expertness. Cognitive-behaviour therapists should thus be prepared to emphasize different aspects of themselves with different clients in the bond domain, without adopting an inauthentic facade, and to monitor transactions in this domain throughout therapy.

How can this best be done? One way would be to administer a portion of Lazarus's (1981) Life History Questionnaire which focuses on clients' expectations regarding therapy. The items: 'How do you think a therapist should interact with his or her clients?' and 'What personal qualities do you think the ideal therapist should possess?' are particularly relevant and could usefully provide impetus for further exploration of this issue at the outset of therapy. If the client has had therapy previously, the current therapist could usefully explore what aspects of the previous therapist(s)' interactive style and behaviour were deemed by the client to be both helpful and unhelpful. Particular emphasis should be placed on the exploration of the instrumental nature of previous therapeutic bonds since statements such as: 'He was warm and caring' are of little use unless the client evaluated these qualities positively and attributed therapeutic progress to these factors.

Furthermore, and for similar reasons, we have found it helpful to explore clients' accounts of people in their lives who have had both positive and negative therapeutic influence on their personal development. Such exploration may provide the therapist with important clues concerning which types of therapeutic bonds to promote actively with certain clients and which bonds to avoid developing with others.

Therapeutic style is another aspect of the bond domain which requires attention. Interpersonally-orientated psychotherapists (e.g. Anchin and Kiesler 1982) have argued that clinicians need to be aware that therapeutic styles have a 'for better or worse' impact on different clients. Cognitive-behaviour therapists tend to be active and directive in their style of conducting therapy. This therapeutic style may not be entirely productive with both passive clients and, as Beutler (1983) has argued, clients who are highly reactive to interpersonal influence. Clients who tend to be passive in their interpersonal style of relating may 'pull' an increasingly active style from their therapists who may in turn reinforce these clients' passivity with their increased activity. Clients whose psychological problems are intrinsically bound up with a passive style of relating are particularly vulnerable in this regard. It is important that cognitive-behaviour therapists be aware of the danger of becoming enmeshed in such unproductive vicious circles which have unfortunate self-fulfilling prophecy implications for their passive clients. These therapists need to engage their clients productively at a level which constructively encourages increased activity on their part without threatening them by adopting an overly passive style of practising CBT.

Beutler (1983) has argued that all approaches to psychotherapy can be viewed as a process of persuasion and this is particularly true of cognitive-behavioural approaches to psychotherapy which aim, in part, to 'persuade' clients to re-evaluate and change their dysfunctional cognitive processes. As such, cognitive-behaviour therapists need to be especially careful in working with clients for whom such persuasive attempts may be perceived as especially threatening (i.e. highly reactant clients). Here it is important that therapists execute their strategies with due regard to helping such clients to preserve their sense of autonomy, emphasizing throughout that these clients are in control of their own thought processes and decisions concerning whether or not to change them. At present, the above suggestions are speculative and await full empirical enquiry, but our clinical work has led us to question the desirability of establishing the same therapeutic bond with all clients and of practising cognitive-behaviour therapy in an unchanging therapeutic style.

## Goals

The major concern of cognitive-behaviour therapists in the goal domain of the alliance is to ensure that there is agreement between therapist and client on the client's outcome goals for change. A prerequisite of such agreement concerns clients and therapists arriving at a shared understanding of the clients' most relevant problems as defined by the client (Meichenbaum and Gilmore 1982). Difficulties may occur here when the therapist uncritically accepts the client's initial accounts of his or her problem since such accounts may well be biased by the client's internalized values, e.g. the views of significant others in the client's life. In addition, although most cognitive-behaviour therapists consider that early goal-setting with the client is important, clients' initial statements about their goals for change may well be coloured by their psychological disturbance as well as by their internalized values concerning what these goals should be. Cognitive-behaviour therapists need to walk a fine line between uncritically accepting clients' initial goals for change and disregarding them altogether. A helpful solution here involves establishment and maintenance of a channel of communication between client and therapist which deals with metatherapy issues (i.e. issues concerning matters relating to therapy itself). Dryden and Hunt (1985) have referred to the activities that occur within this channel as involving negotiations and renegotiations about therapeutic issues. Cognitive-behaviour therapists need to take the main responsibility for keeping this communication channel open in order to monitor clients' goals over time and to determine the reasons for shifts in these goals.

Pinsof and Catherall (in press) have made the important point that clients' goals occur (implicitly or explicitly) in reference to their most important relationships and their therapists need to be mindful of the impact that these systems are likely to have on both the selection of such goals and the client's degree of progress towards goal attainment. Adopting this focus may well possibly mean involving parts of the client's interpersonal system in therapy itself. It also suggests that future theorizing in the cognitive-behaviour therapies could profitably assign a more central role to interpersonal issues (cf. Kwee and Lazarus, this volume; Safran 1984). This discussion on the goal domain of the alliance in the cognitive-behaviour therapies is not meant to be exhaustive. However, issues in this domain do not have that many implications for the practice of cognitive-behaviour therapy. It is the task domain where such issues become particularly salient.

## Tasks

Cognitive-behavioural approaches to psychotherapy, as outlined in this book, tend to subscribe to the following therapeutic process. Initially, having agreed to offer help to the client, the therapist attempts to structure the therapeutic process for the client and begins both to assess his or her problems in cognitive-behavioural terms and also to help the client to view his or her problems within this framework. Goals are elicited based on a cognitive-behavioural assessment and therapeutic strategies and techniques are implemented to effect the desired changes. Finally, obstacles to client change are analyzed and, it is hoped, overcome, and therapeutic gains are stabilized and maintained.

Therapists have tasks to execute at each stage in the cognitive-behavioural therapeutic process and these will now be outlined.

**Structuring** Effective cognitive-behaviour therapy depends in part on each participant clearly understanding their respective responsibilities in the therapeutic endeavour and upon each agreeing to discharge these responsibilities in the form of carrying out therapeutic tasks. It is the therapist's major responsibility to help the client to make sense of this process by providing an overall structure of mutual responsibilities and tasks. It is important to stress that structuring occurs throughout therapy and not just at the outset of the process. Sensitive clinicians who pay attention to alliance issues will structure the process using language which the client can understand and analogies which make sense to each individual person. Thus, it is often helpful to discover client's hobbies and interests so that apt and personally meaningful structuring statements can be made. Thus, if a client is interested in golf, ascertaining how that person learned the game may be valuable in drawing parallels between the processes of learning coping skills and learning golfing skills. Both involve practice and failures can be realistically anticipated in each activity.

**Assessment and conceptualization of clients' problems** During the assessment process, cognitive-behavioural therapists traditionally attempt to gain a full understanding of the cognitive and behavioural variables that are maintaining their clients' problems. During this stage two issues become salient from an alliance theory perspective. First, it is important for therapist and client to arrive at a shared *definition* of the client's problems (i.e. what these problems are). Second, as Meichenbaum and Gilmore (1982) have noted, it is important for them to negotiate a shared *conceptualization* of the client's problem (i.e. an explanation of what accounts for the existence of these problems) so that they can work productively together in the intervention stage of therapy.

When working towards shared problem conceptualization, we argue that it is important for therapists to use, wherever possible, the client's language and concepts, particularly when providing alternative explanations of their problems. This helps therapists to aim work within the range of what clients will accept as plausible conceptualizations of their problems. If clients' own theories about the origins of their problems and, more particularly, what maintains them (which are embodied in the language they use to describe their problems) are ignored, then the clients may well resist accepting their therapists' conceptualizations. As Golden (1985) has noted, sometimes cognitive-behaviour therapists often have to initially accept, for pragmatic purposes, a client's different (i.e. to the therapist's) conceptualization of his or her problems in order to arrive later at a shared one. In addition, cognitive-behaviour therapists may well privately (i.e. to themselves) conceptualize a client's problems in cognitive-behavioural terms (e.g. negative self-statements) while publicly (to the client) using the client's conceptualization (e.g. negative self-hypnosis). To what extent the effectiveness of CBT is based on negotiation or on the unilateral persuasion attempts of the therapist is a matter for future enquiry.

Another important issue here involves what types of cognitions feature in therapists' conceptualizations of clients' problems. As noted earlier, many seem to share the notion that cognitions are hierarchically ordered and that more enduring results occur when 'deeper' levels of cognitions (e.g. irrational beliefs, personal rules of living, attitudes, superordinate constructs, etc.) are changed. How important is it, in clinical practice, to treat these theoretically different types of schemata as distinct, or can therapists profitably disregard such differences and use a general term, e.g. schema, in discussing with clients the conceptualization of their problems? Alliance theory would predict that the important issue here concerns whether or not the therapist and client have a shared agreement of both the meaning of a given 'schema term' and whether it in fact accounts for the existence of the client's problems.

**Therapeutic strategies and techniques**   Once the therapist and client have come to a mutually agreed understanding of the client's problems, the therapist then discusses various treatment strategies with the client. Therapeutic strategies are broad statements of intent which serve to mediate between the assessment of the client's problems and their goals for change. Thus, if the assessment has revealed that a client's depression is based on a dysfunctional underlying assumption, the therapeutic strategy would be to modify this assumption. Therapeutic techniques then come into the picture as prescribed activities which serve to implement a chosen strategy.

Goldfried (1982) considers that it is at the level of therapeutic strategies that therapists of diverse orientations can speak a common language. This point is also relevant when different cognitive-behavioural approaches are considered. Thus, instead of arguing whether they should modify an irrational belief, superordinate personal construct or underlying basic assumption, all of which reflect a deep cognitive level, cognitive-behavioural therapists interested in integration may speak amongst themselves of modifying a deep cognitive schema (schema being a neutral term which is more likely to be accepted by cognitive-behavioural therapists of all schools). Of course, therapists who would maintain that there are real differences between, for example, 'irrational' beliefs and underlying basic assumptions would disagree with this line of reasoning. Not all cognitive-behaviour therapists will seek to adopt an integrative stance. However, those who choose to do so will probably, as Goldfried suggests, develop a common nomenclature at the strategy level.

With regard to dealing with this issue with clients, we would again recommend using the language and concepts of the clients as much as possible in developing a treatment plan. For clients who seem to be more comfortable with conceptualizing their problems in terms of 'irrational beliefs', for example, the language of RET would be appropriate. With clients who, on the other hand, view their problems more in terms of 'rules', we would recommend either the language of cognitive appraisal therapy or Jaremko's cognitive-behaviour modification.

The next step for cognitive-behavioural therapists would be to develop a comprehensive list of such strategies and a corresponding list of therapeutic techniques which are deemed to best implement such strategies. In this way cognitive-behaviour therapists will be able to choose from a range of techniques to implement a single strategy depending upon salient client factors.

A number of alliance issues are relevant here; the most important of which concerns the links between tasks and goals. First, cognitive-behaviour therapists should preferably help their clients to see the connection between the latter's goals and the therapeutic strategies which are intended to mediate between problems and goals. Second, therapists need to choose the most relevant techniques available which serve to implement selected therapeutic strategies. Apart from the fact that clients need to understand how executing particular therapeutic tasks will help them achieve their goals, it is desirable for therapists to employ particular techniques that clients have selected (from a range of possible procedures) rather than unilaterally selecting techniques themselves without client consent. Additionally, assuming that a number of techniques all have equal therapeutic potency (i.e. their execution would result in clients achieving their goals) techniques should be used which are congruent with a particular client's learning style. Whilst some clients learn best through action, others learn best through reading bibliotherapy texts, etc. Selecting techniques to maximize clients' different learning styles is an important area for future development in the cognitive-behavioural therapies.


**Overcoming obstacles to change and stabilizing and maintaining progress**

Finally, cognitive-behavioural therapists will often encounter 'resistance' to client progress. We have already briefly noted the general approach that cognitive-behavioural therapists employ in dealing with this issue. Alliance theory argues that in addition therapists need to scan the three major domains (bonds, goals, and tasks) to determine whether the reason(s) for such 'resistance' can be located in one or more domains or where the domains interact. Thus, for example, in our experience 'resistance' can often occur when clients do not fully understand how the execution of certain homework assignments is relevant to achieving their therapeutic goals.

Finally, the long-term success of cognitive-behavioural therapy as stressed in particular by Platt, Prout and Metzger (this volume) depends in large part on clients successfully internalizing a wide range of coping skills that they can use to prevent the development of future psychological problems. Thus it is important for clients to understand that their future personal development is largely in their own hands. CBT practitioners need to encourage clients to accept and discharge their responsibility of learning and applying strategies and techniques that will help them to achieve and maintain their therapeutic goals.


## Conclusion

We have examined some of the commonalities and differences among the CBT approaches. A broadly based framework which we consider to be consistent with the various CBT approaches has been proposed.

In chapter 1, Wessler discussed some of the important theoretical issues in CBT. Of particular importance is the Zajonc–R. Lazarus debate over the primacy of affect. We expect the primacy of cognition versus affect debate to be one of the issues that shape the future of CBT theory. Also, perhaps CBT in the future will move more in the direction outlined by Kwee and A. Lazarus, where all modalities and their interactions are dealt with. Indeed we included Kwee and Lazarus's multimodal chapter in this book to show how one of the founding fathers of CBT, Arnold Lazarus, has sought to go beyond the cognitive-behavioural tradition.

Our own view is that it is not important to resolve whether cognitions influence affect or affect influences cognitions. More important is to determine which methods (cognitive, affective, and behavioural) work best with which clients under what conditions. We suspect that regardless of whether or not we see a proliferation of CBT approaches in the future, there will probably be greater convergence in terms of the clinical procedures of CBT therapists.

# Note

1  These descriptions are based on Ellis's and Meichenbaum's writings on what they say they do, which may or may not be what they actually do in practice.

# References

Anchin, J.C. and Kiesler, D.J. (eds) (1982) *Handbook of interpersonal psychotherapy.* New York: Pergamon.

Beutler, L.E. (1983) *Eclectic psychotherapy: A systematic approach.* New York: Pergamon.

Bordin, E.S. (1979) The generalizability of the psychoanalytic concept of the working alliance. *Psychotherapy: Theory, Research and Practice, 16,* 252–260.

Dorn, F.J. (1984) *Counseling as applied social psychology: An introduction to the social influence model.* Springfield, IL: Thomas.

Dryden, W. (1984a). Issues in the eclectic practice of individual therapy. In W. Dryden (ed.) *Individual therapy in Britain.* London: Harper and Row.

Dryden, W. (1984b) Rational-emotive therapy. In W. Dryden (ed.) *Individual therapy in Britain.* London: Harper and Row.

Dryden, W. and Hunt, P. (1985) Therapeutic alliances in marital therapy. II. Process issues. In W. Dryden (ed.) *Marital therapy in Britain*, vol. 1: *Context and therapeutic approaches.* London: Harper and Row.

Dush, D.M., Hirt, M.L. and Schroeder, H. (1983) Self-statement modification with adults: A meta-analysis. *Psychological Bulletin, 94(3),* 408–422.

Ellis, A. (1973) *Humanistic psychotherapy: The rational-emotive approach.* New York: McGraw-Hill.

Gibran, K. (1923) *The prophet.* New York: Knopf.

Golden, W.L. (1983) Resistance in cognitive-behaviour therapy. *British Journal of Cognitive Psychotherapy, 1(2),* 33–42.

Golden, W.L. (1985) An integration of Ericksonian and cognitive-behavioral hypnotherapy in the treatment of anxiety disorders. In E.T. Dowd and J.M. Healy (eds) *Case studies in hypnotherapy.* New York: Guilford Press.

Goldfried, M.R. (1980) Toward the delineation of therapeutic change principles. *American Psychologist*, *35*, 991–999.

Goldfried, M.R. (1982) On the history of therapeutic integration. *Behavior Therapy*, *13*, 572–593.

Kiesler, D. (1966) Some myths of psychotherapy research and the search for a paradigm. *Psychological Record*, *65*, 110–136.

Lazarus, A.A. (1967) In support of technical eclecticism. *Psychological Reports*, *21*, 415–416.

Lazarus, A.A. (1981) *The practice of multimodal therapy*. New York: McGraw-Hill.

Meichenbaum, D. (1972) Cognitive modification of test anxious college students. *Journal of Consulting and Clinical Psychology*, *39*, 370–380.

Meichenbaum, D. (1977) *Cognitive-behavior modification: An integrative approach*. New York: Plenum.

Meichenbaum, D. and Gilmore, J.B. (1982) Resistance from a cognitive behavior perspective. In P.L. Wachtel (ed.) *Resistance*. New York: Plenum.

Miller, R.C. and Berman, J.S. (1983) The efficacy of cognitive behavior therapies: A quantitative review of the research evidence. *Psychological Bulletin*, *94(1)*, 39–53.

Pinsof, W.M. and Catherall, D.R. (in press) The integrative psychotherapy alliance: Family, couple and individual therapy scales. *Journal of Marital and Family Therapy*.

Safran, J.D. (1984) Assessing the cognitive-interpersonal cycle. *Cognitive Therapy and Research*, *8*, 333–347.

Strong, S.R. and Claiborn, C.D. (1982) *Change through interaction*. New York: Wiley-Interscience.

Wessler, R.L. (1983) A critical appraisal of therapeutic outcome studies. *British Journal of Cognitive Psychotherapy*, *1(1)*, 39–46.

Woodworth, R.S. (1929) *Psychology* (rev. edn). New York: Holt, Rinehart and Winston.

# SUBJECT INDEX

treatment techniques, 270–2
interpersonal skills, deficits in, 279–87
interrelatedness of modalities of functioning, 326
intrinsic gain cycle, 339–40, 347–8, 349
intrinsic loss cycle, 339, 340, 346–7, 349
'irrational'
    RBT definition of, 177
    RET definition of, 133
'irrational' beliefs, 141, 161, 207–8, 365, 375
    as appraisals, 15–16
    biological tendency towards, 133–4
    disputing, 147, 148–51, 161, 185, 190–1,
        305, 356–7, 358, 366–7
    of therapists, 158–9
    negative, 139–40
    positive, 137–8

jealousy, 251
job satisfaction, lack of, 77

labelling of clients as resistant, 84, 248, 332
labels for treatment procedures, improper, 356
language and meaning, 20–2, 211
learning of skills/habits, 175
loneliness, unavoidable, 103–4
loss, experience of, 103, 104, 202, 204–5
love/approval, obsessive need for, 144
'low frustration tolerance', 145

madonna-whore complex, 251–2, 253
maladaptive behaviour *see* behaviour, mixed
    adaptive/maladaptive; *see also under*
    *individual headings, e.g.* avoidance
    behaviour; undercontrol, behavioural
managers, humans as, 6–8, 23
marital problems, 215, 237
marital therapy, 239–40, 250–6
marriage, seen as oppressive, 120–1, 122
martyrs, 207
matching processes, 95
means-end thinking, 267
memory, 19, 114, 274
messages, distortion/misunderstanding of, 208
metaphorical techniques, 115, 124, 215, 239, 259–60
metatherapy issues, 372; *see also* feedback, from client
misconception hypothesis, 11–72
misinterpretation of interventions, 84
mismatch between therapist and client, 157

modalities *see* BASIC I.D.
mood induction, 306
motivation
    client's, 211–12, 219, 278
    human, 228, 229
Multimodal Life History Questionnaire, 211, 212, 353, 370
Multimodal Therapy, 198, 214, 320–53
    compendium of major techniques, 336–7
    conceptualizing clients' problems, 327–31
    historical development, 320–2
    modality profile, 344–5
    overcoming obstacles to client progress, 341–2
    strategies of treatment, 333–4, 349
    theoretical concepts, 322–7
    therapeutic relationships, 231–3
multiple personalities, 116
'musturbation', 16, 137–8, 139–40

negative thoughts, 5, 16, 18, 36, 66–7, 205
    'letting go' of, 300–1
neo-Hullian paradigm, 320
'nervous stomach', 86–8
neuropsychiatry, 2

obesity, 218–19, 307
observations, nonevaluative, 136
obsessive-compulsive patterns, 104–5, 108
obstacles to client progress, overcoming, in
    cognitive-behavioral approaches, 53–4, 83–
    6, 115–16, 157–60, 187–8, 217–19, 248–50,
    276–9, 309–13, 341–2, 374
    clients obstacles, 159–60
    'relationship' obstacles, 157
    therapist obstacles, 157–9
    *see also* resistance
Occam's Razor, 322
order underlying stream of consciousness, 93;
    *see also* cognitions, organization of
overactivity, 343
overcontrol, behavioural, 42–3
overcontrolling attitude, 101–2, 121, 124, 125
    of husband, 251, 254

pain
    cognitive therapy approach to, 77
    hypnotherapeutic approach to, 200, 291
    radical behaviourist approach to, 53
panic attacks, 71, 72, 78, 85, 119, 124, 125
paradox
    cognitive, 332, 360–1
    behavioural 360

stimulus-response paradigm, 2–3, 322–3
Stoic philosophers, 129–30
strategies of treatment in cognitive-behavioural approaches, 46–7, 73–5, 109–115, 146–9, 160, 177–9, 212–13, 236–40, 269–70, 298–304, 333–40, 349, 374–6
stress cycle, 50, 52
stress inoculation training, 49–53
structural cognitive therapy, 92–125
    conceptualizing clients' problems, 99–106
    historical development, 92
    overcoming obstacles to client progress, 115–16
    strategies of treatment, 109–15
    theoretical concepts, 92–9
    therapeutic relationship, 107–9
    treatment techniques, 115
stutterers, 232
style, therapeutic
    active-directive, 143, 145
    and tightening/loosening of client's constructs, 242–3
    client's expectations of, 370
    collaborative/co-operative, 73–4, 75, 107–8, 110–11, 197, 210, 298
    exploratory, 112
    formal v. informal, 369–70
    need for flexibility in 210–11, 333, 370–1
    variation in, 366
success of interventions, explanations for, 26, 335
successive approximation, 311
suicidal impulses, 245
survival needs and cognition, 9–10
symbolic representations, 11
symptom relief, focus on, 293
systems theory, 321–2, 325–7, 353

tacit processes *see* unconscious cognitive processes
tasks, therapeutic, 372–6
    graded, 82, 88
TAT cards, 273, 274, 275, 283
techniques *see* treatment techniques; *see also under individuals headings e.g.* imagery techniques; metaphorical techniques
termination of therapy, 85
terminology
    client's, defining, 77
    shared between client and therapist, 142, 211, 374, 375
test anxiety, 183, 307, 366–7

theoretical bases of cognitive-behavioural approaches, 32–8, 61–2, 64–5, 92–9, 132–4, 170–2, 198–203, 228–31, 262–5, 296–7, 322–7, 364–5
therapeutic relationship *see* relationship, therapeutic
therapists *see under individual headings, e.g.* rapport-building skills, therapist's; warmth, therapist's
thinking *see under* problem-solving
'thought stopping', 300
thoughts *see* automatic thoughts; cognitions; negative thoughts; *etc.*
threat, perception of, 68–9, 202, 204, 249
threats to vital interests, cognitive response to, 64–5
three-systems model, 330
time projection, 218
time-limited intervention *see* short-term therapy
tracking technique, 341
transference, 235–6
    and therapeutic goals, 236
treatment plan, formulation of, 74
treatment techniques in cognitive-behavioural approaches, 47–53, 75–83, 115, 149–57, 180–7, 214–16, 240–8, 270–2, 304–9, 336–7, 366–8
    mutual agreement on, 375–6
    *see also under individual headings, e.g.* imagery techniques; metaphorical techniques
'troublesomeness', subjective
    as criterion for intervention, 205, 213
    of behaviours, 206–7
    of emotions, 205–6
    of thoughts 207–8
truth/falsity of appraisals, 18; *see also* errors in thinking/logic

unconscious cognitive processes, 2, 9, 19–20, 113–14, 323–5, 364–5
    and hypnoanalysis, 292
    and problem-solving processes, 94
    operation of, 94–5
    unearthing, 19–20, 22–3, 237–8
undercontrol, behavioural, 42, 43
'uniformity myth', 356
unwilling clients, 278

validational role of therapist, 235
values, 23, 199, 207, 214, 215; *see also* cultural norms/values; personal rules of living

*Index compiled by Peva Keane*

# INDEX OF NAMES